THE ETERNAL HIGH PRIEST OF THE COVENANTAL OATH

Remember the Days of Old,
Consider the Years of All Generations.
Ask Your Father and He Will Inform You,
Your Elders, and They Will Tell You.

Deuteronomy 32:7

THE GENEALOGY OF HIGH PRIESTS
IN LIGHT OF GOD'S ADMINISTRATION
IN THE HISTORY OF REDEMPTION

THE ETERNAL HIGH PRIEST OF THE COVENANTAL OATH

ABRAHAM PARK

CLC International
Multi-Language Media
Foreign Language Christian Resources

The Eternal High Priest of the Covenantal Oath

Published by Multi-Language Media,

an imprint of CLC Publications

U.S.A.

P.O. Box 1449, Fort Washington, PA 19034

UNITED KINGDOM

CLC International (UK)

Unit 5, Glendale Avenue, Sandycroft, Flintshire, CH5 2QP

ISBN (hardcover): 978-1-61958-324-5

ISBN (e-book): 978-1-61958-325-2

CONTENTS

Foreword

Dr. Luder G. Whitlock, Jr

It was a great privilege to visit Pyungkang Cheil Church in Seoul, Korea in 2013 during the remarkable ministry of Dr. Abraham Park, author of the History of Redemption Series. As the chairman of Knox Theological Seminary at that time, it was one of the great honors of my life to award the honorary Doctor of Divinity degree to him in recognition of his global ministry. Dr. Park was a faithful servant of God, used globally to advance the Gospel. I was captivated by the global missionary vision of this church and its commitment to reach the world with the Gospel.

The most important thing for him was to know God's will, and he developed an acute sensitivity to God's guidance. Pyungkang Cheil Church was one of the most vibrant congregations that I have ever visited and that was because of the powerful ministry of Dr. Park, who was not only a profoundly spiritual pastor but a gifted teacher who took the whole counsel of God seriously. That led him to emphasize the history of redemption in his preaching and teaching ministry. Since the publication of the first volume of the History of Redemption Series books in 2007, the fact that many scholars, including Dr. Bruce Waltke, one of the finest Old Testament scholars in the world, warmly endorsed this work attests to its value.

This theme of redemptive history provided a framework for the entire Bible so that his congregation could understand what they believed and why. He avoided the weakness of many pastors today who love and preach the Scriptures but fail to equip their congregations with the big picture of God's plan and their place in it. As a result, although they clearly understand some basic truths, they fail to understand why biblical events unfolded as they did and how that should shape our understanding of the Scriptures and the church. Dr. Park taught the big picture so that his church members knew how all the smaller parts fit together.

Book 6 of the History of Redemption Series provides an excellent example of Dr. Park's carefully developed methodology. He begins with an exposition of Deuteronomy and the sermons, or farewell addresses, of Moses, delivered in the plains of Moab just before the Israelites entered Canaan. He reminds us of God's command in Deuteronomy 32:7, to "remember the days of old, consider the years of all generations." He uses this to help the reader understand God's history of redemption by the threefold command to remember, consider and ask: remember the past, reflect on the future, and decide or act in the present. God has been faithful to His covenant and He calls His people to faithfulness so that they may receive the abundance of His blessings.

The Eternal High Priest of the Covenantal Oath addresses the Chronicler's genealogy as it is organized from a priestly perspective following the 70-year Babylonian captivity. It encourages the people of God, using the genealogies of the Old Testament, to remember their spiritual roots and the imperative of spreading God's word to the nations. It also reveals the importance of restoring worship as a priority for God's people as they returned to their homeland and started to rebuild. The Chronicler's genealogy pointed to Jesus Christ, the promised eternal high priest first prophesied in Genesis 3:15. It explains the development of the priestly system that required sacrifices and culminated in the sacrifice of the eternal high priest, Jesus. Book 6 of the History of Redemption Series shows how the development of the priestly system reaches its climax in the ministry of Jesus, the great high priest. The Christo-centric nature of the Scriptures is plainly revealed. It becomes apparent that the shedding of His blood was necessary in order for our sins to be forgiven. Apart from the death and resurrection of Jesus, we would be condemned to remain outside the Promised Land or the New Jerusalem of Revelation 21 and 22. Dr. Park shows how an accurate understanding of the Jewish context, especially of early Christianity, is essential to an accurate interpretation of the Scriptures. They provide the framework for understanding the message of the New Testament. Important but seldom understood Biblical truths are clearly explained and accompanied by colored illustrations and a set of charts that will be invaluable to the reader who may otherwise fail to gain an understanding of the comprehensive Biblical and secular history that is presented. Additional information is available regarding priestly garments and music. There may be a temptation to ignore them but that would be unwise.

As a young Christian, I would have benefited immensely from these volumes. As a new believer, I read the Bible seriously and memorized verses but it was not until I entered theological school that I began to grasp the significance of Biblical theology and redemptive history. In these volumes, Dr. Park makes redemptive history accessible to the lay Christian. Perhaps most significant is the lesson that today's Christians should remember God's work in history, how He has been faithful to those who trust in Him. That lesson should motivate contemporary Christians to renounce the world and all its temptations, trusting the Lord and obediently following Him. In doing so, the promises of God are assured and our sins are forgiven through the eternal sacrifice of Jesus.

Considering the history of Christianity in Korea, especially periods of great spiritual blessing, would it be too much to hope that attention to this volume, preferably the whole series, might be used to bring a new period of Scriptural understanding and spiritual blessing. More Christians need to read books like this one. I hope this volume touches off a new wave of interest in the Bible and illumines the path for God's people everywhere.

Dr. Whitlock is recognized as one of the top five most influential seminary presidents in the latter half of the 20th century, and he served as the executive director for the publication of the ***New Geneva Study Bible****. He received his D.Min. from Vanderbilt University.*

Dr. Bruce K. Waltke

Book 6 in the History of Redemption Series, *The Eternal High Priest of the Covenantal Oath: the Genealogy of High Priests in Light of God Administration in the History of Redemption* comprehensively teaches what the Holy Spirit revealed about the doctrine of the priesthood.

The Holy Spirit graciously used the renowned late Reverend Abraham Park, D. Min., D.D., to give His Church a treasure on this important, albeit often neglected, doctrine.

Scholars heretofore researched aspects of this subject, but none has organized the subject so comprehensively, systematically, and diachronically (i.e., from Genesis to Revelation) as this work.

For example, to my knowledge, this is the first time the generations of the seventy-seven high priests, from the time of Aaron, when Israel was founded as a holy nation, to Phannias (AD 70), when God terminally destroyed the Jerusalem temple, has been systematically organized.

And more than that, the study is enhanced by lucid writing and visual spread-sheets and charts. This labor of love is further enhanced by the author's passion for his subject and all things godly, and by his application of the truth to the Christians.

Dr. Waltke is professor emeritus of Regent College in Vancouver, BC, Canada and distinguished professor emeritus of Knox Theological Seminary in Ft. Lauderdale, FL. He is the award-winning author of ***Genesis: A Commentary*** *and* ***An Old Testament Theology****, as well as an authoritative two-volume commentary on Proverbs. Dr. Waltke also was involved in the* ***New American Standard*** *and* ***New International Version*** *translations of the Bible. He received his Th.D. from Dallas Theological Seminary and his Ph.D. from Harvard University.*

Preface

The entire history of God's work of creation, the fall of mankind, redemption, and, in the end, the consummation of the new heaven and the new earth is called the history of redemption. Jesus Christ stands at the center of redemptive history; and the sixty-six books of Scripture, from beginning to end, record God's administration of redemption with Jesus Christ at its core. The history of the Bible includes the Old Testament era of the patriarchs, the era of Egypt and the exodus, the era of the forty-year wilderness journey, the era of the judges and the monarchy, the era of the Babylonian exile and return, the intertestamental era, and the New Testament era. These are all part of God's great history of redemption. Since Moses' final words of exhortation encourage us to "remember the days of old, consider the years of all generations" (Deut 32:7), we therefore need to have a deep understanding of God's redemptive history that is contained in the years of every successive generation from the very beginning.

The only way mankind could meet with God again after being banished from Eden was the redemptive movement through the altar where sacrifices were made. This altar evolved from personal altars during the generations of the patriarchs to the altar of the tabernacle during the wilderness era. It continued to evolve, becoming the altar in Solomon's temple during the generations of the monarchs and then the altar of Zerubbabel's temple in the postexilic era. However, despite the daily sacrifices that were offered repeatedly on these altars, these sacrifices could not resolve the fundamental issue of sin.

At last, Jesus Christ came as the culmination of the redemptive movement of the altar. He said, "The Son of Man has come to seek and to save that which was lost" (Luke 19:10), and, "It is not the will of your Father who is in heaven that one of these little ones perish" (Matt 18:14). As Jesus proclaimed these words, He continued to carry out the movement of redemption without rest (John 5:17). Finally, Jesus Christ—the eternal high priest—achieved eternal atonement on the cross once and for all (Heb 7:27; 9:12, 26; 10:2, 10, 14; see also Rom 6:10; 1 Pet 3:18). He also fulfilled the promise of the seed of the woman and completed the redemptive movement to seek and save the lost (Gen 3:15).

Jesus Christ, who gave His own body as a sacrifice, resurrected and ascended to heaven (Heb 4:14). Even now, He is at the right hand of God's throne as the high priest who supplicates without rest in order to find those who are lost (Rom 8:34; Col 3:1; Heb 1:3; 8:1; 1 Pet 3:22). Jesus is truly the only eternal high priest who came according to the order of Melchizedek (Heb 2:17; 3:1; 4:14–15; 5:5, 10; 6:20; 7:11, 17; 9:11). He is the one and only high priest of the covenantal oath (Ps 110:4; Heb 7:20–21).

Many high priests are mentioned in the Bible. The ministry of the high priest reveals Jesus, who is the true high priest. Just as the high priests represented the people of Israel before God, their genealogy and history also represent the genealogy and history of all Israel. It is unfortunate that throughout history, even to the present, many have overlooked the genealogy and history of the priests and high priests. Scholars around the world have researched this subject in part, but there has never been a study that diachronically (i.e., through time) and systematically organizes the voluminous seventy-seven generations of the high priests, from the time of Aaron until the destruction of Jerusalem in AD 70, in a biblically relevant method. For an unqualified person such as myself, putting together the contents of this uncharted field of study was an overwhelming task. I am truly grateful and humbled knowing that it was solely by the help of God's good hand that I was able to organize the genealogy of the high priests using the manuscripts I had drafted forty-five years ago as a foundation.

I hope that this book will become a basic textbook in this field of study so that it will not only lighten the workload of research for its readers but also become a catalyst for more extensive research in this field and broaden the knowledge of many Christians. It is my prayer that this elderly servant's studies will encourage fellow researchers to produce even greater work to benefit both the church of Korea and the global theological world.

Like a ginseng digger who carefully searches for centuries-old wild ginseng deep in the mountains, I sought and searched with all my heart, soul, and mind to understand the mysteries of God's redemptive administration (Eph 3:9) from the Holy Scriptures. I carefully retraced the steps of our forefathers of faith that were hidden deep within "the years of all generations" (Deut 32:7). Many times I could not hold back the tears as I noticed the unchanging love and grace at work within those generations. The more I wrote, the sadder and more regretful I felt, knowing that the inadequacies of my writing and conceptualizing skills may prevent the administration of redemption in the years of the generations and the God-given inspirations from being fully communicated. Now that the book is being published, I realize that I have not been able to put in writing all that I wanted to say. Thus I am sorrowful before God because I have been unable to properly express the inspired Word that burns greatly in my heart. Nevertheless, I earnestly hope that the God who perfects all things will allow the powerful work of the Holy Spirit to work in everyone who reads this book to understand the administration of the "mystery which has been hidden from the past ages and generations" (Col 1:26).

It is truly a sad reality that some churches and ministers in Korea today are being condemned for having fallen prey to materialism and mammonism. During Jesus' day, the Pharisees also loved money (Luke 16:14), and the scribes devoured widows' houses (Mark 12:40; Luke 20:47). However, Job, the pure and righteous man of the East, confessed, "I have not put my trust in gold or said to pure gold, 'You are my security.' I have not celebrated my great wealth or the riches my hands had gained" (Job 31:24–25, NCV). Human beings are just sojourners who have nothing to call their own here on Earth (1 Chr 29:15). We are just "vapor that appears for a little while and vanishes" (Jas 4:14). We are here but for a short moment, like a passing shadow that disappears without a trace (see 1 Pet 2:11). Afterward, the judgment of God will certainly come (Rom 2:16; Heb 9:27; Rev 20:12–13). I did not realize this when I was young; but as I age, the words "conduct yourselves in fear during the time of your stay on earth" ring true to my heart (1 Pet 1:17).

All human beings are imperfect, frail, and full of flaws. It is certainly not our Lord's wish that we criticize and deride one another. We must respect one another and go forth together toward a better conclusion. Romans 14:10 states, "You, why do you judge your brother? Or you again, why do you regard your brother with contempt? For we will all stand before the judgment seat of God." Those who rashly judge and condemn others based solely on rumors without confirming the veracity of those statements will not be able to escape great shame and the fearful judgment of God should those rumors turn out to be untrue. We must inscribe the words of Matthew 12:36–37 deep within our hearts: "Every careless word that people speak, they shall give an accounting for it in the day of judgment. For by your words you will be justified, and by your words you will be condemned." Christians who have been redeemed through the precious blood of Jesus must regard others as more important than themselves (Phil 2:3) and absolutely refrain from denouncing one another (Rom 2:1). Before we recklessly judge and condemn others, we must delve deeper into the Bible so we can live upright lives every day following the righteous Word of God. Since the Word of God is upright (Ps 19:8; 33:4), the righteous will walk in His ways, "but transgressors will stumble in them" (Hos 14:9). It is my earnest hope and desire that our God, who withholds no good thing from those who walk uprightly (Ps 84:11), will enable all who live upright lives to understand the amazing administration of redemptive history.

Finally, I would like to extend my sincere gratitude to all who have supported the effort, both materially and spiritually, to publish this precious book. I would especially like to give my wholehearted thanks to all who have worked so hard to translate the History of Redemption Series into various languages such as English, Japanese, Chinese, Indonesian, Spanish, Russian, German, Khmer (Cambodian), Urdu (Pakistan), and Hebrew. If I have just one wish as I approach the end of this life, which was saved without cost through the blood of Christ, it is that God would be glorified through the History of Redemption Series. Like the great confession of Apostle Paul, it is my earnest hope that the blessed aroma that exalts only Jesus Christ would overflow in every cell of my body, whether by life or by death (Phil 1:20).

By returning to the Word of God alone, the church of Korea will receive the great blessing of Joseph's fruitful branches that run over the wall (Gen 49:22). I earnestly hope that the History of Redemption Series will become a channel through which the Word of God will be fully preached, not only in Korea, but throughout the world (Rom 15:19; Isa 11:9; Hab 2:14). It is also my earnest desire that the series will become the fragrance that leads people to the life of Christ that saves all nations of the world (2 Cor 2:15–16). May this book bring abundant blessings and benefits to all our brothers and sisters who love the Word of God. I prayerfully hope that God will use this book as an instrument for His glory.

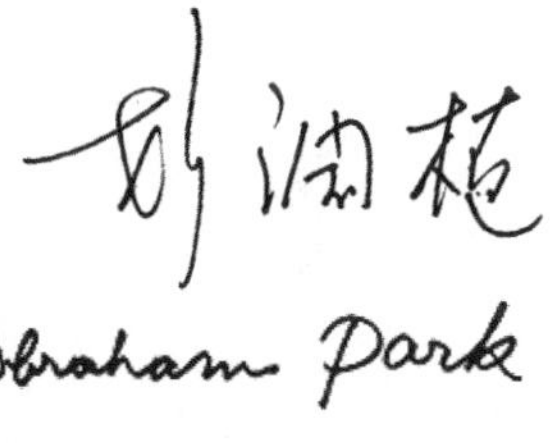

Reverend Abraham Park

An insignificant member of the body of Jesus Christ
on the sojourner's path to heaven
May 17, 2011

עמלק
מדבר צין הוא קדש
ים המלח
הר ההר
עתר
עיר כרמיל
שבט
קדש ברנע
מדבר סין
מדבר פארן
מדבר שור
באר שבע
שבט שמעון
שבט
גת
ארץ פלשתים
אשקלון
פתם
אלכסנדרי
לוח המסעות במדבר
אשר על פי ה׳ יסעו ועל פי ה׳ יחנו
א״ רעמסס טו״ רתמה כט״ חור הגדגד
ב״ סכת טז״ רמן פרץ ל״ יטבתה
ג״ אתם יז״ לבנה לא״ עברנה
ד״ פיהחירת יח״ רסה לב״ עציןגבר
ה״ מרה יט״ קהלתה לג״ מדבר צין
ו״ אילם כ״ הרספר לד״ הרההר
ז״ ים סוף כא״ חרדה לה״ צלמנה
ח״ מדבר סין כב״ מקהלת לו״ פונן
ט״ דפקה כג״ תחת לז״ אבת
יוד״ אלוש כד״ תרח לח״ דיבן גד
יא״ רפידם כה״ מתקה לט״ עלמן דבלתימ
יב״ מדבר סיני כו״ חשמנה מ״ הרי עברים
יג״ קברות התאוה כז״ מסרות מא״ ערבת מואב
יד״ חצרות כח״ בני יעקן

PART

I

Consider the Years of All Generations

CHAPTER

1

THE BOOK OF DEUTERONOMY: MOSES' HISTORIC FAREWELL DISCOURSE

Deuteronomy is the last book of the Pentateuch (Genesis, Exodus, Leviticus, Numbers, and Deuteronomy). It is comprised of the sermons Moses preached to the second generation of Israelites while they were in the wilderness at the plains of Moab, just before their entry into the land of Canaan. Moses reaffirmed the Sinaitic covenant through the covenant of the plains of Moab in Deuteronomy 29 as he reflected upon history and reiterated the law. The name "Deuteronomy" means "second law" in Greek and alludes to a book that records and expounds God's Word a second time (see Deut 17:18–20).[1] After the Israelites first received God's Word (see Exod 19:1–Num 10:10), they journeyed through the wilderness for almost forty years. Now that they were about to enter the Promised Land, Moses expounded the Word once again to this new generation.

---

1 The Greek title of "Deuteronomy" in the Septuagint is *Deuteronomion* (second law). This originated from the expression "a copy of this law" in Deuteronomy 17:18.

The Hebrew title for the book of Deuteronomy comes from the opening words in Deuteronomy 1:1, אֵלֶּה הַדְּבָרִים (*elleh haddevarim*), meaning "these are the words." This clearly shows that Deuteronomy is the Word of God proclaimed through Moses.

In its introduction Deuteronomy reveals the time, location, and audience for its message. Moses proclaimed this message to the second generation of Israelites on the wilderness journey on the first day of the eleventh month in the fortieth year. They were "across the Jordan in the wilderness, in the Arabah opposite Suph" (Deut 1:1; see also Deut 1:2–3). More specifically, it was after they had defeated Sihon king of the Amorites and Og king of Bashan (Deut 1:4). This was about two months and ten days before Israel's entry into Canaan (see Josh 4:19). After his discourse, Moses the man of God went up Mount Pisgah, where his life of 120 years came to an end (Deut 34:1–7). Deuteronomy is the law that Moses reiterated to the new generation right before his death. Hence it was as weighty and solemn as a will passed to the succeeding generation.

By this time all the men over the age of twenty who had been numbered in the first census (603,550; Num 1:46), except Joshua and Caleb, had died; this was before they crossed over the brook Zered (Num 14:26–35; 26:64–65; 32:13; Deut 2:13–15). Thus the audience for this farewell sermon was mostly made up of those born in the wilderness who had not been numbered during the first census because they had been under the age of twenty at the time. The majority of this generation had not personally experienced the 430 years of slavery in Egypt (Exod 12:40–41), nor had they experienced God's living works of salvation that had led their fathers through the great miracles of the exodus and the parting of the Red Sea. They had not witnessed the magnificent scene at Mount Sinai when God Himself had inscribed the Ten Commandments on the stone tablets in the midst of the glorious fire (Deut 11:2–6). For these reasons, God commanded Moses to expound God's laws again by preaching his farewell sermon to the second generation who were waiting for their imminent entry into Canaan.

The recurring theme of Deuteronomy is that God had been faithful in keeping His covenant with Israel's forefathers, despite their unbelief and wickedness (Deut 4:31; 7:9; 9:5; 29:13). Thus Deuteronomy is not merely a repetition of the law; it also explains how the history of Israel unfolded within God's covenant so the Israelites could understand the law in application to the new circumstances they faced in the new generation. Moreover, understanding God's law gave Israel a clear vision and prepared them for what was to happen in the future once they entered into the Promised Land.

Moses' farewell sermons can be classified broadly into two parts: Deuteronomy 1–30 and 31–34. In Deuteronomy 1–30, Moses reminisces about Israel's past and reiterates the law. Deuteronomy 31–34 records the emergence of Joshua as the new leader, the last two poems written by Moses the man of God as he looked into the future of Israel before his death ("the song of witness" in Deuteronomy 32 and "the blessing of the twelve tribes" in Deuteronomy 33), and Moses' final moments (Deut 34). This is the conclusion of the book of Deuteronomy as well as the entire book of the law.

Deuteronomy 1–30 records Moses' three sermons. His first sermon (Deut 1:1–4:43) is a recollection of God's work of salvation as experienced in the wilderness journey, which spans from the exodus until Israel's arrival at the borders of the Promised Land, Canaan. His second sermon is a reiteration of the law (Deut 4:44–26:19), which lays out the principles of the covenant (Deut 4:44–11:32) and the detailed rules and regulations for life in the Promised Land (Deut 12:1–26:19). His third sermon (Deut 27:1–30:20) explains how the Israelites must prepare for entry into Canaan. Moses gives his prophetic counsel, telling the Israelites that they will soon set foot in the Promised Land—the land promised to Abraham, Isaac, and Jacob—and when they enter that land, they must live as descendants of the covenant.

Deuteronomy 31–34 records the following events: Moses' commissioning of Joshua (Deut 31:2–8, 23), the documentation of the expounded law in a book (Deut 31:9, 24), the reading of this book and the education of children (Deut 31:9–13), the charge regarding the safekeeping of this book (Deut 31:10–13, 25–29), the song of witness and Moses' instructions regarding Israel (Deut 31:14–22, 30; 32:1–47), and Moses' blessings for the twelve tribes (Deut 33:1–29). Finally, Moses called Israel "Jeshurun"[2] and concluded with an inspirational message of blessings for Israel, the truly blessed people who had been saved among all nations of the world (Deut 33:29; see also Deut 33:5, 26; Isa 44:1–2).

According to Deuteronomy 3:23–27, Moses pleaded with God with all his heart that he might enter the land of Canaan. Nevertheless, God resolutely rejected his plea, saying, "Enough! Speak to Me no more of this matter." Here the word "more" is יָסַף (*yasaf*) in Hebrew and means "to add," "to increase," or "to prolong"; it indicates that Moses had prayed numerous times that he might enter Canaan.

Thus Moses went up to Mount Nebo, in the land of Moab, opposite Jericho, and met his solemn end (Deut 32:48–52; 34:1–12). God showed Moses the entire land: "Gilead as far as Dan, and all Naphtali and the land of Ephraim and Manasseh, and all the land of Judah as far as the western sea, and the Negev and the plain in the valley of Jericho, the city of palm trees, as far as Zoar" (Deut 34:1–3). This was the entire land of Canaan that had been promised to Israel.

Moses was 120 years old when he died. He was buried in the valley, in the land of Moab, opposite Beth-peor, but "no man knows his burial place to this day" (Deut 34:5–6; see also Jude 1:9). Until Moses died "his eye was not dim, nor his vigor abated" (Deut 34:7). The Israelites wept thirty days for Moses (Deut 34:8).

---

2 *Jeshurun* originates from the word יָשַׁר (*yashar*), meaning "straight, upright, horizontal, joyful"; it thus means "righteous one, upright one, one who stands straight." The Septuagint (LXX) translates the word as "beloved," and Calvin follows this translation. This was a blessed name for the Israelites, meaning "a people whom God sees as righteous" and "a people loved by God."

CHAPTER

2

MOSES' SONG OF CELEBRATION: THE SONG OF WITNESS

After Moses preached his three sermons, he commissioned Joshua as the new leader, just as God had commanded (Deut 31:1–8, 23). Then God gave His final command to Moses to write a song of witness for the future of Israel (Deut 31:19–22) so that, He said, "this song may be a witness for Me against the sons of Israel" (Deut 31:19).

When the Israelites entered Canaan and ate and were satisfied and became prosperous, they would turn to other gods and serve them, spurning God and breaking His covenant (Deut 31:20–21; see also Deut 32:15). Then when many evils and troubles came upon them, this song would testify before them as a witness, since it would not be forgotten from the lips of their descendants (Deut 31:19, 21).

Songs are effective vehicles to deliver specific ideologies or teachings because they are familiar to people, are easy to follow and memorize, and stay in people's memories for a long time. Though Israel would sin and become corrupt, this song that someone had memorized and sung would act as a witness to confirm Israel's sins against God. The New International Version translates the first part of Deuteronomy 31:21, "When many disasters and calamities come on them, this song will testify against them, because it will not be forgotten by their descendants."

Although the subject of the song of witness is Israel's betrayal and God's judgment (Deut 31:16–18), when in the distant future evils and troubles befell the children of Israel because of their rebellion and disobedience, this song—as the embodiment of God's providential love—would serve to remind them of their covenant with God so that they could repent and return to the path of recovery.

Amazingly, Moses was able to write and teach this magnificent song of witness to the assembly of Israel on the same day God commanded it (Deut 31:22). He read all the words of the song in their hearing (Deut 31:30). Joshua also spoke all the words of this song in the hearing of the people along with Moses (Deut 32:44), and the words were also probably communicated indirectly through the elders and officers of the twelve tribes (Deut 31:28; see also Deut 31:9).

This song of witness (Deut 32:1–43) that Moses left behind before he breathed his last contains the experiences of faith from his entire life. The song pulsates with the joys and sorrows that he had shared with Israel and exudes earnest hope for his beloved children of Israel. As clear as a view through a telescope, the song is a panoramic prophecy of Israel's future. Indeed, the fire of God's unchanging love that is founded upon His covenant surges from within this song like an erupting volcano.

CHAPTER

3

Remember the Days of Old, Consider the Years of All Generations

In the beginning of the song of witness, Moses first summoned the heavens and the earth (Deut 32:1; see also Deut 4:26; 30:19; 31:28; Ps 19:1; Isa 1:2). Then he vividly compared God's teachings to the falling rain, the dew, the droplets on the fresh grass, and the showers on the herbs. He proclaimed that God's Word is the source of blessings and life (Deut 32:2). In the main body of the song, he severely rebuked the Israelites for their sin of defying and betraying God, who is faithful and without injustice (Deut 32:3–6).

Moses then appealed to Israel with three commands, as written in Deuteronomy 32:7: "Remember the days of old, consider the years of all generations. Ask your father, and he will inform you, your elders, and they will tell you."

This is a summary of how Israel, after they betrayed and left God, could come to realize their sins and fully recover. They must remember the days of old and consider the years of all generations; if they were still unsure, they were to ask their fathers and elders. Moses was making a heartrending plea to Israel to listen to the fathers and the elders, for they would have many things to explain and tell about the days of old and the years of all generations. Even though God knew that Israel would leave Him in unbelief, He still held them close, pleaded with them, and exhorted them with affectionate words. These words reflect His plaintive heart, deep thoughts, and upright teachings.

FIRST COMMAND

"Remember the days of old"

זְכֹר יְמוֹת עוֹלָם

olam yemoth zekhor

Remember

Moses commanded Israel to "remember" so that they would reflect and think about past events. "To remember" means not to forget past events. The word *zakar* (זָכַר, "remember") in Hebrew appears fifteen times in Deuteronomy alone (Deut 5:15; 7:18 [twice]; 8:2, 18; 9:7, 27; 15:15; 16:3, 12; 24:9, 18, 22; 25:17; 32:7). In addition, phrases like "do not forget" and "so that you do not forget" are repeated numerous times (Deut 4:9; 6:12; 8:11, 14; 9:7; 25:19; 31:21). This special warning and entreaty not to forget God's laws is ever so earnestly repeated. Israel must remember God's miraculous grace that He had bestowed upon them; they must not forget the covenant (Deut 4:23). They must remember that God is the only Savior (Deut 4:37–39); they must be careful not to forget this (Deut 6:12–13). They must remember in detail each and every event (Deut 11:2–7). Above all, they must remember—and remember well (Deut 7:18–19)—how they had been slaves in Egypt and how God had freed them (Deut 5:15; 7:8–11; 8:14; 15:15; 24:18). They were to remember not only God's grace but also how they had disobeyed God (Deut

9:7). God commanded them to remember all the days of their lives (Deut 16:3), keep the words of the law in their hearts, and command their children to observe these words carefully (Deut 32:46).

A servant, who is indebted to his master for his life, will be motivated to be faithful to his master as long as he remembers the grace he has received from him (Ps 116:12). A person who vividly remembers God's miraculous grace and clearly inscribes the memory of His promise of the eternal covenant in his heart will stand firm in faith. He will overflow with thanksgiving and joy, and praises will not cease from his heart (Ps 111:2–4).

The days of old

The "days of old" to be remembered encompass quite a long period of time. The word Moses used for the "days of old" is not the commonly used קֵדְמָה (*qadmah*), which refers to the past (Ps 77:5, 11; 143:5; Isa 51:9; Lam 1:7), but יְמוֹת עוֹלָם (*yemoth olam*). *Yemoth olam* is a combination of the words *yemoth*, the plural form of יוֹם (*yom*, "day"), and *olam* (עוֹלָם, "forever"). The word עוֹלָם (*olam*) refers to a "long duration," whether in the past or the future. A long duration in the future is translated as "all your days" and "forever" (Deut 23:6; 29:29; Ps 21:4; Isa 51:8), and a long duration in the past is translated as the "days of old" and "ages" (Ps 77:5; Eccl 1:10; Isa 63:9, 11). For this reason Micah 5:2 translates *yemoth olam* as "long ago" to describe the Messiah, who is self-existent and eternal.

Hence, the days of old can be traced back to the birth of the nation of Israel and furthermore to the creation of Adam and Eve. Moses' intent was for all to remember the entire history of redemption from the beginning until now. Thus the "days of old" include the creation of the universe and the fall of Adam and Eve in the garden of Eden, Cain's gruesome murder and the unbelieving deeds of his descendants, the completely sinful state of the generation during Noah's time, the pride of the people who built the tower of Babel, the covenant of the torch made with Abraham (Gen 15) and the consequent 430 years of slavery of the Israelites in Egypt, their liberation from slavery and the glorious exodus, and the forty years of trial in the wilderness. Therefore, the command to "remember the days of old" means to remember everything that God has done from the very beginning until now.

Here it is notable that the word יְמוֹת (*yemoth*), the plural form of יוֹם (*yom*, "day"; see Ps 77:5), is used instead of שְׁנוֹת (*shenoth*), the plural form of the word שָׁנָה (*shanah*, "year"), when referring to the "days of old." The days of old to be remembered include every single day of the past. The days of old are the historical foundation and the roots that brought Israel into existence. God, who is the source of Israel's blessings and sovereign over their history, would guide their future from the foundation of the world until they entered the Promised Land and for eternity.

When we backtrack through the entire course of history in which the God of the covenant has been with mankind, we will discover the footprints of His providence in each day of the days of old. These are the times that must be remembered and cherished in our hearts.

SECOND COMMAND

"Consider the years of all generations"

בִּינוּ שְׁנוֹת דּוֹר־וָדוֹר

dor-wador shenoth binu

The years of all generations

Many fathers and mothers died before the second generation that was born in the wilderness heard Moses preach his farewell sermon. Moses described the "years of all generations" as God's work of salvation experienced by the parents, grandparents, and generations of ancestors before the second generation.

The Hebrew word for generations, דּוֹר־וָדוֹר (*dor-wador*), literally means "generations and generations" and can be translated as "repeated generations." Adding the word שְׁנוֹת (*shenoth*), meaning "years," the phrase becomes שְׁנוֹת דּוֹר־וָדוֹר (*shenoth dor-wador*), meaning "years of the repeated generations," and refers to the entire history of the people of Israel. Oxford Dictionaries defines the word "generation" (דּוֹר, *dor*) as "all of the people born and living at about the same time" and "the average period, generally considered about thirty years, in which children grow up, become adults, and have children of their own."[3]

Thus the years of all generations in this context are the years from one generation to the next as well as all subsequent generations. The phrase emphasizes that these years and generations are compactly connected to each other within a time span that Moses refers to as the "days of old." In other words, it refers to the generations of ancestors that make up the days of old as well as the history of salvation that God fulfilled through them in each generation.

The "generations" refer to the genealogy, for genealogy records all the generations from the ancestors down to the descendants. Accordingly, the command to "consider the years of all generations" can also be translated as a command to consider the genealogy. These generations are the footprints of the ancestors of Israel, which are recorded in the genealogy. Hence the instruction is to carefully study the genealogies, the positive and negative attributes of the people who lived in these generations, and discover and understand the will of God who worked in their midst.[4]

---

3 *Oxford Dictionaries*, s.v. "Generation," https://en.oxforddictionaries.com/definition/generation (accessed July 11, 2018).

4 Yong-kook Won, *Deuteronomy* (Seoul: Lifebook, 1993), 503.

Consider

The command to "consider" (בִּין, *bin*, "discern, observe") the years of all generations means "to fully understand." The years of all generations contain events and matters that need to be observed carefully, studied thoroughly, pondered deeply, and cherished in the heart. In other words, this is an exhortation to observe God's redemptive history and understand its historical value and meaning. God is also exhorting His people to discern good and evil within the history of redemption and reflect upon them from a redemptive-historical perspective.

Prophet Jeremiah said to the people of Israel, "Stand by the ways and see and ask for the ancient paths, where the good way is" (Jer 6:16). The New Living Translation translates, "Stop at the crossroads and look around. Ask for the old, godly way." This is a command to learn and understand where the path is and to walk in it. In the phrase "ancient paths," the word "ancient" is the noun עוֹלָם (*olam*), meaning "long duration" or "forever," and the word "paths" is דְּרָכִים (*derakhim*), the plural form of דֶּרֶךְ (*derekh*), meaning "way."

Thus a simple translation of the phrase "see and ask for the ancient paths, where the good way is" would be "ask toward the ancient ways; find and walk toward the eternal paths." In short, the "ancient paths" and the "good way" refer to the laws of the Lord, which were the foundations of life for the ancestors of faith. This is a command to forsake our own thoughts, cease from pursuing the steps of the people of this world, and live a life that follows the Word of God. This path is the good way, the blessed way, and the way of the covenant (Deut 28–30; Ps 1).[5] The "ancient paths" are the ways of life in which one believes in the promise of the Messiah (Gen 5:29; 15:6; 49:18; Job 19:25–27).[6]

---

5 J. A. Thompson, *The Book of Jeremiah,* The New International Commentary on the Old Testament (Grand Rapids, MI: Wm. B. Eerdmans Publishing Co., 1980), 260–261.

6 Peter C. Craigie, *Jeremiah 1–25,* vol. 26, Word Biblical Commentary (Dallas, TX: Word, Incorporated, 1991), 106.

Therefore, this is a path that follows only the Word of God (see 1 Tim 1:18). It is the path of first love and eternal life.[7] This path is narrow, so few find it (Matt 7:13–14), but God promised to sow light for the righteous and gladness for the upright in heart who follow this path (Ps 97:11). Those who forsake this path and turn to another will find affliction and be deprived of peace; they will ultimately lose their lives and blessings to the enemy (Ps 7:3–5; Jer 6:16–19).

THIRD COMMAND

"Ask your father, and he will inform you,
your elders, and they will tell you"

שְׁאַל אָבִיךָ וְיַגֵּדְךָ זְקֵנֶיךָ וְיֹאמְרוּ לָךְ

lakh weyomeru zeqeneykha weyaggedekha avikha sheal

Ask

Moses' third command is an earnest plea not to be passive about inquiring of the elders and fathers, who can easily and attentively answer any question. This is evident in the meaning of the Hebrew word for "ask," which is שְׁאַל (*shaal*), meaning "to ask" or "to question." It refers to "persistent questioning," implying that one must seek with all his strength to receive a precise answer, just as a beggar would plead and beg for food. For parents this is an emphasis on the importance of education in the home and training in faith. It also implores that children need to take an interest in and actively learn about the great things that the Lord has done. At the same time, it is a rebuke against

7 Byung-Kyu Lee, *Commentary on Jeremiah and Lamentations* (Seoul: Yum Kwang, 1995), 90–91.

a rebellious generation that is apathetic and ungrateful for the great works that God has done for them.

If we ask the fathers and elders about the days of old and the years of all generations, they will surely explain them to us. Who, then, are these fathers and elders? The fathers and elders are people who are familiar with the days of old and the years of all generations. They are living witnesses to the history of Israel; they have either experienced it firsthand or been well educated about it. They will help the generation after them recall and remember the days of old and the years of all generations. They will properly explain the years of all generations and the genealogy of faith to their descendants, attesting to God's good works throughout history.

Father

The word "father" is אָב (*av*) in Hebrew. It usually refers to a parent but more broadly refers to an ancestor or forefather (Gen 15:15; Matt 3:9), the ancestor of a nation (Gen 10:21; Deut 26:5), a founder (Gen 4:20; Job 38:28), or a ruler (Gen 45:8).
The following are instances of the usage of the word "father" in the Bible.

***First*, "father" refers to the head of the household.**
Parents must teach the Scriptures to their children and raise their children in the faith (Deut 6:6–9; Job 1:5). Moses came from a blessed family in which he greatly benefited from his parents' teachings. Three prominent figures—Moses the leader of Israel, Miriam the prophetess, and Aaron the high priest—came from this one family at a time when Israel was without hope under Egypt's oppression. This fact attests to the great influence of family upbringing under their father, Amram, and mother, Jochebed. Hebrews 11 also records what they did in faith in order to save Moses (Heb 11:23).

Just before his death, David fully passed down the covenant faith to Solomon his son (1 Chr 22:9–13). He assembled all the rulers of Israel and proclaimed that God had chosen Solomon out of all his sons to sit on the throne of the kingdom of the Lord over Israel (1 Chr 28:5). Then David advised his son for the last time, saying, "As for you, my son Solomon, know the God of your father, and serve Him with a whole heart and a willing mind" (1 Chr 28:9). David confidently committed himself to be a role model of faith. He exhorted his son to follow not a distant God but the "God of [his] father," that is, the God of David. David desired for Solomon to understand how much he loved God and how faithfully he had kept His laws so that Solomon would come to know and love God as much as he did.

Like David, all fathers must be able to speak to their beloved children with confidence. When we teach our children well and raise them in faith so that faith is transmitted to their descendants, then the verse that says "grandchildren are the crown of old men, and the glory of sons is their fathers" will be fulfilled (Prov 17:6).

***Second,* "father" refers to the patriarchs of faith or the forefathers of the covenant who have carried on the genealogy of faith in each of the generations.**

Adam, the recipient of the first covenant, as well as Enoch, Noah, Shem, Abraham, Isaac, Jacob, and Joseph, the heirs of God's covenants, are all our spiritual fathers and models of faith.

Genesis 15:15 states, "As for you, you shall go to your fathers in peace." Here the word "fathers" is אָב (*av*) in Hebrew and refers to Abraham's forefathers of faith and ancestors.

"Father" also refers to the forefathers of faith who teach and guide spiritually as prophets, masters, instructors, and teachers (2 Kgs 2:12; 6:21; 13:14; 1 Cor 4:15; 1 Tim 1:2, 18; 2 Tim 1:2; Titus 1:4; 1 Pet 5:13).

***Third,* "father" refers to God the Father.**

Deuteronomy 32:6 states, "Is not He your Father who has bought you? He has made you and established you." As such, "father" is also a designation for God (Isa 64:8). The word "father" implies that God is the Creator who formed Israel (Isa 43:1; 44:2, 24; Mal 2:10; Luke 3:38), the One who saved Israel from Egypt (Isa 43:2–3), the One who protects and nurtures Israel (Isa 1:2; Jer 31:9), and the One who is worthy to be honored by Israel (Ps 135:3–4; Mal 1:6). God is Israel's eternal Father and Savior (Ps 89:26; Isa 63:16).

Elders

The Hebrew word for "elders" is זָקֵן (*zaqen*), a special term referring to the aged, an old man, the leader of a city, the representative of a tribe, the influential person (patriarch) in a family, and an elder (Gen 50:7; Exod 3:16, 18; 4:29; 12:21; 17:5–6; 18:12; 19:7; 24:1; Lev 4:15; Num 11:16; Josh 23:2; 1 Sam 8:4–5). Elders were not just the elderly. They were wise and ethical leaders who held administrative and judicial offices (Deut 21:1–9; Josh 20:4; Ruth 4:9, 11) and presided over the affairs and issues of the community (Deut 19:12; 22:15; 25:7–10).

***First*, *zaqen* generally refers to "elders."**

Ezekiel 7:26 refers to elders as people who offer counsel. During Moses' time elders were representatives of the twelve tribes of Israel. Together with Moses they led the people into Canaan (Exod 24:14; Deut 5:23; Josh 8:33; 23:2) and assisted Aaron the high priest by participating in the sacrificial rite (Lev 9:1–2). They also taught and proclaimed the Word (Deut 27:1; 31:9–11, 13, 28). Moreover, they arbitrated and adjudicated over problems among the people (Deut 21:18–21; Prov 31:23). After entry into Canaan, they always stood by the leader (Josh 7:6; 8:10) and also represented the people in their request for a king (1 Sam 8:4–5). They assisted the kings during the monarchical era (1 Chr 21:16) and served as their advisors (1 Kgs 12:6–8; 20:7–8). The elders maintained their roles throughout the period of exile in Babylon (Jer 29:1; Ezek 8:1) as well as after the return (Ezra 10:8, 14). During the New Testament era, elders taught the Word of God and nurtured the saints (1 Tim 3:2; Titus 1:7–9; Jas 5:14; 1 Pet 5:1–4).

***Second, zaqen* refers to the "priests" and the "Levites."**
The word *zaqen* refers to people with the ability to teach the Word of God. The *zaqen* were leaders of Israel who could properly pass down God's covenant faith to their descendants. In this sense *zaqen*, the leaders of the law, also included the priests and the Levites. The descendants could inquire of them about the days of old and years of all generations. The *zaqen* were the spiritual pioneers who guided the people with the Word throughout history (Lev 10:11; Deut 33:10). They also preserved the covenant of the Lord and resuscitated the faith of the people even in tumultuous times that shook the nation's foundations.

Fathers and elders were helpers who aided others in recalling the days of old and remembering the years of all generations. For those elders (*zaqen*) the Word of God was not just knowledge but wisdom attained from God's living work that was deeply rooted in their lives. This is why the people diligently inquired and learned from them. Leviticus 19:32 states, "You shall rise up before the grayheaded and honor the aged, and you shall revere your God; I am the LORD." Proverbs 16:31 also states, "A gray head is a crown of glory; it is found in the way of righteousness" (see Prov 20:29).

Former days

We make our inquiries of the fathers and elders, and the subject of our inquiries is God's work of redemption within the days of old and the years of all generations. In Deuteronomy 4:32, the people of Israel were told, "Indeed, ask now concerning the former days which were before you, since the day that God created man on the earth, and inquire from one end of the heavens to the other. Has anything been done like this great thing, or has anything been heard like it?" Here the word "ask" is שָׁאַל (*shaal*) and is the same word used in Deuteronomy 32:7. God is commanding Israel not only to ask the fathers and the elders but also to ask of their "history" that had occurred within time (former days) and space (from one end of the heavens to the other).

The New Jerusalem Bible translates Deuteronomy 4:32, "Put this question, then, to the ages that are past, that have gone before you, from when God created the human race on earth." This passage personifies "the ages that are past" as though they have returned from the former days to provide answers and testify about the redemptive work God has done. Moses is urging Israel to confront and directly question history about the former days since creation.

From one end of the heavens to the other

This expression refers to the realm in which all redemptive-historical lives existed. The Israelites were to look into the great history in the actual places where their forefathers had experienced God's sovereign works, and those places would testify and reveal historical truths. No place in all of Israel's history, from one end of the heavens to the other, is untouched by God's boundless grace. The entire universe and the world within, all of which were created by God's hand, are full of His lovingkindness and providence so that the salvation of the elect may be consummated. God's eyes have always been upon the places inhabited by Israel, His covenant people, and He has tirelessly intervened in every moment of their lives.

The history of redemption is a progressive movement in which God's covenant is being fulfilled within history. At the heart of this movement are fathers and elders who explain the days of old and the years of all generations and descendants who ask in order to recall and consider them. Israel would be perfected as God's holy people through this process of remembering, considering, asking, and explaining about the days of old and the years of all generations (Exod 19:5–6; Deut 7:6; 14:2; 26:18–19). For this reason God revealed His purpose for choosing Abraham in Genesis 18:19: "I have chosen him, so that he will direct his children and his household after him to keep the way of the LORD by doing what is right and just, so that the LORD will bring about for Abraham what he has promised him" (NIV). Ultimately it was through these covenant people that the genealogy of Jesus Christ, the son of Abraham and David, was introduced to history (Matt 1:1).

The genealogy, which uses only names to summarize the rich history of the covenant people, becomes the compass that points us to the direction and the way mankind must walk from the beginning of history to its conclusion. Therefore, by studying the genealogies in the Bible, we can relive the emotions of the experience of the blessings of Immanuel in our present day so that our faith can come alive with a clear vision for the future.

The Bible is filled with accounts of the "days of old," which we must remember, and the "years of all generations," which we must consider. We must certainly ask the fathers and elders about God's mysterious and profound providence of salvation contained within history, and we must attentively listen to their precise explanations. Even today we must ask the countless fathers and elders who are living and breathing within history and speaking to us in faith. We must ask and ask again about the days of old and the years of all generations so that we may recognize the current state of our faith. Then God's profound redemptive providence will spring forward through the many years and the hundreds of generations and stir up the same inspiration and excitement, generating great courage, hope, and comfort for us today.

We must do more than just remember, consider, and ask about the days of old and the years of all generations. Instead of keeping the knowledge to ourselves, we must open our mouths to speak, and we must take action. We must properly teach the godly descendants of faith who will remain until the day of our Lord's return. This is the reason God has left us on this earth. It is by His redemptive providence that He preserves the descendants of the covenant until the end of the world (Gen 18:18–19; 45:7).

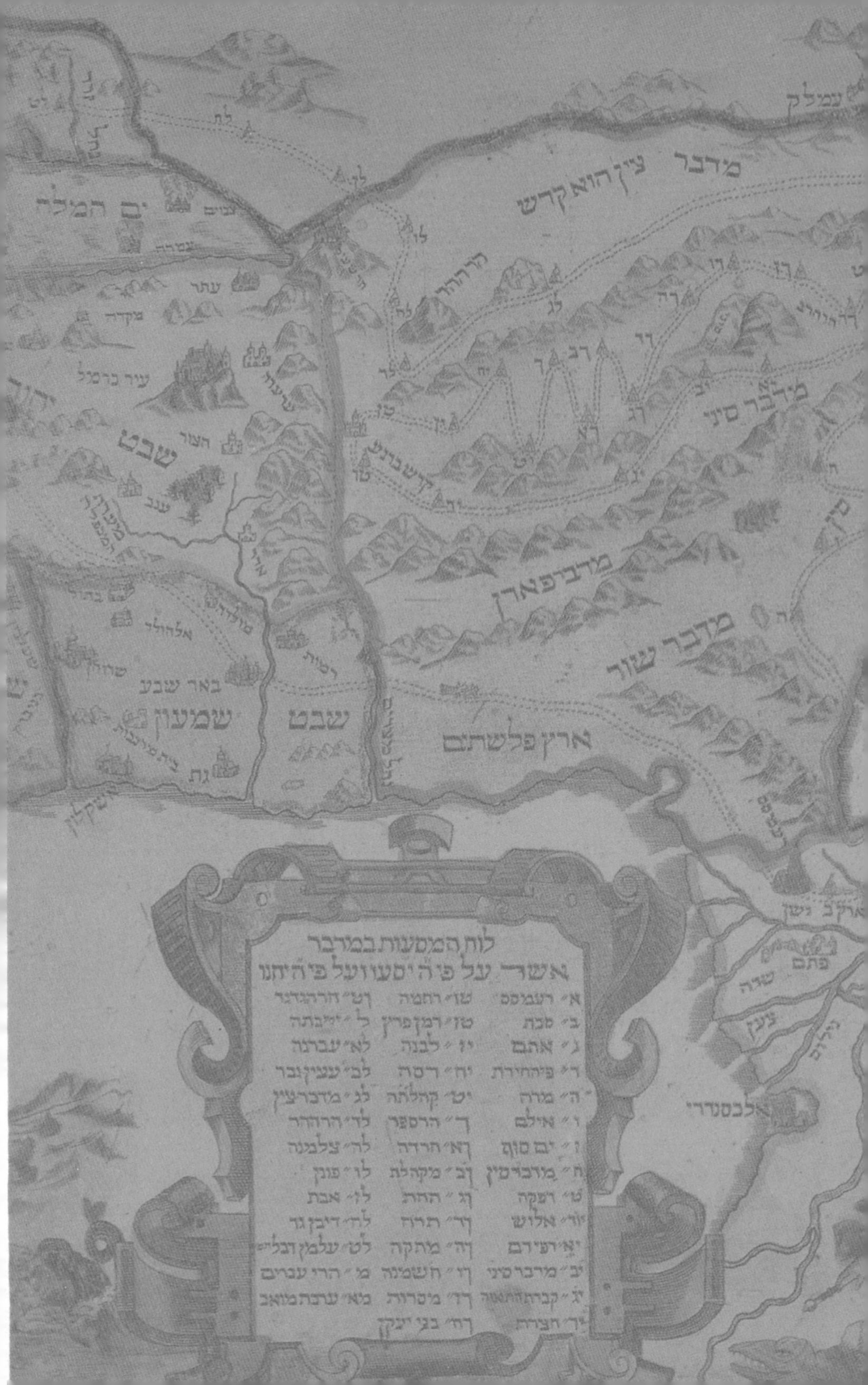

ים המלח
עמלק
מדבר צין הוא קדש
מדבר סיני
מדבר פארן
מדבר שור
ארץ פלשתים
עיר כרמל
עתר
שבט
שבט שמעון
באר שבע
גת
אשקלון
גשן
פתם
אלכסנדרי
לוח המסעות במדבר
אשר על פי ה׳ יסעו ועל פי ה׳ יחנו
א״ רעמסס | טו״ רתמה | ךט״ חרהגדגד
ב״ סכת | טז״ רמן פרץ | ל״ יטבתה
ג״ אתם | יז״ לבנה | לא״ עברנה
ד״ פיהחירת | יח״ רסה | לב״ עציון גבר
ה״ מרה | יט״ קהלתה | לג״ מדבר צין
ו״ אילם | ך״ הרספר | לד״ הרההר
ז״ ים סוף | ךא״ חרדה | לה״ צלמנה
ח״ מדבר סין | ךב״ מקהלת | לו״ פונן
ט״ דפקה | ךג״ תחת | לז״ אבת
יו״ אלוש | ךד״ תרח | לח״ דיבן גד
יא״ רפידם | ךה״ מתקה | לט״ עלמן דבלי״
יב״ מדבר סיני | ךו״ חשמנה | מ״ הרי עברים
יג״ קברות התאוה | ךז״ מסרות | מא״ ערבת מואב
יד״ חצרות | ךח״ בני יעקן

PART

II

The Chronicler's Genealogies

PART II

The command to "remember the days of old and consider the years of all generations" in Deuteronomy 32:7 was proclaimed in the plains of Moab just before Israel's entry into Canaan. Thus the "years of all generations" here refers primarily to the history of redemption spanning the time from the creation until just prior to the entry into Canaan. The Chronicler recounts not only the "years of all generations" mentioned in Deuteronomy 32:7 but the entire history of redemption, which includes the subsequent generations until the return from Babylonian exile. The entire account is told from the perspective of a priest. The books of Chronicles proclaim that the dark past has been cleared after the return from the Babylonian exile and a new era of the chosen people has begun. Moreover, by proclaiming that the Israelites are the heirs of the covenant in the final period of the Old Testament history, the Chronicler heightens the eager expectation for the Messiah, who comes according to the covenant.

The books of Chronicles can be divided into four major sections: first, the history from Adam to King Saul (1 Chr 1:1–9:44); second, the history of King David (1 Chr 10:1–29:30); third, the history of King Solomon (2 Chr 1:1–9:31); and fourth, the history from after Solomon's death until the Babylonian exile (2 Chr 10:1–36:23).

Even within the books of Chronicles, the genealogies recorded in chapters 1–9 are the most essential encapsulation of redemptive history. Thus the Chronicler's genealogies are the condensed summary of the history of redemption in the Old Testament.

CHAPTER

4

THE CHARACTERISTICS OF THE CHRONICLER'S GENEALOGIES

The genealogies in 1 Chronicles 1–9 largely consist of three parts.

***First*, the genealogies consist of the house of David** (1 Chr 1:1–3:24).
The genealogy of the chosen people of Israel begins with Adam and progresses down to the house of David through the tribe of Judah. The genealogy of the royal house of David passes through the period of the southern kingdom of Judah to Zerubbabel, who returned after the Babylonian exile (1 Chr 3:19), and to the seven sons of his descendant, Elioenai (1 Chr 3:24).

***Second*, the genealogies consist of the twelve tribes of Israel (1 Chr 4:1–8:40).**
The Chronicler documents the genealogies of the twelve sons of Jacob, the ancestors of Israel's twelve tribes, and the genealogy of each tribe until before the return from exile. Emphasis is placed upon the tribe of Levi, which was to carry out the immense and difficult task of restoring temple-centered worship during the chaotic postexilic period. The tribes of Judah and Benjamin, the two that made up the southern kingdom of Judah, were emphasized more than the rest. The

records of the tribes of Zebulun and Dan were completely omitted.

Third, **the genealogies consist, by tribes, of the postexilic generation (1 Chr 9:1–44).**
First Chronicles 9:1–9 lists the people of the southern kingdom of Judah who returned from exile. The list of the priests who returned from exile is recorded in 1 Chronicles 9:10–13, while the list of the Levites who returned is recorded in 1 Chronicles 9:14–34. This is connected to Nehemiah's list of people who returned from exile (Neh 11:3–24).

The emphasis on the priests and the Levites in these genealogical records highlights that worshiping God and living a God-centered life are crucial to Israel recovering its status as God's chosen nation.

The Chronicler's genealogies with the aforementioned structure possess the following characteristics.

1. The Chronicler's Genealogies Encapsulate the Entire Old Testament History in Names

They are a summary of the entire Old Testament history

The word "chronicles" in Hebrew is דִּבְרֵי הַיָּמִים (*divre hayyamim*) and means "the matter of the days." The Vulgate, the Latin translation of the Bible, calls the books of Chronicles "a chronicle of the whole of sacred history." The Chronicler's genealogies encapsulate the entire flow of the Old Testament history of redemption using just names. The period covered by the genealogies spans approximately 3,600 years, which starts with Adam and includes the period of the united monarchy; the period of the divided monarchy, centered mainly on the southern kingdom of Judah; and the period following the second return from the Babylonian exile. Altogether, the Chronicler's genealogies form a summarized account of the entire Old Testament history and also provide a redemptive-historical interpretation of that history.

They contain the most number of names

Most of the Chronicler's genealogies are made up solely of names, from the people mentioned in Genesis to the generation that returned from the Babylonian exile. Names are the basic and most essential elements of biblical genealogies. A name reveals information about a person's life and the relationships he or she has with other people. A name gives us a glimpse into the history of a person's nation and the nations connected to it.

In the Chronicler's genealogies, the number of persons recorded is just as important as the names recorded. The following is an examination of the number of persons recorded in 1 Chronicles 1–9.[8]

First Chronicles 1 (vv. 1–54) records the genealogy from Adam to Jacob, *a total of 191 persons* (165 men, 3 women, 12 chiefs, 11 families).

First Chronicles 2 (vv. 1–55) records the genealogy of the tribe of Judah, *a total of 161 persons* (133 men, 13 women, 15 families).[9]

First Chronicles 3 (vv. 1–24) records the genealogy of David and his descendants, *a total of 89 persons* (80 men, 9 women).

First Chronicles 4 (vv. 1–43) records the genealogies of the tribe of Judah and the tribe of Simeon, *a total of 148 persons.* The tribe of Judah (vv. 1–22) had a total of 108 persons (96 men, 7 women, 5 families), and the tribe of Simeon (vv. 24–42) had a total of 40 persons (40 men).

First Chronicles 5 (vv. 1–26) records the genealogies of the tribes to the east of the Jordan (Reuben, Gad, and half tribe of Manasseh), *a total of 60 persons* (60 men).

---

8 Repeated names were counted once, and names of families, chiefs, and tribeswomen were included (different names for the same person were counted two times).

9 Chelubai (Caleb) and Ephrath (Ephrathah) were counted two times.

First Chronicles 6 (vv. 1–81) records the genealogy of the Levites, *a total of 119 persons* (107 men, 1 woman, 11 tribes).

First Chronicles 7 (vv. 1–40) records the genealogies of the northern tribes (Issachar, Benjamin, and Naphtali) and the central tribes (Manasseh, Ephraim, and Asher), *a total of 140 persons* (134 men, 6 women). The tribe of Issachar (vv. 1–5) had 16 persons, the tribe of Benjamin (vv. 6–12) had 31 persons, the tribe of Naphtali (vv. 13) had 6 persons, the tribe of Manasseh (vv. 14–19) had 22 persons (20 men, 2 women), the tribe of Ephraim (vv. 20–29) had 21 persons (20 men, 1 woman), and the tribe of Asher (vv. 30–40) had 44 persons (42 men, 2 women).

First Chronicles 8 (vv. 1–40) records the genealogy of the tribe of Benjamin, *a total of 128 persons* (124 men, 4 women).

First Chronicles 9 (vv. 1–44) records the genealogy of those who settled in Jerusalem after the return from the exile in Babylon, *a total of 123 persons* (122 men, 1 woman). There were 28 persons from the tribes of Judah and Benjamin (vv. 3–9), 19 priests (vv. 10–13), and 35 Levites (vv. 14–34). Lastly, there were 41 persons (40 men, 1 woman) in the genealogy of King Saul (vv. 35–44), the first king of Israel.

2. The Chronicler's Genealogies Employ Both Linear and Segmented Genealogical Formats

Linear genealogies generally use a linear descending format, beginning with one ancestor and listing down to a particular descendant, or a linear ascending format, which lists up from a specific descendant to a particular ancestor. First Chronicles 1:1–4, which lists the generations from Adam to Noah's three sons—Shem, Ham, and Japheth—and 1 Chronicles 1:24–27, which lists from Shem to Abraham, are both written in a linear descending format. The genealogy in 1 Chronicles 6:49–53 is also written in the linear descending format, listing downward from Aaron to Ahimaaz, while 1 Chronicles 6:33–47 is written in the linear ascending format, listing upward from Heman to Levi.

Aside from these few examples of linear genealogies, most of the Chronicler's genealogies employ the segmented format. Some examples of segmented genealogies that appear in 1 Chronicles include the genealogy of the descendants of Japheth (1 Chr 1:5–7), the genealogies of the descendants of Ham (1 Chr 1:8–16), the genealogies of the descendants of Shem (1 Chr 1:17–23), the genealogies of the descendants of Ishmael (1 Chr 1:29–31), the genealogies of the descendants of Esau (1 Chr 1:35–42), the genealogies of the descendants of Judah (1 Chr 2:3–8), the genealogies of David (1 Chr 2:9–17), the genealogies of the descendants of David (1 Chr 3:1–9), the genealogies of the descendants of Simeon (1 Chr 4:24–37), and the genealogies of the descendants of the high priest and Levi (1 Chr 6:1–30).

3. Despite Some Gaps, the Genealogies Manifest an Uninterrupted Progression of Redemptive History

Omissions exist in the Chronicler's genealogies, which means that they do not list every physical descendant within the lineage. Within God's redemptive-historical administration, certain parts of the linear genealogy were boldly omitted, and certain parts were emphasized. People carried on the genealogy even during critical times when the lack of an heir threatened to discontinue the genealogy (1 Chr 2:33–41).

Likewise, the segmented genealogies also do not list every family member. At times only those who were necessary or relevant within redemptive history were selectively chosen and recorded. This will be closely examined in the next section.

The genealogy—which began with Adam, passed through Noah, and came down to Abraham and David—appears to have been cut off with the destruction of the southern kingdom of Judah. However, God continued the genealogy with the people who returned from exile (1 Chr 9), thereby showing that the work of redemption was not disrupted but continued even through the period of exile in Babylon.

4. The Chronicler's Genealogies Are Linked to the Genealogy of Jesus Christ

The books of Chronicles are the last books of the Hebrew Bible. Thus the Chronicler's genealogies are directly linked to the genealogy of Jesus Christ that appears in Matthew 1, the first book of the New Testament. The Chronicler's genealogies recapitulate the redemptive history in the Old Testament, while Matthew 1 uses the genealogy to introduce Jesus Christ as the central figure of the redemptive history (the genealogy) that has progressed thus far. All the genealogies in the Old Testament anticipate the coming of the Messiah. The genealogy of Jesus Christ in Matthew 1 is a firm link between the Old and New Testaments. It acts as the gateway that leads the old into the new, because it is essentially the digest of the Old Testament as well as the basis for the New Testament.

5. There Are Two Kinds of Genealogies in the Books of Chronicles

In the Chronicler's genealogies, two Hebrew words are used primarily to signify *genealogy*: יַחַשׂ (*yahas*) and תּוֹלְדֹת (*toledoth*).

יַחַשׂ (*yahas*)

The word *yahas* means "enrolled in the genealogies." This term signifies that one has been verified regarding his lineage and numbered in the census. It also confirms that the individual has been acknowledged as part of God's chosen people of Israel and enrolled in the genealogy. *Yahas* is used mainly in the genealogies that were recorded during the postexilic period such as those found in the books of Ezra, Nehemiah, and Chronicles.

The genealogy of the tribe of Simeon

> These were their settlements, and they have their genealogy [יַחַשׂ] (1 Chr 4:33).

The genealogy of the tribe of Gad

> All of these were enrolled in the genealogies [יַחַשׂ] in the days of Jotham king of Judah and in the days of Jeroboam king of Israel (1 Chr 5:17).

The genealogy of the tribe of Benjamin

> They were enrolled by genealogy [יַחַשׂ], according to their generations, heads of their fathers' households, 20,200 mighty men of valor (1 Chr 7:9).

The genealogy of the tribe of Asher

> All these were the sons of Asher, heads of the fathers' houses, choice and mighty men of valor, heads of the princes. And the number of them enrolled by genealogy [יַחַשׂ] for service in war was 26,000 men (1 Chr 7:40).

The official genealogy of all Israel

> All Israel was enrolled by genealogies [יַחַשׂ]; and behold, they are written in the Book of the Kings of Israel (1 Chr 9:1).

The genealogy of the gatekeepers

All these who were chosen to be gatekeepers at the thresholds were 212. These were enrolled by genealogy [יָחַשׂ] in their villages (1 Chr 9:22).

The genealogical enrollment in which Rehoboam is recorded

The acts of Rehoboam, from first to last, are they not written in the records of Shemaiah the prophet and of Iddo the seer, according to genealogical [יָחַשׂ] enrollment? (2 Chr 12:15).

תּוֹלְדֹת (*toledoth*)

The word *toledoth* is derived from the word יָלַד (*yalad*), which means "to bear." Thus *toledoth* means "birth," "descendant," "genealogy," or "the history of a certain event or person." The word *toledoth* emphasizes the fact that the genealogy originates from one specific ancestor and bears contents that are central to the history of redemption.

The genealogies of Ishmael

These are their genealogies [תּוֹלְדֹת]: the firstborn of Ishmael (1 Chr 1:29).

The genealogy of the tribe of Issachar

With them by their generations [תּוֹלְדֹת] according to their fathers' households were 36,000 troops of the army for war (1 Chr 7:4).

The genealogy of the tribe of Benjamin

They were enrolled by genealogy, according to their generations [תּוֹלְדֹת], heads of their fathers' households, 20,200 mighty men of valor (1 Chr 7:9).

The genealogy of the people of the tribe of Benjamin who settled in Jerusalem

> Their relatives according to their generations [תּוֹלְדֹת] [were] 956. All these were heads of fathers' households according to their fathers' houses (1 Chr 9:9).

The genealogy of the Hebronites

> As for the Hebronites, Jerijah the chief (these Hebronites were investigated according to their genealogies [תּוֹלְדֹת] and fathers' households, 1 Chr 26:31).

Besides these instances, the word תּוֹלְדֹת (*toledoth*) is used three more times in the books of Chronicles. At times, it is translated as "generations" when it is more suitable in the context than the word "genealogy" (1 Chr 7:2; 8:28; 9:34).

6. "All Israel" Is the Focus of the Genealogies

An extensive genealogy is used in 1 Chronicles 1–9 to summarize and document the long history that spans from Adam (the progenitor of mankind) to Abraham, from Abraham to King David, and from King David to the return from the Babylonian exile. All Israel emerges as one covenantal people whom God had called by name according to His sovereign choice. Except for those of Dan and Zebulun, the lineages of every tribe are briefly introduced in the genealogies. These genealogies represent the history of "all Israel." First Chronicles 9:1 states, "All Israel was enrolled by genealogies; and behold, they are written in the Book of the Kings of Israel." Phrases like "all Israel" (כָל־יִשְׂרָאֵל, *khal-yisrael*), "all the men of Israel," or "assembly of Israel" are used frequently in the books of Chronicles. A total of fifty-two instances of such variant forms can be found in the books of Chronicles.[10] Additionally, thirty-three instances are found in the books of Kings, four in the book of Ezra, and three in the book of Nehemiah.

7. The Tribes of Judah and Levi Are the Focus of the Genealogies

When many people are listed in a genealogy, it means either that the family was important from a redemptive-historical perspective or that it had flourished. The Chronicler's genealogies are centered on the twelve tribes of Israel. The focus, however, is on the tribe of Judah, to which King David belonged, and the tribe of Levi, to which the high priests belonged.

This emphasis is justified, because the tribe of Judah not only produced King David but also the promised seed, Jesus Christ (Gen 49:10; Heb 7:14). The genealogy in 1 Chronicles 1–3 documents all the descendants from Adam to King David as well as King Solomon and the kings of the southern kingdom of Judah. It lists David's descendants all the way down to the postexilic period, even into the early 400s BC. The tribe of Simeon, which had settled among the tribe of Judah, is also documented in 1 Chronicles 4:24–43.

It is noteworthy that all the people from Abraham to the last Davidic descendant documented by the Chronicler became the foundation for the genealogy of Jesus Christ in Matthew 1.

In terms of structure, the genealogy of the tribe of Levi (priests) stands at the center of the Chronicler's genealogies. First Chronicles 6 contains a total of eighty-one verses and is the longest among the genealogies in 1 Chronicles 1–9. In addition, 1 Chronicles 23–26 documents the order of temple service for the Levites, which was

---

10 1 Chr 9:1; 10:7; 11:1, 4, 10; 12:38; 13:2; 5, 6, 8; 14:8; 15:3; 16:3; 17:6; 18:14; 19:17; 21:5; 28:8; 29:21, 23, 25, 26; 2 Chr 1:2 (twice); 6:3 (twice), 13, 29; 7:3, 6, 8; 9:30; 10:1, 3, 16 (twice); 11:3, 13; 12:1; 13:4, 15; 18:16; 28:23; 29:24 (twice); 30:1, 5, 6, 25; 31:1; 35:3, 18

systematized by King David just before his death.

All of 1 Chronicles 6 is a record of the descendants of Levi. Chapter 9 lists the names of the priests (1 Chr 9:10–13), the Levites (1 Chr 9:14–16, 17–34), and the gatekeepers for the entrance of the tent of meeting (1 Chr 9:17–34)—all who had settled in Jerusalem after returning from the exile. Among the genealogies of the twelve tribes in the books of Chronicles, the genealogy of the tribe of Levi is the longest and most detailed. It even appears twice (1 Chr 23:1–24).

As evident in the chiastic structure of the genealogies in chapters 1–9, the genealogies of the high priests and the Levites in 1 Chronicles 6 are positioned at the center of the genealogies of the twelve tribes.

The chiastic structure of the Chronicler's genealogies

A 1 Chronicles 1:1–54; the world before Israel (the root of Israel)
B 1 Chronicles 2:1–2; all the sons of Israel
C 1 Chronicles 2:3–4:23; Judah, the tribe of King David
D 1 Chronicles 4:24–5:26; the tribes of Israel
E 1 Chronicles 6:1–47; the descendants of the high priest and Levi
F 1 Chronicles 6:48–49; duties of the priests
F' 1 Chronicles 6:50–53; the high priests
E' 1 Chronicles 6:54–81; the descendants of Levi in the settlements
D' 1 Chronicles 7:1–40; the tribes of Israel
C' 1 Chronicles 8:1–40; Benjamin, the tribe of King Saul
B' 1 Chronicles 9:1[a]; all of Israel that has been counted
A' 1 Chronicles 9:1[b]–34; reconstruction of Israel

The chiastic structure demonstrates that the genealogy of the tribe of Levi in chapter 6 is at the center in a symmetrical structure, preceded by five tribes—Judah, Simeon, Reuben, Gad, and the half tribe of Manasseh—and followed by six tribes—Issachar, Benjamin, Naphtali, the half tribe of Manasseh, Ephraim, and Asher. This structure emphasizes the importance of the Levites and the priests in the history of Israel.

CHAPTER

5

THE ADMINISTRATION OF REDEMPTION IN EACH CHAPTER OF THE CHRONICLER'S GENEALOGICAL SECTION

1. First Chronicles 1

Content

1 Chronicles 1:1–4	The genealogy from Adam to Noah's three sons (Shem, Ham, and Japheth)
1 Chronicles 1:5–23	The genealogy of Noah's descendants
1 Chronicles 1:24–27	The genealogy from Shem to Abraham
1 Chronicles 1:28–34	The genealogy from Abraham to Israel (Jacob)
1 Chronicles 1:35–54	The genealogy of Esau

Special characteristics

The list of names in the genealogy in 1 Chronicles 1 is almost identical to those in the Genesis genealogies. However, it contains two notable differences, aside from slight variations in some of the names.

***First*, the genealogy of the sons of Shem is different.**

Genesis 10:22–23 states, "The sons of Shem were Elam and Asshur and Arpachshad and Lud and Aram. The sons of Aram were Uz and Hul and Gether and Mash." On the other hand, 1 Chronicles 1:17 states, "The sons of Shem were Elam, Asshur, Arpachshad, Lud, Aram, Uz, Hul, Gether and Meshech." The main difference in these two verses is seen in the last four names, Uz, Hul, Gether, and Mash (Meshech), which are named as Aram's sons (Shem's grandsons) in Genesis but as Shem's sons in 1 Chronicles. The Hebrew word בֵּן (*ben*), which is translated as "son" in the books of Chronicles, primarily refers to a biological son, but it is also frequently used to refer to a descendant (e.g., Gen 31:28; Exod 12:24). Therefore, both sons and descendants of Shem may be called בֵּן (*ben*).

***Second,* the genealogy of the sons of Eliphaz is different.**

First Chronicles 1:36 states, "The sons of Eliphaz were Teman, Omar, Zephi, Gatam, Kenaz, Timna and Amalek." Here the name that differs from the Genesis account is "Timna." According to Genesis 36:12, Timna was Eliphaz's concubine, who gave birth to his son Amalek. On the contrary, 1 Chronicles 1 lists Timna as if she were Eliphaz's son. This warrants the presumption that Timna received an inheritance like the other sons of Eliphaz and formed a clan.

Redemptive-historical administration

The genealogy in 1 Chronicles 1 begins with Adam. It shows that Adam is the root of the people of Israel, and it was their duty to obey the Word of God that was given to Adam (see Gen 2:17; Hos 6:7). The Chronicler's genealogies span from the beginning (Adam) to the return from the Babylonian exile, showing that God's work of redemption through Israel has continued without halting. Thus the Chronicler's genealogies are a continuous reminder of God's administration of redemption in each generation.

In 1 Chronicles 1, the genealogies of Isaac (1 Chr 1:34) and Ishmael (1 Chr 1:28–31) are separated as are the genealogies of Esau (1 Chr 1:35–42) and Jacob (1 Chr 2:1–4). Abraham's genealogy is succeeded by Isaac (1 Chr 1:34) and Isaac's by Jacob (1 Chr 2:1).

Only descendants who possess God's promise will be enrolled in the genealogy that inherits God's covenant. Romans 9:6–8 states, "They are not all Israel who are descended from Israel; nor are they all children because they are Abraham's descendants, but: 'through Isaac your descendants will be named.' That is, it is not the children of the flesh who are children of God, but the children of the promise are regarded as descendants." Therefore, it was not Ishmael and Esau but Isaac and Jacob, sons born through God's promise, who were the legitimate heirs of the covenant (Gen 17:18–19; 25:23; 28:13–14).

2. First Chronicles 2

Content

1 Chronicles 2:1–2	The twelve sons of Israel
1 Chronicles 2:3–17	The genealogy from Judah to David
1 Chronicles 2:18–55	The genealogy of the other sons of Judah

Special characteristics

Save for a few major differences and some omissions, the genealogy in 1 Chronicles 2 is similar to other genealogies in the Bible.

***First,* the sons of Zerah**

First Chronicles 2:6 states, "The sons of Zerah were Zimri, Ethan, Heman, Calcol and Dara; five of them in all." First Kings 4:31 states that among the sons of Zerah, "Ethan the Ezrahite, Heman, Calcol, and Darda [Dara]" were Solomon's contemporaries. Their names were mentioned in reference to Solomon's wisdom. Zerah was named in the list of Jacob's seventy family members who went down to Egypt in 1876 BC (Gen 46:12), and Ethan, Heman, Calcol, and Darda (Dara) were recorded as Solomon's contemporaries (970–930 BC). Hence there is a gap of more than nine hundred years between Zerah and the four men.

Furthermore, Ethan was a descendant of Merari (1 Chr 6:44; 15:17) and is the author of Psalm 89 (Ps 89 introduction). Heman the Kohathite (1 Chr 6:33) is the author of Psalm 88 (Ps 88 introduction) and the "king's seer to exalt him according to the words of God" (1 Chr 25:5). Calcol and Darda (Dara) were listed as Ethan and Heman's brothers (1 Kgs 4:31; 1 Chr 2:6). Considering their duties, it is certain that they belonged to the tribe of Levi (1 Chr 15:16–17, 19; 25:1, 5). Nevertheless, these four men were listed in 1 Chronicles 2:6 as sons of Zerah from the tribe of Judah. This is probably because they dwelt in the land of the tribe of Judah and were assimilated into the family of Zerah of the tribe of Judah (see Judg 17:7).[11]

Ethan in particular is introduced as an "Ezrahite" (1 Kgs 4:31), which is אֶזְרָחִי (*ezrahi*) in Hebrew. This word is derived from the word זֶרַח (*zerah*), meaning "dawning" or "shining." The word *zerah* and the name "Zerah" in 1 Chronicles 2:6 are the same in Hebrew. Therefore, the word "Ezrahite" can be construed as being synonymous with the phrase "Zerah's son." The title of Psalm 88 reads, "A Psalm of the sons of Korah . . . A Maskil of Heman the Ezrahite," while the title for Psalm 89 reads, "A Maskil of Ethan the Ezrahite." The fact that both Ethan and Heman are called "Ezrahite" (אֶזְרָחִי) also supports this view. These men probably shined brightly and were greatly renowned in their day for their wisdom in serving God.

In First Kings 4:31, the other three men besides Ethan—Heman, Calcol, and Darda—are specifically listed as the "sons of Mahol"

---

11 Carl Friedrich Keil and Franz Delitzsch, *Commentary on the Old Testament*, vol. 3 (Peabody, MA: Hendrickson, 1996), 41.

(בְּנֵי מָחוֹל, *bene mahol*, "sons of dance"). The name מָחוֹל (*mahol*) is derived from the word חוּל (*hul*), meaning "to dance" or "to writhe," which is used in the Bible to refer to dancing while praising the Lord (2 Sam 6:14; Ps 30:11; 87:7; 149:3; 150:4; see also Exod 15:20; Jer 31:4, 13; Lam 5:15). Here the word בֵּן (*ben*) is not used to mean a biological son; rather, it is an expression that refers to members of a certain association or a professional guild. In the expression "sons of the prophets" (2 Kgs 2:3, 5, 7, 15; 4:1, 38; 9:1), the word "son" is also בֵּן (*ben*) in Hebrew, but it is more appropriate to accept its meaning as "group of prophets" (1 Sam 10:5; 19:20; 1 Kgs 20:35) rather than as "sons of the prophets."

Among those with various God-given musical talents (singing, dancing, and playing instruments), it is likely that those with special talent in dancing were referred to as the "sons of Mahol."[12] Even among the Ezrahites, only Heman, Calcol, and Darda were described as the "sons of Mahol," because they were dancers before God.

Although Ethan, Heman, Calcol, and Darda (Dara) were not biological brothers, they came especially together for the purpose of serving God better. They were called Ezrahites because their wisdom brought them such great renown that it was even compared to that of Solomon (1 Kgs 4:31).

Zimri, who is recorded as Zerah's firstborn in 1 Chronicles 2:6, is זִמְרִי (*zimri*) and means "praising with singing." The sons of Mahol (Heman, Calcol, Darda) served God with dancing, and Zimri served through singing praises.

According to their genealogies and their duties, these four persons (Ethan, Heman, Calcol, and Darda) were from the tribe of Levi. They were called Ezrahites or the sons (בֵּן, *ben*, "descendant") of Zerah because they assimilated with the descendants of Zerah from the tribe of Judah.

---

12 Simon J. DeVries, *1 Kings, Word Biblical Commentary*, vol. 12 (Dallas: Word, 2003), 74.

***Second*, the son of Carmi**

First Chronicles 2:7 states, "The son of Carmi was Achar, the troubler of Israel, who violated the ban." The person named "Achar" in this passage refers to Achan, the one who stole a mantle, two hundred shekels of silver, and a bar of gold fifty shekels in weight according to the account in Joshua 7. In the quest to find the culprit Achan, one of the twelve tribes was taken by lot first, and then one family was taken from that tribe.

Joshua 7:17–18 states that the family of the Zerahites was chosen from the tribe of Judah; and from them Achan the son of Carmi, the grandson of Zabdi was chosen. Here we must focus on the expression "the family of the Zerahites." The word "family" is מִשְׁפָּחָה (*mishpahah*) in Hebrew and is frequently used to denote a subdivision of a large group such as a tribe or nation (see Judg 18:19; "a family"). This is equivalent to a community of extended families.

However, note that the word "tribe" is not attached to the names Zabdi, Carmi, and Achan. Thus Carmi must have been Achan's biological father and Zabdi Carmi's biological father; Zerah was not Zabdi's biological father but an ancestor who preceded Zabdi and his sons many generations.

The name "Zerah" appears in the list of Jacob's seventy family members who entered Egypt in 1876 BC (Gen 46:12), whereas Achan, who had entered Canaan, was part of the second generation of Israelites in the wilderness journey. Accordingly, Achan's father, Carmi, took part in the exodus and was part of the first generation of the wilderness journey. Achan's grandfather, Zabdi, most likely lived during the end of the slavery period in Egypt. Thus there is a large time gap of about four hundred years between Zerah and Zabdi.

Why did the Chronicler emphasize Achan? God was using Achan's life (Achar) as an example for the Jews who had returned from exile so that they would not harbor greed or lie to God but live sanctified lives. Another example was Judah's firstborn, Er. First Chronicles 2:3 states, "Er, Judah's firstborn, was wicked in the sight of the LORD, so He put him to death" (Gen 38:7). Let us reflect upon the kind of example of faith that we are setting for others as we consider the context in which our names will be recorded in the genealogies.

***Third*, the gap between Ram and Amminadab**

First Chronicles 2:10 states, "Ram became the father of Amminadab," and Matthew 1:4 states, "Ram was the father of Amminadab." Ram was Hezron's second son (1 Chr 2:9), and Hezron's name was among those of the seventy family members who entered Egypt with Jacob (Gen 46:12). Accordingly, Hezron and his son Ram lived during the early part of the 430-year sojourn in Egypt.

On the other hand, Nahshon, who is frequently mentioned as being Amminadab's son (Exod 6:23), was a leader (prince, chief, head of his father's household) of the tribe of Judah during the post-exodus wilderness era (Num 2:3; 10:14). Nahshon's father, Amminadab, lived during the exodus and was part of the latter period of the 430-year life in Egypt. Therefore, a period of about 430 years in Egypt was omitted from the genealogy between Ram and Amminadab.

***Fourth*, the gap between Salma (Salmon) and Boaz**

First Chronicles 2:11 states, "Nahshon became the father of Salma, Salma became the father of Boaz," and Matthew 1:5 states, "Salmon was the father of Boaz by Rahab."

As we have examined, Nahshon was a leader during the forty-year wilderness journey, and his son Salma lived around 1406 BC, during the period of the entry into Canaan. However, Boaz lived during the end of the period of the judges. Boaz married Ruth and fathered Obed. Obed was the father of Jesse, the father of David, and thus Obed was David's grandfather (Ruth 4:13, 17, 22).

Therefore, about three hundred years of the period of judges were omitted between Salma and Boaz. The period of judges was a spiritually dark period in which faith was not transmitted and the people did what was right in their own eyes (Judg 17:6; 21:25).

***Fifth*, the family of Hezron**

First Chronicles 2 provides a detailed account of the family of Hezron, the son of Perez from the tribe of Judah. The record of his family is in the following order: the descendants of Ram, who was Hezron's second son (1 Chr 2:10–17); the descendants of Chelubai (Caleb; 1 Chr 2:9), who was the third son (1 Chr 2:18–20); the descendants of Segub and Ashhur, who were Hezron's sons from his second wife (1 Chr 2:21–24); the descendants of Jerahmeel, who was Hezron's firstborn (1 Chr 2:25–41); then again the descendants of Chelubai's (Caleb's) firstborn, Mesha, and of his two concubines (Ephah and Maacah; 1 Chr 2:42–49); and the descendants of Chelubai's (Caleb's) other wife, Ephrathah (Ephrath; 1 Chr 2:19, 50–55). Hezron was able to raise a large family by the exceptional grace of God.

Redemptive-historical administration

In some instances in 1 Chronicles 2, certain people's names were changed according to God's redemptive-historical administration. The book of Genesis primarily uses the name "Jacob," while the Chronicler's genealogy prefers to use the name "Israel" to refer to the same person (1 Chr 5:1, 3; 6:38; 7:29). First Chronicles 1:34 states, "Abraham became the father of Isaac. The sons of Isaac were Esau and Israel." First Chronicles 2:1 also states, "These are the sons of Israel: Reuben, Simeon, Levi, Judah, Issachar, Zebulun." Why is Jacob listed as Israel?

First, from the perspective of the inheritance of God's covenant, the new name "Israel" given amid God's blessings is more meaningful than "Jacob," a name with no regard for faith (Gen 32:28).

Second, the name "Israel" was an individual's name as well as the name of the nation (1 Chr 2:7; 4:10). This is because the nation of Israel was built upon the twelve sons of Israel.

Even Achan is recorded by a different name in the Chronicler's genealogies. Joshua 7:1 refers to him as "Achan, the son of Carmi," while 1 Chronicles 2:7 records, "The son of Carmi was Achar."

"Achan" is עָכָן (*akhan*) in Hebrew and means "troublemaker"; "Achar" is עָכָר (*akhar*) in Hebrew and means "he that brings troubles." This shows that the whole nation of Israel was troubled because of Achan (Josh 7:1–26).

The significance of these names that have been changed in the list in 1 Chronicles 2 lies in their relationship to the entire community of Israel. The name "Israel" was an honorable name that became the name of the nation, whereas "Achar" became a name that disgraced the nation.

3. First Chronicles 3

Content

1 Chronicles 3:1–9	Sons of David
1 Chronicles 3:10–16	Genealogy from Solomon to Zedekiah
1 Chronicles 3:17–24	Descendants of Jehoiachin (Jeconiah)

Special characteristics

***First,* the sons of David**

David ruled in Hebron for seven years and six months (2 Sam 2:11; 5:5; 1 Chr 3:4) and in Jerusalem for thirty-three years (2 Sam 5:5; 1 Chr 3:4). The Chronicler's genealogies differentiated sons born in Hebron and sons born in Jerusalem (1 Chr 3:1–9). The following is a comparison of differing records of David's sons from different books of the Bible.

The six sons born to him in Hebron:

2 Samuel 3:2–5		1 Chronicles 3:1–4
Amnon	the son of Ahinoam the Jezreelitess	Amnon
Chileab	the son of Abigail, the widow of Nabal the Carmelite	Daniel
Absalom	the son of Maacah, the daughter of Talmai, king of Geshur	Absalom
Adonijah	the son of Haggith	Adonijah
Shephatiah	the son of Abital	Shephatiah
Ithream	the son of Eglah, specially noted as "David's wife" (2 Sam 3:5; 1 Chr 3:3)	Ithream

The thirteen sons born to him in Jerusalem:

	2 Samuel 5:13–16	1 Chronicles 3:5–8	1 Chronicles 14:4–7
1	Shammua	Shimea	Shammua
2	Shobab	Shobab	Shobab
3	Nathan	Nathan	Nathan
4	Solomon	Solomon	Solomon
	** by Bath-shua (Bathsheba means "daughter of the oath") the daughter of Ammiel (1 Chr 3:5)*		
5	Ibhar	Ibhar	Ibhar
6	Elishua	Elishama	Elishua
7		Eliphelet	Elpelet
8		Nogah	Nogah
9	Nepheg	Nepheg	Nepheg
10	Japhia	Japhia	Japhia
11	Elishama	Elishama	Elishama
12	Eliada	Eliada	Beeliada
13	Eliphelet	Eliphelet	Eliphelet

A son named "Jerimoth" is not recorded in the genealogy

Second Chronicles 11:18 states, "Rehoboam took as a wife Mahalath the daughter of Jerimoth the son of David and of Abihail the daughter of Eliab the son of Jesse." Mahalath (born to Jerimoth and Abihail) became the wife of Rehoboam, the first king of the southern kingdom of Judah. She gave birth to Jeush, Shemariah, and Zaham (2 Chr 11:18–19). Based on 1 Chronicles 3:9, which mentions "the sons of the concubines," it is likely that Jerimoth was one of the sons born to David by a concubine.

***Second*, the sons of Josiah**

First Chronicles 3:15 states, "The sons of Josiah were Johanan the firstborn, and the second was Jehoiakim, the third Zedekiah, the fourth Shallum." Shallum was another name for Jehoahaz (2 Kgs 23:30; 2 Chr 36:1; Jer 22:11).

Jehoahaz succeeded Josiah (609b[13]–608 BC) as king at the age of twenty-three (2 Kgs 23:31; 2 Chr 36:2). However, after three months he was taken captive to Egypt, and Jehoiakim ascended the throne in his place (2 Kgs 23:31, 34; 2 Chr 36:2–4). Jehoiakim became king at the age of twenty-five and ruled for eleven years (608–597 BC; 2 Kgs 23:36; 2 Chr 36:5). Then his son Jehoiachin succeeded him (597 BC) at the age of eighteen (2 Kings 24:6; 2 Chr 36:8–9, NIV). He ruled for three months and ten days and was taken captive to Babylon (2 Kings 24:8–15; 2 Chr 36:9–10). Then Zedekiah became king at the age of twenty-one and ruled for eleven years (597–586 BC; 2 Kings 24:18; 2 Chr 36:11; Jer. 52:1).

Calculations based on these historical records reveal that Jehoahaz was born when Josiah was sixteen years old (632 BC), and Zedekiah was born when Josiah was thirty years old (618 BC); thus Zedekiah was Jehoahaz's younger brother. Accordingly, the genealogy in 1

---

13 The *b* following the year denotes the second half of the year. Similarly, when an *a* is seen after a year, it denotes the first half of the year. This notation is used throughout this book. (Refer to Abraham Park's fourth book of the History of Redemption Series, *God's Profound and Mysterious Providence*, 57–58.)

Chronicles 3:15 was not recorded in the order of birth. The younger brother, Zedekiah, was probably recorded before his older brother, Jehoahaz, in 1 Chronicles 3:15 because Zedekiah ruled much longer (eleven years) than Jehoahaz (three months).

***Third*, the sons of Zerubbabel**

Including Zerubbabel himself, seven generations of Zerubbabel's lineage are listed in 1 Chronicles 3:19–24: Zerubbabel, Hananiah, Shecaniah, Shemaiah, Neariah, Elioenai, and Hodaviah. If one generation is reckoned to be approximately twenty-five years, then Hodaviah, the last generation listed in this genealogy, must have been born around 420 BC. This is based on the assumption that Zerubbabel was born around 570 BC and that twenty-five years were subtracted for each subsequent generation until Hodaviah. Zerubbabel's birth year is conjectured to have been around 570 BC, because he was the leader of the Israelites in the first return from Babylon, which took place just after the decree proclaimed by King Cyrus of Persia in 538 BC (Ezra 2:1–2). Since one has to be at least thirty years old to become a leader, Zerubbabel must have been born before 568 BC.

Considering all these circumstances, Hodaviah must have been born around 420 BC. Since Hodaviah's six younger brothers (Eliashib, Pelaiah, Akkub, Johanan, Delaiah, and Anani; 1 Chr 3:24) are recorded in the genealogy, his youngest brother, Anani, must have been born sometime in the early years of 400 BC. This is around the time the books of Chronicles were written by Ezra, who is believed to be the author. This shows that the Chronicler's genealogies are valuable references that record all Zerubbabel's descendants to the seventh generation without any omissions.

Redemptive-historical administration

First Chronicles 3:10–16 enumerates the kings of the southern kingdom of Judah, the descendants of David. In this passage, 1 Chronicles 3:11 mentions "Joram his son, Ahaziah his son, Joash his son."

Here the record of Athaliah (840–835[b]), who made herself queen and ruled for six years, was omitted between Ahaziah and Joash.

This was because Athaliah, the daughter of King Ahab of the northern kingdom of Israel, was not a monarch from the line of David (2 Kgs 8:18, 26–27; 2 Chr 21:6). She opposed God and repeatedly performed evil acts. Worst of all, she attempted to block the path of the coming Messiah by destroying the royal seed of the house of Judah (2 Kgs 11:1; 2 Chr 22:10).

First Chronicles 3:17–24 records the Davidic lineage after the return from the Babylonian exile. The Davidic covenant, which promised that the Messiah would come as a descendant of David (2 Sam 7:12–16; 1 Chr 17:11–14), proceeded uninterrupted even through the Babylonian exile and the return therefrom. This affirmed that the covenant would persist until the coming of the Messiah. At times God's administration of redemptive history may seem buried in secular history, yet it has never ceased, and it will eventually resurface at the forefront of history.

4. First Chronicles 4

Content

1 Chronicles 4:1	Main lineage of the tribe of Judah (Perez-Hezron-Carmi-Hur-Shobal)
1 Chronicles 4:2–8	The genealogy of the inhabitants of Zorah, Etam, and Tekoa
1 Chronicles 4:9–10	The background of Jabez's birth and prayer
1 Chronicles 4:11–14	The genealogy of the inhabitants of Recah and Ge-harashim
1 Chronicles 4:15–20	The genealogy of the other main leaders of the tribe of Judah

1 Chronicles 4:21–23	The main descendants of the line of Shelah, Judah's son
1 Chronicles 4:24–27	The basic genealogy of the tribe of Simeon
1 Chronicles 4:28–33	The settlements of the tribe of Simeon
1 Chronicles 4:34–38[a]	The main leaders of the tribe of Simeon
1 Chronicles 4:38[b]–43	The conquests of the leaders of the tribe of Simeon

Special characteristics

First, the sons of Judah

First Chronicles 4:1 states, "The sons of Judah were Perez, Hezron, Carmi, Hur and Shobal." The five men listed as "sons of Judah" were not brothers; they were fathers and sons. Judah fathered Perez (Gen 46:12; Num 26:20; Ruth 4:12; 1 Chr 2:4; Matt 1:3; Luke 3:33), Perez fathered Hezron (Gen 46:12; Num 26:20–21; Ruth 4:12, 18; 1 Chr 2:4–5; Matt. 1:3; Luke 3:33), and Hezron fathered Caleb (1 Chr 2:18). However, 1 Chronicles 4:1 lists Carmi in place of Caleb. "Carmi" is כַּרְמִי (*karmi*) in Hebrew and means "vineyard." Considering the fact that Hur is listed as Caleb's son in 1 Chronicles 2:19 and Shobal as Hur's son in 1 Chronicles 2:50, Carmi and Caleb must be the same person, whose name was written differently in different places in the genealogy.

Second, the record of Jabez

Jabez is unique among the descendants of Judah in that there is a detailed personal account about him. First Chronicles 4:9 states, "Jabez was more honorable than his brothers, and his mother named him Jabez saying, 'Because I bore him with pain.'" The word "honorable" in Hebrew is in the niphal (passive) stem of the participial form of the word כָּבַד (*kavad*) and means "held in honor." Jabez received more honor than his brothers. His name, "Jabez," יַעְבֵּץ (*yabets*), originates from the word עָצַב (*atsav*), which means "to hurt," "to suffer," or "to grieve." The root of this word is related to the pain of labor (Gen 3:16). The word indicates that his mother gave birth to him amidst great sorrow, reflecting the unfortunate circumstance of his birth. This word is also used in Isaiah 14:3 to express the sorrow of the people of Israel taken into captivity in Babylon.

Jabez's sorrowful birth in 1 Chronicles 4:9 is reminiscent of the sorrow felt by the people of Israel as they were taken into Babylonian exile. The great honor he received in adulthood is reminiscent of the glory that came after the Israelites' return from exile.

Jabez was a man of prayer, despite the unfortunate circumstances surrounding his birth. First Chronicles 4:10 states, "Jabez called on the God of Israel, saying, 'Oh that You would bless me indeed and enlarge my border, and that Your hand might be with me, and that You would keep me from harm that it may not pain me!' And God granted him what he requested." Here in the request "Oh that You would bless me indeed" he repeats the word בָּרַךְ (*barakh*, "to kneel, bless"), making it an earnest plea: "Please bless me without fail." If we earnestly pray even in unfortunate situations, God will certainly answer our prayers.

There were three requests in Jabez's prayer. First Jabez prayed, "Enlarge my border." Israel had returned from exile, but they were still under attack from the surrounding nations. Thus it was a prayer for national prosperity and strength. Next he prayed that God's hand might be with him (see Neh 2:8, 18). If God's hand is with us, we will have no need for worry or concern. Lastly he prayed, "Keep me from harm that it may not pain me." When Jabez prayed for these things, God granted him all he asked for.

Jabez was honorable because he prayed even in the midst of pain and sorrow. He did not forget to pray to God, even though he lived within the hopeless state of inescapable captivity. Jabez had faith in God's absolute sovereignty; he believed that all things depended on God.

The Chronicler gives a detailed account of Jabez because the circumstances of the people returning from the exile were very similar to the circumstances surrounding Jabez's birth. This was to instill hope in the people of Israel that although they were in the midst of trouble and anxiety, if they prayed earnestly like Jabez did, then God would surely grant them glory.

Redemptive-historical administration

In 1 Chronicles 4:17, a Gentile woman, Bithia, is introduced as the wife of Mered. She is recorded as the daughter of the Pharaoh of Egypt. The name "Bithia" is בִּתְיָה (*bithyah*) in Hebrew, which is a combination of the word בַּת (*bath*, "daughter") and יָה (*yah*, shortened form of Yahweh) and means "daughter of Yahweh." She was a Gentile, but she believed in God and was assimilated into the community of the covenant people. The inclusion of the name of a Gentile woman in the Chronicler's genealogy demonstrates that the rights of covenantal inheritance are not derived from physical descent but from faith.

In addition, 1 Chronicles 4 lists the tribe of Simeon right after the tribe of Judah, preceding all the other remaining tribes. Among Jacob's twelve sons, Simeon and Levi were cursed, because they had maliciously used the rite of circumcision to take vengeance upon the Shechemites; Simeon and Levi had killed them with the sword for defiling their sister, Dinah (Gen 34:24–27; 49:5–7).

The tribe of Simeon was greatly debilitated for a long time after this incident. Even a simple comparison of the first and second censuses taken in the wilderness (59,300 persons and 22,200 persons, respectively) shows a significant decrease of 37,100 persons (Num 2:13; 26:14). Simeon was also excluded from Moses' blessings upon the tribes (Deut 33). Even during the conquest of the land of Canaan, the tribe of Simeon did not receive an inheritance of its own but was granted a portion of the inheritance of the tribe of Judah (Josh 19:1–9).

After many years, in the days of King Hezekiah, the thirteenth king of Judah (715–686 BC), a work of recovery and growth began for the enfeebled tribe of Simeon. First Chronicles 4:38 states, "Their fathers' houses increased greatly" (YLT, "The house of their fathers have broken forth into a multitude"). Thus the tribe of Simeon sought bigger pastures: "they went to the entrance of Gedor, even to the east side of the valley," and "they found rich and good pasture, and the land was broad and quiet and peaceful" (1 Chr 4:39–40). The tribe of Simeon also finished conquering the land of their inheritance, which their ancestors had been unable to do. First Chronicles 4:41 states, "These [descendants of Simeon], recorded by name, came in the days of Hezekiah king of Judah, and attacked their tents and the Meunites who were found there, and destroyed them utterly to this day, and lived in their place, because there was pasture there for their flocks." This shows that the Simeonites, who were once the weakest tribe, had fulfilled, albeit belatedly, God's command to "utterly destroy" the Canaanites (Deut 7:1–2). Thus God's grace and special providence restored them from a previously dark history.

Why was the conquest of the tribe of Simeon recorded in detail in 1 Chronicles 4? This was an urgent plea to the people returning from Babylon to overcome their dark past through proactive faith as the Simeonites had done and to blaze new trails for the future of the covenant people.

Through the accounts of Jabez from the tribe of Judah and the Simeonites in 1 Chronicles 4, God was emphasizing spiritual reformation, recovery of faith, an active prayer life, and acts of faith for those who had returned from captivity in Babylon.

5. First Chronicles 5

Content

1 Chronicles 5:1–10	The main genealogy of the tribe of Reuben and its settlements
1 Chronicles 5:11–17	The main genealogy of the tribe of Gad and its settlements

1 Chronicles 5:18–22	The battle and victory of the two and a half tribes to the east of the Jordan (Reuben, Gad, and the half tribe of Manasseh)
1 Chronicles 5:23–24	The main settlements and heads of the half tribe of Manasseh
1 Chronicles 5:25–26	The sins of the two and a half tribes to the east of the Jordan and their exile to Assyria

Special characteristics

***First,* the account of Reuben, Jacob's firstborn, losing his birthright**

First Chronicles 5:1–2 speaks of "the sons of Reuben the firstborn of Israel (for he was the firstborn, but because he defiled his father's bed, his birthright was given to the sons of Joseph the son of Israel; so that he is not enrolled in the genealogy according to the birthright. Though Judah prevailed over his brothers, and from him came the leader, yet the birthright belonged to Joseph)." The reason for the loss of Reuben's birthright and the consequences of this loss are clearly revealed at the opening of the genealogy in 1 Chronicles 5.

The Bible reiterates numerous times that Reuben is the firstborn of Israel (Exod 6:14; Num 1:20; 26:5; 1 Chr 5:1, 3). Using various expressions, Genesis 49:3 alone indicates five times that Reuben is the firstborn: "my firstborn," "my might," "the beginning of my strength," "preeminent in dignity," and "preeminent in power."

Nevertheless, Genesis 49:4 explains in detail why he lost his birthright: "Because you went up to your father's bed; then you defiled it." The phrase "defile the bed" is a Hebrew euphemism referring to unlawful sexual relations. This refers to how Reuben lay with his father's concubine, Bilhah (Gen 35:22). Bilhah (בִּלְהָה, "gentle," "simple") was Rachel's maid and the mother of Dan and Naphtali (Gen 29:29; 30:3–8). Reuben possessed uncontrollable lust that caused him to lie with his father's concubine and defile his father's bed. Ultimately, Satan caused him to lose his birthright by attacking his greatest weakness. According to the law, having relations with the wife of one's own father was like "uncovering the nakedness of the father," which was a grave sin punishable by death (Lev 18:6–8; 20:11; Deut 22:30; 27:20).

***Second*, the account of the history of the tribe of Reuben**

The tribe of Reuben was exiled to Assyria when Tilgath-pilneser III, the king of Assyria, attacked the northern kingdom of Israel (2 Kgs 15:29; 1 Chr 5:26). First Chronicles 5:6 states, "Beerah his son, whom Tilgath-pilneser king of Assyria carried away into exile; he was leader of the Reubenites." According to 1 Chronicles 5:7–10, the chiefs of the tribe of Reuben—Jeiel, Zechariah, and Bela—settled "as far as the entrance of the wilderness from the river Euphrates." The account also tells us that in the days of King Saul, these three kinsmen of Beerah were victorious in battle against the Hagarites and settled in all the lands east of Gilead. The word "kinsman" (אָח, *ah*) in 1 Chronicles 5:7 must be understood as also referring to the Reubenites at large. Even though Jeiel, Zechariah, and Bela are recorded as being Beerah's brothers who lived at the time the northern kingdom of Israel was destroyed (1 Chr 5:6–7), they were actually contemporaries of King Saul (1 Chr 5:10).

The Chronicler contrasts 1 Chronicles 5:6 with 5:7–10 to instill hope in the Israelite community that even though they now endured the tragedy of exile, they would experience amazing recovery and growth after their return. On the other hand, the contrasting passages also clearly show that although the Israelites had been blessed with prosperity in the past for trusting in God, they would certainly receive judgment if they turned to idols and disobeyed God's Word.

***Third*, the word regarding the victory and fall of the three tribes**

According to 1 Chronicles 5:18, the tribes of Reuben, Gad, and the half tribe of Manasseh had 44,760 valiant men, skillful in battle. These tribes obtained great victory in battle against the Hagrites, Jetur, Naphish, and Nodab. They took 50,000 camels, 250,000 sheep, 2,000 donkeys, and 100,000 men. They were victorious in battle because they trusted in God and cried out to Him, and He heard their cries and helped them. First Chronicles 5:20 states, "They were helped against them, and the Hagrites and all who were with them were given into their hand; for they cried out to God in the battle, and He answered their prayers because they trusted in Him."

Nevertheless, the ultimate reason for their victory was that the battle was from God. First Chronicles 5:22 states that "the war was of God." Thus there will surely be victory in wars that are of God, that is, wars that God initiates.

Nevertheless, even after obtaining such great victories, these three tribes fell when Assyria attacked Israel. They were carried away into exile by Tilgath-pilneser (Pul) king of Assyria and brought to Halah, Habor, Hara, and to the river of Gozan (1 Chr 5:26). This was because they had sinned by playing the harlot with foreign gods, so God stirred up the spirit of the Assyrian king to attack Israel (2 Kgs 17:7–18). First Chronicles 5:26 states, "So the God of Israel stirred up the spirit of Pul, king of Assyria, even the spirit of Tilgath-pilneser king of Assyria, and he carried them away into exile, namely the Reubenites, the Gadites and the half tribe of Manasseh, and brought them to Halah, Habor, Hara and to the river of Gozan, to this day."

The stark contrast between the victory and fall of these three tribes served as a powerful lesson to warn the postexilic generations against repeating past transgressions of unfaithfulness. We too have to bear in mind that if we become intoxicated in our momentary victories and turn to idol worship with coveting of every kind, the wrath of God will suddenly strike, and the day of destruction will come upon us (Col 3:5–6).

Redemptive-historical administration

The genealogy in 1 Chronicles 5 begins with Reuben's loss of his birthright (1 Chr 5:1–2). Because Reuben lay with Bilhah, his father's concubine, and defiled his father's bed (Gen 35:22; 49:3–4), the right of the firstborn went to the descendants of Joseph (Gen 49:22–26). This is mindful of the fact that Joseph was the spiritual firstborn and that

Jacob's seventy family members were saved through Joseph (Gen 45:7, 46:27, 47:12, 50:21). However, the second part of 1 Chronicles 5:1 states that Reuben's "birthright was given to the sons of Joseph the son of Israel; so that he [Joseph] is not enrolled in the genealogy according to the birthright." This demonstrates that it is not Joseph but actually Judah, the fourth son, who is the firstborn according to the genealogy.[14] It also reveals that from the tribe of Judah will come not only King David but also the ruler, that is, the Messiah (Gen 49:8–10; see also Isa 9:7; Jer 23:5; Ezek 34:23; Matt 1:1).

Reuben's loss of the birthright is in direct contrast to Joseph's life, which reflects the qualities of a firstborn; Joseph rose to be second in command in Egypt and saved his people. At the same time, it also reveals how the legitimacy of the covenant inheritance was transmitted through the tribe of Judah.

Reuben was Jacob's firstborn. If he had not sinned, he would have received a double portion of the inheritance and the authority to rule over the family (Deut 21:15–17). Isaac's son Esau was the firstborn by birth, but he despised his birthright (Gen 25:34) and did not receive the blessings of the firstborn (Gen 27:22–23, 35–36). Thus the birthright eventually went to Jacob (see Heb 12:16–17). Although Reuben was the legal firstborn, the blessing of the double portion within the birthright went to Joseph (Gen 48:5), and the scepter of the ruler went to Judah (1 Chr 5:1–2).

A father's bed is his authority and his secret. Reuben committed the grave sin of adultery as well as that of challenging his father's authority. David's son Absalom also committed the sin of disgracing

---

14 Three kinds of firstborn are mentioned in the Bible: (1) the physical firstborn (literally born first); (2) the firstborn according to genealogy, i.e., the one given the honor due the firstborn (in this case Judah, Jacob's fourth born, since Reuben was disqualified for dishonoring his father's bed, and Simeon and Levi, the second and third born, were disqualified for using circumcision as a tool of murder [see Gen 34 and Jesus' genealogy, Matt 1:2-3]); and (3) the spiritual firstborn (in this case Joseph, Gen 37:5-10). (Refer to Abraham Park's second book of the History of Redemption Series, *The Covenant of the Torch*, 261-266.)

his father's wives (2 Sam 12:11–12; 16:21–22), and he met a tragic end. As Absalom fled on his mule, his hair, which was his pride (2 Sam 14:25–26), was caught in the branches of an oak. Then Joab, the commander of David's army, speared him in the heart, and the ten young men who carried Joab's armor surrounded Absalom and struck him to death (2 Sam 18:9–15, NIV).

We must note that the Chronicler's genealogies stress the importance of the loss and the acquisition of the birthright. The account of how Reuben, Jacob's firstborn, lost his birthright teaches an important lesson that we must all deeply ponder: no matter how preeminent and powerful a person may be, a momentary sin of "adultery" can strip a person of all the blessings that God had prepared and stored up for him.

6. First Chronicles 6

Content

1 Chronicles 6:1–15	Genealogy of the high priest
1 Chronicles 6:16–30	Genealogy of the tribe of Levi Descendants of Levi: vv. 16–19 Descendants of Gershom (Gershon): vv. 20–21 Descendants of Kohath: vv. 22–28 Descendants of Merari: vv. 29–30
1 Chronicles 6:31–47	Genealogy of the descendants of Levi who ministered as musicians Beginning of the ministry of the musicians: vv. 31–32 Genealogy of Heman: vv. 33–38 Genealogy of Asaph: vv. 39–43 Genealogy of Ethan: vv. 44–47

1 Chronicles 6:48–49	Duties of the Levites, the priests, and the high priests
1 Chronicles 6:50–53	Genealogy of the high priests (from Aaron to King David's period)
1 Chronicles 6:54–81	Cities settled by the tribe of Levi

Special characteristics

First, the account of Azariah

The list of the high priests in 1 Chronicles 6:1–15 makes special mention of Azariah's deeds. First Chronicles 6:10 states, "Johanan became the father of Azariah (it was he who served as the priest in the house which Solomon built in Jerusalem)." Azariah lived at a time when Solomon's temple had become the center of people's lives and religion. This emphasized to the postexilic generations that the temple must be the focus of their religion and lives.

The genealogy of the high priests ends in 1 Chronicles 6:15 with the deportation to Babylon. This shows that the tragic exile to Babylon resulted because the temple was not the central focus of the Israelites' lives.

Second, the account of the service of song

The ark of the covenant, which had been taken away during Samuel's time, was kept in Kiriath-jearim. David finally brought it to the city of David in Jerusalem and placed it in a tent (2 Chr 1:4). First Chronicles 6:31 records the incident with the expression "the ark rested there." It was at this time that David appointed people over the service of song in the house of the Lord. The representatives of those who ministered with song were Heman, Asaph, and Ethan. Heman was a descendant of Kohath (1 Chr 6:33–38), Asaph was a descendant of Gershom (Gershon; 1 Chr 6:39–43), and Ethan was a descendant of Merari (1 Chr 6:44–47). As such, God selected leaders over the service of song evenly from among the descendants of the three sons of Levi.

***Third*, the account of the Levites who were appointed**
First Chronicles 6:31 states, "These are those whom David appointed over the service of song in the house of the LORD." The word "appointed" is in the hiphil (causative) stem of the verb עָמַד (*amad*) and means "to establish." First Chronicles 6:48 also states, "Their kinsmen the Levites were appointed for all the service of the tabernacle of the house of God." Here the word "appointed" is נָתַן (*nathan*), and it also means "to establish." This means that the duties of the Levites, whatever they may have been, were all necessary for God's glory. Each person was appointed through an official appointment process, and God advised the Levites to be faithful and work with a great sense of calling.

Redemptive-historical administration

First Chronicles 5 gives an account of the three tribes that settled to the east of the Jordan River. Instead of following with the account of the tribes to the west of the Jordan, chapter 6 gives an account of the tribe of Levi first. Within the tribe of Levi, the genealogy of the high priests appears first (1 Chr 6:1–15) and is repeated again in 1 Chronicles 6:49–53. This is because the high priests were spiritual representatives of the people and held the most important positions in the tabernacle (temple). First Chronicles 6:49 states, "Aaron and his sons offered on the altar of burnt offering and on the altar of incense, for all the work of the most holy place, and to make atonement for Israel, according to all that Moses the servant of God had commanded." By emphasizing the priestly office to the postexilic generations, God is revealing that the remnant of Israel has the same priestly duty to save the whole world. In Exodus 19:6, God said to Israel, "You shall be to Me a kingdom of priests and a holy nation" (see 1 Pet 2:9; Rev 1:6; 5:10).

7. First Chronicles 7

Content

1 Chronicles 7:1–5	The genealogy of the tribe of Issachar
1 Chronicles 7:6–12	The genealogy of the tribe of Benjamin
1 Chronicles 7:13	The genealogy of the tribe of Naphtali
1 Chronicles 7:14–19	The genealogy of the half tribe of Manasseh
1 Chronicles 7:20–29	The genealogy of the tribe of Ephraim
1 Chronicles 7:30–40	The genealogy of the tribe of Asher

Special characteristics

***First*, Zelophehad had only daughters.**

First Chronicles 7:15 states, "The name of the second was Zelophehad, and Zelophehad had daughters." In this account it appears as if Zelophehad is Manasseh's second son. However, Numbers 27:1 states, "The daughters of Zelophehad, the son of Hepher, the son of Gilead, the son of Machir, the son of Manasseh, of the families of Manasseh the son of Joseph, came near." Hence Zelophehad was not Manasseh's second son. The word "second" used here is שֵׁנִי (*sheni*), and besides meaning "second," it also means "another." Thus a more accurate rendering of the original text for the sentence "The name of the second was Zelophehad" in 1 Chronicles 7:15 would be "The name of another was Zelophehad."

Zelophehad had five daughters and no sons (Josh 17:3). Since only men were able to receive inheritances from their parents at that time, there was a risk that Zelophehad's inheritance would be lost. Hence his five daughters asked Moses to give them their father's inheritance, since Zelophehad had no sons. Moses inquired of God regarding the matter, and God commanded that the inheritance be given to daughters in cases where there is no son. Numbers 27:8 states, "You shall speak to the sons of Israel, saying, 'If a man dies and has no son, then you shall transfer his inheritance to his daughter.'"

Then the people from the tribe of Manasseh raised the issue of their ancestors' inheritance being transferred to another tribe in the case that the daughters of Zelophehad married men from another tribe. Seeing the validity of this issue, Moses said, "This is what the LORD has commanded concerning the daughters of Zelophehad, saying, 'Let them marry whom they wish; only they must marry within the family of the tribe of their father.' Thus no inheritance of the sons of Israel shall be transferred from tribe to tribe, for the sons of Israel shall each hold to the inheritance of the tribe of his fathers" (Num 36:6–7).

This incident is emphasized in 1 Chronicles 7 in order to teach all postexilic generations the importance of preserving the inheritances of the ancestors.

***Second*, Ephraim's two sons were killed by the men of Gath.**
Besides Shuthelah, Ephraim had other sons named Ezer and Elead. However, they were killed by the Gathites, men born in the land of Gath, because they were trying to take their livestock. Ephraim mourned many days, and his relatives came to comfort him (1 Chr 7:21–22). He had another son after this, and he named him Beriah. The name "Beriah" is בְּרִיעָה (*beriah*) in Hebrew and means "in misfortune" (1 Chr 7:23).

Beriah was the son born to Ephraim when his family was in extreme sorrow due to the disastrous incident. However, one of Beriah's direct descendants was Joshua, Moses' successor and leader of the conquest of Canaan (1 Chr 7:27). Our God has boundless compassion and is always with His people through every time of sorrow and pain while making provisions for them for a brighter future.

Redemptive-historical administration

The genealogy of the tribe of Ephraim in 1 Chronicles 7 ends with Joshua. He was the leader during the period of the Canaan conquest, and his life came to a close at the age of 110 in 1390 BC (Josh 24:29).

Approximately one thousand years passed from Joshua's death until the recording of the Chronicler's genealogies after the return from the Babylonian exile. Yet the Chronicler's genealogies end with Joshua without recording any more descendants from the Ephraimites after him, revealing a great redemptive-historical administration to the postexilic generations.

The Chronicler's genealogy of the tribe of Ephraim testifies to the fact that Joshua, the great leader in the conquest of Canaan, had been born to the line of Ephraim after Ephraim underwent the pain and suffering of losing his two sons, Ezer and Elead, to the Canaanites. This gave hope to the people, who were experiencing pain and suffering in various ways after the return from the exile, that there would be another work of victory like that of the conquest of Canaan.

The emergence of Joshua is a foreshadowing of the coming of Jesus Christ, who comes to destroy Satan, our adversary, and resolve all issues involving tragedy and pain. Ezer and Elead were killed by the men of Gath, who had been "born in the land" (1 Chr 7:21). The word "land" is אֶרֶץ (*erets*), and the people "born in the land" refer to the "indigenous peoples." They were natives of the land of Canaan and had lived there for generations. By conquering the land of Canaan, therefore, Joshua destroyed and overcame an old enemy of the family. The name "Joshua" in Hebrew is יְהוֹשֻׁעַ (*yehoshua*), meaning "the LORD is salvation." Joshua had been born into a family of tragedy, but he became the family's hope and comfort. Today for mankind living among sin, death, tears, pain, and suffering, Jesus is our only hope and comfort. There is nothing on Earth upon which we can place our hope (see Eccl 1:2). Only Jesus Christ is the source of living hope (1 Tim 1:1). Only Jesus Christ, the mystery of God, is our eternal hope of glory (Col 1:27).

8. First Chronicles 8

Content

1 Chronicles 8:1–5	The genealogy of Benjamin and the sons of Bela
1 Chronicles 8:6–28	The genealogy of the descendants of Ehud
1 Chronicles 8:29–33	The genealogy of Saul
1 Chronicles 8:34–40	The genealogy of Jonathan

Special characteristics

***First*, the names of Benjamin's sons are recorded differently than in other passages.**

The passages in Genesis 46:21, Numbers 26:38–40, 1 Chronicles 7:6–8, and 1 Chronicles 8:1–5 all record the names of Benjamin's sons differently. Reasons for this may be explained as follows: one person may have had two different names; not all sons were listed but only the important ones were selectively recorded; or even the descendants from subsequent generations were included in the genealogy. The following is a chart of their names.

Benjamin's sons and descendants	
Genesis 46:21	"The sons of Benjamin: *Bela* and *Becher* and *Ashbel*, *Gera* and *Naaman*, *Ehi* and *Rosh*, *Muppim* and *Huppim* and *Ard*."
Numbers 26:38–40	"The sons of Benjamin according to their families: of *Bela*, the family of the Belaites; of *Ashbel*, the family of the Ashbelites; of *Ahiram*, the family of the Ahiramites; of *Shephupham*, the family of the Shuphamites; of *Hupham*, the family of the Huphamites. The sons of Bela were *Ard* and *Naaman*: of Ard, the family of the Ardites; of Naaman, the family of the Naamites."

First Chronicles 7:6–8	"The sons of Benjamin were three: *Bela* and *Becher* and *Jediael*. The sons of Bela were five: *Ezbon*, *Uzzi*, *Uzziel*, *Jerimoth* and *Iri*. They were heads of fathers' households, mighty men of valor, and were 22,034 enrolled by genealogy. The sons of Becher were *Zemirah*, *Joash*, *Eliezer*, *Elioenai*, *Omri*, *Jeremoth*, *Abijah*, *Anathoth* and *Alemeth*. All these were the sons of Becher."
First Chronicles 8:1–5	"Benjamin became the father of *Bela* his firstborn, *Ashbel* the second, *Aharah* the third, *Nohah* the fourth and *Rapha* the fifth. Bela had sons: *Addar*, *Gera*, *Abihud*, *Abishua*, *Naaman*, *Ahoah*, *Gera*, *Shephuphan* and *Huram*."

***Second*, the account of Shaharaim**

Shaharaim (שַׁחֲרַיִם, "two dawns" or "double dawn") had two wives, Hushim and Baara (1 Chr 8:8), but he sent them away. The phrase "sent away" in 1 Chronicles 8:8 means to divorce and drive them away. Then Shaharaim went to the country of Moab and married Hodesh and had children (1 Chr 8:8–10).

First Chronicles 8 makes a contrast between the lineage begotten through an Israelite wife (1 Chr 8:11–28) and that begotten through a Moabite woman (1 Chr 8:8–10) and emphasizes how God's inheritance was passed down through the children born through the Israelite wife. This sounded an alarm for the postexilic generations. In those days the problem of intermarriage with Gentiles was a serious rebellion against God. It was an act of disobedience against God's Word and considered a roadblock in the path of the coming of the Messiah, who was to come through the lineage of faith (Ezra 9:1–2; Neh 13:23–29). The genealogy in 1 Chronicles 8 teaches that the Israelites were not to intermarry with Gentiles in order to become a lineage that continued the heritage of God's inheritance.

Redemptive-historical administration

The genealogy of Benjamin was already recorded in 1 Chronicles 7:6–12. Why is it recorded again in such detail in 1 Chronicles 8:1–40?

First, it was because the first king of Israel was from the tribe of Benjamin (1 Sam 10:21; 1 Chr 8:33).

Second, it was because the tribe of Judah and the tribe of Benjamin constituted the southern kingdom of Judah during the period of the divided monarchy. Only the tribe of Benjamin, choosing not to side with the northern kingdom of Israel, remained with the tribe of Judah to form the southern kingdom of Judah and inherited the Davidic covenant (1 Kgs 12:21; 2 Chr 11:12; 15:2).

Third, the tribe of Benjamin represented a significant number of the generations that returned from the exile (Neh 11:7–9, 31–36). The record in Nehemiah 11:4 highlights the tribes of Benjamin and Judah among those who settled in Jerusalem.

The tribe of Benjamin, rather than choosing to retain their tribal pride or interests, chose to remain on the side that preserved the legitimacy of covenantal succession. Paul, who would be used greatly as an apostle in the future, was also from the tribe of Benjamin (Rom 11:1). He described himself in Philippians 3:5 as "circumcised the eighth day, of the nation of Israel, of the tribe of Benjamin, a Hebrew of Hebrews; as to the Law, a Pharisee." We must also choose at all times to continue the legitimacy of God's covenant and be faithful to the work of building God's kingdom.

9. First Chronicles 9

Content

1 Chronicles 9:1–9	Those who returned from exile and settled in Jerusalem

1 Chronicles 9:10–13	The priests who returned from exile
1 Chronicles 9:14–34	The Levites who returned from exile
1 Chronicles 9:35–44	The genealogy of Saul

Special characteristics

***First*, the record of the sons of the temple servants (Nethinim; KJV)**
First Chronicles 9:2 (KJV) mentions the Nethinims (temple servants) along with the priests and the Levites as it introduces the people who returned from the Babylonian exile. "Nethinim" in Hebrew is נְתִינִים (*nethinim*) and means "people who have been bestowed" or "temple servants" (most modern English Bibles translate "Nethinim" as "temple servants"). When Ezra was returning from the Babylonian exile, he completely halted the march and gathered all the returning exiles at the river that runs to Ahava. During the three-day camp there, they examined the people and the priests and found that there were no Levites among them. He called the nine leading men as well as Joiarib and Elnathan, men of insight, and had them perform a thorough search "at the place Casiphia" (Ezra 8:17). As a result, thirty-eight Levites from three families (represented by Sherebiah, Hashabiah, and Jeshaiah) and two hundred twenty temple servants joined the ranks of the returning exiles (Ezra 8:15–20). Ezra 8:20 states that the leading men brought people "also of the Nethinim, whom David and the leaders had appointed for the service of the Levites, two hundred and twenty Nethinim. All of them were designated by name" (NKJV). The Nethinim were able to join the ranks of the Levites returning from exile probably because they had lived together in the settlements of the Levites.

The Levites were known to have been entrusted with the service of the house of the Lord (Num 3:6–9; 1 Chr 23:3–5). Although the Nethinim were called "temple servants," there was a distinction between them and the Levites. The unique characteristic of the genealogy of the Nethinim is that they were not of pure Jewish descent; they were

Gentiles who served in the temple (Ezra 2:43–54; Neh 7:46–56). Although the Nethinim were not Israelites by blood, they had become Israelites fundamentally by rooting deep down into the Lord-fearing faith.

The Nethinim returned from exile and settled in Ophel (Neh 3:26; 11:21). Ophel was considered a part of the "holy city," as it was a region connected to the southern valley of the temple of Jerusalem.

Second, the list of those returning from exile

The list of the returning exiles recorded in 1 Chronicles 9:3 includes the sons of Judah, the sons of Benjamin, the sons of Ephraim, and the sons of Manasseh. First Chronicles 9:4–9 contains accounts only of the sons of Judah and Benjamin. This is because these two tribes that formed the southern kingdom of Judah also played a leading role in establishing a theocratic nation after the return from exile (Ezra 1:5; 4:1).

Third, the list of the priests returning from exile

First Chronicles 9:13 introduces the genealogy of the priests who returned from exile: "1,760 very able men for the work of the service of the house of God."

The expression "very able men" is גִּבּוֹרֵי חֵיל (*gibbore hel*) in Hebrew. The word גִּבּוֹרֵי (*gibbore*) means "warrior" or "mighty man," and the word חֵיל (*hel*) is the construct form of חַיִל (*hayil*), meaning "ability." Thus the phrase "very able men" means "men with ability" or "men of strength." People who serve in God's temple must be "people with strength." However, the strength used to serve in the temple must not be human strength but strength given by God. First Peter 4:11 states, "Whoever speaks, is to do so as one who is speaking the utterances of God; whoever serves is to do so as one who is serving by the strength which God supplies; so that in all things God may be glorified through Jesus Christ, to whom belongs the glory and dominion forever and ever. Amen."

***Fourth*, singers among the leaders of the Levites who returned from exile**

First Chronicles 9:33 states, "These are the singers, heads of fathers' households of the Levites, who lived in the chambers of the temple free from other service; for they were engaged in their work day and night." They were descendants of Heman, Asaph, and Ethan, who served as singers during the Davidic era (1 Chr 6:33, 39, 44). They continued to perform well the duties of the singers even after the return from exile.

Here the word "chambers" is לִשְׁכָּה (*lishkah*) in Hebrew and refers to a room connected to the temple (Neh 10:38; Ezek 40:17, 45). In addition, the word "engaged" is עֲלֵיהֶם (*alehem*), which was formed by combining the preposition עַל (*al*) with a third-person masculine plural pronoun suffix; thus it literally means "over them." In other words, there was always work over the singers, meaning that they lived in the chambers connected to the temple and were dedicated solely to doing God's work. They were always preparing in order to be able to properly perform their duties as singers. Hence they were ready to sing praises to God at any time. They were the very people mentioned in Psalm 84:4, which states, "How blessed are those who dwell in Your house! They are ever praising You. Selah."

Redemptive-historical administration

First Chronicles 9:32 states, "Some of their relatives of the sons of the Kohathites were over the showbread to prepare it every sabbath." Here the word "showbread" represents Jesus Christ, the bread of life. Jesus said in John 6:48, "I am the bread of life."

Just as the showbread was replaced with new loaves every Sabbath (Lev 24:8), all saints must go to church every Lord's Day and be renewed through Jesus Christ, the bread of life. We enjoy physical and spiritual peace and rest, and receive new strength to obtain victory in this world by the Word of God preached through God's servants. Thus we must arm ourselves every Lord's Day with the sword of the Spirit, the Word of God (Eph 6:17).

God promised that He would give us the hidden manna. Revelation 2:17 states, "He who has an ear, let him hear what the Spirit says to the churches. To him who overcomes, to him I will give some of the hidden manna, and I will give him a white stone, and a new name written on the stone which no one knows but he who receives it." I pray in the name of the Lord that our families and churches may receive the "hidden manna" and triumph at all times with ever-renewing faith.

ים המלח
מדבר צין הוא קדש
עמלק
מדבר סיני
מדבר פארן
מדבר שור
ארץ פלשתים
שבט
שבט
שמעון
באר שבע
עיר כרמל
ארץ גשן
פתם
אלכסנדרי
לוח המסעות במדבר
אשר על פי ה׳ יסעו ועל פי ה׳ יחנו
א׳ רעמסס טו׳ רתמה כט׳ חר הגדגד
ב׳ סכת טז׳ רמן פרץ ל׳ יטבתה
ג׳ אתם יז׳ לבנה לא׳ עברנה
ד׳ פי החירת יח׳ רסה לב׳ עצין גבר
ה׳ מרה יט׳ קהלתה לג׳ מדבר צין
ו׳ אילם כ׳ הר ספר לד׳ הר ההר
ז׳ ים סוף כא׳ חרדה לה׳ צלמנה
ח׳ מדבר סין כב׳ מקהלת לו׳ פונן
ט׳ דפקה כג׳ תחת לז׳ אבת
י׳ אלוש כד׳ תרח לח׳ דיבן גד
יא׳ רפידם כה׳ מתקה לט׳ עלמן דבלתים
יב׳ מדבר סיני כו׳ חשמנה מ׳ הרי עברים
יג׳ קברות התאוה כז׳ מסרות מא׳ ערבות מואב
יד׳ חצרות כח׳ בני יעקן

PART

III

The Duties of the Priests and Levites

PART III

The Chronicler's genealogies in 1 Chronicles 1–9 encapsulate the entire history of redemption, and the genealogy of the Levites (priests) in 1 Chronicles 6 stands at the center of these genealogies. God established the priests from the tribe of Levi and set them apart so they would be focused solely on serving God (Num 3:5–10). When God established the priesthood, He entered into a covenant with the priests and Levites and made it a perpetual statute (Exod 27:21; 28:1–3; Neh 13:29; Jer 33:21; Mal 2:4–5, 8). Moreover, He established laws regarding offerings and consecrated the priests (Lev 1–8). The laws regarding the offerings and the priestly covenant will be discussed in detail in upcoming volumes of the History of Redemption Series.

This chapter will examine the duties of the Levites and the priests with a focus on their twenty-four divisions. First Chronicles 22–29 contains the account of David's last will and testament to Solomon, who would succeed him on the throne, and to the people of Israel before his impending death (1 Chr 22:6, 17; 23:1–2). David's last words were mostly regarding the construction of the temple and the laws for the sacrifices to be offered in the temple. Chapter 22 provides details about the preparations for the construction of the temple as well as words to encourage the construction work. Chapter 23 documents the genealogies of the Levites who were to serve in the house of the Lord, while chapter 24 records the genealogies of the priests and the remainder of the Levites. Chapters 25 and 26 document the genealogies of the musicians and the gatekeepers, respectively. After organizing the duties and the structure of the Levites who were to serve in the temple as well as the priests, David restructured the military system and administrative organizations (1 Chr 27:1–4). This reveals David's wholehearted faith, which placed the temple and offerings to God above national defense or administration.

In his latter years, David made thorough preparations with all his heart and strength to fulfill his lifelong desire to build the temple. First Chronicles 22:5 states, "David said, 'My son Solomon is young and inexperienced, and the house that is to be built for the Lord shall be exceedingly magnificent, famous and glorious throughout all lands. Therefore now I will make preparation for it.' So David made ample preparations before his death." With great zeal and all his strength, David joyfully provided all the materials needed for the construction of the temple in great abundance (1 Chr 29:2). Besides all these materials, he also gave gold and silver from his own possessions for the temple (1 Chr 29:3–5).

David's zeal for God's temple did not end with material preparations. He also made detailed preparations for the offering of sacrifices and the temple services to be rendered after the temple was built. Despite his advanced age, he devoted his heart to organizing the divisions of the priests and the Levites who would serve in the temple as well as delegating and structuring their duties. David truly lived a blessed life that sought only to glorify God even until the last moment of his life.

The following are the characteristics of the temple service order that David structured with the Levites at the center.

First, **David structured the temple service order just before his death.** The details of the pattern of Solomon's temple were made clear to David in writing from the hand of the Lord (1 Chr 28:12, 19). Thus David was able to prepare thoroughly all the materials that would be needed to build the temple according to the pattern God had shown him. "He set stonecutters to hew out stones to build the house of God" (1 Chr 22:2). He "prepared large quantities of iron to make the nails for the doors of the gates and for the clamps" (1 Chr 22:3). He procured "more bronze than could be weighed" (1 Chr 22:3) as well as "timbers of cedar logs beyond number" (1 Chr 22:4). He also prepared one hundred thousand talents of gold and one million talents of silver (1 Chr 22:14). Then David gave his son Solomon the plan for the temple that God had shown him (1 Chr 28:11–12). He explained the divisions of the priests and the Levites and all their duties (1 Chr 28:13). He also explained all the plans for the utensils to be used in the temple and even for the weight of gold to be used for all the utensils for every kind of service (1 Chr 28:14–18).

Not only did David wholeheartedly prepare for the materials needed for the construction of the temple, but he also organized the Levites, priests, musicians, and gatekeepers into twenty-four divisions so they could devote themselves to the service of the temple.

Even in his twilight years, with death just before him (1 Chr 23:1), David beheld with faith the glorious temple that would be built according to God's covenant and the offerings to be made therein. He prepared without ceasing so that these works would progress flawlessly. David's devotion, fervent zeal, and resplendent faith with which he meticulously prepared in advance for the succeeding generation is like a fragrant aroma permeating through the ages.

***Second*, the temple service order was commanded by God.**

When David was passing on the throne to his son in his latter years, he gathered and numbered all the leaders of Israel, along with the priests and the Levites, and organized the divisions for service in the house of the Lord (1 Chr 23–26).

God instructed David regarding the temple's size and plans, and the weight for the gold and silver that would be used for the utensils. Likewise, the organization of the Levites, priests, musicians, and gatekeepers to serve in the temple also came from God, not from David (2 Sam 7:21; 1 Chr 17:19; 28:12–13, 19). In 2 Chronicles 29:25, Hezekiah wanted to establish the Levites as temple musicians as had been done during David's time, because that system had come from God. The second half of 2 Chronicles 29:25 states, "The command was from the Lord through His prophets." This phrase in Hebrew is כִּי בְיַד־יְהוָה הַמִּצְוָה בְּיַד־נְבִיאָיו (*ki veyad-yhwh hammitswah beyad-neviayw*), and it literally means "because that command was through the hand of the Lord and the hand of the prophets." In other words, David did not organize the musicians of his own accord; the organization of the musicians was instituted at God's command and was thus of divine origin. It was God who spoke through David, Gad the seer, and Nathan the prophet.

That is why David made it a point to explain in detail to his son Solomon the plans for the temple and "also for the divisions of the priests and the Levites and for all the work of the service of the house of the Lord and for all the utensils of service in the house of the Lord" (1 Chr 28:13).

***Third*, the temple service order was organized into twenty-four divisions for each duty.**

When David counted all the Levites over the age of thirty to serve in the temple, the total came to 38,000 (1 Chr 23:3). This number is four times higher than the 8,580 Levites who were numbered by Moses in the wilderness of Sinai in 1445 BC (Num 4:48) about 475 years prior to Solomon's reign (970 BC).

The 38,000 Levites numbered in 1 Chronicles 23:4–5 were divided according to their duties. There were 24,000 to oversee the work of the house of the Lord, 6,000 officers and judges, 4,000 gatekeepers, and 4,000 musicians playing instruments that David had provided. These priests, Levites, musicians, and gatekeepers were organized into twenty-four divisions.

According to the law of Moses, the age requirement for service in the tent of meeting was from thirty to fifty years of age (Num 4:3, 23, 30, 47; 8:25). Nevertheless, the Levites were allowed to enter the tent from twenty-five years of age in order to learn the work of the tent of meeting for five years (Num 8:24). In his final words, however, David requested to have them thoroughly trained from twenty years of age, for ten years, so they could officially serve in the temple by the time they were thirty years old (1 Chr 23:24, 27). In accordance with David's last words, the Levites were numbered from age twenty and upward and were allowed to serve in the temple (1 Chr 23:32).

CHAPTER

6

THE TWENTY-FOUR DIVISIONS: A Complete System for Ministering in the Temple

David organized the divisions of Levites, priests, musicians, and gatekeepers so that proper temple sacrifices could be offered in an orderly manner. The unique aspect of this is that they were divided into twenty-four divisions according to their households (1 Chr 23–26).

Divisions refer to classifications within the military or a religious organization based on one's birth, rank, or duties. The word "division" is מַחֲלֹקֶת (*mahaloqeth*) in Hebrew and means "order," "course," or "division" (1 Chr 23:6; 26:1). It is derived from the word חָלַק (*halaq*), which means "to divide" or "to allot." With regard to the distribution of land, *mahaloqeth* can also mean "allotment" or "portion" (Josh 18:10; Ezek 48:29).

The word "division" also refers to the order of rotation for the priests and the Levites, which was put in place so that the work of the temple could be carried out more effectively. Each division served twice a year for one week at a time; the exchange of divisions took place on the Sabbath day. Levites entering service would come in on the Sabbath, and those completing their service would go out on the Sabbath. Accounts exist of priests coming in and going out on the Sabbath day during the time when the high priest Jehoiada overthrew Athaliah and made Joash king in 835 BC (2 Kgs 11:5, 7, 9; 2 Chr 23:4, 8). Since each of the twenty-four divisions served in the temple for one week at a time, the rotation for each division occurred every 168 days (24 divisions × 7 days = 168 days).

In addition to serving twice a year for one week each, all those who served in the temple within the twenty-four divisions went up to Jerusalem for the three great feasts and served together in the temple. The three great feasts that God commanded through Moses were the Passover (Feast of Unleavened Bread), the Feast of Weeks (Pentecost, Feast of the Harvest, Feast of the First Fruits of the Wheat Harvest), and the Feast of Booths (Feast of Tabernacles, Feast of Ingathering). Every Israelite man over the age of twenty was required to keep these three annual feasts (Exod 23:14–17; 34:23; Deut 16:16); therefore, those who served in the temple—the Levites, priests, musicians, and gatekeepers—must have all participated.

From their inception during the days of David, the twenty-four divisions of priests continued in their service until the deportation to Babylon. The twenty-four divisions that David instituted probably rotated about eight hundred times during a period of about three hundred seventy years, which spanned from the dedication of Solomon's temple to its destruction by the Babylonians. Since the cycle of the twenty-four divisions rotated in their regular order for such an extended period of time, the Israelites would have been very familiar with this system of temple service.

The priestly division that was serving at the time of the destruction of Solomon's temple (the seventh day of the fifth month [Av] in 586 BC; 2 Kgs 25:8; 2 Chr 36:19) was that of Jehoiarib.[15] The division of Jehoiarib was again serving at the time when Herod's temple was destroyed

15 Heinrich W. Guggenheimer, trans., *Seder Olam: the Rabbinic View of Biblical Chronology* (Lanham, MD: Rowman & Littlefield, 1998), 264.

(the ninth day of the fifth month [Av] in AD 70). It is evident from specific records of the divisions serving in the temple that were preserved in history that the system of the twenty-four divisions was considered very important.

David divided the priests by lot into twenty-four divisions because he foresaw that the number of priests would increase as the sacrifices and worship services became centralized in the temple after its construction. David wanted to ensure that no household was left out from fulfilling its temple service duties by having all households take turns equally.[16]

This system of divisions was a fair and reasonable method, since the order of rotation was decided by lot and not by any particular order of distinction or superiority; it was not partial to any one household (1 Chr 24:5–7; 25:8–9; see also 1 Chr 26:13–16). This system was strictly implemented during Solomon's time (2 Chr 8:14). However, the system barely survived thereafter; it was sustained by spurts of religious revival during the reformation eras (i.e., reformation by the high priest Jehoiada during the time of King Joash, by King Hezekiah, and by King Josiah; 2 Chr 23:18; 29:25; 31:2; 35:4–5) until it was restored during the days of Ezra and Nehemiah. Ezra 6:18 states, "Then they appointed the priests to their divisions and the Levites in their orders for the service of God in Jerusalem, as it is written in the book of Moses." The system was then carried out even until Jesus' time (Luke 1:5, 8–9). Whether or not the system of the twenty-four divisions was enforced or neglected depended largely on the religious and spiritual state of each era.

In his latter years, David divided the Levites into four orders—the ministers of the temple, the priests, the musicians, and the gatekeepers—and structured each of them into twenty-four divisions. We will examine that organizational structure and the history of each order as they appear in Israel's history.

---

16 Richard L. Pratt, *1 & 2 Chronicles: A Mentor Commentary* (1998; repr., Fearn: Mentor, 2006), 253-254.

CHAPTER

7

TWENTY-FOUR DIVISIONS OF THE LEVITES: MINISTERS OF THE TEMPLE

1 Chronicles 23:6–23; 24:20–31

❖ systematically organized for the first time in history ❖

1. The Origin of the Levites

Levi was Jacob's third son

Levi was the third son born to Jacob by his first wife, Leah (Gen 35:23). As soon as Levi was born, Leah confessed, "This time my husband will become attached to me, because I have borne him three sons" (Gen 29:34). The name "Levi" is לֵוִי (*lewi*) in Hebrew and means "to join" or "to be attached." The name reflects Leah's hope to be joined with her husband through this child.

Levi massacred the Shechemites

Levi and his brother Simeon massacred the Shechemites when they were on their way back to Canaan with their father, Jacob. When their younger sister, Dinah, was raped by Shechem the son of Hamor,

Levi and Simeon deceived the Shechemites by saying that they would allow Shechem to marry Dinah if all the men of Shechem received circumcision. Instead, they killed all the men with the sword on the third day after their circumcision (Gen 34:24–31). Because of this incident, the sons of Levi received the curse that they would be scattered throughout the land of Canaan (Gen 49:5–7).

The Levites dedicated themselves to God during the incident of the golden calf

When the people of Israel made for themselves a golden calf and worshiped it at the foot of Mount Sinai, the tribe of Levi followed God's command and dedicated themselves to Him by slaughtering their brothers, friends, and neighbors with righteous indignation (Exod 32:25–29). After this incident the Levites lived scattered in forty-eight cities among the twelve tribes (Num 35:2–8), teaching God's statutes and laws and performing their duties in sacrificial offerings. The Levites did not have an inheritance of their own because God Himself became their inheritance (Deut 10:9).

The Levites' duty was to assist in offering sacrifices

On Mount Sinai God commanded Moses, "Bring the tribe of Levi near and set them before Aaron the priest, that they may serve him" (Num 3:6). God also commanded, saying, "You shall thus give the Levites to Aaron and to his sons; they are wholly given to him from among the sons of Israel" (Num 3:9).

From that time the Levites served before the tent of meeting to perform their duties for Aaron and the whole congregation of Israel (Num 3:7–8). They assisted in the priestly duties performed by the sons of Aaron, took care of all the furnishings of the tent of meeting, and were in charge of transporting the tabernacle.

2. Levitical Duties

The consecration ceremony of the Levites, the ministers of the temple

According to the law, the Levites had to go through two ceremonial rites to become eligible to serve the Lord.

***First*, the Levites were to undergo a cleansing ceremony (Num 8:6–7).** To begin, the Levites were sprinkled with purifying water. Then their whole bodies were shaved using a razor. Finally, their clothes were washed (Num 8:7). The "purifying water" in this passage, literally translated as "water of sin," was made by mixing the ashes that remained after burning an "unblemished red heifer in which is no defect and on which a yoke has never been placed" into water; it was also called the "water to remove impurity" (Num 19:2, 9). Ezekiel 36:25 refers to this water as "clean water."

***Second*, the Levites were presented before God as a wave offering (Num 8:11).**
The Hebrew word for "wave offering" is תְּנוּפָה (*tenufah*), which is derived from the word נוּף (*nuf*), meaning "to move to and fro" or "to lift." This is an offering method in which the offerings—oftentimes the breast part of the animal or the firstfruits of the harvest—were "waved." The offering was laid on the hands of the priest. Then the priest, standing before the altar of the Lord, moved his hands, along with the offering, in a horizontal motion, forward toward the sanctuary and backward toward himself. In other words, the offering was "waved" in a repeated motion of pushing forward and pulling backward. The forward motion signified that the offering was first offered to God; then the backward motion signified that God had returned it to the priests as a gift (Exod 29:24, 26–27; Lev 7:30–34; 8:27–29; 9:21; 10:14–15; 14:12, 21, 24; 23:11–12, 15–17, 20; Num 6:20; 8:11, 13; 18:11, 18, etc.).

God commanded that the Levites be offered as a wave offering for the descendants of Israel. Offering up living Levites in a wave offering was different from killing an animal and offering it (Num 8:11, 13). In order for the Levites to be offered as a wave offering, two bulls first had to be offered as a sin offering and a burnt offering to make atonement for them. The Levites were to lay their hands on the heads of the bulls, and then Moses was to offer one for a sin offering and the other for a burnt offering to the Lord to make atonement for the Levites. The Levites then stood before Aaron and his sons to be presented as a wave offering to the Lord (Num 8:12–13). After that the Levites were finally able to enter the tent of meeting to serve God (Num 8:14–15).

The Levites who were presented before God as a wave offering were returned to Aaron as a gift (Num 8:10–13). Numbers 8:19 states, "I have given the Levites as a gift to Aaron and to his sons from among the sons of Israel, to perform the service of the sons of Israel at the tent of meeting and to make atonement on behalf of the sons of Israel." Numbers 18:6 also states, "Behold, I Myself have taken your fellow Levites from among the sons of Israel; they are a gift to you, dedicated to the Lord, to perform the service for the tent of meeting." In this manner the Levites were "wholly given to him [Aaron] from among the sons of Israel" in accordance with Numbers 3:9. Hence the Levites were set apart from among the sons of Israel and dedicated to God; they totally belonged to God and were His possessions (Num 8:14). They served God but were also given to the priests as a gift (Num 3:9; 8:19) and became ministers of the temple, assisting the priests (Num 3:6; 1 Chr 23:28).

The relationship between the Levites and the priests reflects the relationship between the saints and Christ. The Levites, who belonged to the priests, became people who served God in the temple. Likewise Christians, who were purchased by Jesus' blood and thus belong to God (Acts 20:28; 1 Cor 6:20), must strive to live lives that glorify only Christ, whether by life or by death (Phil 1:20).

The twofold obligation of the Levites (obligations to Aaron and to the congregation)

The division of obligations between Aaron, the priests, and the Levites was strict. The Levites were to "attend to your [Aaron's] obligation and the obligation of all the tent" (Num 18:3). The priests were to "attend to the obligations of the sanctuary and the obligations of the altar" (Num 18:5).

Numbers 18:1–3 states, "The Lord said to Aaron, '. . . Bring with you also your brothers, the tribe of Levi, the tribe of your father, that they may be joined with you and serve you, while you and your sons with you are before the tent of the testimony. And they shall thus attend to your obligation and the obligation of all the tent.'" The expression "your obligation" refers to Aaron's obligation, that is, a priestly obligation. Numbers 3:7 states, "They [the Levites] shall perform the duties for him [Aaron] and for the whole congregation before the tent of meeting, to do the service of the tabernacle," referring to the twofold obligations of the Levites.

Here "obligation" refers to the task or duty for which a person is responsible. In Hebrew it is מִשְׁמֶרֶת (*mishmereth*) and derives from the word שָׁמַר (*shamar*), meaning "to guard"; thus it means "something to be carefully observed and kept." It is important to note that the meaning of the word implies a duty that must be performed throughout one's lifetime. The Levites have been called to perform their duties not just one time but faithfully throughout their lives.

In Numbers 18:4, God said to Aaron, "They shall be joined with you and attend to the obligations of the tent of meeting, for all the service of the tent; but an outsider may not come near you." Only priests anointed by God could touch the furnishings that had been sanctified as holy and stood before the altar (Num 4:15–20). Although the Levites could join the priests and keep their obligations in the tent of meeting and the tent, they could not come near the furnishings of the sanctuary or the altar (Num 18:3).

The following is a detailed look at the duties of the Levites.

***First*, they assisted with Aaron's duties (obligations) before the tent of meeting (Num 3:7; 18:3–4).**

Aaron's duties (obligations) refer to the religious duties performed by Aaron and his sons, the priests, in the sanctuary (Exod 29:1, 9, 30, 44; 30:30; 31:10; 40:13–15; Num 3:3, 10; 18:1, 7; 25:13). Their most important and mandatory tasks were lighting the lamps, maintaining the lamps, burning incense, and setting out the showbread. Numbers 4:16 states, "The responsibility of Eleazar the son of Aaron the priest is the oil for the light and the fragrant incense and the continual grain offering and the anointing oil—the responsibility of all the tabernacle and of all that is in it, with the sanctuary and its furnishings."

The Levites assisted the priests in performing "Aaron's duties" and took care of the whole sanctuary. Thus the essential duty of the Levites was to assist the priests so that the offerings would be made to God without any problems. Numbers 3:6 states, "Bring the tribe of Levi near and set them before Aaron the priest, that they may serve him." The word "serve" is שָׁרַת (*sharath*) in Hebrew and refers to the act of serving a king.

The Hebrew word שָׁרַת (*sharath*) was used when Abishag the Shunammite was called to nurse and "serve" King David (1 Kgs 1:4). It was also used when Elisha followed Elijah and "ministered" to him (1 Kgs 19:21). This word was used often to speak of serving a king, a priest, or a person in the highest position. The word stands in contrast to its synonym *avad* (עָבַד; Gen 15:13; Isa 14:3) in that it emphasizes the distinction and honor of the person being served, while *avad* simply describes a lowly slave serving his master. Therefore, God's command to the Levites to serve the high priest and the priests implies that God wanted the Levites who were consecrated holy by God to uphold their service to the priests with great honor and a willing spirit and to give thanks to Him who had bestowed the duty (see Num 16:9–10).

The Levites were to "be joined" with the priests in performing the duties before the tent of meeting (Num 18:2, 4). The word "join" is לָוָה (*lawah*) in Hebrew and means "to twist," "to interlock," or "to become one." This means that when the Levites assisted with Aaron's duties and attended to the duties of the tent, they were to serve and follow the priests wholeheartedly so that the priestly duties could be performed smoothly.

As David had established, the 24,000 Levites who oversaw the work of the house of the Lord during Solomon's days (1 Chr 23:3–4) performed their service in the house of God by assisting with the purification of all the holy things (1 Chr 23:28). They were also in charge of "the showbread, and the fine flour for a grain offering, and unleavened wafers, or what is baked in the pan or what is well-mixed, and all measures of volume and size" (1 Chr 23:29). They also stood every morning and evening to thank and praise the Lord (1 Chr 23:30). Likewise they stood before the Lord whenever the burnt offerings were offered on the Sabbaths, new moons, and fixed festivals, according to the number set by the ordinance concerning them; these were offered continually before the Lord. Furthermore, they were to keep charge of the tent of meeting and the holy place, and also assist the sons of Aaron, their relatives, for the service of the house of the Lord (1 Chr 23:31–32).

***Second*, they were to perform the duties for the whole congregation before the tent of meeting (Num 3:7–8).**

Regarding the location in which the Levites served, Numbers 3:7 states that the Levites were to perform the duties "before the tent of meeting, to do the service of the tabernacle." The "tent of meeting" in Hebrew is אֹהֶל מוֹעֵד (*ohel moed*; Exod 29:30, 42, 44; 33:7; 40:12). The Hebrew word אֹהֶל (*ohel*) means "tent," and מוֹעֵד (*moed*) means "appointed time," "place," or "meeting." Thus *ohel moed* means "appointed place to meet God" or "tent of meeting."

> *It shall be a continual burnt offering throughout your generations at the doorway of the tent of meeting before the Lord, where I will meet with you, to speak to you there. I will meet there with the sons of Israel, and it shall be consecrated by My glory. (Exodus 29:42–43)*

The ark of the covenant was located in the holy of holies inside the tent of meeting (Exod 26:33; 40:3, 20–21). The lampstand, the altar of incense, and the table of showbread were located in the area outside the veil (Exod 40:4–5, 22–27; Lev. 24:3–9), with the veil separating it from the holy of holies (Exod 26:33; 40:3, 20–21). This area was called the tent of meeting or, more specifically, the holy place. The Levites (temple ministers) and laity were prohibited from entering the holy place (Num 1:51; 3:10, 38; 17:13; 18:4, 7, 22–23). Furthermore, only the high priest was allowed to enter the holy of holies, on one day in a year, the Day of Atonement (Lev 16:29–34; 23:27–28; Heb 9:7). The English Standard Version translates Numbers 18:22–23 as saying that the Levites were to serve in the tent of meeting "so that the people of Israel do not come near the tent of meeting, lest they bear sin and die. But the Levites shall do the service of the tent of meeting, and they shall bear their iniquity. It shall be a perpetual statute throughout your generations."

The word "tabernacle" in Numbers 3:7 is מִשְׁכָּן (*mishkan*) in Hebrew and refers to the entire tabernacle. The Levites served in the court of the priests, which is also referred to as "tabernacle" at times, but they could not enter the sanctuary (the holy place) inside the tent of meeting. The tabernacle was distinguished from the tent of meeting and, in this general sense, refers to the court area containing the laver and the altar of burnt offering, where the laity was able to enter (Exod 40:6, 29–30). In the tabernacle the Levites performed various services for the people, such as assisting the laity with sacrifice offerings or preventing them from approaching the tent of meeting:

You shall appoint the Levites over the tabernacle of the testimony, and over all its furnishings and over all that belongs to it. They shall carry the tabernacle and all its furnishings, and they shall take care of it; they shall also camp around the tabernacle. So when the tabernacle is to set out, the Levites shall take it down; and when the tabernacle encamps, the Levites shall set it up. But the layman who comes near shall be put to death. The sons of Israel shall camp, each man by his own camp, and each man by his own standard, according to their armies. But the Levites shall camp around the tabernacle of the testimony, so that there will be no wrath on the congregation of the sons of Israel. So the Levites shall keep charge of the tabernacle of the testimony. (Numbers 1:50–53)

The distinctive character of the Levitical duties

The Levites were consecrated ministers who ensured that all Israel received God's merciful atonement and that no plague would come upon them. Numbers 8:19 states, "I have given the Levites as a gift to Aaron and to his sons from among the sons of Israel . . . to make atonement on behalf of the sons of Israel, so that there will be no plague among the sons of Israel by their coming near to the sanctuary."

Although the priests offered the sacrifices for the atonement of sin, the Levites served in the tabernacle and assisted the priests in performing the sacred service. In so doing, they helped obtain atonement for the sins of Israel and made sure that no plagues would befall them. In other words, God's holiness and glory were preserved through the Levites, while the people were able to avoid the wrath of God. This was the Levites' definitive and most important duty. Numbers 8:16 explains, "They are wholly given to Me from among the sons of Israel. I have taken them for Myself instead of every first issue of the womb, the firstborn of all the sons of Israel."

After God protected Israel's firstborns from the tenth plague just prior to the exodus (Exod 12:29–30), He proclaimed that every firstborn of the womb among the sons of Israel, both of man and of beast, belonged to Him (Exod 13:2). Then God declared regarding the Levites, "I have taken them for Myself instead of every first issue of the womb, the firstborn of all the sons of Israel" (Num 8:16), to signify that He had chosen the Levites to replace the firstborns of Israel. Thus the Levites worked on behalf of all the sons of Israel; they served in the temple all their lives on behalf of all the firstborn of the twelve tribes (Num 3:41, 45; 8:17–19). The sons of Israel were able to escape the plagues of God's wrath because the Levites were offered in the place of all the firstborn of Israel (Num 8:19).

God commanded the Israelites to give their tithes to the Levites as an inheritance in return for their Levitical service in the tabernacle (Num 18:21). In turn, the Levites offered a tenth of their tithes as a heave offering (KJV, Num 18:26) to God. Then the heave offering was given to Aaron the priest so it could be given to the priests serving in the tent of meeting as their compensation (Num 18:26–31). Thus the heave offering and the wave offering that were given as an inheritance to the priests became their perpetual allotment;[17] the first ripe fruits offered to God were also given to them. God instituted this as an everlasting covenant of salt to the priests and their descendants (Num 18:8–19).

3. The Genealogy of the Twenty-Four Divisions of the Levites

David set apart 24,000 Levites to oversee the work of the house of the Lord and divided them into divisions according to the sons of Levi: Gershon, Kohath, and Merari (Exod 6:16; 1 Chr 23:6). First Chronicles 23:24 states, "These were the sons of Levi according to their fathers'

---

17 "Allotment": the portion of pay, such as a ration or stipend, for one's duty and service

households, even the heads of the fathers' households of those of them who were counted, in the number of names by their census, doing the work for the service of the house of the Lord, from twenty years old and upward." Here "fathers' households" refers to the leading families within the lineage of the firstborns. Taking a census according to the fathers' households meant that the Levites were counted and enrolled in the genealogy in a systematic way according to their lineage, not in a random, arbitrary way.

The divisions of the Levites were chosen by casting lots within God's sovereign administration (Prov 16:33). First Chronicles 24:31 states, "These also cast lots just as their relatives the sons of Aaron in the presence of David the king, Zadok, Ahimelech, and the heads of the fathers' households of the priests and of the Levites—the head of fathers' households as well as those of his younger brother." The order of the twenty-four divisions of the Levites was also chosen by lot just like that of the priests; this in turn enabled them to perform their duties in an equitable environment, with no distinctions awarded to any of the clans. Therefore, they were able to perform their duties according to God's will, without being swayed by special privileges or vested rights.

The Twenty-Four Divisions of the Levites in 1 Chronicles 23:7–23

Gershon (1 Chr 23:7)

1	Libni (1 Chr 6:17)	Ladan	Jehiel / יְחִיאֵל / "God lives"
2			Zetham / זֵתָם / "olive tree"
3			Joel / יוֹאֵל / "the Lord is God"
			1 Chr 23:8
4		Shimei	Shelomoth / שְׁלֹמוֹת / "abundant peace, peace"
5			Haziel / חֲזִיאֵל / "vision of God"
6			Haran / הָרָן / "mountaineer"
			1 Chr 23:9
7	Shimei		Jahath / יַחַת / "God will snatch up, recovery, growth"
8			Zina (Zizah) / זִינָא (זִיזָה) / "abundant, fat"
9			Jeush / יְעוּשׁ / "he comes to help"
10			Beriah / בְּרִיעָה / "excellent, received plague"
			1 Chr 23:10–11

The Twenty-Four Divisions of the Levites Reorganized in 1 Chronicles 24:20–31

Kohath (1 Chr 23:12)

11	1	Hebron	Jeriah / יְרִיָּה / "the Lord wants to see"
12	2		Amariah / אֲמַרְיָה / "the Lord has spoken, the Lord has proclaimed"
13	3		Jahaziel / יַחֲזִיאֵל "God sees, God gives a vision"
14	4		Jekameam / יְקַמְעָם / "may kinsman establish, let the people be established"
			1 Chr 23:19; 24:23

15	5	Uzziel			Micah / מִיכָה / "who is like God" 1 Chr 23:20; 24:24
	6				(added) Shamir / שָׁמוּר "thorn, adamant, flint" 1 Chr 24:24
16	7				Isshiah / יִשִּׁיָּה / "whom the Lord lends, may the Lord forget" 1 Chr 23:20; 24:25
	8				(added) Zechariah / זְכַרְיָה "the Lord remembers" 1 Chr 24:25
17	9	Amram	Moses (1 Chr 23:13–15)	Gershom	Shebuel (Shubael) / שְׁבוּאֵל "captive of God" 1 Chr 23:16; 24:20
	10				(added) Jehdeiah / יֶחְדְּיָהוּ "may the Lord give joy" 1 Chr 24:20
18	11			Eliezer	Rehabiah / רְחַבְיָה / "the Lord enlarged" 1 Chr 23:17; 24:21
	12				(added) Isshiah / יִשִּׁיָּה / "whom the Lord lends, may the Lord forget" 1 Chr 24:21
	13	Izhar			Shelomith (Shelomoth) / שְׁלֹמִית "abundant peace, peace" 1 Chr 23:18; 24:22
19	14				(added) Jahath / יַחַת / "God will snatch up, recovery, growth" 1 Chr 24:22
Merari (1 Chr 23:21; 24:26)					
20	**15**	Mushi			Mahli / מַחְלִי / "sickness" 1 Chr 6:19; 23:23; 24:30
21	**16**				Eder / עֵדֶר / "flock, herd" 1 Chr 23:23; 24:30
22	**17**				Jeremoth (Jerimoth) / יְרֵימוֹת "high place, the highest One" 1 Chr 23:23; 24:30

23	18	Mahli	Eleazar / אֶלְעָזָר / "God has helped" 1 Chr 23:21; 24:28
24	19		Kish / קִישׁ / "power, arrow" 1 Chr 23:21; 24:29
	20		Jerahmeel / יְרַחְמְאֵל "may God have compassion" 1 Chr 24:29
	21	(added) Jaaziah *presumed to be a descendant of Merari (1 Chr 24:26–27)	Beno / בְּנוֹ / "his son" 1 Chr 24:27
	22		Shoham / שֹׁהַם "Carnelian" (a type of gemstone) 1 Chr 24:27
	23		Zaccur / זַכּוּר / "one who is remembered" 1 Chr 24:27
	24		Ibri / עִבְרִי / "a Hebrew" 1 Chr 24:27

First Chronicles 24 lists the twenty-four divisions of the priests and the Levites who assisted the priests in the temple. However, the list of the twenty-four divisions in 1 Chronicles 24:20–31 is a repetition of the record in 1 Chronicles 23:6–23. The difference in the second list is that the ten divisions from the line of Gershon recorded in 1 Chronicles 23:7–11 are missing. Also, four divisions of Hebron's descendants are missing from the line of Kohath, and three divisions of Mushi's descendants are missing from the line of Merari. Besides these, the list continues to their sons' generations.

Jaaziah is not recorded in 1 Chronicles 23:21 but is recorded only in 1 Chronicles 24:26–27. The Chronicler recorded Jaaziah on an equal level with Mahli and Mushi, because Jaaziah's household grew large and occupied four of the twenty-four divisions alongside Mahli and Mushi. Normally only one person was recorded from each of the households of the sons of Levi (1 Chr 24:21, 24–25, 29). If a household had no son, then it might not be represented at all (1 Chr 24:28). For Jaaziah's household, however, four of his descendants are recorded, suggesting that his household flourished. Considering the fact that Jaaziah's son Beno is recorded twice in 1 Chronicles 24:26–27, it seems that Beno thrived the most among all Jaaziah's sons and became the representative for the household.

In conclusion, with the passage of time, 1 Chronicles 24:20–30 omitted ten divisions from the line of Gershon among the twenty-four divisions originally listed in 1 Chronicles 23:6–23. However, it preserved the twenty-four divisions by incorporating ten more divisions: five from the line of Kohath (Shamir, Zechariah, Jehdeiah, Isshiah, and Jahath; 1 Chr 24:20, 21, 22, 24, 25) and five from the line of Merari (Jerahmeel, Beno from the house of Jaaziah, Shoham, Zaccur, and Ibri; 1 Chr 24:26–27, 29).

4. The History of the Levitical Duties

Moses' days

The duties of the Levites in the tent of meeting were twofold, and both responsibilities involved physical labor. First, they were to camp on the west, south, and north sides of the tabernacle to guard it (Num 3:14–37). Second, they were charged with the task of carrying all the furnishings of the tabernacle and the tent when the camp set out (Num 4:1–33).

Numbers 3 lists Gershon, Kohath, and Merari in the order of their birth. Numbers 4, on the other hand, lists the descendants of Kohath first, which reflects not genealogical priority but priority in the importance of the tabernacle furnishings that the Kohathites were charged with carrying. Before the Israelites settled in Canaan, the life of the Kohathites in the wilderness revolved around the tabernacle. When the camp set out to move, the sons of Kohath carried on their shoulders all the most holy things in the tabernacle, such as the ark of the covenant, the table of the showbread, the lampstand, the altar, the utensils, and so on (Num 4:4–15).

The sons of Gershon were in charge of transporting the following items: the curtains of the tabernacle, the tent of meeting with its covering and the covering of porpoise skin on top of it, the screen for the doorway of the tent of meeting as well as the hangings of the court, the screen for the doorway of the gate of the court that is around the tabernacle and the altar, the hangings of the court and their cords, and all the equipment for their service (Num 4:21–28).

The sons of Merari were in charge of transporting the foundation units needed to set up the tabernacle, such as the boards of the tabernacle, its pillars, and its pegs (Num 4:29–33).

The sons of Gershon and the sons of Merari always carried the tabernacle and set out before the sons of Kohath so that the tabernacle would be set up before the Kohathites arrived with the holy objects (Num 10:17, 21).

Although they were all descendants of Levi, only Aaron and his sons were given the priesthood, thus creating a strict hierarchical relationship in which the other Levites were effectively subordinated to the sons of Aaron in terms of their duties. An incident that resulted from such a relationship is documented in Numbers 16, which records how a faction made up of a Levite named Korah and several Reubenites named Dathan, Abiram, and On conspired to rebel against Moses and Aaron. Two hundred and fifty leaders of the congregation, men of renown, joined this faction and rose up against Moses and Aaron, saying, "You have gone far enough, for all the congregation are holy, every one of them, and the Lord is in their midst; so why do you exalt yourselves above the assembly of the Lord?" (Num 16:3).

Korah, the leader of the rebellion, was a son of Kohath, a Levite who had received the great blessing of serving God in close proximity to Him in the tabernacle. Moses emphasized the Kohathites' honorable position by repeatedly addressing them as "sons of Levi" (Num 16:7–8) and thus rebuked them, saying, "Is it not enough for you that the God of Israel has separated you from the rest of the congregation of Israel, to bring you near to Himself, to do the service of the tabernacle of the Lord, and to stand before the congregation to minister to them; and that He has brought you near, Korah, and all your brothers, sons of Levi, with you? And are you seeking for the priesthood also?" (Num 16:9–10). In other words, what they did was against the Lord. They had spurned the Lord (Num 16:11, 30).

Despite Moses' rebukes, Korah would not repent. Instead he assembled all the congregation against Moses and Aaron at the doorway of the tent of meeting. Instantly the glory of the Lord appeared to the entire congregation (Num 16:19). In Numbers 16:21, God spoke to Moses and Aaron, saying, "Separate yourselves from among this congregation, that I may consume them instantly." In obedience the people got back from around the dwellings of Korah, Dathan, and Abiram (Num 16:27). As soon as Moses finished speaking, the ground split open, and the earth swallowed up the households of Dathan and Abiram and all the men who belonged to Korah, along with their possessions. The earth then closed over them, and they were buried alive (Num 16:31–33). In addition, fire came forth from the Lord and consumed the 250 who were offering the incense (Num 16:35). Even in this situation, the immature congregation grumbled against Moses and Aaron, saying that they had caused the death of the Lord's people. Consequently they were struck with a plague, and 14,700 people died (Num 16:41–50).

In order to stop the people's grumblings, God commanded them to take rods with the names of the twelve tribes written on them and place them in the tent of meeting in front of the ark of the testimony. The next day God caused only the rod of the house of Levi with Aaron's name on it to sprout and put forth buds, thereby confirming before all Israel that God had chosen Aaron and his sons as priests (Num 17:1–11).

David's and Solomon's days

After the Israelites settled in Canaan, the status of the Levites in terms of their role and activities went into drastic decline throughout the period of the judges. It was only during the time of Samuel that their importance was slowly recognized again, and their original calling was finally reaffirmed during King David's time (1 Chr 15:2–15).

During the days of David and Solomon, the role of the Levites became much more systematic and specialized than it had been during the days of Moses. Ever since the exodus, which had ended Israel's slavery and 430-year sojourn in Egypt, God was with Israel as He dwelt in the tabernacle throughout their wilderness journey. In 2 Samuel 7:6, the Lord said, "I have not dwelt in a house since the day I brought up the sons of Israel from Egypt, even to this day; but I have been moving about in a tent, even in a tabernacle." Also in 1 Chronicles 17:5, He said, "I have not dwelt in a house since the day that I brought up Israel to this day, but I have gone from tent to tent and from one dwelling place to another."

With the construction of a permanent temple, however, the Levitical duties involving disassembling and transporting the tent became unnecessary. For this reason David said, "The Lord God of Israel has given rest to His people, and He dwells in Jerusalem forever. Also, the Levites will no longer need to carry the tabernacle and all its utensils for its service" (1 Chr 23:25–26). Thus the sons of Levi were ordered to "keep charge of the tent of meeting, and charge of the holy place, and charge of the sons of Aaron their relatives, for the service of the house of the Lord" (1 Chr 23:32).

The institution of the twenty-four divisions, prepared during David's days, was stringently implemented during Solomon's time. Second Chronicles 8:14 states, "According to the ordinance of his father David, he [Solomon] appointed the divisions of the priests for their service, and the Levites for their duties of praise and ministering before the priests according to the daily rule, and the gatekeepers by their divisions at every gate; for David the man of God had so commanded."

Hezekiah's days

Hezekiah, the thirteenth king of the southern kingdom of Judah, began a religious reformation and cleansed the temple as soon as he ascended the throne. Second Chronicles 29:3 states, "In the first year of his reign, in the first month, he opened the doors of the house of the Lord and repaired them." The "first month" of Hezekiah's first regnal year refers to the month of Nisan in 715 BC, when he began his sole reign. Hezekiah commanded the priests and the Levites to open the doors of the house of the Lord, which had been closed as a result of his father Ahaz's wicked reign (2 Chr 28:24–25). Hezekiah commanded them to light the lamps of the temple that had been put out and begin burning incense and offering sacrifices in the holy place once again (2 Chr 29:3–7, 11). The following reforms concerning the Levites were instituted during Hezekiah's days.

***First*, fourteen Levites, two from each of the seven sons of Levi, rose to cleanse the temple.**

After Hezekiah commanded the cleansing of the temple of the Lord, he encouraged the people, telling the Levites, "My sons, do not be negligent now, for the Lord has chosen you to stand before Him, to minister to Him, and to be His ministers and burn incense" (2 Chr 29:11). Then fourteen Levites arose (2 Chr 29:12–14). They assembled their brothers, consecrated themselves, and cleansed the temple of God (2 Chr 29:15). Knowing that Hezekiah had commanded them "by the words of the Lord," the Levites followed his command and did everything accordingly (2 Chr 29:15).

Since the Levites were prohibited from entering the sanctuary, the priests went in to the inner part of the house of the Lord and brought out every unclean thing to the court of the temple. Then the Levites carried it out to the Kidron valley (2 Chr 29:16). The work of cleansing the temple was carried out through such close cooperation between the priests and the Levites (2 Chr 29:16–19).

***Second*, the Levites also helped skin the burnt offerings because the priests were too few.**

The consecration of the Lord's temple began on the first day of the first month. On the eighth day of the month, they entered the porch of the Lord. Then they consecrated the house of the Lord in eight days and finished on the sixteenth day of the first month (2 Chr 29:17). As soon as the consecration of the temple was complete, King Hezekiah ordered the sin offering and the burnt offering for all Israel to be offered in the consecrated temple (2 Chr 29:20–24).

After Hezekiah made the offering to God with praises and worship (2 Chr 29:25–30), he commanded the assembly to bring sacrifices and thank offerings. The assembly brought seventy bulls, one hundred rams, and two hundred lambs as burnt offerings to the Lord as well as six hundred bulls and three thousand sheep as consecrated offerings (2 Chr 29:31–33).

The priests, however, were too few in number to skin all the burnt offerings; therefore, their brothers the Levites assisted until the work was completed (2 Chr 29:34). This was because the Levites were "more conscientious to consecrate themselves than the priests" (2 Chr 29:34). The New King James Version translates this, "The Levites were more diligent in sanctifying themselves than the priests." The word "conscientious" is יִשְׁרֵי לֵבָב (*yishre levav*) in Hebrew and means the "heart is upright"; it is translated as "more conscientious" (NIV, NASB), "more upright in heart" (KJV, RSV), and "more diligent" (NKJV).

***Third*, the service of the house of the Lord was established again through the cooperation of the Levites.**

Through the proactive service and cooperation of the Levites in the days of Hezekiah, sacred services like offering sacrifices in the temple and praising God with singing and playing of instruments were able to be reinstituted so that the entire system of sacred temple services was wholly restored. Second Chronicles 29:35 states, "Thus the service of the house of the Lord was established again." The phrase "established again" is תִּכּוֹן (*tikkon*) and is in the niphal (passive) stem of the word כּוּן (*kun*), meaning "to stand firm" and "to be established." Hence temple sacrifice and other related rites were completely reestablished at this time.

Second Chronicles 29:36 states, "Then Hezekiah and all the people rejoiced over what God had prepared for the people, because the thing came about suddenly." Although they presented a great number of offerings all at once, they were able to carry out the service in an orderly manner, because God had prepared the conscientious Levites. King Hezekiah and all the people rejoiced greatly, for everything came about entirely by God's grace and providence.

Hezekiah conferred with the princes and all the assembly, and they decided to celebrate the Passover in the second month. He thus proclaimed that all Israel, from Beersheba to Dan, should come to Jerusalem to celebrate the Passover to the Lord (2 Chr 30:1, 5). They were unable to celebrate the Passover in the first month, as prescribed, "because the priests had not consecrated themselves in sufficient numbers, nor had the people been gathered to Jerusalem" (2 Chr 30:3). Indeed, Israel had not been able to celebrate the Passover as it had been prescribed for a long time (2 Chr 30:5).

Originally the people slaughtered their own Passover lambs (Exod 12:6; see Lev 1:2–9), but in Hezekiah's day many people had not consecrated themselves. Thus the Levites slaughtered the lambs for them, and the priests received the blood from the Levites and sprinkled it according to the law of Moses (2 Chr 30:15–17). Likewise the Levites had also slaughtered the sacrifice on behalf of the assembly during Josiah's days (2 Chr 35:1, 11) as well as the days immediately after the return from the Babylonian exile (Ezra 6:19–20).

Then Hezekiah spoke encouragingly to all the Levites who showed good insight in the things of the Lord. The people ate for the appointed seven days, sacrificing peace offerings and giving thanks to God (2 Chr 30:22). They then celebrated another seven days with joy (2 Chr 30:23). All Hezekiah's religious reforms—the cleansing of the temple and the reestablishing of the system of sacred services and the order of the musicians—were "good, right, and true" before God (2 Chr 31:20). In every work he performed in the service of the house of God and in seeking God according to the law and commandment, Hezekiah worked with all his heart; therefore, he prospered (2 Chr 31:21). The faithful devotion of the Levites provided the foundational support for all this work.

Josiah's days

In the eighth year of his reign (at about sixteen years of age), Josiah began to seek the God of his father David. In the twelfth year of his reign (at about twenty years of age), he began a religious reformation that purged all the idols in Judah and Jerusalem (2 Chr 34:1–7). In the eighteenth year of his reign (at around twenty-six years of age), he finished purging the land and the temple, and repaired the temple (2 Chr 34:8). At this time the Levite doorkeepers hired workers with money that the people offered for the temple repairs. The foremen who supervised the work were also Levites (2 Kgs 22:4–6; 2 Chr 34:9–12). The Levites who were skilled musicians also participated (2 Chr 34:12), and some Levites took leading roles as scribes, officials, and gatekeepers (2 Chr 34:13).

While celebrating the Passover, Josiah commanded the Levites who taught all Israel and who were holy to the Lord, saying, "Put the holy ark in the house which Solomon the son of David king of Israel built; it will be a burden on your shoulders no longer. Now serve the Lord your God and His people Israel" (2 Chr 35:3).

The statement "it will be a burden on your shoulders no longer" reveals that the ark had been moved around to different places according to the greedy desires of the evil kings of the past, such as Ahaz, Manasseh, and Amon. Ahaz, adding to his excessive idolatry, destroyed the temple utensils (2 Kgs 16:10–18; 2 Chr 28:22–25); Manasseh built various idols and altars inside the temple (2 Kgs 21:3–9; 2 Chr 33:3–9); and Manasseh's son Amon also committed evil deeds like his father (2 Kgs 21:20–21; 2 Chr 33:22–23). Josiah's reforms, however, brought the ark of the covenant to its permanent place (the holy of holies) so that the Levites no longer needed to carry it around (2 Chr 35:3).

After consecrating themselves the Levites slaughtered the Passover sacrifices for the congregation and skinned them (2 Chr 35:6, 11). Once the sacrifices were offered, they cooked them according to the ordinance and "carried them speedily" (רוּץ, *ruts,* "to run," "to rush upon") to all the lay people so that the food was distributed evenly (2 Chr 35:13). Afterward the Levites prepared portions for themselves and for the priests, because the priests were offering the burnt offerings and the fat until night (2 Chr 35:14). Moreover, the musicians and the gatekeepers were able to stay at their stations and did not have to depart, because the Levites prepared their portions as well (2 Chr 35:15). Not only were the Levites faithful in their own duties, but they were also unwavering in their commitment to the role of supporting the priests.

On that day the Levites worked long hours, and their workload was heavy, but they all faithfully carried out their duties. "All the service of the Lord was prepared on that day" (2 Chr 35:16). The sons of Israel who were present at that time also celebrated the Feast of Unleavened Bread for seven days. There had not been a time in the history of Israel since the days of the prophet Samuel (or since the times when the judges ruled Israel) when the Passover had been celebrated in such a grand scale by the entire nation as it was in the days of Josiah (2 Kgs 23:21–23; 2 Chr 35:17–18).

Postexilic days

The role of the Levites became the foundation upon which the restoration of the temple and the spiritual revival of the Israelites were to take place after the return from the Babylonian exile. The book of Nehemiah reveals that the Levites who returned from the exile played a significant role in awakening the souls of all the people of Israel (Neh 8–9). During Nehemiah's time, however, temple services were almost cut off, because the Levites could not carry out their duties due to economic hardships (Neh 13:10–11).

The Levites performed the following duties during the postexilic period.

First, Mattithiah (מַתִּתְיָה, "gift from God"), the firstborn of Shallum the Korahite, was in charge of the things that were baked in pans (1 Chr 9:31; see also 1 Chr 23:29).

Second, some of the sons of the Kohathites were in charge of preparing the showbread every Sabbath (1 Chr 9:32; see also 1 Chr 23:29).

Third, it is stated that the singers, who were heads of fathers' households of the Levites, uniquely "lived in the chambers of the temple free from other service; for they were engaged in their work day and night" (1 Chr 9:33). This shows how devoted they were in carrying out their duties to the best of their abilities so that they would not be disgraced before God.

Fourth, some people were put in charge of the storehouses for the offerings and tithes to the Lord, and their task was to distribute evenly to their kinsmen (Neh 13:11–13). Nehemiah appointed three people over the storehouse: Shelemiah the priest, Zadok the scribe, and Pedaiah of the Levites. He appointed Hanan the son of Zaccur, the son of Mattaniah, to be second in charge. These men were appointed because they were all considered reliable (Neh 13:13).

Fifth, the Levites taught the people the law of God (Neh 8:7–9). The Levites, like the scribes and judges, also played the role of Israel's spiritual leaders who taught God's Word (1 Chr 23:4). Records from the past reveal that nine Levites along with five officials and two priests were sent out to teach in the various cities of Judah during the third year of the reign of King Jehoshaphat (2 Chr 17:7–9). It is quite likely that the Levites made up the majority of the people sent out to teach, because they were skillful at teaching God's Word.

During the third return from the Babylonian exile, the people gathered in front of the Water Gate and asked Ezra the scribe to read from the book of the law. Ezra read from the book of the law from early morning until midday, while the people listened attentively. When Ezra blessed the Lord, the people answered, "Amen, Amen!"

while lifting up their hands; then they bowed low and worshiped the Lord with their faces to the ground (Neh 8:1–6).

At that time the Levites interpreted the law for the people and taught them so that they understood. Nehemiah 8:7–9 states, "Jeshua, Bani, Sherebiah, Jamin, Akkub, Shabbethai, Hodiah, Maaseiah, Kelita, Azariah, Jozabad, Hanan, Pelaiah, the Levites, explained the law to the people while the people remained in their place. They read from the book, from the law of God, translating to give the sense so that they understood the reading. Then Nehemiah, who was the governor, and Ezra the priest and scribe, and the Levites who taught the people said to all the people, 'This day is holy to the Lord your God; do not mourn or weep.'"

The Levites also gathered around Ezra the scribe so "that they might gain insight into the words of the law" (Neh 8:13). Moreover, the Levites lived scattered among the cities of Israel and served also as officers and judges (1 Chr 23:4). This indicates that the Levites carried out the task of teaching and guiding the people of Israel to live sanctified and righteous lives in accordance with the Word of God.

The faith and service of the Levites that we have examined thus far provide a good example of how lay leaders today should serve God.

5. The Tribe of Levi and the General Assembly of the Firstborn

The tribe of Levi was offered to God in the place of every firstborn among the sons of Israel. Numbers 3:12 states, "Behold, I have taken the Levites from among the sons of Israel instead of every firstborn, the first issue of the womb among the sons of Israel. So the Levites shall be Mine" (Num 8:16, 18). God even commanded that the cattle of the Levites be offered instead of every firstborn among the cattle of the sons of Israel (Num 3:41). Thus the tribe of Levi became an assembly of the firstborns to replace the firstborn sons of Israel. In other words, they were entirely dedicated for the work of redeeming all Israel.

Preciseness characterizes God's principle of redemption. The total number of Israel's firstborns was 22,273 (Num 3:43), but the number of Levites was only 22,000 (Num 3:39). Since there were 273 fewer Levites than the firstborn of Israel, that's exactly the number of Israel's firstborns that could not be redeemed by the Levites. In order to redeem the 273 firstborns of Israel, God commanded that five shekels be paid as a ransom for each person; therefore, 1,365 shekels were collected and given to Aaron and his sons in accordance with God's command (Num 3:46–51).

In reality, however, the number of Levites was 7,500 from the family of Gershon (Num 3:21–22), 8,600 from the family of Kohath (Num 3:27–28), and 6,200 from the family of Merari (Num 3:33–34). That comes to a total of 22,300 Levites. Then why does Numbers 3:39 state that there were 22,000 Levites? The additional 300 were the firstborn from the tribe of Levi. They were excluded from the number of the Levites who were to redeem the firstborn of the other tribes because they needed to be redeemed as the firstborn of the tribe of Levi.

God set apart Israel from the Gentiles and said in Exodus 4:22, "Israel is My son, My firstborn." Hence the tribe of Levi as an assembly that replaces all God's firstborn prefigures the general assembly of the firstborn, that is, the saints who will be saved in the last days (Heb 12:23).

We enter into the general assembly of the firstborn only through Jesus Christ. He is the firstborn and the firstfruit (firstborn) of the resurrection (Rom 8:29; 1 Cor 15:20, 23; Heb 1:6; see also Col 1:18). The saints will be able to enter the general assembly of the firstborn by believing in Jesus Christ, the true firstborn.

CHAPTER

8

Twenty-Four Divisions of the Priests

1 Chronicles 25:1–31

❖ systematically organized for the first time in history ❖

1. The Origin of the Priesthood

The priests were set apart from among the tribe of Levi in order to carry out the tasks related to sacred services. The high priest, the chief of the priests, represented the people of Israel before God.

The word "priest" in Hebrew is כֹּהֵן (*kohen*). This word appears for the first time in Scripture in relation to Melchizedek. In Genesis 14:18, Melchizedek is introduced as "a priest of God Most High."

Although the expression "priest" is not used in their case, Cain and Abel brought offerings to God (Gen 4:1–5). Noah also offered sacrifices to God when he came out of the ark (Gen 8:20). Abraham, Isaac, and Jacob offered sacrifices to God as well (Gen 12:7; 13:4; 22:13; 26:25; 35:3).

The office of the priesthood officially began after the tabernacle was completed in the days of Moses. Moses' older brother, Aaron, was the first to receive the priesthood (i.e., Aaron was the first high priest).

According to the law, unless there were grounds for disqualification, the firstborn in the line of the high priest succeeded the high priesthood, which was an inherited office tenured for life (Exod 29:29; Lev 21:16–23; Num 25:11–13). The ordination of the priest was performed by anointing him with oil (Exod 28:41; 29:29; 30:30). The qualifications included being consecrated (Exod 29:7–9, 19–21, 31–34; 30:30–33), having no physical defect (Lev 21:16–23), and wearing garments that were emblems of holiness (Exod 28:2–43; 29:29).

Among the priests, the high priest in particular managed the holy place and oversaw the service and the money (Exod 30:7–9; Lev 24:3–4; 2 Kgs 12:10; 22:4; 2 Chr 24:12). He also sought God's will by using the Urim and the Thummim (Exod 28:30; Lev 8:8; Num 27:21). He entered the holy of holies one day a year, on the Day of Atonement; on the tenth day of the seventh month, the high priest entered the holy of holies to offer a sin offering for himself and another for the people (Lev 16; Heb 9:7). During New Testament times, the high priest also acted as the chief of the Sanhedrin (Matt 26:57; Acts 5:21).

2. The Consecration of the Priest

A person must be a Levite by blood in order to become a priest. Not only did one have to be from the tribe of Levi among the twelve tribes, but he also had to be a descendant of Aaron in order to become a priest (Exod 28:1; 29:9).

Special consecration was required for those who were ordained as priests. It was mandatory for a priest to have a consecrated marriage, live a consecrated life, meet physical requirements for consecration, and eat consecrated food. No one could carry out the duties of a priest without meeting these qualifications.

The consecrated marriage of the priest

The absolute criterion for the priesthood was the Aaronic lineage. The priest had to be a descendant of Aaron, and the office was automatically passed down from father to son (Exod 40:12–15). Only the covenant "sons of Aaron" were allowed to officiate at the sacred service. Therefore, God commanded strict regulations for the marriages of the priests in order to preserve the pure lineage of the covenant priests:

> *They shall not take a woman who is profaned by harlotry, nor shall they take a woman divorced from her husband; for he is holy to his God. You shall consecrate him, therefore, for he offers the food of your God; he shall be holy to you; for I the Lord, who sanctifies you, am holy. (Leviticus 21:7–8)*

According to the provisions of the law, the priests, who had been set apart and consecrated to God, had to take a wife who had not been with another man. In other words, she had to be a virgin from among the priests' own people, that is, an Israelite (Lev 21:14). Ezekiel 44:22 specifies that the priests' wives must be "virgins from the offspring of the house of Israel."

The priests were forbidden from marrying the following types of women: a harlot (זֹנָה, *zanah*, "prostitute"), a defiled woman (חָלָל, *halal*, a woman who had been defiled through incest or other sexual relations forbidden by God; Gen 49:4; Lev 18:6–23), a divorced woman (גָּרַשׁ, *garish*, a woman driven out by her husband because her purity was in doubt), or a widow (אַלְמָנָה, *almanah*, a woman who lived alone because her husband died; Lev 21:7, 14; Ezek 44:22). Nevertheless, priests were allowed to marry the widows of priests. Ezekiel 44:22 states, "They shall not marry a widow or a divorced woman but shall take virgins from the offspring of the house of Israel, or a widow who is the widow of a priest."

These regulations on consecrated marriage also applied to the high priest. Leviticus 21:13–15 states, "He shall take a wife in her virginity. A widow, or a divorced woman, or one who is profaned by harlotry, these he may not take; but rather he is to marry a virgin of his own people, so that he will not profane his offspring among his people; for I am the Lord who sanctifies him." The only difference between the case of the high priest and that of the priest was that the high priest had to marry only a virgin and could not take a widow as wife, even the widow of a priest.

These strict regulations, which were established to preserve the holiness of the household of the priest, also applied to a priest's daughter. According to the law, adulterers were burned with fire in the following cases: when a man married a woman and her mother (Lev 20:14) or when the daughter of a priest profaned herself by harlotry. If a daughter who was a direct descendant of a priest profaned herself by harlotry, she profaned her father. Consequently, she must be burned with fire (Lev 21:9).

Strict regulations on priestly marriages demonstrate the importance of the preservation of a consecrated genealogy. The following excerpt from the first volume of Josephus's book *Against Apion* confirms this fact:

> *This is our practice, not only in Judea; but wheresoever any body of men of our nation do live: and even there an exact catalogue of our priests' marriages is kept: I mean at Egypt and at Babylon; or in any other place of the rest of the habitable earth, whithersoever our priests are scattered. For they send to Jerusalem the ancient names of their parents in writing, as well as those of their remoter ancestors: and signify who are the witnesses also. But if any war falls out, . . . those priests that survive them compose new tables of genealogy, out of the old records, and examine the circumstances of the women that remain. For still they do not admit of those that have been captives; as suspecting that they have had conversation with some foreigners. But what is the strongest argument of our exact management in this matter is what I am now going to say; that we have the names of our High priests from father to son set down in our records, for the interval of two thousand years. And*

> *if any of these have been transgressors of these rules, they are prohibited to present themselves at the altar, or to be partakers of any other of our purifications. And this is justly, or rather necessarily done.* (Apion 1.32–37)

The consecrated life of a priest (impurity and purity)

Numbers 19 records the method of preparing the ash water used to remove the impurity that resulted from touching a corpse and the method of purifying oneself from such impurities. Numbers 19:20 states, "The man who is unclean and does not purify himself from uncleanness, that person shall be cut off from the midst of the assembly, because he has defiled the sanctuary of the Lord; the water for impurity has not been sprinkled on him, he is unclean." God established this cleansing ritual as a perpetual statute (Num 19:21), not only for the Israelites, but also for the Gentiles living among them (Num 19:10).

There were three ways to become unclean, according to Numbers 19.

First, a person who touched a corpse was unclean for seven days (Num 19:11–13). Second, when a person died in a tent, anyone who entered the tent and anyone who was inside the tent was unclean for seven days (Num 19:14); every open vessel that was uncovered inside the tent at the time of the death was also unclean (Num 19:15). Third, anyone in the open field who touched one who had been slain with a sword or who had died naturally, or anyone who touched a human bone or a grave was unclean for seven days (Num 19:16). All this uncleanness was related to death, because death is the result of sin (Rom 6:23).

If a priest came into contact with what was unclean, then he also became unclean (Num 19:7). Anything an unclean person touched became unclean, and anyone who touched that thing was also unclean until evening (Num 19:22).

Priests whose duties included performing the holy ritual of offering sacrifices to God and purifying what was unclean must not have any uncleanness. Since cleanness was absolutely mandatory for priests, they were forbidden from going near a dead person or attending funerals. The only exceptions were for the priests' parents, children, brothers, and virgin sisters who had never been married (Lev 21:1–4; Ezek 44:25–27). Nonetheless, the high priest, on whose head the anointing oil had been poured and who had been consecrated to wear the garments, was forbidden from approaching any dead bodies, even those of his father or his mother (Lev 21:10–12). He was forbidden from mourning even the deaths of his own children (Lev 10:1–7). When Nadab and Abihu were killed for offering strange fire, Moses commanded Aaron and his sons Eleazar and Ithamar, "Do not uncover your heads nor tear your clothes, so that you will not die and that He will not become wrathful against all the congregation" (Lev 10:6).

God also forcefully warned the holy priests not to make any baldness on their heads or shave off the edges of their beards in order to mourn the dead as in the idol-worshiping customs of the Gentiles. Leviticus 21:5 states that the priests were not to "make any baldness on their heads, nor shave off the edges of their beards, nor make any cuts in their flesh." In Israel the beard represented dignity and honor, so shaving or plucking off the beard was a sign of great indignity or dishonor (2 Sam 10:4–5; Isa 50:6). The command regarding the beard, the hair, and the cutting of the skin applied not only to the priests but also to the congregation (Lev 19:27–28; see also 2 Sam 10:4; Isa 7:20).

For human beings who cannot escape being tarnished by uncleanness, God prepared a way to recover their purity through the offering of an "unblemished red heifer in which is no defect and on which a yoke has never been placed" (Num 19:2). The priest must sprinkle some of its blood toward the front of the tent of meeting seven times, then burn its hide, flesh, blood, and refuse along with cedar wood, hyssop, and scarlet material (Num 19:2–6). The ashes of the heifer were kept outside the camp and used to make the water for removing impurity (Num 19:9). In order to make this water that removed the impurities of the Israelites, they needed to sacrifice an unblemished red heifer without defect and on which a yoke had never been placed. This prefigured the atoning sacrifice of Jesus Christ, the unblemished One, who is without defect and knows no sin (see Matt 27:4; Mark 14:55; Luke 23:4, 14–15, 22, 41, 47; John 8:46; 18:38; 2 Cor 5:21; Heb 4:15; 7:26; 1 Pet 2:22; 1 John 3:5). The red color of the heifer is reminiscent of the crimson blood that Jesus Christ shed on the cross (John 19:34; Heb 9:12–14; 12:24).

> *If the blood of goats and bulls and the ashes of a heifer sprinkling those who have been defiled sanctify for the cleansing of the flesh, how much more will the blood of Christ, who through the eternal Spirit offered Himself without blemish to God, cleanse your conscience from dead works to serve the living God? (Hebrews 9:13–14)*

Physical requirements of the consecrated priest

A priest could not carry out his priestly duties if he had any defects on his body. Leviticus 21:21 states, "No man among the descendants of Aaron the priest who has a defect is to come near to offer the Lord's offerings by fire; since he has a defect, he shall not come near to offer the food of his God."

Leviticus 21:16–20 provides a list of twelve defects that disqualified one from being a priest. The following could not become a priest: a blind man or a lame man, he who had a disfigured face or any deformed limb, a man who had a broken foot or broken hand, a hunchback or a dwarf, or one who had a defect in his eye or eczema or scabs or crushed testicles.

Additionally, a person could not become a priest if he was not qualified to participate in the assembly of the Lord. Deuteronomy 23:1 regulates, "No one who is emasculated or has his male organ cut off shall enter the assembly of the Lord." The Revised Standard

Version translates, "He whose testicles are crushed or whose male member is cut off shall not enter the assembly of the Lord." Anyone whose male organ had been damaged could not enter the holy assembly of the Lord. Due to their inability to fulfill the male reproductive function, they were not able to participate in the assembly of God's holy people.

The assembly of Israel was totally different from gatherings established by human promises of personal gain. No one of illegitimate birth could enter the assembly of the Lord, not even his descendants, even to the tenth generation (Deut 23:2). The Ammonites and the Moabites could not enter the assembly of the Lord forever (Deut 23:3). Thus the assembly of the Lord was thoroughly set apart.

The word "assembly" is derived from the Hebrew verb קָהַל (*qahal*), which means "to call together" or "to convoke." The nominative קָהָל (*qahal*) originally referred to adult males who were able to wield weapons, and by extension it included all male Israelites gathered to participate in the battles of the Lord, in sacrifice rituals, and in court adjudications (Judg 20:2; 2 Chr 20:5). All men of Israel had to appear before the Lord, in the place that He appointed, for the three feasts (Passover, Feast of Weeks, and Feast of Tabernacles), that is, three times a year (Exod 23:14–17; 34:22–23; Deut 16:16). This was the covenant community, a people who had been called by God and received the covenant on Mount Sinai (Deut 4:10; 5:22; 9:10; 10:4; 18:16).

Those who could not serve in the priesthood because of a physical defect were still part of the division of priests. Thus they were allowed to receive a food portion of the most holy and the holy:

> *He may eat the food of his God, both of the most holy and of the holy, only he shall not go in to the veil or come near the altar because he has a defect, so that he will not profane My sanctuaries. For I am the Lord who sanctifies them.* (Leviticus 21:22–23)

We are truly grateful, however, that in the New Testament era, God's atoning grace through Jesus Christ enables both the physically challenged and women to participate in the work of the kingdom of God (see Isa 35:5–6; 56:4–8; Luke 14:13, 21; John 5:2–9; Gal 3:28–29).[18]

The consecrated food of the priests

The food that the priests are allowed to eat is called the food of the most holy. The expression "most holy" is קָדְשֵׁי הַקֳּדָשִׁים (*qadshe haqqodashim*) in Hebrew (Lev 21:22; 2 Chr 31:14; Ezek 42:13). Note that the root word קֹדֶשׁ (*qodesh*) is used twice, in order to stress the highest importance, thus signifying "the holiest among the holies." It means that the food the holy priest eats in the holy place must be treated as holy (Lev 10:17; 14:13; Ezek 42:13). The "most holy" refers to the priests' portions from the sin offering, the guilt offering, and the grain offering as well as the bread of the Presence (Lev 2:3, 10; 6:16–18, 29; 7:6–10; 24:8–9). Besides the most holy gifts, the priests could eat other holy gifts along with their descendants. These included the breast of the wave offering and the thigh of the heave offering from the sacrifices given in the peace offering. They also included "all the best of the fresh oil and all the best of the fresh wine and of the grain, the first fruits of those which they [the sons of Israel] give to the Lord" (Num 18:12; see Lev 7:29–34; Num 18:8–13).

However, any priest or his descendant who approached the holy gifts while his body was in the state of uncleanness would be cut off from before God (Lev 22:2–3). The following are cases when priests or laymen could not eat the holy gifts:

18 Joong-Eun Kim, "Priests' Index of Ethics (Lev 21–22)," *Christian Philosophy 33*, no. 12 (Seoul: The Christian Literature Society of Korea, 1989), 220–21.

- A priest who was a leper or who had a discharge (Lev 22:4)
- A priest who touched anything made unclean by a corpse, had a seminal emission, or touched any swarming insects or unclean person and had not bathed in water (Lev 22:4–6)
- A layman (i.e., stranger or foreigner), a sojourner with the priest, or a hired man (Lev 22:10, 13)
- A priest's daughter who was married to a layman (Lev 22:12)

Nevertheless, a slave bought by a priest with his money and those who were born in his house could eat of the holy gifts (Lev 22:11). If a priest's daughter became a widow or divorced and had no children and returned to her father's house as in her youth, then she could eat of the holy gifts (Lev 22:13). Also, if a man unintentionally ate a holy gift, then he must add to it a fifth of it and give the holy gift to the priest (Lev 22:14).

Apostle Peter states in 1 Peter 2:5 that all Christians have been given priesthood: "You also, as living stones, are being built up as a spiritual house for a holy priesthood, to offer up spiritual sacrifices acceptable to God through Jesus Christ." For Christians nothing is more glorious than to be called holy priests of God. We are priests who make up the body (church) of Christ.

We are Christians who have been entrusted with the holy priesthood through the atoning grace of our Lord Jesus Christ. Henceforth, we must present our bodies as living sacrifices, acceptable to God (Rom 12:1).

God requires consecration from those who have been granted holy priesthood through God's covenant in Jesus Christ. This requirement of consecration teaches how we must serve God. Christians with spiritual priesthood in Jesus Christ must live lives that are consecrated in all aspects (1 Pet 1:15–16). Leviticus 20:26 states, "You are to be holy to Me, for I the Lord am holy; and I have set you apart from the peoples to be Mine" (see also Lev 11:44; 19:2).

Living a consecrated life should be the utmost priority for those who have been redeemed by the precious blood of Jesus Christ. The word "consecrated" means "declared sacred" or "set apart." First, consecration entails cutting off all worldly things for God (Neh 13:22). Second, it refers to becoming like Christ (Rom 8:29; Eph 2:10; Col 3:10). Third, it refers to changing our whole lives to be God-centered (Gal 1:15; Titus 2:14). Fourth, it refers to living godly lives before our holy God (Lev 11:44–45; 19:2; 20:7, 26; 21:8; 22:9, 16; 1 Thess 4:7; 1 Pet 1:16). Just as Daniel made up his mind that he would not defile himself and risked his life to keep this resolution (Dan 1:8), blessed Christians must be consecrated by separating themselves every day from the counsel of the wicked, the path of sinners, and the seat of scoffers (Ps 1:1).

The strict regulations for consecration that God commanded the priests to keep in the Old Testament era serve as a prototype for the lives of the saints who have become "holy priests" in Jesus Christ in the end time. We must be absolutely consecrated in all aspects of our lives. The following are some aspects of our lives that require such consecration: a life of worship (sacrifice) in spirit and in truth; a consecrated marriage life that is pleasing to God; a godly life that is set apart from sin (uncleanness) but always drawing closer to the Word of God; and a life of eating and drinking solely for the glory of the Lord. In all these aspects, we must strive to be found spotless and blameless so that we may be able to stand before our returning Lord (2 Pet 3:14).

Daniel was without error or fault in speech and in all aspects of his life (Dan 6:4). A consecrated saint is without blemish. A consecrated saint is the quintessential believer. No matter what we do, only when we live consecrated lives that are spotless and blameless can we overcome sin and the world and be victorious. In order to meet the second coming Christ, we must be made spotless and blameless in our character, morals, and the faithfulness of our conduct.

The uncleanness of our bodies is connected to the uncleanness of our hearts; our souls are defiled and diseased by it. Apostle Peter said, "Abstain from fleshly lusts which wage war against the soul" (1 Pet 2:11). Apostle Paul also commanded, "Flee immorality. Every other sin that a man commits is outside the body, but the immoral man sins against his own body" (1 Cor 6:18). Christians waiting for the second coming of the Lord must overcome the lusts of the flesh with living faith. They must consecrate themselves by repenting of all sins committed both knowingly and unknowingly. A sinner must be cleansed from the uncleanness of sin in order to draw near to God, and this is possible only through the Word of the living God. Leviticus 22:6 states, "A person who touches any such shall be unclean until evening, and shall not eat of the holy gifts unless he has bathed his body in water." This refers to purifying oneself from fleshly uncleanness by the washing of the water, as stated in Ephesians 5:25–26: "Christ also loved the church and gave Himself for her, so that He might sanctify her, having cleansed her by the washing of water with the word" (see Titus 3:5).

We must listen to and meditate on the Word of the living God in order to overcome sin and become pure, spotless, and blameless. When we see, hear, and read the holy Word of God, He gives us hearts of repentance, casts away our unclean thoughts, and changes our evil habits. When we are consecrated as such, then we are able to meet God. Psalm 119:9 also states, "How can a young man keep his way pure? By keeping it according to Your word." Jesus also said that those who hear the voice of the Son of God—God's Word—will live (John 5:25).

Our spirits, souls, and bodies must become spotless and blameless through the Word of the living God in order that we may be able to stand in glorification before the God of glory (Phil 1:10–11; 1 Thess 3:13; 5:23; 1 Tim 6:14; Heb 4:12–13; 2 Pet 3:14). Only those who live consecrated lives, pursuing peace and holiness with all men, will truly be able to see the Lord:

> *Pursue peace with all men, and the sanctification without which no one will see the Lord. (Hebrews 12:14)*

3. The Priestly Duties

The reason God distinguished Israel as His chosen people among all the nations was to establish them as the priestly kingdom (Exod 19:5–6). In order to accomplish this, God not only gave them laws through Moses but also erected the sanctuary in the midst of Israel so that He would be the center of their lives. He also established priests and Levites to assist them so that together these men could lead and guide the religious lives of the people.

By presiding over all the sacrifices and offerings given in service to God, the priests had the task of overseeing the people's lives of worship. Meanwhile, the Levites assisted with the priestly duties in the tabernacle. They also lived scattered across the cities of Israel and took on duties to assist in the people's religious lives.

Israel's institution of the priesthood is laid out in Exodus 28–29. In the wilderness God made specific commands to Moses regarding the ordination of Aaron and his sons (Nadab, Abihu, Eleazar, and Ithamar), the holy garments they were to wear, and the process for the ordination ceremony of the priests. Deuteronomy 33:10 introduces two important duties that the priests must carry out.

The duty to interpret and teach the Word of God (law) to the people of Israel

The first half of Deuteronomy 33:10 states, "They shall teach Your ordinances to Jacob, and Your law to Israel." Among the priestly duties, interpreting and teaching the Word of God was an important duty that did not cease throughout the ages (1 Sam 12:23; Neh 8:7–9; Jer 18:18; Ezek 7:26).

King Jehoshaphat, in the third year of his reign, sent five officials, two priests, and nine Levites to teach the law, and the specific list of names identifying these men leaves a strong impression. Five officials (Ben-hail, Obadiah, Zechariah, Nethanel, and Micaiah) were sent to various cities to teach, and nine Levites (Shemaiah, Nethaniah, Zebadiah, Asahel, Shemiramoth, Jehonathan, Adonijah, Tobijah, and Tobadonijah) as well as two priests (Elishama and Jehoram; 2 Chr 17:7–8) were also sent with them. "They taught in Judah, having the book of the law of the Lord with them; and they went throughout all the cities of Judah and taught among the people" (2 Chr 17:9). The priests possessed the authority to interpret the law, and the Levites were adept at teaching the Word. It seems that the officials were both skillful at administrative tasks and knowledgeable in the law and thus traveled with the Levites and also taught the Word.

Moreover, the priests possessed the ultimate authority on all issues regarding the law. They taught the sons of Israel all the statutes that the Lord had spoken to them through Moses so that the people could distinguish between the holy and the profane and between the unclean and the clean (Lev 10:8–11). Ezekiel 44:23 states, "They shall teach My people the difference between the holy and the profane, and cause them to discern between the unclean and the clean."

Regarding the qualifications for a true priest, Prophet Malachi said, "True instruction was in his mouth and unrighteousness was not found on his lips; he walked with Me in peace and uprightness, and he turned many back from iniquity. For the lips of a priest should preserve knowledge, and men should seek instruction from his mouth; for he is the messenger of the Lord of hosts" (Mal 2:6–7).

The duty to offer incense to the Lord and burnt offerings on the Lord's altar

The latter part of Deuteronomy 33:10 states, "They shall put incense before You, and whole burnt offerings on Your altar." The work relating to sacrificial offerings was a duty exclusively entrusted to the priests (Exod 29:1, 9, 29, 44; 30:30; 40:13–15; Num 3:3, 10; 18:1, 7; 25:12–13). The priests had to be without physical defect in order to carry out these duties (Lev 21:16–21). However, even a priest who was disqualified from approaching the altar due to physical defects could still eat the holy gifts (Lev 21:22–23).

The greatest reason the priests burned incense before God and offered whole burnt offerings was to resolve the sins of the people as well as their own:

> *The Lord said to Aaron, "You and your sons and your father's household with you shall bear the guilt in connection with the sanctuary, and you and your sons with you shall bear the guilt in connection with your priesthood." (Numbers 18:1)*

Broadly, there were two types of sins that the priests were to bear.

First, to bear the sins "in connection with the sanctuary" meant to atone for the sins committed by those other than the priests and the Levites, namely, the entire congregation of the sons of Israel (Lev 16:15–19).

Second, because even the priests who appeared holy also had sins, they must bear the sins "in connection with [their] priesthood" (Lev 16:6, 11; see also Lev 4:3). What are the sins connected to the priesthood? These refer to the priest's careless performance of his duties without being conscientious and faithful. On the Day of Atonement each year, the priest made atonement for the holy gifts and consecrated them, and this included atonement for himself (Lev 16:6, 11, 17, 24). Hebrews 7:27 states that Jesus did not need, "like those high priests, to offer up sacrifices, first for His own sins and then for the sins of the people"; and Hebrews 9:7 states that the high priest "offers for himself and for the sins of the people."

The priests also ministered inside the holy place.

First, Aaron and his sons commanded the sons of Israel to bring clear oil from beaten olives to be used for lighting the seven lamps in the holy place (Exod 27:20–21; Lev. 24:1–4). God commanded that when they lit the lamps, they were to make sure that the seven lamps shone in the front of the lampstand (Num 8:1–3).

Second, so the lamps would burn continually, Aaron and his sons kept them in order from evening to morning in the tent of meeting, outside the veil that is before the testimony (Exod 27:21; Lev 24:3–4). This was a perpetual statute throughout their generations for the sons of Israel (Exod 27:21). The priests could not rest peacefully from evening until morning in order to carry out this duty; they had to keep awake inside the tent of meeting at all times. Even during the hours when all the people of Israel were asleep and the camp was covered in darkness because the lights had gone out, the light in the tent of meeting burned brightly. It is likely that the priests kept watch, staying awake all through the night while meditating on the Word and praying for the welfare of the people. The priests were the lamps of the covenant watching over the people of Israel even during the dark night (see 1 Sam 3:3).

Third, when Aaron the high priest trimmed and lit the lamps every morning and evening, he was to burn fragrant incense on the altar of incense. Exodus 30:7–8 states, "Aaron shall burn fragrant incense on it; he shall burn it every morning when he trims the lamps. When Aaron trims the lamps at twilight, he shall burn incense. There shall be perpetual incense before the Lord throughout your generations." The fragrant incense used in the tent of meeting was first made by Moses as commanded by God (Exod 30:34–38), and later God commanded Bezalel, Oholiab, and all who were wise of heart to make it (Exod 31:2, 6, 11; 37:29).

Fourth, every Sabbath the priests were to set twelve cakes (loaves of bread) on the pure gold table in two rows, with six in each row (Lev 24:5–6, 8). It was an everlasting covenant for the sons of Israel (Lev 24:8). They were also to place pure frankincense on each row to be a memorial portion for the bread, as an offering by fire to the Lord (Lev 24:7). God commanded that the priests eat the holy bread of the Presence and burn the frankincense as an offering in place of the bread they ate. This was an eternal statute (Lev 24:9).

Fifth, when the tabernacle was moved, Aaron and his sons packed up the ark of the testimony, the dishes, the pans, the sacrificial bowls, the jars for the drink offering, the lampstand and all its utensils, the altar of incense, and all the utensils of service (Num 4:5–16). When the priests were done preparing these things to be moved, the Levites carried them on their shoulders (Num 4:15, 27, 31–32). Regarding the related duties of the Levites, Numbers 3:8 states, "They shall also keep all the furnishings of the tent of meeting, along with the duties of the sons of Israel, to do the service of the tabernacle."

Besides the duties mentioned above, the priests also acted as judges (Num 5:12–31; Deut 17:8–9; Ezek 44:24), blessed communities and individuals (Num 6:22–27), summoned the congregation (Num 10:1–2, 7–8), blew the trumpets as a warning of war (Num 10:9), and encouraged the soldiers during battles (Deut 20:2–4).

4. The Organization of the Twenty-Four Priestly Divisions

Along with the preparations for the construction of the temple, David classified the Levites who were to take on the holy duties and organized the priests into twenty-four divisions.

In the priesthood there were the high priest, the priests of the second order (2 Kgs 23:4; 25:18), and the other priests (2 Kgs 12:7; 2 Chr 26:20; Neh 3:1).

The genealogy of the twenty-four divisions opens with the words, "Now the divisions of the descendants of Aaron were these" (1 Chr 24:1). According to 1 Chronicles 23:13, Aaron "was set apart to sanctify him as most holy, he and his sons forever, to burn incense before the Lord, to minister to Him and to bless in His name forever." However, while Aaron's four sons, Nadab, Abihu, Eleazar, and Ithamar were serving along with him, Nadab and Abihu committed the sin of offering strange fire before the Lord, which He had not commanded them, and died before their father (Lev 10:1–2; Num 3:4; 26:61; 1 Chr 24:2). Because they did not have any children, the priesthood was passed thereafter to the lineage of Eleazar and Ithamar.

During David's time, Zadok of the sons of Eleazar and Ahimelech of the sons of Ithamar served as priests and divided their offices for their ministry between themselves (1 Chr 24:3). Moreover, when the lots were cast for the twenty-four divisions, because the sons of Eleazar were greater in number than the sons of Ithamar, sixteen heads of families were chosen from the household of Eleazar and eight heads of families from the household of Ithamar. Hence a total of twenty-four heads of families became the heads of the twenty-four divisions (1 Chr 24:4):

> *Shemaiah, the son of Nethanel the scribe, from the Levites, recorded them in the presence of the king, the princes, Zadok the priest, Ahimelech the son of Abiathar, and the heads of the fathers' households of the priests and of the Levites; one father's household taken for Eleazar and one taken for Ithamar. (1 Chronicles 24:6)*

The priests chosen for the twenty-four divisions were called "officers of the sanctuary" and "officers of God" (1 Chr 24:5). The expression "officers of the sanctuary" is שָׂרֵי־קֹדֶשׁ (*sare-qodesh*) in Hebrew and means "consecrated officials." The expression "officers of God" is שָׂרֵי הָאֱלֹהִים (*sare hoelohim*) and means "officials of God." These officers were responsible for assisting the king and the high priest in managing all things related to the temple.

The following were chosen for the twenty-four divisions.

1st Division	**Jehoiarib** / יְהוֹיָרִיב	"the LORD contends, whom the LORD defends" 1 Chr 24:7
2nd Division	**Jedaiah** / יְדַעְיָה	"the LORD knows" 1 Chr 24:7, Ezra 2:36; Neh 7:39
3rd Division	**Harim** / חָרִם	"consecrated, dedicated" 1 Chr 24:8, Ezra 2:39; Neh 7:42
4th Division	**Seorim** / שְׂעֹרִים	"barley" 1 Chr 24:8
5th Division	**Malchijah** / מַלְכִּיָּה	"my king is the LORD" 1 Chr 24:9
6th Division	**Mijamin** / מִיָּמִן	"right [luck], from the right hand" 1 Chr 24:9
7th Division	**Hakkoz** / הַקּוֹץ	"thorn bush" 1 Chr 24:10
8th Division	**Abijah** / אֲבִיָּה	"the LORD is my Father" 1 Chr 24:10
9th Division	**Jeshua** / יֵשׁוּעַ	"the LORD is salvation" 1 Chr 24:11
10th Division	**Shecaniah** / שְׁכַנְיָה	"the LORD has taken up His abode" 1 Chr 24:11
11th Division	**Eliashib** / אֶלְיָשִׁיב	"God restores, God recovers" 1 Chr 24:12
12th Division	**Jakim** / יָקִים	"He [the LORD] lifts up, whom God sets up" 1 Chr 24:12
13th Division	**Huppah** / חֻפָּה	"the LORD covers, canopy" 1 Chr 24:13
14th Division	**Jeshebeab** / יֶשֶׁבְאָב	"father's seat, dwelling of the father" 1 Chr 24:13
15th Division	**Bilgah** / בִּלְגָּה	"cheerfulness, gleam" 1 Chr 24:14

16th Division	**Immer** / אִמֵּר	"prominent, lamb" 1 Chr 24:14, Ezra 2:37; Neh 7:40
17th Division	**Hezir** / חֵזִיר	"swine" 1 Chr 24:15
18th Division	**Happizzez** / הַפִּצֵּץ	"dispersion, he has shattered" 1 Chr 24:15
19th Division	**Pethahiah** / פְּתַחְיָה	"freed by the LORD, the LORD has opened [the womb]" 1 Chr 24:16
20th Division	**Jehezkel** / יְחֶזְקֵאל	"God strengthens" 1 Chr 24:16
21st Division	**Jachin** / יָכִין	"He will establish" 1 Chr 24:17
22nd Division	**Gamul** / גָּמוּל	"who has received [benefits], weaned" 1 Chr 24:17
23rd Division	**Delaiah** / דְּלָיָה	"the LORD has drawn, the LORD has pulled out" 1 Chr 24:18
24th Division	**Maaziah** / מַעַזְיָה	"consolation of the LORD, the LORD is my refuge" 1 Chr 24:18

5. The History of the Priestly Duties

The period of the wilderness and subsequent settlement in Canaan

As the leader of the exodus, Moses was the first person to play the role of the priest. According to Exodus 24, he made offerings to God himself, since he was from the tribe of Levi. When the Sinaitic covenant was ratified, he took the blood of the sacrifice and put half of the blood in basins, and the other half he sprinkled on the altar. He then took the book of the covenant and read it before the people and sprinkled the blood on the people (Exod 24:5–8).

God allowed Moses to enter the holy of holies. Moses was not able to enter the holy of holies on the Day of Atonement, but he was allowed to enter it on other days. Exodus 25:22 states, "There I will meet with you; and from above the mercy seat, from between the two cherubim which are upon the ark of the testimony, I will speak to you about all that I will give you in commandment for the sons of Israel." In fact, Moses entered the holy of holies three times when he placed the twelve rods of the twelve tribes before the ark of the testimony. He went in once to place the rods before the ark of the testimony (Num 17:7); the next day he went in to bring out the rods (Num 17:8); and he went in again to place Aaron's rod that budded before the ark of the testimony (Num 17:10–11). Moses was a special priest.

Later Moses received the message, "Bring near to yourself Aaron your brother, and his sons with him, from among the sons of Israel, to minister as priest to Me—Aaron, Nadab and Abihu, Eleazar and Ithamar, Aaron's sons" (Exod 28:1). Moses then ordained Aaron and his sons so that they could serve as priests (Exod 29:1–9) and thus institutionalized the priesthood.

The "Levitical priests" carried the ark of the covenant when they entered Canaan (Josh 3:3; 8:33). After settling in Canaan, there was a clear differentiation between the Levites and the priests (Josh 21:1–42). Joshua set up the tent of meeting at Shiloh (Josh 18:1), and Shiloh became Israel's center of faith during the period of the judges.

Statutes regarding the priesthood became ineffective due to increasing spiritual disorder during the period of the judges. A man named Micah from the hill country of Ephraim made idols and consecrated his son as his priest (Judg 17:5). Later he consecrated a young Levite as a priest for his house (Judg 17:12). Afterward, at the proposal of the tribe of Dan, this young Levite priest left the house of Micah to become the priest for the whole tribe of Dan (Judg 18:19–20). It was indeed a corrupt era when the holy ministers moved from place to place based on financial circumstances.

During the latter part of the judges' era, the sons of Ithamar, Aaron's fourth son, served as high priest. Eli, a descendant of Ithamar, served as high priest, and his sons served as priests (1 Sam 1:3, 9). However, Eli's sons, Hophni and Phinehas, lay with the women who served at the doorway of the tent of meeting (1 Sam 2:22) and took the sacrifices for themselves before they were offered to God (1 Sam 2:12–17). Hence they were killed in battle against the Philistines, and the ark of the covenant was taken by the Philistines (1 Sam 4:11). Upon hearing this news, Eli fell backward from his seat and broke his neck and died (1 Sam 4:17–18).

The period of the united monarchy

Ahijah, Eli's grandson, served as priest during the reign of King Saul (1 Sam 14:3). Saul wanted to inquire of Ahijah about the outcome of the war, but he stopped, as the war turned out to his advantage (1 Sam 14:18–19). When Saul sought to attack the Philistines that night, Ahijah suggested that they inquire of God whether it was His will or not; Saul agreed, and they inquired of God (1 Sam 14:36–37). As such, at the time priests were the channels through whom inquiry was made regarding God's will.

During the latter years of his reign, Saul chased after David like a bloodthirsty hound. Driven into a corner, David fled to Ahimelech the priest in the land of Nob and received great help (1 Sam 21:1–9). Ahimelech was a priest from the line of Ithamar and the great-grandson of Eli (Eli, Phinehas, Ahitub, Ahimelech; 1 Sam 14:3; 22:9, 11, 20). David, who had fled to Ramah and received the prophet Samuel's help, was now seeking the priest's help. David had been hungry for a long time in the midst of this unforeseeable, life-threatening situation and requested, "Give me five loaves of bread, or whatever can be found" (1 Sam 21:3). Ahimelech, after checking to be sure that the men had kept themselves from women, gave them the bread of the Presence that had been removed from before the Lord on the Sabbath day (1 Sam 21:3–6). First Samuel 21:6 states, "The priest gave him consecrated bread; for there was no bread there but the bread of the Presence which was removed from before the Lord, in order to put hot bread in its place when it was taken away." The bread of the Presence was the most holy bread placed before the Lord every Sabbath in two rows ("piles"; ESV) of six on the pure gold table. As an everlasting covenant, the household of the high priest was to eat them in the holy place (Lev 24:5–9). Besides the bread, David also received from Ahimelech the sword of Goliath, which had been wrapped in a cloth and placed behind the ephod (1 Sam 21:9).

At that time Nob was where the priests lived, where the sanctuary in which offerings were made to God was located, and where the ephod was kept. For this reason Nob was called the "city of the priests" (1 Sam 22:19). David, whose life was in danger, had fled to the land of Nob in order to receive accurate guidance from God through the priests regarding his future path (1 Sam 22:10, 15).

Nevertheless, when David left the land of Nob and took refuge in the forest of Hereth, Doeg the Edomite (1 Sam 21:7), the chief of Saul's shepherds, told King Saul what Ahimelech had done for David. As a result, Ahimelech and all the priests of his father's household were falsely accused of treason and brutally killed (1 Sam 22:17–18). Eighty-five priests of God, men who wore the linen ephod, were killed along with men and women, children and infants, and even the animals (1 Sam 22:19).

Two high priests served during the time of King David: Abiathar, a descendant of Ithamar, and Zadok, a descendant of Eleazar (2 Sam 15:35; 20:25). Abiathar the high priest had helped David during Absalom's rebellion (2 Sam 15:24–26; 17:15–16), but King Solomon dismissed him from the office of high priest for conspiring with David's son Adonijah in his attempt to usurp the throne (1 Kgs 1:7; 2:27, 35). After this the position of the high priest was monopolized by the descendants of Zadok from the line of Eleazar (see Ezek 44:15).

King Solomon finished constructing the temple; hence a permanent temple was established during his time (1 Kgs 6:37–38). The priests then carried the ark of the covenant into the appointed place, and when the priests came out of the holy place, the cloud and the glory of the Lord filled the temple (1 Kgs 8:1–11).

The period of the divided monarchy (with focus on the sou-thern kingdom of Judah)

After Solomon's death the kingdom was divided into the northern kingdom of Israel and the southern kingdom of Judah. King Jeroboam of the northern kingdom of Israel made a golden calf in Dan and Bethel; he drove out the sons of Levi and made priests of men who were not from the tribe of Levi (1 Kgs 12:28–31; 13:33; 2 Chr 13:9). Jeroboam gave the priesthood to anyone who came with a young bull and seven rams (2 Chr 13:9). He even committed the sin of burning incense, which was supposed to be done by the priests (1 Kgs 13:1).

In comparison, the southern kingdom of Judah kept the statutes regarding the priesthood better than the northern kingdom of Israel.

Hezekiah's time: *enrollment of the priestly genealogy and statutes regarding the most holy things*

After removing the idols and successfully observing the Passover feast, King Hezekiah reassigned the priests and Levites—who had been inactive for many years—to their divisions and duties (2 Chr 31:2). When he led the religious reformation, he rectified the temple services and restructured the organization of the priests and the Levites. It was at this time that King Hezekiah guaranteed the livelihood of the priests and the Levites with the most holy things so that they could devote themselves to the law of the Lord and faithfully carry out their duties (2 Chr 31:4–19). These were the most innovative reforms put in place, never before attempted by any of the preceding kings.

The "most holy things" were the most sacred things and most consecrated things. In Hebrew the phrase is קָדְשֵׁי הַקֳּדָשִׁים (*qadshe haqqodashim*), where the Hebrew word for "holy," קָדַשׁ (*qadash*), is used twice to emphasize "utmost holiness." Ezekiel 42:13 states that the place where the most holy things were kept was also a holy place. The priests and the Levites received as their due the most holy things that were left over after making offerings to God (Lev 7:35–36; Num 18:8–32; Deut 18:1–5). Second Chronicles 31:14 states that the most holy things were the portion of the priests and the Levites who were near to the Lord as they served in His temple (Ezra 2:63; Neh 7:65; Ezek 42:13). Hezekiah collected tithes so that the priests and the Levites could receive the most holy things; he also prepared a place to store these things and an overseer to manage them meticulously (2 Chr 31:11–15). Second Chronicles 31:11–12 states, "Hezekiah commanded them to prepare rooms in the house of the Lord, and they prepared them. They faithfully brought in the contributions and the tithes and the consecrated things."

The details are as follows.

First, the king commanded all the people of Jerusalem to give the portion due to the priests and the Levites (2 Chr 31:4).

Second, as soon as the king gave orders, the people of Israel brought "the first fruits of grain, new wine, oil, honey, and of all the produce of the field" in abundance. They also brought the tithe of everything in abundance (2 Chr 31:5–7).

Third, when the priests and the Levites had eaten enough and still had plenty left over (2 Chr 31:10), Hezekiah prepared rooms to store what was left over (2 Chr 31:11). At the same time he set an officer over the temple storage rooms to manage the contributions. Conaniah the Levite was the officer in charge of them, his brother Shimei was second, and ten overseers (Jehiel, Azaziah, Nahath, Asahel, Jerimoth, Jozabad, Eliel, Ismachiah, Mahath, and Benaiah) also assisted (2 Chr 31:12–13).

Fourth, he put Kore (קוֹרֵא, "one who cries out"), the son of Imnah the Levite, the keeper of the eastern gate, in charge of distributing the contributions for the Lord and the most holy things equally among the brothers (2 Chr 31:14). He had six persons under his authority (Eden, Miniamin, Jeshua, Shemaiah, Amariah, and Shecaniah). They went to the cities where the priests lived and faithfully distributed the portions to their brothers, whether great or small (2 Chr 31:15).

Fifth, he meticulously managed the genealogies of the priests and the Levites in order to distribute the most holy things to them (2 Chr 31:16–19). Second Chronicles 31:16–19 records in detail the classifications of the people eligible to receive the most holy things by various criteria. Notably, the first criterion that qualified someone for the most holy things was that one must be enrolled in the genealogy. During Nehemiah's days a thorough search was conducted into the ancestral registrations, or genealogies, of those who had participated in the first return. It was discovered that some priests (the sons of Habaiah/Hobaiah, the sons of Hakkoz, and the sons of Barzillai) could not verify their genealogical enrollment. The governor commanded them that they "should not eat from the most holy things until a priest stood up with Urim and Thummim" (Ezra 2:63; see Ezra 2:61–63; Neh 7:63–65). Those who were not enrolled in the genealogy, who falsified their genealogy, or who did not maintain their genealogy were strictly forbidden from eating the most holy things offered in the temple. All the most holy things, whatever they were, were distributed strictly according to the criteria of the genealogical records.

Second Chronicles 31:16–19 lists the following people as those eligible to receive the most holy things.

First, men over the age of three[19] who were enrolled in the genealogy (2 Chr 31:16) were eligible. Here the word "enrollment" is יַחַשׂ (*yahas*) and means "to reckon genealogically," "to have registered," or "to be enrolled by genealogy." Most babies are weaned by the age of three. Thus it is presumed that babies were enrolled in the genealogy starting at three years, when they became eligible to receive their portions.

19 Most versions (ESV, KJV, NIV, NLT, RSV, etc.) have translated this as "three years old." Some translations, including the NASB, have rendered this figure as "thirty."

Second, those who entered the house of the Lord every day to carry out their duties according to their divisions (2 Chr 31:16) were eligible. It is presumed that the priests received extra portions, besides what was written in the genealogy, according to the types of duties performed and amount of time served when they went to the temple to serve according to their divisions.

Third, the priests who were recorded in the genealogies according to their fathers' households (2 Chr 31:17) were eligible. The priests were enrolled in the genealogy according to their fathers' households, and the most holy things were distributed according to the genealogy.

Fourth, the Levites twenty years old and older who were listed according to their duties and divisions (2 Chr 31:17) were eligible. In accordance with the twenty-four divisions institutionalized by David, the Levites had to be twenty years old or older in order to enter the temple and serve (1 Chr 23:24–27). It is presumed that they received extra portions according to the types of duties done and the amount of time served when they went to the temple to serve.

Fifth, the little children, wives, and sons and daughters of the whole assembly who were enrolled in the genealogy (2 Chr 31:18) were eligible. Here the "whole assembly" indicates the entire community of priests and Levites who served in the temple. The most holy things were distributed not only to all the priests and the Levites serving in the temple but also to the families they supported. The reason the families of the priests and the Levites were included in the distribution is given in 2 Chronicles 31:18 in the following phrase: "for [כִּי, *ki*, "indicator of cause or reason"] they consecrated themselves faithfully in holiness." The word "consecrated" is יִתְקַדְּשׁוּ־קֹדֶשׁ (*yithqaddeshu-qodesh*), where the Hebrew word קֹדֶשׁ (*qodesh*), meaning "holy" or "to set apart," is repeated as an indication of how faithfully the assembly had consecrated and dedicated themselves. Additionally, the word "faithfully" is אֱמוּנָה (*emunah*), meaning "fidelity" or "truthfulness." Thus this is an emphasis on the fact that the families of the priests and Levites were taken care of because the priests and the Levites dedicated themselves before God in holiness and were truthful people without any deceit.

Sixth, the sons of Aaron who were in the pasture lands of their cities to every male among the priests and to everyone enrolled in the genealogies of the Levites (2 Chr 31:19) were eligible. Some Levites lived in the outskirts of the cities in which the priests resided. Their names were enrolled sequentially in the genealogies of the Levites, and they received their portions of the most holy things based on this genealogy. Only males were to be included in the census in Israel (Num 1:2; 3:15; Ezra 8:3), and only these men were enrolled in the genealogies and remembered by the descendants. Thus all the Levites were remembered, and not one was left out when they received their portions of the most holy things and the tithes. Regardless of whether they dwelt in the cities or in the pasture lands, all Levites and priests received their portion of the most holy things. This is evidence that Hezekiah had sincere consideration for them.

Josiah's time

King Josiah discovered the book of the law in the eighteenth year of his reign (when he was approximately twenty-six years old) while he was repairing the temple. He and all the people entered into a covenant before God to obey Him and keep His commandments, testimonies, and statutes with all their hearts and all their souls (2 Kgs 22:3–8; 23:1–3). Josiah began a thorough religious reformation after he established this covenant.

He started by commanding Hilkiah the high priest, the priests of the second order, and the doorkeepers to bring out from the temple of the Lord all the vessels that had been made for Baal, Asherah, and all the host of heaven. Then those vessels were to be burned outside Jerusalem in the fields of the Kidron and their ashes carried to Bethel (2 Kgs 23:4). He also tore down the houses of the male cult prostitutes that were in the temple where the women had woven hangings for the Gentile goddess Asherah (2 Kgs 23:7).

One of the prominent acts among Josiah's religious reformation was the expulsion and punishment of the priests who worshiped idols.

First, he expelled the priests who burned incense in the high places and worshiped idols. These were priests who had been established by the previous kings of Judah and who burned incense in the high places in the cities of Judah and in the surrounding area of Jerusalem (2 Kgs 23:5). Josiah also expelled those who burned incense to Baal, the sun, the moon, the constellations, and all the host of heaven (2 Kgs 23:5).

Second, he brought all the priests from the cities of Judah and punished the priests of the high places so that they could not go up to the altar of God in Jerusalem (2 Kgs 23:8–9). Josiah defiled the high places where the priests had burned incense, from Geba to Beersheba, and stopped the idol-worshiping rituals in the high places scattered around the cities. He also destroyed the high places of the city gate (2 Kgs 23:8).

This religious reformation led to the revival of true worship, as all the people came up to Jerusalem to worship. This was the last flame of Israel's spiritual reformation.

The restoration of the twenty-four priestly divisions after the return from Babylon

The twenty-four divisions of priests were disbanded when the temple of Jerusalem was burned on the seventh day of the fifth month in 586 BC (2 Kgs 25:8–9) and all the people of Judah were taken captive. Hence after the return from the exile, some who claimed to be descendants of the priests could not find their genealogy. The governor considered such persons unclean and excluded them from the priesthood. He said that they should not eat from the most holy things until a priest stood up with Urim and Thummim (Ezra 2:61–63; Neh 7:63–65). Thus the organization of the priests in Israel fell apart due to the chaotic period of the Babylonian exile.

It was during such times that God showed through Prophet Ezekiel a vivid and definite vision of the resurrection of the chosen people. Ezekiel prophesied to the Israelites in the exile that the new temple would be built (Ezek 40–43) and that worship would be restored (Ezek 44–46). Both of these elements of Ezekiel's prophecy would serve as a symbol of the promise that God would return to His people and dwell among them.

Ezekiel 44 contains ordinances for the priests in the new temple (Ezek 44:15–31). The most important ordinance here is that only the sons of Zadok would be allowed into the priesthood (Ezek 44:15; see also Ezek 40:46; 43:19). The reason for this is given: "The Levitical priests, the sons of Zadok, . . . kept charge of My sanctuary when the sons of Israel went astray from Me" (Ezek 44:15).

The other Levites, those not of the sons of Zadok, committed the following abominable acts (Ezek 44:6): First, they brought foreigners, who were uncircumcised in heart and flesh, into the temple (Ezek 44:7). Second, they did not keep watch over the holy things themselves but set foreigners to keep charge in their place (Ezek 44:8). Third, not only did they make the people worship idols, but they themselves also worshiped idols (Ezek 44:10, 12).

As a result, the Levites were allowed to minister before the people only in slaughtering the burnt offerings (Ezek 44:11, 14) and were not allowed to draw near the most holy things (Ezek 44:13). God said, "The sons of Zadok, who kept charge of My sanctuary when the sons of Israel went astray from Me, shall come near to Me to minister to Me; and they shall stand before Me to offer Me the fat and the blood" (Ezek 44:15). Thus only the sons of Zadok were able to enter the sanctuary and draw near the table of the Lord (Ezek 44:16).

Along with the reconstruction of Zerubbabel's temple after the first return from the Babylonian exile, the divisions of the priests and the Levites were reinstated in order to restore the temple sacrifice system as in the days of David. Ezra 6:18 states, "They appointed the priests to their divisions and the Levites in their orders for the service of God in Jerusalem, as it is written in the book of Moses."

Amazingly, this twenty-four division system was preserved even until the New Testament times (Luke 1:5, 8). Zacharias, John the Baptist's father, was part of the division of Abijah, which was the eighth division out of the twenty-four (1 Chr 24:10). The division of Abijah had been restored and named after its predecessor, Abijah. Luke 1:8 states that Zacharias "was performing his priestly service before God in the appointed order of his division." Here the expression "appointed order of his division" is ἐν τῇ τάξει τῆς ἐφημερίας αὐτοῦ (*en tē taxei tēs ephēmerias autou*) in Greek and means that the priests carried out their priestly duties for a fixed time according to the appointed order (1 Chr 24:19). In addition, Luke 1:9 states, "According to the custom of the priestly office, he was chosen by lot to enter the temple of the Lord and burn incense." Here the word "custom" refers to "a long-established practice or example" (see Ruth 4:7). Simply put, it means "a habitual practice" or "as was usually practiced for a long time" (see Mark 10:1; Luke 2:42). This means that the twenty-four-division system in which the priests served in the temple for one week twice a year was still in effect during the New Testament period, and Zacharias from the division of Abijah was performing his priestly duties in this manner (Luke 1:8).

In his autobiography the Jewish historian Josephus introduces himself as a priest from the division of Jehoiarib, which was the first of the twenty-four divisions of priests (*Life of Flavius Josephus*). He also mentions that the names and orders of the divisions from David's time were well preserved even until the New Testament era (*Antiquities of the Jews* 7.366; hereafter *Ant.*).

For the Israelite community in the postexilic period, the most urgent need was probably the establishment of the temple service system centered on the rebuilt temple of Zerubbabel. Examination of the names of priests in the sealed document in Nehemiah 10:1–8 and the lists of priests in Nehemiah 12:1–7 and 12:12–21 reveal clear traces of the reorganization of the twenty-four divisions after the return from Babylon. Nehemiah 12 lists the names of the priests and Levites after the first return from exile. It accurately documents the list of the priestly households (Neh 12:1–7), the list of the Levites (Neh 12:8–9), the list of the high priests (Neh 12:10–11), and the list of the priests who were heads of fathers' households in the days of Joiakim the high priest (Neh 12:12–21). Joiakim's generation had succeeded that of the high priest Jeshua (also spelled "Joshua") who had returned from the Babylonian exile (Neh 12:10, 26). The priests and Levites from this period were also recorded (Neh 12:12–21, 22–26).

A total of 4,289 priests from four divisions—Jedaiah (973), Immer (1,052), Pashhur (1,247) and Harim (1,017)—out of the original twenty-four divisions came back during the first return from exile (Ezra 2:36–39; Neh 7:39–42). According to 1 Chronicles 9:12 and Nehemiah 11:12, Pashhur was the son of Malchijah (fifth priestly division; 1 Chr 24:9).

The priests who returned along with Joshua (Jeshua) in the first return from the exile were reorganized under the twenty-two heads of the priests (Neh 12:1–7). These twenty-two priests were referred to as "heads of the priests and their kinsmen" (Neh 12:7). The word "head" is רֹאשׁ (*rosh*) in Hebrew and means "elder," "chief," or "leader," thus referring to the leaders of the priests. It is presumed that only twenty-two heads of the priests were recorded here, because the twenty-four divisions had not yet been completely restored.

Here we must take note of the record in Nehemiah 12:6. Many Bible versions have translated this verse as "Shemaiah, Joiarib, Jedaiah," but the King James Version and the New American Standard Bible followed the original Hebrew script and translated it as "Shemaiah and Joiarib, Jedaiah." They placed the conjunction "and" between Shemaiah and Joiarib in order to differentiate the first sixteen priests from the latter six priests. These latter six priests were not included in the list of the signers of the sealed document in Nehemiah 10:3–9.

According to Nehemiah 12:1–21, twenty-two heads of priests were recorded for the days of the high priest Jeshua (Neh 12:1–7). For Jeshua's son Joiakim's generation, the names of twenty priests who belonged to the twenty heads of the fathers' households were recorded (Neh 12:12–21). For the generation of Joiakim's son Eliashib, the names of twenty-one priests who signed the sealed covenant document after the reconstruction of the city wall were recorded (Neh 10:1–8).

The following changes took place in the organization of the priestly divisions for each period after the return from exile.

	Nehemiah 12:1–7		Nehemiah 12:12–21		Nehemiah 10:2–8
	The first generation of high priests in the postexilic period		The second generation of high priests in the postexilic period		The third generation of high priests in the postexilic period
	Joshua (515–490 BC)		**Joiakim** (490–470 BC)		**Eliashib** (470–333 BC)
	The heads of the priests and their kinsmen (twenty-two persons)		Households and the heads of the households (twenty persons)		The priests who sealed the covenant (twenty-one persons)
1	Seraiah (v. 1)	1	of Seraiah, Meraiah (v. 12)	1	Seraiah (v. 2)
2	Jeremiah (v. 1)	2	of Jeremiah, Hananiah (v. 12)	2	Azariah (v. 2)
3	Ezra (v. 1)	3	of Ezra, Meshullam (v. 13)	3	Jeremiah (v. 2)
4	Amariah (v. 2)	4	of Amariah, Jehohanan (v. 13)	4	Pashhur (v. 3)
5	Malluch (v. 2)	5	of Malluchi, Jonathan (v. 14)	5	Amariah (v. 3)
6	Hattush (v. 2)		4 households omitted	6	Malchijah (v. 3)
7	Shecaniah (v. 3)			7	Hattush (v. 4)
8	Rehum (v. 3)			8	Shebaniah (v. 4)
9	Meremoth (v. 3)			9	Malluch (v. 4)
10	Iddo (v. 4)	6	of Iddo, Zechariah (v. 16)	10	Harim (v. 5)
11	Ginnethoi (v. 4)	7	of Ginnethon, Meshullam (v. 16)	11	Meremoth (v. 5)
12	Abijah (v. 4)	8	of Abijah, Zichri (v. 17)	12	Obadiah (v. 5)
13	Mijamin (v. 5)	9	of Miniamin, of Moadiah, Piltai (v. 17)	13	Daniel (v. 6)
14	Maadiah (v. 5)			14	Ginnethon (v. 6)
15	Bilgah (v. 5)	10	of Bilgah, Shammua (v. 18)	15	Baruch (v. 6)
16	Shemaiah (v. 6)	11	of Shemaiah, Jehonathan (v. 18)	16	Meshullam (v. 7)
17	Joiarib (v. 6)	12	of Joiarib, Mattenai (v. 19)	17	Abijah (v. 7)
18	Jedaiah (v. 6)	13	of Jedaiah, Uzzi (v. 19)	18	Mijamin (v. 7)
19	Sallu (v. 7)	14	of Sallai, Kallai (v. 20)	19	Maaziah (v. 8)
20	Amok (v. 7)	15	of Amok, Eber (v. 20)	20	Bilgai (v. 8)
21	Hilkiah (v. 7)	16	of Hilkiah, Hashabiah (v. 21)	21	Shemaiah (v. 8)
22	Jedaiah (v. 7)	17	of Jedaiah, Nethanel (v. 21)		
			New households added (Neh 12:14–15)		
		18	of Shebaniah, Joseph (v. 14)		
		19	of Harim, Adna (v. 15)		
		20	of Meraioth, Helkai (v. 15)		

* The shaded numbers refer to the priests who sealed the covenant.

As evident from the chart, the four households that were included in the days of Joshua (Jeshua)—Hattush, Shecaniah, Rehum, and Meremoth (Neh 12:2–3)—were omitted in the process of organizing the twenty-four divisions during the days of Joiakim. At the same time, three households—Shebaniah, Harim, and Meraioth (Neh 12:14–15)—were added. In addition, for the two separate households named Mijamin and Maadiah from Joshua's time (Neh 12:5), the list for Joiakim's generation provides only one household head, Piltai, as being "of Miniamin, of Moadiah" (Neh 12:17). This demonstrates that the two households Mijamin and Maadiah were later listed as "Miniamin" and "Moadiah" and combined into a single household under the headship of Piltai. Thus there were two fewer priestly divisions during the days of the high priest Joiakim than during the days of Joshua (Jeshua).

Nehemiah 10:1–8 shows that the priestly divisions that had been reorganized with twenty-two heads of priests after the first return were later amended and supplemented during Ezra and Nehemiah's nationwide movement for repentance and reforms of faith. After the third return from Babylon, the wall of Jerusalem was rebuilt (Neh 6:15), and before its dedication Ezra read from the book of the law. Upon hearing Ezra's recitation, all the people cried in repentance (Neh 8:5–9) and kept the Feast of Booths in a holy manner (Neh 8:13–18). Through nationwide fasting and repentance and through the prayers of the Levites, the whole assembly of Israel was able to agree upon a firm covenant before God; and the leaders, the Levites, and the priests affixed their seals upon this covenant document (Neh 9:38).

The names of the twenty-one priests on the sealed covenant document in Nehemiah 10:1–8 were not individual names but names of households. This is evident from the fact that most of the twenty-one names (sixteen out of twenty-one; "Azariah" has the same meaning as "Ezra") matched the names on the list of the heads of the priests and their kinsmen who came in the first return from exile (Neh 12:1–7). Moreover, two names—Malchijah and Pashhur (Pashhur is a descendant of Malchijah; 1 Chr 9:12; Neh 11:12)—from the covenant document were identical with two of the names listed in the twenty-four priestly divisions from the days of David (see 1 Chr 24:9). Only three names—Obadiah, Daniel, and Baruch—were new additions.

As seen above, the twenty-four priestly divisions underwent continuous reorganization after the return from Babylon. It is particularly noteworthy that Ezra consecrated the priestly genealogy by making public the list of priests who married foreign women after the second return from exile (Ezra 10:18–22). This incident serves as an example of the ongoing restructuring of the twenty-four priestly divisions. After the return from Babylonian exile, the priestly divisions were restructured and supplemented on many different occasions over several years. As Josephus commented (*Ant.* 7.366), it seems that the divisions were fully restored, even taking on the original names of the twenty-four divisions from the days of King David.

Although the temple of Zerubbabel and the city wall were rebuilt and the Promised Land was now inhabitable for the people of Israel, threats from Gentile nations continued. While the nation was in this situation, the nationwide movement for repentance and sanctification led by the two leaders Ezra and Nehemiah became the lamp that would illuminate the darkened path of history.

The Israelites realized and confessed that the afflictions coming from the oppression of the Gentile kings were their due punishment for the sins of forgetting their covenant with God and not keeping the law. The leaders of the people placed their seal on the covenant document, and the people made a resolution "to keep and to observe all the commandments of God [their] Lord, and His ordinances and His statutes," and they stated, "We will not give our daughters to the peoples of the land or take their daughters for our sons" (Neh 10:28–30).

While they were fasting and repenting, determined to keep the covenant, all the people prayed first and foremost that their relationship with God might be restored (Neh 9:1–38). The leaders and the people were all united in their efforts to purify the lineage and bring about a spiritual awakening. By so doing, the covenant community of Israel was able to overcome the historical darkness of the intertestamental period and rise again to prepare the path of the coming Messiah.

As time passed, however, the priests became extremely corrupt. They abused the privileges of the priesthood, forsook the Word of God, and violated the covenant (Neh 13:23–29). This was exactly what Prophet Malachi had prophesied:

> *"The lips of a priest should preserve knowledge, and men should seek instruction from his mouth; for he is the messenger of the Lord of hosts. But as for you, you have turned aside from the way; you have caused many to stumble by the instruction; you have corrupted the covenant of Levi," says the Lord of hosts. (Malachi 2:7–8)*

At the time there was not one "messenger of the Lord of hosts" to teach the law to the people and adjudicate justly. In fact, the priests actually encouraged the people to go astray from the right path and indulge in deeds that were against the law. Even today if the priests (religious leaders) go astray from the law (Word), they cannot properly teach the saints. The moment a priest betrays his fundamental faith in the covenant, many saints will also lose their direction and drift away from the right path—into instant corruption.

The amazing fact is that despite the corruption of the high priests and the priests, God, in His administration of redemption, preserved the system of the twenty-four divisions. At about the time when Jesus was to be born, Zacharias, a priest from the division of Abijah, was righteous in the sight of God and blameless in the law (Luke 1:5–6). God allowed him to father a son named John the Baptist, who would be the one to prepare the way for the coming of Jesus Christ.

CHAPTER
9

Twenty-Four Divisions of the Musicians

1 Chronicles 25:1–31

❖ systematically organized for the first time in history ❖

1. The Duties and Origin of the Musicians

The duties of the musicians

The musicians were entrusted with the duty to "prophesy" through music. First Chronicles 25:1 states, "David and the commanders of the army set apart for the service some of the sons of Asaph and of Heman and of Jeduthun who were to prophesy with lyres, harps and cymbals." Singing praises is the act of proclaiming God's prophetic Word through song (see 1 Chr 25:2–3); therefore, the musicians were also called "seers" (2 Chr 29:30—Asaph; 1 Chr 25:5—Heman; 2 Chr 35:15—Jeduthun). God is enthroned upon the praises of His people (Ps 22:3). He delights in those who have His Word richly dwelling within them, singing psalms and hymns and spiritual songs, and praising Him with gratitude in their hearts (Ps 56:4; Eph 5:19; Col 3:16).

More specifically, what kind of duty is the ministry of praise? First Chronicles 16:4 states, "He appointed some of the Levites as ministers before the ark of the Lord, even to celebrate and to thank and praise the Lord God of Israel." Here the work before the ark of the Lord is specifically described with three verbs: "to celebrate," "to thank," and "to praise." These three actions appear similar, but each word broadens the depth and width of our understanding of the meaning of praise.

First, the verb "to celebrate" comes from the active hiphil stem of the Hebrew word זָכַר (*zakhar*) and means to "remember" or "meditate on" something after seeing a certain sign (Gen 9:15). It also means "to celebrate" publicly (Esther 9:28), "to mention," as to outwardly express the thoughts of the heart (Jer 20:9, KJV), or "to boast" (Ps 20:7). When we put all this together, the expression means to remember God's work, proclaim His achievements, celebrate them, and boast of them by promulgating them far and wide.

Second, the verb "to thank" is יָדָה (*yadah*) in Hebrew and is derived from the word יָד (*yad*), meaning "hand." It thus means "to show thanks with the hands extended." If the word is used in the hiphil (causative) stem with an active voice, then it means "to confess one's sins" (Prov 28:13), "to praise" someone (Ps 49:18), to thank and praise God (Ps 107:8; 109:30). This type of praise of thanksgiving usually refers to singing accompanied by instruments (2 Chr 5:13; Ps 43:4; 71:22).

Third, the verb "to praise" is הָלַל (*halal*) in the piel (intensive) stem and means "to be boastful," "to rejoice in someone," and "to applaud." This refers to the act of lifting up one's voice and praising God's preeminent power and His greatness.

A company of musicians was assembled for the first time when the ark of the covenant was brought up by King David

David was the first person in Israel's history to inaugurate the singing and the playing of various instruments during worship.

Musicians were first assembled to proclaim God's glory when David moved the ark of the covenant from the house of Obed-edom to the city of David (2 Sam 6:10–15; 1 Chr 13:13–14; 15:1–28). After David prepared a place for the ark and pitched a tent for it, he chose the sons of Aaron and the Levites to be entrusted with the honorable task of carrying up the ark (1 Chr 15:1–15). In the past David had experienced the shocking death of Uzza at Perez-uzza when he had first attempted to bring up the ark (1 Chr 13:1–11). Through this event David had thoroughly realized that God's ark had to be carried by the Levites on their shoulders. Hence this time he made the Levites carry the ark according to the law (1 Chr 15:2, 13–15; Num 4:5–15; Deut 10:8; 31:25).

David gathered up Aaron's descendants and Levites, and he selected a total of 862 of their relatives, including 120 relatives of Uriel, 220 relatives of Asaiah, 130 relatives of Joel, 200 relatives of Shemaiah, 80 relatives of Eliel, and 112 relatives of Amminadab (1 Chr 15:4–10). Then he called Zadok and Abiathar the priests and the six heads of the fathers' households (Uriel, Asaiah, Joel, Shemaiah, Eliel, and Amminadab) and instructed them to consecrate themselves and their relatives that they could carry the ark of God on their shoulders with the poles thereon (1 Chr 15:11–15).

Then David commanded the six heads of the fathers' households whom he had chosen to appoint singers and musicians to raise sounds of joy with instruments of music (1 Chr 15:16).

First, the Levites appointed as the chiefs of the musicians Heman the son of Joel, and from his relatives, Asaph the son of Berechiah, and the Merarite Ethan the son of Kushaiah. Then they appointed a total of fourteen more, including their relatives of the second rank—Zechariah, Ben, Jaaziel, Shemiramoth, Jehiel, Unni, Eliab, Benaiah, Maaseiah, Mattithiah, Eliphelehu, and Mikneiah—and the gatekeepers Obed-edom and Jeiel (1 Chr 15:17–18).

Second, the three chiefs and the fourteen were further divided into three groups by instruments (cymbals, harps, and lyre; 1 Chr

15:19–21).[20] The first group was chosen to sound aloud the cymbals of bronze (Heman, Asaph, and Ethan). The second group was to lead with harps tuned to "*alamoth*"[21] (1 Chr 15:20; Zechariah, Aziel, Shemiramoth, Jehiel, Unni, Eliab, Maaseiah, and Benaiah). The third group was to lead with lyres tuned to the "sheminith"[22] (Mattithiah, Eliphelehu, Mikneiah, Obed-edom, Jeiel, and Azaziah). In particular Obed-edom, who appears in 1 Chronicles 15:18, 21, was a blessed man in whose house the ark of the covenant rested for three months following the Perez-uzza incident that had halted the transport of the ark (1 Chr 13:13–14). David entrusted him with the two important duties of gatekeeper (1 Chr 15:18; 26:1, 4–5) and instrument player.

Third, Chenaniah, a skillful singer, was put in charge (made conductor) of the singers to give instruction in singing (1 Chr 15:22).

Fourth, four men—Berechiah, Elkanah, Obed-edom, and Jehiah—were gatekeepers for the ark. Their duty was to keep guard so that no one could touch or draw near to the ark (1 Chr 15:23, 24).

Fifth, seven priests (Shebaniah, Joshaphat, Nethanel, Amasai, Zechariah, Benaiah, and Eliezer), were appointed to blow the trumpets before the ark of God (1 Chr 15:24).

At this time the Levites who were carrying the ark, the singers, and Chenaniah the leader of the singers were all set apart by being dressed in robes of fine linen (1 Chr 15:27). All Israel brought up the ark with shouting and the sound of the horn שׁוֹפָר (*shofar*, "ram's horn"), trumpets, loud-sounding cymbals, harps, and lyres (2 Sam 6:15; 1 Chr 15:27–28).

---

20 Ben (בֵּן), who appears in 1 Chronicles 15:18, is uniquely omitted in verses 19–21, reintroducing the names of people appointed for each part, and Azaziah is included instead (1 Chr 15:21).

21 Alamoth (עֲלָמוֹת) refers either to the voices of young women or to the soprano or falsetto of boys (see Ps 46:1).

22 The "eighth key" (שְׁמִינִית, *sheminith*) in music denotes the lowest and gravest note sung by men's voices (*basso*). This means that the lyre was played in a very low key (see Ps 6, 12).

David wore the linen ephod (2 Sam 6:14; 1 Chr 15:27) and was so moved that he danced and leaped with joy (2 Sam 6:14; 1 Chr 15:29). David's wife Michal, who was watching him from the window, despised him in her heart and said, "He uncovered himself today in the eyes of his servants' maids as one of the foolish ones shamelessly uncovers himself" (2 Sam 6:20; see also 1 Chr 15:29). Michal mocked David and despised his actions, using the expression "in the eyes of his servants' maids" or, as the NIV translates, "in full view of the slave girls of his servants." David responded by saying that he had performed his deeds "before the Lord," and added, "I will become even more undignified than this, and I will be humiliated in my own eyes. But by these slave girls you spoke of, I will be held in honor" (2 Sam 6:21–22, NIV). From this time on, Michal was childless until the day she died (2 Sam 6:23).

Organization of the First Levite Musicians That David Assembled (1 Chr 15:16–28; 16:4–6)		
Chiefs		
Cymbals	Heman / הֵימָן	"faithful, sincere" 1 Chr 15:17, 19
	Asaph / אָסָף	"gatherer, one who gathers and piles up" 1 Chr 15:17, 19; 16:5
	Ethan / אֵיתָן	"permanence" 1 Chr 15:17, 19
Deputy Chiefs		
Harps	Zechariah / זְכַרְיָה	"the LORD remembers" 1 Chr 15:18, 20; 16:5
	Ben / בֵּן	"son" 1 Chr 15:18
	Jaaziel (Aziel) יַעֲזִיאֵל (עֲזִיאֵל)	"made bold by God" 1 Chr 15:18, 20
	Shemiramoth שְׁמִירָמוֹת	"name of heights" 1 Chr 15:18, 20; 16:5
	Jehiel / יְחִיאֵל	"may God live" 1 Chr 15:18, 20; 16:5
	Unni / עֻנִּי	"afflicted, oppressed" 1 Chr 15:18; 15:20
	Eliab / אֱלִיאָב	"God is father" 1 Chr 15:18, 20; 16:5
	Benaiah / בְּנָיָה	"the LORD had built up" 1 Chr 15:18, 20; 16:5
	Maaseiah / מַעֲשֵׂיָה	"work of the LORD" 1 Chr 15:18, 20
Lyres	Mattithiah / מַתִּתְיָה	"gift from the LORD" 1 Chr 15:18, 21; 16:5
	Eliphelehu אֱלִיפְלֵהוּ	"may God distinguish him, my God sets him apart" 1 Chr 15:18, 21
	Mikneiah / מִקְנֵיָהוּ	"possession of the LORD" 1 Chr 15:18, 21
	Obed-edom עֹבֵד אֱדוֹם	"servant of Edom, worshiper of Edom" 1 Chr 15:18, 21; 16:5

	Jeiel (Jehiel) / יְעִיאֵל (יְחוּאֵל)	"carried away by God, God preserves" 1 Chr 15:18, 21; 16:5
	*another person by the same name was recorded after the ark was placed	
	Azaziah / עֲזַזְיָה	"the LORD is mighty" 1 Chr 15:21
	*added as one of the leaders for the instrument	
Conductor	Chenaniah / כְּנַנְיָה	"the LORD establishes, the LORD gives strength" 1 Chr 15:22
	Priests	
Those who blow trumpets before the ark	Shebaniah / שְׁבַנְיָה	"increased by the Lord, the Lord makes flourish" 1 Chr 15:24
	Joshaphat / יוֹשָׁפָט	"the Lord has judged" 1 Chr 15:24
	Nethanel / נְתַנְאֵל	"given of God" 1 Chr 15:24
	Amasai / עֲמָשַׂי	"burdensome" 1 Chr 15:24
	Zechariah / זְכַרְיָה	"the Lord remembers" 1 Chr 15:24
	Benaiah / בְּנָיָה	"the Lord built up" 1 Chr 15:24; 16:6
	Eliezer / אֱלִיעֶזֶר	"God is help" 1 Chr 15:24
	Jahaziel / יַחֲזִיאֵל	"God sees, God gives visions" 1 Chr 16:6
	*added after the ark of the covenant was placed	
	Gatekeepers	
Gate-keepers before the ark	Berechiah / בֶּרֶכְיָה	"the Lord blesses" 1 Chr 15:23
	Elkanah / אֶלְקָנָה	"God has taken possession" 1 Chr 15:23
	Obed-edom עֹבֵד אֱדוֹם	"servant of Edom, worshiper of Edom" 1 Chr 15:24
	Jehiah / יְחִיָּה	"may the Lord live" 1 Chr 15:24

Reorganization of the musicians after the ark of the covenant was placed inside the tent

Once the ark of the covenant was safely placed in the city of David, David offered burnt offerings and peace offerings before God. He distributed to everyone in Israel a loaf of bread, a portion of meat, and a raisin cake and commemorated this day as a national celebration (1 Chr 16:1–3). Then he reorganized the Levite musicians as people specially set apart to minister before the ark of the Lord (1 Chr 16:4–6).

David next appointed ten musicians (Asaph, Zechariah, Jeiel, Shemiramoth, Jehiel, Mattithiah, Eliab, Benaiah, Obed-edom, and Jeiel). They played harps and lyres while Asaph the chief (the conductor) played loud-sounding cymbals (1 Chr 16:5). The priests, Benaiah and Jahaziel, were always before the ark and blew the trumpets at each of the appointed times (1 Chr 16:6; see Num 10:1–8).

David also appointed Asaph and his relatives to recite the psalm of thanksgiving, which David had written himself (1 Chr 16:7–36). The song had been written in remembrance and praise of God's power and His covenant (1 Chr 16:8–22; Ps 105:1–15). It urged all nations—even those of the Gentiles—to worship God (1 Chr 16:23–33; Ps 96:1–13) and praise the lovingkindness of God who had saved Israel (1 Chr 16:34–36; Ps 106:1, 47–48).

After David had safely placed the ark of the covenant, he left Asaph and his relatives before the ark of the covenant of the Lord to minister before it continually. David organized all duties relating to the sacred service (1 Chr 16:37–42). First Chronicles 6:31–32 records that Heman, Asaph, and Ethan (1 Chr 6:33, 39, 44) were appointed to minister with song before the tabernacle of the tent of meeting until Solomon had built the temple, and they served in their office according to their order (1 Chr 6:32). After this, just before his death, David again systematized the musicians into the twenty-four divisions to promote their efficiency (1 Chr 25).

2. Organization of the Twenty-Four Divisions of the Musicians

David divided the Levites who would assist the priests in the temple into twenty-four divisions according to the households of Gershon, Kohath, and Merari (1 Chr 23:6–23). Then he also divided the four thousand musicians (1 Chr 23:5) into twenty-four divisions (1 Chr 25:1–31).

David appointed musicians who would minister in the temple according to God's command. Second Chronicles 29:25 states, "He then stationed the Levites in the house of the Lord with cymbals, with harps and with lyres, according to the command of David and of Gad the king's seer, and of Nathan the prophet; for the command was from the Lord through His prophets."

David differentiated the musicians according to their positions. The total number of musicians was four thousand (1 Chr 23:5), and he set the order by which the sons of Asaph, Heman, and Jeduthun would serve in the temple as musicians (1 Chr 25:1). The musicians were under a meticulous organizational structure with a clear hierarchical order. They were placed under the following hierarchical order: King David; then Heman, Asaph, and Jeduthun; then the chiefs of the twenty-four divisions; then two hundred eight-eight people; and finally, four thousand musicians (1 Chr 25:1–7).

Heman, Asaph, and Ethan (Jeduthun)[23]—three chiefs (conductors)

According to his genealogy, Heman was the twentieth-generation descendant of Izhar, the son of Kohath; he was Samuel's grandson and Joel's son (1 Chr 6:33–38; see 1 Sam 8:1–2). Samuel's son, Joel, had

23 It is presumed that "Ethan" and "Jeduthun" refer to the same person (1 Chr 6:44, 15:17, 19; 25:1). It is likely that "Ethan," as it is recorded in the genealogy, was his given name, and "Jeduthun," which means "to praise," was a nickname given after he was entrusted with the duty of a musician.

not followed after the deeds of his father, but his grandson Heman followed Samuel's footsteps and became a godly person. Although Heman was the descendant of a powerful chief, he did not regard singing in the house of God a lowly duty but an honorable one. Heman wrote Psalm 88.

Asaph was a descendant of Gershon, but the Bible refers to him as "Heman's brother" (1 Chr 6:39). This is probably because they had the same duties, although they were from different households. Asaph performed his duties at Heman's right hand (1 Chr 6:39), and the twelve psalms he wrote are included in the book of Psalms (Ps 50; Ps 73–83). Asaph is recorded in the genealogy as the fifteenth-generation descendant of Levi's son Gershon (1 Chr 6:20, 39–43).

Ethan was a descendant of Merari (1 Chr 6:44). He is recorded in the genealogy as the thirteenth-generation descendant of Levi's son Merari (1 Chr 6:44–48). He performed his duties at Heman's left hand (1 Chr 6:44). Psalm 89 was written by Ethan.

The twenty-four representatives of each division

The twenty-four representatives of the divisions were Asaph's four sons (Zaccur, Joseph, Nethaniah, and Asharelah), Jeduthun's six sons (Gedaliah, Zeri, Jeshaiah, Hashabiah, Mattithiah, and Shimei [conjectured; 1 Chr 25:17]) and Heman's fourteen sons (Bukkiah, Mattaniah, Uzziel, Shebuel, Jerimoth, Hananiah, Hanani, Eliathah, Giddalti, Romamti-ezer, Joshbekashah, Mallothi, Hothir, and Mahazioth) (1 Chr 25:2–4).

Asaph's sons prophesied (1 Chr 25:2), Jeduthun's sons prophesied with the harp (1 Chr 25:3), and Heman's sons lifted up the horn to exalt God (1 Chr 25:5, KJV).

The 288 people who were trained and skillful in singing—skilled musicians

Twelve were chosen from each of the divisions of musicians, including the chiefs; they were instructors of music, 288 persons in all (1

Chr 25:7). These 288 persons were "trained in singing to the Lord . . . all who were skillful."

Here the word "trained" is לָמַד (*lamad*) in Hebrew and means "to prick or strike with a rod" and thus connotes "to train" or "to educate." This demonstrates that those who were appointed as singers underwent hard training. Also, the word "skillful" (בִּין, *bin*, "to discern, to have insight, be acquainted with") denotes a person who is "proficient" or even "a teacher." This means that there were 288 skillful teachers who had attained a high level of artistic proficiency such that they could instruct in singing.

The four thousand musicians—grand orchestra and choir

The four thousand musicians comprised the twenty-four divisions; and after intense training and professional instruction, 288 persons skillful in singing were established as chiefs (conductors) over the twenty-four divisions. Thus the musicians were also divided into twenty-four divisions so they could serve according to their rotation order. They cast lots for their order of service, "all alike, the small as well as the great, the teacher as well as the pupil" (1 Chr 25:8).

The following is the first to the twenty-fourth order of the division.

1	**Joseph** / יוֹסֵף Asaph's second son	"He increases" 1 Chr 25:2, 9
2	**Gedaliah** / גְּדַלְיָה Jeduthun's first son	"the LORD is great" 1 Chr 25:3, 9
3	**Zaccur** / זַכּוּר Asaph's first son	"pure, remembered" 1 Chr 25:2, 10
4	**Izri (Zeri)** / יִצְרִי (צְרִי) Jeduthun's second son	"the LORD has built" 1 Chr 25:3, 11
5	**Nethaniah** / נְתַנְיָה Asaph's third son	"given of the LORD" 1 Chr 25:2, 12
6	**Bukkiah** / בֻּקִּיָּה Heman's first son	"proved of the LORD, the LORD has emptied" 1 Chr 25:4, 13

7	**Jesharelah (Asharelah)** יְשַׂרְאֵלָה (אֲשַׂרְאֵלָה) Asaph's youngest son	"God holds, right with God" 1 Chr 25:2, 14
8	**Jeshaiah** / יְשַׁעְיָה Jeduthun's third son	"salvation of the LORD" 1 Chr 25:3, 15
9	**Mattaniah** / מַתַּנְיָה Heman's second son	"gift of the LORD" 1 Chr 25:4, 16
10	**Shimei** / שִׁמְעִי Jeduthun's youngest son	"my being heard" 1 Chr 25:17
11	**Azarel (Uzziel)** / עֲזַרְאֵל Heman's third son	"God has helped" 1 Chr 25:4, 18
12	**Hashabiah** / חֲשַׁבְיָה Jeduthun's fourth son	"the LORD had taken account, the LORD has considered" 1 Chr 25:3, 19
13	**Shubael (Shebuel)** שׁוּבָאֵל (שְׁבוּאֵל) Heman's fourth son	"turn back, O God!, captive of God" 1 Chr 25:4, 20
14	**Mattithiah** / מַתִּתְיָה Jeduthun's fifth son	"gift of the LORD" 1 Chr 25:3, 21
15	**Jerimoth (Jeremoth)** יְרִימוֹת (יְרֵימוֹת) Heman's fifth son	"He is Most High" 1 Chr 25:4, 22
16	**Hananiah** / חֲנַנְיָה Heman's sixth son	"the LORD has been gracious" 1 Chr 25:4, 23
17	**Joshbekashah** / יָשְׁבְּקָשָׁה Heman's eleventh son	"a hard seat, to live in misfortune" 1 Chr 25:4, 24
18	**Hanani** / חֲנָנִי Heman's seventh son	"gracious, merciful" 1 Chr 25:4, 25
19	**Mallothi** / מַלּוֹתִי Heman's twelfth son	"I have uttered, I spoke" 1 Chr 25:4, 26
20	**Eliathah** / אֱלִיאָתָה Heman's eight son	"God has come, You are my God" 1 Chr 25:4, 27
21	**Hothir** / הוֹתִיר Heman's thirteen son	"abundance" 1 Chr 25:4, 28

22	**Giddalti** / גִּדַּלְתִּי Heman's nineth son	"I magnify God, I make great" 1 Chr 25:4, 29
23	**Mahazioth** / מַחֲזִיאוֹת Heman's fourteenth son	"visions, observation" 1 Chr 25:4, 30
24	**Romamti-ezer** / רוֹמַמְתִּי עֶזֶר Heman's tenth son	"I have exalted the Helper, I have made lofty help" 1 Chr 25:4, 31

* Twelve persons, including the above individuals from each division, constituted a total of 288 (1 Chr 25:7).

3. The History of the Musicians' Duties

Solomon's days

The ark of the covenant was the testimonial object of the covenant made between God and the people of Israel on Mount Sinai. This ark, passed down for about five hundred years since Moses' time, was placed in the temple that was built during Solomon's time (1 Kgs 8:1–6, 21; 2 Chr 5:2–7; 6:11). It became the symbol that legitimized Solomon's temple as the one that succeeded the Davidic covenant.

When the ark was moved from the tabernacle to the temple, the Levitical singers—Asaph, Heman, Jeduthun, and their sons and kinsmen—wore linen garments and stood east of the altar with cymbals, harps, and lyres. Also standing with them were 120 priests blowing trumpets. Then the trumpeters and singers made themselves heard with one voice to praise and give thanks (2 Chr 5:12–13). Asaph, Heman, and Jeduthun were the three great musicians appointed by David just before his death (1 Chr 25:1).

David assigned to them the instruments they were to play (1 Chr 15:16–24; see also Ps 33:2; 57:8; 71:22; 108:2; 144:9; 150:3–5). The "cymbals" (מְצֶלֶת, *metseleth*) were made of bronze and were the only percussion instruments played by the temple musicians (1 Chr 15:16; 25:1; 2 Chr 5:12–13). The "harp" (נֵבֶל, *nevel*) was a stringed instrument with a wooden frame and twelve strings; it was played by plucking the strings with the finger (1 Kgs 10:12; 1 Chr 15:16; 25:1; 2 Chr 5:12; 9:11). The "lyre" (כִּנּוֹר, *kinnor*) varied in shape and number of strings; it produced the most elegant sound out of all the stringed instruments (1 Kgs 10:12; 1 Chr 15:16; 25:1; 2 Chr 5:12; 9:11; Dan 3:5, 7, 10, 15) and was played by plucking the strings with the finger or a plectrum (1 Sam 16:16, 23; 18:10). Lastly, the "trumpet" (חֲצֹצְרָה, *hatsotserah*) refers to any tube-like instrument that is played by blowing air through it (1 Chr 15:23–24; 2 Chr 5:12–13).

The musicians blew the trumpets, sounded the cymbals, and played all the instruments, praising the Lord in a loud voice, saying, "He indeed is good for His lovingkindness is everlasting" (2 Chr 5:13). At that time the temple was filled with the cloud so that the priests could not stand to minister (2 Chr 5:14). The cloud that filled the temple had also appeared during Moses' time when the tabernacle was dedicated; it represented the holy presence of God's glory (Exod 40:34–35; see Exod 16:10; Num 16:42).

Jehoshaphat's days

During the reign of Jehoshaphat, the fourth king of the southern kingdom of Judah, at one time the musicians marched ahead of the army, singing praises to the Lord, and achieved great victory against the enemy (2 Chr 20:1–30).

In 2 Chronicles 20, the sons of Ammon and Moab and Mount Seir joined together in an attack against Judah (2 Chr 20:1, 10, 22). King Jehoshaphat and the people of Judah were powerless against the onslaught of the enemy; they did not know what to do. All they could do was to look to the Lord and pray (2 Chr 20:12). Verse 13 states, "All Judah was standing before the Lord, with their infants, their wives and their children." Even the little children sought the help of the Lord as Judah prayed with fasting (2 Chr 20:3–4). Then God answered through Jahaziel (descendant of Asaph), saying, "Do not fear or be dismayed because of this great multitude, for the battle is not yours but God's" (2 Chr 20:15).

At this, King Jehoshaphat bowed his head with his face to the ground; then all Judah and the inhabitants of Jerusalem fell down before the Lord, worshiping the Lord. Some Levites from the Kohathites and the Korahites stood up to praise the Lord God of Israel with a very loud voice (2 Chr 20:18–19).

Jehoshaphat consulted with the people and assembled musicians who sang to the Lord and praised Him in holy attire, as they went out before the army. As soon as they sang in a loud voice, "Give thanks to the Lord, for His lovingkindness is everlasting," God set ambushes against the sons of Ammon, Moab, and Mount Seir (2 Chr 20:21–22). The sons of Ammon and Moab rose up against the inhabitants of Mount Seir and destroyed them completely; then the sons of Ammon and Moab slaughtered one another (2 Chr 20:23). As a result, they all fell dead as corpses on the ground and there was no one who escaped. Furthermore, there was so much spoil that it took three days to gather them all (2 Chr 20:24–25).

On the fourth day, they assembled in the valley of Beracah and called the place "The Valley of Beracah [blessing]" (2 Chr 20:26). The people of Judah returned with Jehoshaphat at their head, and as soon as they reached Jerusalem, they went to the house of the Lord, singing praises. Rather than being carried away by the joy of victory, they first gave thanks to God and sang praises to Him. Second Chronicles 20:28 states, "They came to Jerusalem with harps, lyres and trumpets to the house of the Lord."

As a result, the dread of God fell on all the kingdoms of the lands, and the kingdom of Jehoshaphat was at peace. This was because God gave King Jehoshaphat rest on all sides during his reign (2 Chr 20:29–30).

Hezekiah's days

As soon as Hezekiah began his sole reign, he assembled all the priests and the Levites and purified the temple from the first day until the sixteenth day of the first month (2 Chr 29:3–19). Afterward he revived the divisional system for the musicians that had been established during David's time (2 Chr 29:25–30).

Since Hezekiah had revived the divisions of the musicians, the Levites now stood with the musical instruments of David, and the priests stood with the trumpets (2 Chr 29:25–26). The expression "the musical instruments of David" (2 Chr 29:26–27) refers to the harp, lyre, and the cymbals that were played when the ark of the covenant was carried into the city of David (1 Chr 15:16, 28; 16:5; 23:5).

Then, as Hezekiah had ordered, the priests offered the burnt offering. When the burnt offering was offered, the singers and musicians sang praises to the Lord with the words of David and Asaph the seer, blew the trumpets, and played David's instruments; all this continued until the offering was completely burned. Thanksgiving and praises from the assembly resonated in the temple as if the heavens and the earth were shaken (2 Chr 29:27–28, 30).

For many years the people of Jerusalem and Judah could not give praise to God because they had been corrupt with idolatry and their hearts had been blotched with sin and darkness. After such a long period, however, the bright rays of the sun finally shone abundantly in their hearts. The whole assembly worshiped (2 Chr 29:28); the king and all who were with him bowed down and worshiped (2 Chr 29:29). The Levites, according to the order of the king and the officials, sang praises to the Lord with the words of David and Asaph the seer; they "sang praises with joy, and bowed down and worshiped" (2 Chr 29:30). Thus, because of Hezekiah's reforms, the whole assembly that had gathered in the temple rejoiced greatly and willingly worshiped God.

Postexilic days

Ezra and Nehemiah's list of those who had returned from the Babylonian exile includes the 128 "singers" from the sons of Asaph the descendant of Levi (Ezra 2:41; Neh 7:44 lists 148 persons; see Neh 12:8). Nehemiah 12:24 states that they were "to praise and give thanks, as prescribed by David the man of God, division corresponding to division."

After the return from the Babylonian exile, these singers sang praises together when the reconstruction of the temple began. Ezra 3:10 states, "When the builders had laid the foundation of the temple of the Lord, the priests stood in their apparel with trumpets, and the Levites, the sons of Asaph, with cymbals, to praise the Lord according to the directions of King David of Israel."

It seems likely that the organization of the musicians was also restored at this time when the other Levites were appointed in their orders for their service (Ezra 6:18). Nehemiah 12:44–47 shows that after the return from exile, the leaders of Judah were taking the necessary measures to distribute the portions required by the law for the Levites. It states, "In the days of David and Asaph, in ancient times, there were leaders of the singers, songs of praise and hymns of thanksgiving to God. So all Israel in the days of Zerubbabel and Nehemiah gave the portions due the singers and the gatekeepers as each day required" (see Neh 11:22–23). In particular, 1 Chronicles 9:33 states, "These are the singers, heads of fathers' households of the Levites, who lived in the chambers of the temple free from other service; for they were engaged in their work day and night." In light of this passage, we can see that they lived in the temple chambers and focused wholeheartedly on carrying out their duties, even working day and night. These are the very people mentioned in Psalm 84:4: "How blessed are those who dwell in Your house! They are ever praising You. Selah."

After Nehemiah rebuilt the wall of Jerusalem, he sought out the Levites from all their places and brought them to Jerusalem; this was to celebrate the dedication with hymns of thanksgiving and songs accompanied by cymbals, harps, and lyres (Neh 12:27). The singers assembled from Beth-gilgal and the fields in Geba and Azmaveth, which were close in proximity to Jerusalem. These people had built themselves villages around Jerusalem so they could immediately respond to calls for temple service as necessary (Neh 12:28–29). The priests and the Levites first purified themselves; then the people, the gate, and the wall were purified. In addition, the multitude of singers who sang praises of thanksgiving were divided into two choirs; one group was led by Ezra and the other by Nehemiah. These two choirs performed a unique celebration by proceeding in opposite directions as they walked on top of the wall while praising and giving thanks. The choir following Ezra was made up of Hoshaiah and half the leaders of Judah, with Azariah, Ezra, Meshullam, Judah, Benjamin, Shemaiah, and Jeremiah (Neh 12:32–34). Some of the sons of the priests also blew trumpets; they were Zechariah, Shemaiah, Azarel, Milalai, Gilalai, Maai, Nethanel, Judah, and Hanani (Neh 12:35–36). They proceeded above the Tower of Furnaces to the Broad Wall and above the Gate of Ephraim by the Old Gate, the Fish Gate, the Tower of Hananel, and the Tower of the Hundred, as far as the Sheep Gate; and they stopped at the Gate of the Guard (Neh 12:31–39).

The choir following Nehemiah included the priests, Eliakim, Maaseiah, Miniamin, Micaiah, Elioenai, Zechariah, and Hananiah, with trumpets; also Maaseiah, Shemaiah, Eleazar, Uzzi, Jehohanan, Malchijah, Elam, and Ezer (Neh 12:41–42). The singers sang loudly under the leadership of Jezrahiah (Neh 12:42). All the people rejoiced greatly so that their sound was heard from afar (Neh 12:43).

Singing praises is truly the most natural response to God's love and grace, and for the recipients of grace, it is indeed the way to repay God for His grace. Praising is also a confession of one's dedication and a prayer that one may be used according to God's will. It embodies the longing for the fulfillment of God's will as well as the exaltation of His glory, power, wisdom, and mercy. Praise is singing of genuine satisfaction and the best, highest, and greatest joy. It is rejoicing and giving thanks for God's reign, which is the greatest blessing bestowed upon all mankind and all creation on Earth. Therefore, we must continually give thanks and forever sing the praises of God's redemption through the sacrifice of Jesus Christ.

> *Through Him then, let us continually offer up a sacrifice of praise to God, that is, the fruit of lips that give thanks to His name. (Hebrews 13:15)*

CHAPTER
10

Twenty-Four Divisions of The Gatekeepers

1 Chronicles 26:1–19

❖ systematically organized for the first time in history ❖

The word "gatekeeper" in Hebrew is שֹׁעֵר (*shoer*) and refers to people who guard the entrance of the temple or the king's palace (1 Chr 9:23-24; 2 Sam 18:26). The temple is a holy place of God's presence and is set apart from the world, so it must be preserved holy. Hence guarding the various gates of the temple was a duty of the utmost importance, and it was entrusted to the Levites.

1. The Importance of the Gatekeepers' Duties

First Chronicles 26 introduces the genealogy of the gatekeepers with "For the divisions of the gatekeepers . . ." (1 Chr 26:1) and ends in verse 19 with "These were the divisions of the gatekeepers of the sons of Korah and of the sons of Merari." The duty of guarding the gates may appear to be a lowly position, but it was a special position entrusted exclusively to the household of the Levites, who had been chosen by God. Moreover, the names of the gatekeepers make up a substantial part of the genealogies. The following is a survey of the importance of the gatekeepers' duties as they were recorded in the genealogies.

The gatekeepers were chosen to guard the house of God and were recorded in the genealogy

First Chronicles 9:22 states, "All these who were chosen to be gatekeepers at the thresholds were 212. These were enrolled by genealogy in their villages, whom David and Samuel the seer appointed in their office of trust."

Those of the tribe of Levi served as gatekeepers for generations, from the end of the wilderness period led by Moses until the days of David. First Chronicles 9:19–20 states, "Their fathers had been over the camp of the Lord, keepers of the entrance. Phinehas the son of Eleazar was ruler over them previously, and the Lord was with him."

About two months prior to Israel's entry into Canaan, those of the second generation of Israelites were struck with a great plague because they had played the harlot with the daughters of Moab and worshiped idols at Shittim. When Phinehas from the tribe of Levi took a spear and struck the man and the woman who had committed adultery, the plague was checked (Num 25:1–8). Then God promised to establish Phinehas and his family as a priestly clan forever (Num 25:13). The fact that Phineas, who had received the covenant of the perpetual priesthood, oversaw the gatekeepers implies that the duty of the gatekeepers had also been entrusted to him within God's covenant.

The gatekeepers were blessed with the duty that was to be passed down the generations without ceasing

We must note that the genealogy of the temple gatekeepers (1 Chr 9:17–27) takes up the largest portion of the Levitical genealogies in 1 Chronicles 9. The gatekeepers who had settled in Jerusalem were Shallum, Akkub, Talmon, Ahiman, and their relatives; among them, Shallum the son of Kore, the son of Ebiasaph, the son of Korah was the chief (1 Chr 9:17–19).

The Bible contains many lists of gatekeepers. The sheer volume of record that the Bible contains about them testifies to the importance of their duty and to the fact that the descendants of the gatekeepers had flourished with the office. Among those whose descendants flourished was Obed-edom, of whom 1 Chronicles 26:5 states, "Ammiel the sixth, Issachar the seventh and Peullethai the eighth; God had indeed blessed him [Obed-edom]." The reason dates back to the incident when Uzzah died while God's ark of the covenant was being transported from the house of Abinadab to the city of David. As a result, David was unwilling to bring up the ark, and it was taken to the house of Obed-edom the Gittite. Despite this fearful situation, by faith Obed-edom (עֹבֵד אֱדוֹם, "servant") looked after God's ark of the covenant for three months, and the Lord blessed Obed-edom and all his household (2 Sam 6:1–12; 1 Chr 13:1–14). Soon news that the Lord had blessed Obed-edom reached King David's ears (2 Sam 6:12), and David went down to Obed-edom's house and joyfully brought up the ark to the city of David (2 Sam 6:12).

Later the descendants of Obed-edom made up thirteen divisions out of the twenty-four divisions of gatekeepers that David had organized (Jehozabad, Joah, Sacar, Nethanel, Ammiel, Issachar, Peullethai, Othni, Rephael, Obed, Elzabad, Elihu, and Semachiah; 1 Chr 26:4–7). All the descendants were "able men with strength for the service" (1 Chr 26:8). Because of the blessings that Obed-edom received, all his descendants also prospered throughout their generations (see Exod 20:6).

The genealogies of the gatekeepers are also found in 1 Chronicles 16:38; 23:5; and 26:1–19. Their genealogies are recorded as well in various places among the genealogies of those who had returned from the Babylonian exile. Their names and numbers are listed according to their families: 1 Chronicles 9:17–27 (212 persons after the return from exile), Ezra 2:42 (139 persons during the construction of the temple of Zerubbabel after the first return), and Nehemiah 11:19 (172 persons during the reconstruction of the wall of Jerusalem).

The mention of the genealogy of the gatekeepers in each subsequent generation demonstrates that the gatekeepers were greatly blessed by God and flourished continually.

As able men (ESV), the gatekeepers received official positions to serve in the Lord's temple

First Chronicles 26:7 states that the gatekeepers "were able men" (ESV, NASB, "valiant men"), and 1 Chronicles 26:8 states that "they and their sons and their relatives were able men with strength for the service." First Chronicles 26:9 also describes them as "valiant men" (ESV, "able men"). The gatekeepers possessed the strength, intelligence, and wisdom to carry out their duty of guarding the temple gates and strictly prohibiting the entry and exit of outsiders. First Chronicles 26:14 particularly describes Zechariah who was chosen to guard the northern gate as "a counselor with insight."

Gatekeepers, like the other Levites, were entrusted with the duty to serve in the house of the Lord. Following the genealogy of the chiefs of the gatekeepers (ninety-three men) in 1 Chronicles 26:1–11, the passage states, "To these divisions of the gatekeepers, the chief men, were given duties like their relatives to minister in the house of the Lord" (1 Chr 26:12).

2. The Organization of the Twenty-Four Divisions of the Gatekeepers (1 Chr 26:1-19)

Although no biblical records explicitly state that the gatekeepers were divided into twenty-four divisions, 1 Chronicles 26:1 and 2 Chronicles 8:14 suggest that they were. Second Chronicles 8:14 states, "According to the ordinance of his father David, he [Solomon] appointed the divisions of the priests for their service, and the Levites for their duties of praise and ministering before the priests according to the daily rule, and the gatekeepers by their divisions at every gate; for David the man of God had so commanded."

The gatekeepers were made up of the descendants of Korah and Merari (1 Chr 26:1, 10, 19; see also 1 Chr 9:19). Among them, those who served as chiefs came from the lineage of Meshelemiah (eighteen persons; 1 Chr 26:9), the lineage of Obed-edom (sixty-two persons; 1 Chr 26:8), and the lineage of Hosah (thirteen persons; 1 Chr 26:11) for a total of ninety-three persons in all. David had summoned four thousand gatekeepers to prepare for temple worship (1 Chr 23:5), so each chief must have overseen forty-three gatekeepers.

The name "Meshelemiah" (מְשֶׁלֶמְיָה) means "the Lord is my happiness" and is also mentioned in its shortened form, "Shelemiah" (שֶׁלֶמְיָה; 1 Chr 26:14). It is listed as "Meshelemiah" in 1 Chronicles 9:21.

First Chronicles 26:13 states, "They cast lots, the small and the great alike, according to their fathers' households, for every gate." On the east gate were six gatekeepers, and four each on the north and the south gates. At the "court" (per NIV; ESV and NRSV, "colonnade"; KJV and NASB, *parbar* [the meaning of the Hebrew word *parbar* is unclear]) on the west were four gatekeepers at the highway and two at the court itself. Also, two gatekeepers were stationed at each of the two storehouses. There was a total of twenty-four persons in seven locations (1 Chr 26:17–18; see also 1 Chr 26:20).

The Gatekeepers from the Sons of Asaph the Korahite (1 Chr 26:1–9)		
	The Line of Meshelemiah מְשֶׁלֶמְיָה	"the LORD is my happiness" 1 Chr 26:1–2, 9
1	**Zechariah (firstborn)** / זְכַרְיָה	"the Lord remembers" 1 Chr 26:2
2	**Jediael** / יְדִיעֲאֵל	"known by God" 1 Chr 26:2
3	**Zebadiah** / זְבַדְיָה	"the Lord had bestowed" 1 Chr 26:2
4	**Jathniel** / יַתְנִיאֵל	"God hires" 1 Chr 26:2
5	**Elam** / עֵילָם	"a high place" 1 Chr 26:3
6	**Johanan** / יְהוֹחָנָן	"the Lord has been gracious" 1 Chr 26:3
7	**Eliehoenai** / אֶלְיְהוֹעֵינַי	"toward the Lord are my eyes" 1 Chr 26:3
	eighteen sons and relatives of Meshelemiah, the "valiant men" 1 Chr 26:9	
	The Line of Obed-edom עֹבֵד אֱדוֹם	"servant of Edom, worshiper of Edom" 1 Chr 26:4
	Shemaiah (firstborn) / שְׁמַעְיָה	"the Lord hears" 1 Chr 26:4
1	**Jehozabad** / יְהוֹזָבָד	"the Lord has bestowed" 1 Chr 26:4
2	**Joah** / יוֹאָח	"the Lord is brother" 1 Chr 26:4
3	**Sacar** / שָׂכָר	"wages, labor, burden" 1 Chr 26:4
4	**Nethanel** / נְתַנְאֵל	"given of God" 1 Chr 26:4
5	**Ammiel** / עַמִּיאֵל	"my kinsman is God" 1 Chr 26:5
6	**Issachar** / יִשָּׂשכָר	"there is recompense" 1 Chr 26:5
7	**Peullethai** / פְּעֻלְּתַי	"laborious, the Lord is reward" 1 Chr 26:5

	The Line of Shemaiah שְׁמַעְיָה	"the Lord hears" 1 Chr 26:6, 7
1	Othni / עָתְנִי	"lion of the Lord" 1 Chr 26:7
2	Rephael / רְפָאֵל	"God has cured" 1 Chr 26:7
3	Obed / עוֹבֵד	"servant, worshiper" 1 Chr 26:7
4	Elzabad / אֶלְזָבָד	"God has given" 1 Chr 26:7
5	Elihu / אֱלִיהוּ	"He is my God" 1 Chr 26:7
6	Semachiah / סְמַכְיָה	"the Lord has sustained" 1 Chr 26:7
	sixty-two sons and relatives of Obed-edom, "able men with strength for the service" 1 Chr 26:8	

The Gatekeepers from the Sons of Merari (1 Chr 26:10–11)		
	The Line of Hosah / חֹסָה	"refuge" 1 Chr 26:10
1	Shimri (firstborn) / שִׁמְרִי	"my guard, my watcher" 1 Chr 26:10
2	Hilkiah / חִלְקִיָּה	"my portion is the LORD" 1 Chr 26:11
3	Tebaliah / טְבַלְיָה	"the LORD has purified" 1 Chr 26:11
4	Zechariah / זְכַרְיָה	"the LORD remembers" 1 Chr 26:11
	thirteen sons and relatives of Hosah 1 Chr 26:11	

During the six-year reign of Athaliah, the wife of King Jehoram and the evil daughter of King Ahab (840–835 BC; 2 Kgs 11:3; 2 Chr 22:12), all the sacrifices and praises offered in the temple were either abolished or defiled. Hence the order of temple duties that had been established by David was destroyed. When Jehoiada the high priest succeeded in overthrowing Athaliah and enthroning Joash, a descendant of David (2 Kgs 11:4–16; 2 Chr 23:1–15), Jehoiada broke down the idols and killed the priests of Baal. He then placed the offices of the house of the Lord under the authority of the Levitical priests (2 Chr 23:18). Furthermore, he restored the Davidic system of the twenty-four divisions and offered burnt offerings as written in the law of Moses—with rejoicing and singing according to the order of David (2 Chr 23:18). Jehoiada not only restored the order for the temple rituals, which had fallen into disuse, but also revived the duties of the gatekeepers. He stationed them in the various gates of the house of the Lord so that no unclean persons could enter (2 Chr 23:19).

Like the other duties of the Levites, the work of the gatekeepers was also restored after the return from Babylon. According to 1 Chronicles 9:17–27, which lists all the gatekeepers after the return from exile, there were 212 gatekeepers in all, including Shallum the chief, Akkub, Talmon, Ahiman, and their relatives (1 Chr 9:17, 22). "By their divisions" (NLT) they guarded the gates of the house of the Lord, that is, the house of the tent (1 Chr 9:23–24). The four chief gatekeepers, who were Levites, held essential positions and were in charge of all the chambers of the temple and treasuries (1 Chr 9:26). Besides the four chief gatekeepers, the other Levites stayed in their inherited villages that had been passed down from their ancestors; they were to "come in every seven days" to be with the others and carry out their duties (1 Chr 9:25). Nehemiah 12:25 also states, "Mattaniah, Bakbukiah, Obadiah, Meshullam, Talmon, and Akkub were gatekeepers keeping watch at the storehouses of the gates." Shallum, who appears in 1 Chronicles 9:17, is the same person as Meshullam in Nehemiah 12:25.

3. The History of the Temple Gatekeepers and Their Duties

Biblical records of the history of the temple gatekeepers show that the duties were important and diverse.

They guarded the temple gates (1 Chr 9:17–27)

The gatekeepers were chosen in order to guard each of the gates in the house of the Lord (1 Chr 26:12–13). They were assigned to each side of the temple—east, west, north, and south—by their divisions and vigilantly guarded the temple (1 Chr 9:23). They were responsible for opening the gates each morning with the key (1 Chr 9:27). The temple was closed at night, and entry and exit was prohibited until it was opened in the morning. The gatekeepers maintained the cleanliness and safety of the temple and guarded the gates all day from anything that could disturb the worship. They also cleaned the areas near the gates and polished the gates.

They guarded and protected the gate in front of the ark of the covenant (1 Chr 15:23–24)

First Chronicles 15:23–24 mentions that four persons guarded the gate in front of the ark of the covenant: "Berechiah and Elkanah were gatekeepers for the ark" (1 Chr 15:23), and "Obed-edom and Jehiah also were gatekeepers for the ark" (1 Chr 15:24). It appears that the duty of these four was to prevent anything from touching or coming close to the ark. Obed-edom mentioned here is a descendant of Merari, a descendant of Ethan (Jeduthun; 1 Chr 15:17, 24; 16:38) and is different from the Obed-edom who had the ark of the covenant in his house for three months (2 Sam 6:10–11; 1 Chr 26:4–5). In addition, the seven priests—Shebaniah, Joshaphat, Nethanel, Amasai, Zechariah, Benaiah, and Eliezer—blew the trumpets before the ark of God (1 Chr 15:24).

After the ark of the covenant was enshrined, David appointed Asaph and his relatives to stay before the ark and minister before it continually. He also appointed Obed-edom, his sixty-eight relatives, Obed-edom the son of Jeduthun, and Hosah as gatekeepers (1 Chr 16:37–38).

They prevented the unclean from entering the temple (2 Chr 23:6, 19)

As Jehoiada the high priest prepared for the coronation of Joash, he commanded, "Let no one enter the house of the Lord except the priests and the ministering Levites; they may enter, for they are holy. And let all the people keep the charge of the Lord" (2 Chr 23:6). He also stationed the gatekeepers by the various gates of the house of the Lord so that no one who was unclean in any way would enter (2 Chr 23:19).

They oversaw and distributed the freewill offerings (2 Chr 31:14)

Second Chronicles 31:14 states, "Kore the son of Imnah the Levite, the keeper of the eastern gate, was over the freewill offerings of God, to apportion the contributions for the Lord and the most holy things." The gatekeepers also oversaw the freewill offerings and distributed the most holy things.

They guarded all the chambers and the treasuries in the temple (1 Chr 9:26; Neh 12:25)

Among the plans for the temple that the Holy Spirit had shown David was a plan "for the storehouses of the house of God and for the storehouses of the dedicated things" (1 Chr 28:12). The gold, silver, treasures, tithes, thanksgiving offerings, and spoils of war were kept in these places (1 Kgs 7:51; 2 Kgs 14:14; 16:8; 18:15; 24:13; 2 Chr 31:11–14).

When David commanded Solomon to build the temple storehouses, he also appointed specific people to oversee these storehouses (1 Chr 26:20–28).

The divisions of the gatekeepers existed during the postexilic era as well. First Chronicles 9:26 states, "The four chief gatekeepers who were Levites, were in an office of trust, and were over the chambers and over the treasuries in the house of God," while Nehemiah 12:25 states, "Mattaniah, Bakbukiah, Obadiah, Meshullam, Talmon and Akkub were gatekeepers keeping watch at the storehouses of the gates." Thus the gatekeepers guarded the temple chambers and storehouses.

They guarded the gate of Shallecheth (1 Chr 26:16)

First Chronicles 26:16 states, "For Shuppim and Hosah it was to the west, by the gate of Shallecheth, on the ascending highway." The gate of Shallecheth (שַׁלֶּכֶת) led to the highway on the west side of the temple. This path was made by King Solomon in order to go up to the temple and was known as "his stairway by which he went up to the house of the Lord" (1 Kgs 10:5; 2 Chr 9:4).

They closed the temple gates on the Sabbath and prevented the merchants from entering (Neh 13:19)

Nehemiah rebuilt the walls of Jerusalem and appointed gatekeepers to guard the city gates (Neh 7:1, 3–4). The gates were guarded especially to prevent commercial activities on the Sabbath. Nehemiah 13:19 states, "It came about that just as it grew dark at the gates of Jerusalem before the sabbath, I commanded that the doors should be shut and that they should not open them until after the sabbath." Nehemiah commanded the Levites that they should purify themselves and come as gatekeepers to sanctify the Sabbath day (Neh 13:22).

Psalm 84 is preceded by the heading, "For the choir director; on the Gittith. A Psalm of the sons of Korah." Korah died in the wilderness after God punished him for challenging Moses' and Aaron's positions and authority (Num 16:1–3, 28–35), but his sons did not die (Num 26:11). Later Korah's descendants served as gatekeepers or singers among the musicians (1 Chr 6:31–38; 25:4–6; 26:1, 19; 2 Chr 20:19). This is why eleven psalms in the book of Psalms bear the heading "sons of Korah" (Ps 42; 44–49; 84; 85; 87; 88).

It is presumed that Psalm 84 was a song written by a gatekeeper among the sons of Korah (1 Chr 9:19; 26:1) who wrote about what he saw and felt in the temple with earnest yearning for the temple (see Ps 84:10). "Gittith" means "joyful melody" and shows the overflowing joy of the psalmist, who was yearning for the temple of the Lord. The psalmist described the temple in various ways: "Your dwelling places" (Ps 84:1), "the courts of the Lord" (Ps 84:2), "Your house" (Ps 84:4), and "Your courts" (Ps 84:10). His desire for the temple above all things in the world was so intense that he envied the sparrows and the swallows that built their nests under the temple eaves and flew around in freedom (Ps 84:1, 3). His soul longed and even fainted for the courts of the Lord (Ps 84:2, KJV).

Why did he long for the temple so much? It is because the temple is where God dwells. By dwelling in the temple, God's people can receive God's blessings, gain His strength, and find the highways of Zion (Ps 84:4–5). Although many difficult and wearisome events and countless temptations come from Satan, we must pass through the valley of tears (or valley of Baca) and overcome with faith to enter into the temple (Ps 84:6–7). Then at last God will bestow upon us the blessing of the spring and of the early rain; He will give the true blessing that all mankind seeks after (Ps 84:6, 12).

As the psalmist inspiringly reminisced upon the time he had served as a gatekeeper in the temple of God, he exclaimed in his praise, "A day in Your courts is better than a thousand outside. I would rather stand at the threshold of the house of my God than dwell in the tents of wickedness" (Ps 84:10).

Truly the temple is the place of God's dwelling. It overflows with life that is as splendid as the sun and salvation that is as secure as a shield; she gleams with the abundant glory of heaven and grace divine (Ps 84:11). God does not turn away from the upright and does not withhold any good thing from them (Ps 84:11). We must draw near to God all the more each time we pass through the numerous valleys of tears in our life's paths as sojourners. If we are empowered from above by the Holy Spirit, then we can surely march onward in victory. We can forget all our sorrows and share in spiritual fellowship with God as we each relish our abundant lives (Col 3:1–4; Rev 7:17).

Concluding Remarks: The Twenty-Four Divisions

We have examined the twenty-four divisions of the Levites, priests, musicians, and gatekeepers. The number "twenty-four" is twice the number "twelve" and signifies "representation." The people in the twenty-four divisions are like the representatives of the nation of Israel. The number "twelve" is used to describe the tribes that make up the nation of Israel, and the expression "the twelve tribes" is often used to represent the whole nation of Israel. In that regard it is interesting that the genealogy of the high priests in 1 Chronicles 6 is also made up of twelve generations before and twelve generations after Zadok.

This concept is developed further in the New Testament, where the book of Revelation introduces the "twenty-four" elders who sit upon the "twenty-four" thrones (Rev 4:4, 10, 5:8, 11:16, 19:4). Again, the number "twenty-four" here is a representative number. The number "twelve" refers to the church of the Old Testament, represented by the twelve tribes of Israel, as well as to the church of the New Testament (see Matt 19:28; Rev 21:12–14), represented by the twelve apostles of Jesus (Matt 10:1; Mark 3:14; Luke 6:13). Thus the twenty-four elders represent the churches of both the Old and New Testaments.

The background for the twenty-four elders is the twenty-four priestly divisions that appear in 1 Chronicles 24:7–19. According to Revelation 5:8, the twenty-four elders take the golden bowls full of the prayers of the saints and bow before the Lamb. They fall down before Him who sits on the throne and worship Him who lives forever and ever (Rev 4:10). They also sing a new song as they worship (Rev 5:9–10). Such roles of the twenty-four elders are reminiscent of the twenty-four divisions of the Old Testament. Ultimately, through the twenty-four divisions, God has shown to us the image of the true life of faith that Christians must live today as we fulfill our calling as the true priesthood (1 Pet 2:9).

מדבר צין הוא קדש
ים המלח
עמלק
מדבר סיני
מדבר פארן
מדבר שור
ארץ פלשתים
שבט
שבט שמעון
באר שבע
עיר כרמל
אלכסנדרי
פתם
לוח המסעות במדבר
אשר על פי ה׳ יסעו ועל פי ה׳ יחנו
א׳ רעמסס | טו׳ רתמה | כט׳ הר הגדגד
ב׳ סכת | טז׳ רמן פרץ | ל׳ יטבתה
ג׳ אתם | יז׳ לבנה | לא׳ עברנה
ד׳ פי החירת | יח׳ רסה | לב׳ עציון גבר
ה׳ מרה | יט׳ קהלתה | לג׳ מדבר צין
ו׳ אילם | כ׳ הר ספר | לד׳ הר ההר
ז׳ ים סוף | כא׳ חרדה | לה׳ צלמנה
ח׳ מדבר סין | כב׳ מקהלת | לו׳ פונן
ט׳ דפקה | כג׳ תחת | לז׳ אבת
י׳ אלוש | כד׳ תרח | לח׳ דיבן גד
יא׳ רפידם | כה׳ מתקה | לט׳ עלמן דבלתימה
יב׳ מדבר סיני | כו׳ חשמנה | מ׳ הרי עברים
יג׳ קברות התאוה | כז׳ מסרות | מא׳ ערבת מואב
יד׳ חצרת | כח׳ בני יעקן

PART

IV

The Genealogy of the High Priests

PART IV

In general, a genealogy is a document that traces the patrilineal descent of a clan and explains its lineage in a way that is easy to understand. It is a historical account of a family that reveals the origins of the clan to honor its lineage. Hence it produces respect for lineal succession and establishes the foundation for filial piety. Likewise, biblical genealogies were recorded during each crucial point in the history of redemption. They thus provide a panoramic view of the immense history of redemption by manifesting the succession of the covenant—the driving force behind the history of redemption—and the processes of its fulfillment.

Various types of genealogies are continuously introduced throughout the Old and New Testaments. The covenant functions as the mighty buttress that upholds all genealogies; therefore, the fulfillment of biblical covenants is clearly revealed through the genealogies. At the core of the covenant is God's love that desires to save sinners after the fall of Adam by sending the Savior to this world. This covenant is the force that propels the great work of redemption. All genealogies in the Bible have their foundation in the covenant; hence they are the first step and the shortcut to learning about the covenant and the history of redemption. This living and dynamic history of redemption that flows through the agency of the divine covenants can be lucidly understood and experienced through the biblical genealogies.

CHAPTER

11

The Genealogy of the High Priests

The book of Genesis, which opens the Old Testament, comprises ten genealogies (*toledoth*). The book of Chronicles, which concludes the Old Testament history, allocates an extensive amount of writing in 1 Chronicles 1–9 and 23–26 for the genealogies. Considering the structure, length, and content of the Chronicler's genealogies, it is evident that its focus is the tribe of Levi, and even among them greater weight is given to the genealogy of the priests.

During Old Testament times, priests played the sacred role of mediator between God and the people of Israel. Unlike the prophets who spoke God's Word, the priests shed the blood of animals and offered sin offerings on behalf of the people so that their sins would be forgiven. One day a year, the high priests entered the holy of holies on the Day of Atonement and ministered to atone for the sins of all the people (Lev 16:1–34; Heb 9:7).

First Chronicles 6:3–15 records the genealogy of the high priests. It contains the names of twenty-three priests from Aaron to Seraiah and his son Jehozadak, who was deported to Babylon in 586 BC when the temple in Jerusalem was destroyed.[24] Moreover, Nehemiah 12:10–11 supplements the record with six priests from the postexilic period, starting with Jeshua (Joshua) and ending with Jaddua, who was from the Persian era. Thus the Bible contains the names of twenty-nine priests solely from the Aaronic line. This genealogy, however, contains omissions and is not a complete genealogy of blood lineage. It is also uncertain whether the twenty-nine people actually performed the high priestly duties as overseers of the temple sacrifices.

1. The Meaning of "High Priest" in Hebrew

The expression "high priest" in Hebrew is כֹּהֵן גָּדוֹל (*kohen gadol*) or כֹּהֵן רֹאשׁ (*kohen rosh*).

Kohen gadol (כֹּהֵן גָּדוֹל)

Kohen gadol is a combination of the words כֹּהֵן (*kohen*), meaning "priest," and גָּדוֹל (*gadol*), meaning "big," "honorable," "great," or "noble." Historically this title was used for the high priest Jehoiada during the time of Joash, the eighth king of the southern kingdom of Judah (2 Kgs 12:10; see 2 Kgs 12:7), as well as the high priest Hilkiah two hundred years later, during the time of Josiah the sixteenth king (2 Kgs 22:4, 8; 23:4). It was also used for the high priest Eliashib during the postexilic era, in the days of Nehemiah (Neh 3:1).

The words "high priest" referring to Jehoiada in 2 Kings 12:7 are הַכֹּהֵן (*hakkohen*) in Hebrew. Translated this word means "the priest,"

---

24 Based on Josephus's writings as well as the *Seder Olam Zutta, the Jewish Encyclopedia* introduces six high priests who are not included in the genealogy of the high priests in the Bible, between Azariah (thirteenth generation) and Shallum (nineteenth generation). Josephus includes six more high priests: Joran, Axiomar, Phideas, Sudeas, Jotham, and Odeas (*Ant.* 10.151–53; 20.227–51), whereas the *Seder Olam Zutta* includes six high priests: Joash, Jehoshaphat, Pedaiah, Zedekiah, Jotham, and Hoshaiah.

but it is translated as "high priest" in order to differentiate it from הַכֹּהֲנִים (*hakkohanim*, plural), which refers to the other priests in the same verse. The same is true in the translation of Nehemiah 3:1, "Eliashib the high priest arose with his brothers the priests." In addition, 2 Chronicles 24:6, which is related to 2 Kings 12:7, uses the word הָרֹאשׁ (*harosh*), meaning "the head," instead of הַכֹּהֵן (*hakkohen*). This clearly reveals that Jehoiada was the high priest, the chief among the priests.

Kohen rosh (כֹּהֵן רֹאשׁ)

Kohen rosh is the combination of the words כֹּהֵן (*kohen*), meaning "priest," and רֹאשׁ (*rosh*), meaning "head," "summit," or "leader." The following are examples of its historical usage.

Kohen rosh was used to refer to:

- Aaron the chief priest (Ezra 7:5)
- Amariah the chief priest from Jehoshaphat's time (2 Chr 19:11)
- Jehoiada the chief priest during Joash's time (2 Chr 24:6)
- Azariah the chief priest during Uzziah's time (2 Chr 26:20)
- Azariah the chief priest during Hezekiah's time (2 Chr 31:10)
- Seraiah the chief priest during Zedekiah's time, when the southern kingdom of Judah fell (2 Kgs 25:18; Jer 52:24)
- Jehoiada, the father of Benaiah, David's chief bodyguard and one of the mighty men (1 Chr 27:5; see 2 Sam 8:18; 1 Chr 12:27, "leader of the house of Aaron")

In addition, in 2 Chronicles 35:8, the high priest Hilkiah and the other officials were referred to as נָגִיד (*nagid*), chiefs in the temple of God. *Nagid* originally signified the king of a nation and was used to refer to kings like David, Solomon, and Hezekiah (2 Sam 5:2; 6:21; 7:8; 1 Kgs 1:35; 2 Kgs 20:5; Dan 11:22). In 1 Chronicles 9:11, *nagid* is translated as "chief officer" of the house of God and in 2 Chronicles 31:13 as "the ruler" of the house of God (KJV).

2. Seventy-Seven Generations of High Priests from the Time of Aaron Until AD 70

❖ Systematically organized for the first time in history

The genealogy of the sons of Levi in 1 Chronicles 6:1–14 begins with Kohath the son of Levi and ends with Jehozadak. Considering the fact that Zadok (1 Chr 6:8)—who served during the days of David and Solomon (2 Sam 15:27, 1 Kgs 2:35)—appears at the center of the genealogy with twelve persons before him (Kohath to Ahitub) and twelve after him (Ahimaaz to Jehozadak), it is clear that a chiastic structure has been built with Zadok at its center. First Chronicles 6:1–14 contains the genealogy of Aaron's son Eleazar and his descendant Zadok; thus it is clear that this genealogy is of a single bloodline.

The history of the high priests parallels the history of the temple. This is because the role of the high priests becomes meaningless without the temple. This fact was demonstrated well when the southern kingdom of Judah fell at the hands of Nebuchadnezzar of Babylon. When the temple in Jerusalem was burned with fire, Seraiah the chief priest and Zephaniah the second priest were struck down and put to death at Riblah in the land of Hamath (2 Kgs 25:9, 18–21).

Ten high priests, from the first high priest, Aaron, to Ahitub, served in the tabernacle that was built in the wilderness of Sinai in 1445 BC (Exod 40:1–38). The high priests who served in Solomon's temple span from Zadok to Seraiah (and his son Jehozadak), who was high priest in 586 BC when the southern kingdom of Judah fell. This is the temple that Solomon built over a period of six years and six months, starting in the fourth year of his reign (1 Kgs 6:37–38; 2 Chr 3:1–2).[25] The high priests from Joshua to Jaddua served in Zerubbabel's temple; its construction began on the twenty-fourth day of the

25 Abraham Park, *God's Profound and Mysterious Providence: As Revealed in the Genealogy of Jesus Christ from the Time of David to the Exile in Babylon* (Hong Kong: Periplus, 2011), 112–13.

sixth month in the second year of the reign of Darius king of Persia and was completed after about four years and five months, on the third day of the month of Adar (twelfth month) in the sixth year of Darius (Hag 1:15; Ezra 6:15–22). Seventeen high priests, including Joseph Caiaphas, served in Herod's temple, which was built by Herod the Great (37 BC–4 BC) between 20 (19) BC and AD 63 (64), over about eighty-three years (see John 2:20).

The history of the high priests continued even after the end of the Old Testament era. It continued through the intertestamental period and Jesus' thirty-three-year life until AD 70, when the temple was completely destroyed by the Roman general Titus (son of the Roman emperor Vespasian). Forty-eight generations of high priests served after the time of Jaddua, the last high priest recorded in the Old Testament. The high priesthood and the period of the high priests' ministry are recorded in detail in the New Testament as well as in *Antiquities of the Jews* and *The Jewish War* written by the Jewish historian Josephus. They are also documented in 1 and 2 Maccabees, the Jewish history books written during the two centuries before Christ.

The history of the high priests spanned about fifteen hundred years, beginning with Aaron in 1445 BC and continuing until AD 70, when Jerusalem fell. The history of the high priesthood includes seventy-four persons but seventy-seven generations. These high priests can be classified into three groups.

First, twenty-nine generations of high priests from Aaron to Jaddua are recorded in the Old Testament. They are subdivided into three groups by the temples in which they served: the tabernacle, Solomon's temple, and Zerubbabel's temple.

Second, nineteen generations (eighteen persons) are listed from Onias I to Antigonus. They are subdivided according to the time period in which they served. Their priesthoods started after the fall of Persia, ran through the Ptolemaic and Seleucid dynasties of the Hellenistic period, and continued until the period of Judean independence.

Third, twenty-nine generations are recorded from the high priest Ananel, whom King Herod appointed, until AD 70, when Jerusalem fell. The high priests from this time period are subdivided according to their appointers.

29 Generations Classified by Temples	
tabernacle of Moses	1445–959 BC / 10 generations
temple of Solomon	959–586 BC / 13 generations
temple of Zerubbabel	515–320 BC / 6 generations

19 Generations Classified by Time Periods	
period of the Ptolemaic and Seleucid rule	320–175 BC / 7 generations
period of the Seleucid rule (extremely wicked high priests)	175–159 BC / 3 generations
interlude in the priesthood	159–152 BC
period of Judean independence (Hasmonean Dynasty)	152–37 BC / 9 generations

29 Generations Classified by Appointers	
appointed by King Herod the Great	37–4 BC / 7 generations
appointed by Herod Archelaus	4 BC–AD 6 / 3 generations
appointed by Quirinius the governor of Syria	AD 6–9 / 1 generation
appointed by Gratus the governor of Judea	AD 15–26 / 4 generations
appointed by Vitellius the governor of Syria	AD 35–39 / 2 generations
appointed by Herod Agrippa I	AD 41–44 / 3 generations
appointed by Herod of Chalcis	AD 44–49 / 2 generations
appointed by Herod Agrippa II	AD 50–66 / 6 generations
chosen by the Zealots by casting lots	AD 67 / 1 generation

Total of seventy-seven generations / 1445 BC–AD 70

The following is a list of the seventy-seven generations of high priests classified according to the above categories.

1. The High Priests Classified by Temples		
Tabernacle of Moses, 1445–959 BC / 10 generations		
1	**Aaron**	1 Chr 6:3, 50; Ezra 7:5
2	**Eleazar**	1 Chr 6:3–4, 50; Ezra 7:5
3	**Phinehas**	1 Chr 6:4, 50; Ezra 7:5
4	**Abishua**	1 Chr 6:4–5, 50; Ezra 7:5
5	**Bukki**	1 Chr 6:5, 51; Ezra 7:4
6	**Uzzi (Uzziel)**	1 Chr 6:5–6, 51; Ezra 7:4
7	**Zerahiah**	1 Chr 6:6, 51; Ezra 7:4
8	**Meraioth**	1 Chr 6:6–7, 52; Ezra 7:3
9	**Amariah**	1 Chr 6:7, 52
10	**Ahitub**	1 Chr 6:7–8, 52
Temple of Solomon, 959–586 BC / 13 generations		
1	**Zadok**	1 Chr 6:8, 53 King David, King Solomon; 2 Sam 8:17; 15:35; 1 Chr 29:22
2	**Ahimaaz**	1 Chr 6:8–9, 53 Zadok's son; 2 Sam 15:27
3	**Azariah**	1 Chr 6:9
4	**Johanan**	1 Chr 6:9–10
5	**Azariah**	1 Chr 6:10–11; 1 Kgs 4:2; Ezra 7:3
6	**Amariah**	1 Chr 6:11; Ezra 7:3 Jehoshaphat, Judah's fourth king 871–847 BC
7	**Ahitub**	1 Chr 6:11–12; Ezra 7:2
8	**Zadok**	1 Chr 6:12; Ezra 7:2
9	**Shallum**	1 Chr 6:12–13; Ezra 7:2
10	**Hilkiah**	1 Chr 6:13; Ezra 7:1 Josiah, Judah's sixteenth king 640–609[b] BC
11	**Azariah**	1 Chr 6:13–14; Ezra 7:1
12	**Seraiah**	1 Chr 6:14; Ezra 7:1 586 BC, just before the fall of Judah
13	**Jehozadak (Jozadak)**	1 Chr 6:14–15; Ezra 3:2, 8; 5:2 period of the Babylonian exile

Temple of Zerubbabel (until the fall of Persia) 515–320 BC / 6 generations		
1	**Joshua (Jeshua)**	Neh 12:10; Hag 1:1, 12, 14; 2:2, 4; Zech 6:11; Ezra 2:2 515–490 BC / 25 years
2	**Joiakim**	Neh 12:10, 12, 26 490–470 BC / 20 years
3	**Eliashib**	Neh 3:1, 20–21, 12:10, 22–23, 13:4–9, 28 470–433 BC / 37 years
4	**Joiada**	Neh 12:10–11, 22, 13:28 433–410 BC / 23 years
5	**Johanan (Jonathan)**	Neh 12:11, 22–23 410–371 BC / 39 years
6	**Jaddua**	Neh 12:11, 22 371–320 BC / 51 years

2. The High Priests Classified by Time Periods

Ptolemaic and Seleucid reigns, 320–175 BC / 7 generations		
1	**Onias I**	son of Jaddua 320–280 BC / 40 years
2	**Simon I**	son of Onias I 280–260 BC / 20 years
3	**Eleazar**	brother of Simon I 260–245 BC / 15 years
4	**Manasseh**	brother of Onias I 245–240 BC / 5 years
5	**Onias II**	son of Simon I 240–218 BC / 22 years
6	**Simon II**	son of Onias II 218–185 BC / 33 years
7	**Onias III**	son of Simon II 185–175 BC / 10 years

Seleucid reign (extremely wicked high priests), 175–159 BC / 3 generations		
1	**Jason**	younger brother of Onias III 175–172 BC / 3 years
2	**Menelaus**	younger brother of Onias III, or brother of Simon (governor of the temple) 172–162 BC / 10 years

3	**Alcimus (Jakim)**	descendant of Aaron 162–159 BC / 3 years

Interlude in the high priesthood, 159–152 BC

Period of Judean independence (Hasmonean era), 152–37 BC / 9 generations

1	**Jonathan Apphus**	youngest son of Mattathias 152–142 BC / 10 years
2	**Simon (III) Thassi**	older brother of Jonathan 142–134 BC / 8 years
3	**John Hyrcanus I**	son of Simon III 134–104 BC / 30 years
4	**Aristobulus I**	first son of Hyrcanus I 104–103 BC / 1 year
5	**Alexander Jannaeus**	younger brother of Aristobulus I 103–76 BC / 27 years
6	**Hyrcanus II**	first son of Alexander Jannaeus 76–67 BC / 9 years
7	**Aristobulus II**	second son of Alexander Jannaeus 67–63 BC / 3 years and 3 months or 3 years and 6 months
8	**Hyrcanus II**	first son of Alexander Jannaeus 63–40 BC / 23 years
9	**Antigonus**	son of Aristobulus II 40–37 BC / 3 years

3. The High Priests Classified According to Appointers

Appointed by Herod the Great, 37–4 BC / 7 generations

1	**Ananel**	from Babylon	37–35 BC / 2 years
2	**Aristobulus III**	grandson of Aristobulus II	35 –34 BC / 1 year
3	**Ananel**	from Babylon	34–30 BC / 4 years
4	**Jesus**	son of Phabi	30–24 BC / 6 years
5	**Simon**	son of Boethus	24–5 BC / 19 years
6	**Matthias**	son of Theophilus	5–4 BC / 1 year
7	**Joasar**	son of Boethus	4 BC / 1 year

Appointed by Herod Archelaus, 4 BC–AD 6 / 3 generations			
1	**Eleazar**	son of Boethus	4 BC / 1 year
2	**Jesus**	son of Sie	4 BC–AD 6 / 10 years
3	**Joasar**	son of Boethus	AD 6 / 1 year
Appointed by Quirinius the governor of Syria, AD 6–9 / 1 generation			
1	**Annas**	son of Seth	AD 6–15 / 9 years
Appointed by Gratus the governor of Judea, AD 15–26 / 4 generations			
1	**Ishmael**	son of Phabi	AD 15–16 / 1 year
2	**Eleazar**	son of Annas	AD 16–17 / 1 year
3	**Simon**	son of Camith	AD 17–18 / 1 year
4	**Joseph Caiaphas**	son-in-law of Annas	AD 18–36 / 18 years
Appointed by Vitellius the governor of Syria, AD 35–39 / 2 generations			
1	**Jonathan**	son of Annas	AD 36–37 / 1 year
2	**Theophilus**	son of Annas	AD 37–41 / 4 years
Appointed by Herod Agrippa I, AD 41–44 / 3 generations			
1	**Simon Cantheras**	son of Boethus	AD 41–42 / 1 year
2	**Matthias**	son of Annas	AD 42–43 / 1 year
3	**Elioneus**	son of Cantheras	AD 43–45 / 2 years
Appointed by Herod of Chalcis, AD 44–49 / 2 generations			
1	**Josephus**	son of Camei	AD 45–48 / 3 years
2	**Ananias**	son of Nedebaius	AD 48–59 / 11 years
Appointed by Herod Agrippa II, AD 50–66 / 6 generations			
1	**Ishmael**	son of Phabi	AD 59–61 / 2 years
2	**Joseph Cabi**	son of Simon	AD 61–62 / 1 year
3	**Annas II**	son of Annas	AD 62 / 3 months
4	**Jesus**	son of Damneus	AD 62–63 / 1 year
5	**Jesus**	son of Gamaliel	AD 63–64 / 1 year
6	**Matthias**	son of Theophilus	AD 64–66 / 2 years

Chosen by the Zealots by casting lots, AD 67 / 1 generation			
1	**Phannias**	son of Samuel	AD 67–70 / 3 years

The following sources were used as reference for the period of service for the high priests not recorded in the Bible.

- The Apocrypha: King James Version.
- Josephus, Flavius and William Whiston. *The Works of Josephus: Complete and Unabridged*. Peabody, MA: Hendrickson, 1996.
- Lightfoot, John. *The Whole Works of the Rev. John Lightfoot, D.D., Master of Catherine Hall, Cambridge*. Edited by John Rogers Pitman. London: J. F. Dove, 1823.
- VanderKam, James C. *From Joshua to Caiaphas: High Priests after the Exile*. Minneapolis: Fortress, 2004.
- Yong-Kuk Wone, *Christology of the Pentateuch* (revised edition). Seoul: Korea Christian Education Research Institute, 1999.

CHAPTER
12

The History of High Priests Classified by Temples

1. The Tabernacle of Moses

Ten generations of high priests between 1445 BC and 959 BC

Moses first constructed the tabernacle with the pattern he received from God on Mount Sinai (Exod 25:9). The tabernacle was completed on the first day of the first month in 1445 BC, one year after the exodus. Upon its completion the cloud covered the tent of meeting, and the glory of the Lord filled the tabernacle (Exod 40:2, 17, 34). From this time on until the temple of Solomon was completed in 959 BC, the tabernacle was a migrating holy place in which the people of Israel made offerings to God. It was a way to show that God dwelt among His people and governed over them (Exod 25:8). The priests and the Levites dedicated themselves to God through the work of transporting the tabernacle each time the Israelite camp set out in the wilderness (Num 4:5–33, 10:17, 21).

Among the high priests listed in 1 Chronicles 6, ten high priests, from Aaron to Ahitub, served in the tabernacle before Solomon's temple was built. Since the high priesthood was a lifetime office, it is most certain that the ten generations of high priests succeeded the office by blood lineage (Num 20:26).

Aaron was born in 1530 BC and served as high priest from 1445 BC. About 486 years passed from the time Aaron began his service as high priest until the temple of Solomon was completed in 959 BC. Under the assumption that the high priesthood was a lifetime office and that one generation is approximately twenty-five to thirty years in length, the time is too long for ten generations. Therefore, it is clear that generations were omitted in the record of these ten generations of high priests, although exact time periods of the omissions are uncertain.

The genealogy of the priest Samuel recorded in 1 Chronicles 6 supports this fact. Among Aaron's descendants, Ahitub—the tenth generation—was the high priest who lived contemporaneously with Samuel. This is because Ahitub was the father of Zadok, who served as a priest during David's time (2 Sam 8:17; 1 Chr 6:8). In addition, among Samuel's ancestors Korah lived contemporaneously with Aaron. This is evident, since Aaron was Amram's son and Korah was the son of Izhar, Amram's brother (Num 16:1; 1 Chr 6:38).

Fifteen generations are listed between Korah and Samuel (1 Chr 6:22–27, 33–38; 1 Sam 1:1), but only eight between Aaron and Ahitub. Hence a comparison with Samuel's genealogy shows that about seven generations were omitted in the genealogy of high priest for this period.

Kohath—1 Chronicles 6:2, 18, 38; 23:12

1 Chr 6:3	**Amram**	**Izhar**	1 Chr 6:38
1 Chr 6:3	**Aaron**	**Korah**	1 Chr 6:37
eight generations recorded		fifteen generations recorded	
1 Chr 6:7–8	**Ahitub**	**Samuel**	1 Chr 6:33

1st Generation

1. Aaron אַהֲרֹן "lofty, exalted"

Aaron was among the three leaders (Moses, Aaron, and Miriam) during the forty years of the wilderness journey and the progenitor of the lineage of the holy high priest (1 Chr 6:3; Exod 28:1; 31:10; 35:19; Lev 6:20–22; Ezra 7:5). Aaron was Miriam's younger brother and Moses' older brother. He was called at the age of eighty-three (Exod 7:7) and became Moses' spokesperson by God's command when Moses made the excuse before God that he was not an eloquent speaker (Exod 4:10–16; 7:1–2).

Aaron married Elisheba, the daughter of Amminadab and the sister of Nahshon (Exod 6:23; 1 Chr 2:10). He and Elisheba had four sons—Nadab, Abihu, Eleazar, and Ithamar (Exod 6:23; 1 Chr 6:3). Among them Nadab and Abihu offered strange fire before God, and fire came out from the presence of the Lord and consumed them. Since they died before the Lord childless, their brothers Eleazar and Ithamar served as priests (Lev 10:1–2; Num 3:4; 26:60–61), and Eleazar succeeded Aaron's high priesthood (Num 20:25–28; Deut 10:6).

Since Aaron died at the age of 123 (Num 33:38–39), just before entry into Canaan (1407 BC), his birth year must have been 1530 BC. God called him at the age of eighty-three along with his brother Moses (Exod 7:7), and he helped lead the Israelites in the exodus in 1446 BC. He served as high priest for thirty-nine years, from 1445 BC, when the tabernacle was completed, until 1407 BC.

When the Israelites fought against Amalek on the path that led to the wilderness of Sinai after the exodus, Aaron, along with Hur, contributed to the victory by holding up Moses' arms (Exod 17:8–13). Then, after the tabernacle was built, Aaron served as the high priest who mediated God's authority to the people. His descendants succeeded the priestly office. For this reason the priests were called the "sons of Aaron" (2 Chr 13:10), the "house of Aaron" (1 Chr 12:27), and the "order of Aaron" (Heb 7:11).

While Moses was up on Mount Sinai for forty days to receive the law, Aaron incited the people to commit idolatry by worshiping a golden calf (Exod 32:1–25). Then God made the sons of Levi kill with their hands their own brothers, friends, and neighbors—about three thousand men (Exod 32:26–28). The disbelief and sin of Aaron and the Israelites led to the tragic deaths of three thousand individuals (Exod 32:28). The next day Moses prayed that his name be blotted out from the book of life in order to atone for the people's sins (Exod 32:30–33). God sought to immediately kill Aaron, who had caused so many people to die, but Moses' intercessory prayer saved his brother from death (Deut 9:20).

In addition, while the Israelites were camping at Hazeroth, Aaron and Miriam spoke against Moses for marrying a Cushite woman (Num 12:1–16). God quickly intervened and rebuked them by exposing their impure intentions, which caused Aaron to once again thoroughly acknowledge the authority of his younger brother Moses. Nevertheless, Aaron had to die without entering into Canaan, because he failed to reveal God's holiness when he disbelieved and disobeyed God's Word during the Meribah rock incident at Kadesh (Num 20:7–13, 22–29; 33:38–39; Deut 10:6; 32:50).

According to God's command, Moses took Aaron and his son Eleazar up Mount Hor. He disrobed Aaron of his holy, high priestly garments (ephod) and put them on Eleazar (Num 20:25–28). Aaron did not take off the garments himself; he was disrobed. Aaron had been appointed as high priest according to God's will and robed with the holy garments. As a result of his disbelief, however, he had to be divested of the high priesthood and the priestly garments.

This occurred on the first day of the fifth month of the fortieth year of the exodus, about eight months prior to the entry into Canaan. Aaron was called at the age of 83, and until the age of 123, for about forty years, he worked hard during the wilderness journey alongside Moses. Unfortunately, his life ended in the wilderness without his being able to set foot in Canaan (Num 33:38–39).

Aaron's death was not a natural death but punishment from God for disobeying His will. As soon as Aaron died, the whole assembly mourned for him for thirty days (Num 20:29). He was the high priest whom the whole assembly had revered for nearly forty years during their long and perilous wilderness journey, but his disbelief and disobedience led to his death in accordance to God's Word. His death must have become the impetus for the Israelites' great fear of God.

2nd Generation

2. **Eleazar**	אֶלְעָזָר	"God has helped"

Eleazar was Aaron and Elisheba's third son (Exod 6:23). His brothers were Nadab, Abihu, and Ithamar (Num 3:2; 26:60; 1 Chr 6:3; 24:1), and he married Putiel's daughter, who gave birth to Phinehas (Exod 6:25). Eleazar succeeded Aaron and became the second high priest in the genealogy of the high priests (1 Chr 6:3–4, 50; Ezra 7:5). He was also the ancestor to Zadok and Ezra (1 Chr 6:3–15; Ezra 7:1–5). In Hebrew the name "Eleazar" is אֶלְעָזָר (*elazar*), a combination of the words אֵל (*el*, "God") and עָזַר (*azar*, "to help, to aid, to support"), and means "God has helped."

The duration of Eleazar's priesthood was from the time the community of faith was formed in the wilderness (1445–1406 BC) until the time of the conquest of and settlement in Canaan (1406–1390 BC). After the Israelites left Egypt and arrived at Mount Sinai, Eleazar was anointed, consecrated, and ordained as priest along with Aaron and his brothers according to the law of God (Exod 28:1, 40–41; 29:9; 30:30; 40:12–15; Num 3:2–3).

When his brothers Nadab and Abihu offered up to God a different fire that God had not commanded and thus were killed (Lev 10:1–2), God, through Moses, prohibited Aaron and the remaining sons—Eleazar and Ithamar—from uncovering their heads and tearing their clothes in mourning. Moses said that only the whole house of Israel should bewail the burning that the Lord had brought about (Lev 10:5–6). According to the law, the high priest who was anointed with "the Lord's anointing oil" (Lev 10:6–7; see Exod 29:6–9) and consecrated to serve only the Lord could not uncover his head or tear his clothes, even when his parents died (Lev 10:7; 21:10–11). So Moses called to Mishael and Elzaphan, the sons of Aaron's uncle Uzziel, to carry out the bodies of Nadab and Abihu, still in their tunics, to the outside of the camp (Lev 10:4–5). Since their older brothers had died, Aaron's third and fourth sons, Eleazar and Ithamar, served as priests (Num 3:4).

Eleazar was ordained as high priest in Aaron's place eight months prior to Israel's entry into Canaan, on the first day of the fifth month in 1407 BC when Aaron the high priest died on Mount Hor (Num 20:25–28).

The second census[26] was taken after the sons of Israel were struck with a plague because of the affair of Baal of Peor in the plains of Moab. God commanded Moses and Eleazar, the son of Aaron the high priest, to take this census (Num 26:1–4).

In addition, when Joshua succeeded Moses, God commanded Moses to lay his hand on Joshua, have him stand before Eleazar and all the congregation, and commission him in their sight (Num 27:18–20). Moreover, Joshua stood before Eleazar so that Eleazar could inquire for him by the judgment of the Urim before the Lord. God commanded that Joshua and all the assembly of Israel must go out and come in at Eleazar's command (Num 27:21). The Urim was a tool used to inquire about the will of God before making an important decision (Exod 28:29–30; see 1 Sam 14:36–42) and was worn on the high priest's garment, in the breastpiece of judgment (Exod 28:15–30). This demonstrates that the authority of the priests had increased from what it had been during Moses' time.

26 The first census was taken during the time when Israel received the Ten Commandments at Mount Sinai in the early part of the journey to Canaan (see Num 1).

Thereafter, Eleazar, along with Joshua, led the second generation of the Israelites in the wilderness into Canaan and helped distribute the inheritance of the land by tribes (Num 34:17; Josh 14:1; 19:51).

Following Joshua's death at the age of 110 and his burial at Timnath-serah (Josh 24:29–30), Eleazar also died and was buried in the hill country of Ephraim, which had been given to his son Phinehas (Josh 24:33).

3rd Generation

3. **Phinehas**	פִּינְחָס	"an oracle, revelation"

Phinehas was Aaron's grandson and Eleazar's son (Exod 6:25; 1 Chr 6:4, 50; 9:20). He was Eleazar's successor and the third high priest in the genealogy of the high priests. First Chronicles 6:4 states, "Eleazar became the father of Phinehas, and Phinehas became the father of Abishua" (see 1 Chr 6:50; Ezra 7:5). The name "Phinehas" in Hebrew is פִּינְחָס (*pinehas*) and means "an oracle" or "revelation."

***First*, Phinehas turned away God's wrath.**

The Israelites brought the wrath of God upon themselves by playing the harlot in the plains of Moab, and 24,000 died by the plague as a result (Num 25:1–3, 9). Meanwhile, Zimri, a leader of the tribe of Simeon, went into his tent with Cozbi, a Midianite woman, and committed adultery. Then Phinehas took a spear and pierced both of them through, and the plague was checked (Num 25:6–9). God testified, "Phinehas the son of Eleazar, the son of Aaron the priest, has turned away My wrath from the sons of Israel in that he was jealous with My jealousy among them, so that I did not destroy the sons of Israel in My jealousy" (Num 25:11).

Due to this incident, God gave Phinehas the covenant of peace and promised him and his descendants the perpetual priesthood (Num 25:12–13). Psalm 106:30–31 states, "Phinehas stood up and interposed, and so the plague was stayed. And it was reckoned to him for righteousness, to all generations forever."

Peace and righteousness reign when sin is resolved and God's wrath disappears. Jesus gave us eternal peace and righteousness by resolving our sins on the cross and taking on God's wrath on our behalf.

***Second*, Phinehas led Israel to victory in the battle against the Midianites.**

The Midianites were the descendants of Abraham born through Keturah (Gen 25:1–2). They colluded with the Moabites on the east side of Canaan and instigated Israel's acts of harlotry and idolatry (Num 22:7; 25:6). Thus God commanded that they "be hostile to the Midianites and strike them" before the Israelites entered Canaan (Num 25:17). The reason was stated by God: "They have been hostile to you [Israel] with their tricks, with which they have deceived you in the affair of Peor and in the affair of Cozbi, the daughter of the leader of Midian, their sister who was slain on the day of the plague because of Peor" (Num 25:18).

Moses selected one thousand people from each tribe for the battle against the Midianites and sent them to the war along with Phinehas, who had holy vessels from the sanctuary and the trumpets for the alarm in his hand (Num 31:3–6). Taking the trumpets for the alarm was commanded in Numbers 10:9: "When you go to war in your land against the adversary who attacks you, then you shall sound an alarm with the trumpets, that you may be remembered before the Lord your God, and be saved from your enemies." Phinehas and the soldiers struck the Midianites and killed their men and the five kings (i.e., Evi, Rekem, Zur, Hur, and Reba) as well as Balaam, son of Beor, who had caused the sons of Israel to sin with his counsel (Num 31:7–11, 16; Josh 13:22).

***Third*, Phinehas resolved the issue of building the altar by the Jordan.**

The six-year-long war to conquer the major footholds in Canaan had ended, and the soldiers from the Transjordanian tribes who had fought in the war could finally return to the land of their inheritance. So they built a great altar on a hill to the west of the Jordan to commemorate God's grace that had protected them until then and to prove that they were also the people of the covenant, like the tribes to the west of the Jordan (Josh 22:10–11, 24–29).

After hearing this news, the tribes to the west of the Jordan gathered at Shiloh to fight against the Transjordanian tribes. They misunderstood and thought that the great altar had been built for the purpose of idol worship (Josh 22:12, 15–20). Thus the sons of Israel sent Phinehas and ten chiefs to the tribes on the east of the Jordan in order to learn the truth about the matter (Josh 22:13–14).

After learning that the purpose of the altar was not for idolatry, Phinehas and the chiefs of the tribes clarified the situation to the tribes west of the Jordan, and the situation was pacified (Josh 22:21–34). Phinehas was a wise mediator who reconciled the people and prevented the division of the community.

***Fourth*, Phinehas led worship during the battle against the tribe of Benjamin.**

During the period of the judges, a certain Levite living in the hill country of Ephraim lived with a concubine, but she played the harlot against him and went back to her father's house. The Levite went to her father's house in order to bring her back (Judg 19:1–3). However, on their way home, certain worthless fellows of the Benjamite tribe raped and abused the concubine all night; they let her go at the approach of dawn, but she died. The Levite brought her body home on a donkey and cut her body into twelve pieces and sent the pieces to all the tribes of Israel (Judg 19:22–29).

Enraged at this, the Israelites sent allied forces of 400,000 men and fought against the 26,700 Benjamites; they lost, with 22,000 men killed in the first battle and 18,000 killed in the second battle (Judg 20:15, 17, 21, 25). Thus all the Israelites went up to Bethel, and there they wept and fasted until evening, offering burnt offerings and peace offerings to God, and inquired of Him. It was Phinehas who led the worship at this time (Judg 20:26–28). After the worship the allied forces of Israel obtained great victory against the Benjamites, and only 600 men from the tribe of Benjamin survived (Judg 20:47).

Phinehas, who was also the ruler over the keepers of the thresholds of the tabernacle (1 Chr 9:19–20), continually restored the relationship between the Israelites and God as well as among the Israelites themselves. In doing so he faithfully fulfilled his role as a mediator who brought stability to Israel. There is no record in the Bible about the death of Phinehas.

From **Abishua** to **Ahitub**

First Chronicles 6 lists the high-priestly lineage from Phinehas's successor to Ahitub (1 Chr 6:4–8, 50–53; Ezra 7:2–5). However, there are no other special records in the Bible regarding their ministry. A comparison with Samuel's genealogy, which is another Levitical lineage, clearly shows that there are omissions between these priests.

We will examine the Hebrew meanings of the names of the priests from Phinehas's successor to Ahitub.

4th Generation		
1. **Abishua**	אֲבִישׁוּעַ	"my father is rich"

Abishua was Phinehas's son (בֵּן, *ben*; 1 Chr 6:4–5, 50; Ezra 7:5). The name "Abishua" is אֲבִישׁוּעַ (*abishua*) in Hebrew and means "my father is rich."

5th Generation		
2. **Bukki**	בֻּקִּי	"the Lord proved"

Bukki was Abishua's son (בֵּן, *ben*; 1 Chr 6:5, 50–51; Ezra 7:4–5). The name "Bukki" is בֻּקִּי (*buqqi*) in Hebrew, a shortened form of בֻּקִּיָּה (*buqqiyyah*), and means "the Lord proved."

6th Generation

3. Uzzi (Uzziel) | עֻזִּי | "strong" (the Lord is strong)

Uzzi was Bukki's son (בֵּן, *ben*; 1 Chr 6:5–6, 51; Ezra 7:4). The name "Uzzi" is עֻזִּי (*uzzi*) in Hebrew. It is derived from the word עָזַז (*azaz*), which means "strong," and thus the name also means "strong."

In the *Antiquities of the Jews*, Josephus recorded that the high priesthood after Uzzi was passed over from the line of Eleazar, Aaron's third son, to Eli in the line of Ithamar, Aaron's fourth son. He explains as follows:

> *The family of Eleazar officiated as high priest at first, the son still receiving that honor from the father which Eleazar bequeathed to his son Phineas; after whom Abiezer his son took the honor, and delivered it to his son, whose name was Bukki, from whom his son Ozi received it; after whom Eli, of whom we have been speaking, had the priesthood, and so he and his posterity until the time of Solomon's reign. (Ant. 5.361–63)*

7th Generation

4. Zerahiah | זְרַחְיָה | "the Lord has risen"

Zeraiah was Uzzi's son (בֵּן, *ben*; 1 Chr 6:6, 51; Ezra 7:4). The name "Zeraiah" is זְרַחְיָה (*zerahyah*) in Hebrew, a combination of the words זָרַח (*zarah*, "rising") and יָהּ (*yah*, shortened form of *Yahweh*), and means "the Lord has risen."

8th Generation

5. Meraioth | מְרָיוֹת | "rebellious"

Meraioth was Zeraiah's son (בֵּן, *ben*; 1 Chr 6:6, 51–52; Ezra 7:3–4). The name "Meraioth" is מְרָיוֹת (*meraywoth*) in Hebrew, derived from the word מְרָיָה (*merayah*, "rebellion"), and means "rebellion."

9th Generation		
6. **Amariah**	אֲמַרְיָה	"the Lord speaks"

Amariah was the son (בֵּן, *ben*) of Meraioth (1 Chr 6:7, 52). "Amariah" is אֲמַרְיָה (*amaryah*) in Hebrew and is a combination of the words אָמַר (*amar*, "say") and יָהּ (*yah*, shortened form of *Yahweh*); it means "the Lord speaks."

10th Generation		
7. **Ahitub**	אֲחִיטוּב	"my brother is goodness"

Ahitub was the son (בֵּן, *ben*) of Amariah (1 Chr 6:7, 52). He is recorded as Zadok's father in 2 Samuel 8:17. Ahitub is אֲחִיטוּב (*ahituv*) in Hebrew and is a combination of the words אָח (*ah*, "brother") and טוּב (*tuv*, "goodness"); it means "my brother is goodness."

The Life of Samuel the Priest and Prophet

Samuel was a great prophet who guided the people and protected the nation of Israel during the transition from the period of the judges to the period of the monarchy. Samuel is שְׁמוּאֵל (*shemuel*) in Hebrew, meaning "asked/heard of God." Samuel's mother, Hannah, was barren, but she received her son, Samuel, by entreating God (1 Sam 1:20). As a priest, prophet, and judge, Samuel's name was greatly praised even by the generations that succeeded him. He was valued as a man of prayer (Ps 99:6), a great leader comparable to Moses (Jer 15:1), and a prophet who prophesied of the coming of Jesus Christ (Acts 3:24).

1. The Background of Samuel's Birth

Samuel was born during the period of the judges, when all types of sin prevailed over the land of Israel and her politics, economy, society, and religion were mired in chaos. Samuel's father, Elkanah, was a descendant of Kohath the son of Levi (1 Chr 6:33–38) and was from Ramathaim-zophim of the hill country of Ephraim (1 Sam 1:1). His mother was Hannah (1 Sam 1:19–20). Elkanah had two wives, Hannah and Peninnah. Hannah was childless, but Peninnah had children (1 Sam 1:2).

Peninnah provoked Hannah bitterly to irritate her (1 Sam 1:6–7). Hannah was so greatly distressed that she went up to the house of God, where she wept in prayer to God and made a vow. She prayed, "O Lord of hosts, if You will indeed look on the affliction of Your maidservant and remember me, and not forget Your maidservant, but will give Your maidservant a son, then I will give him to the Lord all the days of his life, and a razor shall never come on his head" (1 Sam 1:11).

God heard this prayer and remembered Hannah, so He gave her Samuel (1 Sam 1:19–20).

2. Samuel's Genealogy

An examination of Samuel's genealogy shows that he was a descendant of Izhar (Amminadab; 1 Chr 6:22), the son of Kohath, the son of Levi (Exod 6:18; 1 Chr 6:22–28, 34–38). The Bible clearly states that Samuel was a descendant of the tribe of Levi, but some liberal theologians assert that Samuel was an Ephraimite. William Albright states that Samuel belonged to the tabernacle as a Nazirite and was therefore drawn by Levitical tradition into family attachment to the tribe of Levi although he was from the tribe of Ephraim by birth. He argues that the genealogy was a non-historical attempt by the Chronicler to attach Samuel, an Ephraimite, to the Levite genealogy.[27]

Nevertheless, 1 Samuel 1:1 describes Samuel's father, Elkanah, as an Ephraimite not because he was of the sons of Ephraim but because he lived in the hill country of Ephraim. Unlike the other tribes, the Levites did not have their own allotted land but were scattered throughout the nation and lived among the settlements of other tribes in order to carry out their religious duties. Hence the ancestors of Elkanah, who were Levites, probably settled and continued their livelihood in the hill country of Ephraim.[28]

---

27 William F. Albright, "Samuel and the Beginnings of the Prophetic Movement," in ed. Harry M. Orlinsky, *Interpreting the Prophetic Tradition, The Goldenson Lectures*, 1955–1966, *Library of Biblical Studies* (New York: Ktav, 1969), 161.

28 Robert D. Bergen, *1, 2 Samuel: An Exegetical and Theological Exposition of Holy Scripture*, vol. 7, *The New American Commentary* (Nashville: Broadman & Holman, 2001), 64.

Samuel's genealogy is recorded in 1 Chronicles 6:2–28 and repeated in verses 33–38, making it possible to compare and identify people who were called by two different names. Furthermore, the repetition of Samuel's genealogy alludes to its importance. Samuel was a special person because he anointed both Saul and David king (1 Sam 11:14–15; 16:1, 13).

	1 Chronicles 6:33–38	1 Chronicles 6:22–28	1 Samuel 1:1
1	Levi		
2	Kohath	Kohath	
3	Izhar	Amminadab	
4	Korah	Korah	
5	Ebiasaph	Assir, Elkanah, Ebiasaph (Abiasaph; Exod 6:24)	
6	Assir	Assir	
7	Tahath	Tahath	
8	Zephaniah	Uriel	
	"mighty God"	"God of light"	
9	Azariah	Uzziah	
	"the Lord has helped"	"my strength is the Lord"	
10	Joel	Shaul	
	"the Lord is God"	"hope, great"	
11	Elkanah	Elkanah	
12	Amasai	Amasai, Ahimoth	
13	Mahath		
14	Elkanah	Elkanah	
15	Zuph	Zophai	Zuph
	"honeycomb"	"captive, guard"	"honeycomb"
16	Toah	Nahath	Tohu
	"humble, child"	"rest, calm"	"weakness"
17	Eliel	Eliab	Elihu
	"God is God"	"God is father"	"my God"

18	Jeroham	Jeroham	Jeroham
19	Elkanah	Elkanah	Elkanah
20	Samuel	Samuel	Samuel

The following are notable factors in Samuel's genealogy.

A comparison of the genealogies in 1 Chronicles 6:33–38 and 1 Chronicles 6:22–28 reveals that many persons had two names

Izhar (v. 38) is listed as Amminadab (v. 22), Zephaniah (v. 36) as Uriel (v. 24), Azariah (v. 36) as Uzziah (v. 24), and Zuph (v. 35) as Zophai (v. 26). Toah (v. 34) is listed as both Nahath (v. 26) and Tohu (1 Sam 1:1), and Eliel (v. 34) as both Eliab (v. 27) and Elihu (1 Sam 1:1).

Considering the fact that Uzziah (2 Chr 26:1–4), the tenth king of the southern kingdom of Judah, was also called by the name Azariah (2 Kings 14:21; 15:1; 1 Chr 3:12), it is presumable that the Uzziah and Azariah who appear as Samuel's ancestors were also one person with two names. If Uzziah and Azariah are construed as one person with two names, it is reasonable to consider the possibility of others in the genealogy being listed with different names in the corresponding order of another genealogy.

It contains a detailed record of the sons of Korah

Since 1 Chronicles 6:22–23 reads, "Korah his son, Assir his son, Elkanah his son, Ebiasaph his son and Assir his son," the lineage appears to come down in the order of Korah, Assir, Elkanah, Ebiasaph, Assir. However, 1 Chronicles 6:37 reads "the son of Assir, the son of Ebiasaph, the son of Korah" without reference to Assir and Elkanah.

The key to this issue lies in Exodus 6:24, which states, "The sons of Korah: Assir and Elkanah and Abiasaph; these are the families of the Korahites." According to this verse, Assir and Elkanah were brothers with Ebiasaph (Abiasaph). Thus the genealogy in 1 Chronicles 6:37 is a record of blood lineage, while the genealogy in 1 Chronicles 6:22–23 includes Ebiasaph's brothers, Assir and Elkanah.

3. Samuel's Relationship with Eli the Priest

Eli was the high priest during the time of Samuel's birth. As soon as Samuel was weaned, his mother, Hannah, brought him to Shiloh and entrusted him to Eli so that he could grow up in the house of the Lord (1 Sam 1:24–28). Thus Eli was Samuel's guardian and teacher (1 Sam 2:18–20; 3:8–9).

A look into the family of Eli reveals that he belonged to the Aaronic line of priesthood, not from the line of Eleazar but from that of Ithamar (see 1 Chr 24:3–6). His sons, Hophni and Phinehas, were worthless men who did not know the Lord. They despised the offering of the Lord (1 Sam 1:3; 2:12, 17, 34; 4:4, 11, 17). In the end they died in a battle against the Philistines. Upon hearing the news of their deaths, Eli fell back from his chair and broke his neck and died (1 Sam 4:18). At the same time Phinehas's wife was dying as she gave birth, and she named her son Ichabod (אִי־כָבוֹד, "inglorious"; 1 Sam 4:19–21). According to 1 Samuel 14:3 and 22:11, Ichabod had an older brother, Ahitub, who had sons: Ahijah and Ahimelech.

Ahimelech had a son named Abiathar, who was a priest along with Zadok during David's time (2 Sam 8:17). He was the priest who helped David during Absalom's rebellion (2 Sam 15:24–26). During King Solomon's time, however, he participated in Adonijah's rebellion and was divested of the high priesthood (1 Kgs 1:7; 2:35). From this time on, the descendants of Zadok from the line of Eleazar made up the sole lineage that continued the high priesthood.

4. Samuel's Ministry

When Eli the high priest died at the age of ninety-eight, Samuel succeeded him and ministered as a prophet. Samuel's age at this time is believed to have been thirty years old, the minimum age required for service in the temple (1102 BC; 1 Sam 3:19–20; see Num 4:3; 2 Sam 5:4–5; Ezek 1:1; Luke 3:23). Samuel's ministry from this time on included the following.

He was victorious in the battle against the Philistines at Mizpah

Around 1082 BC, when Samuel was fifty years old (see 1 Sam 7:1–2), he led a movement for the spiritual awakening of Israel and gathered the people at Mizpah (1 Sam 7:3–5). There the people drew water and poured it out before the Lord, fasting in repentance (1 Sam 7:6). When the Philistines drew near for battle, Samuel offered up to God a whole burnt offering and cried out to the Lord and prayed (1 Sam 7:7–9). God, who heard this earnest prayer, thundered with a great thunder against the Philistines and confused them and allowed Israel to be victorious (1 Sam 7:10).

Samuel took a stone to commemorate this victory and set it between Mizpah and Shen; he named it "Ebenezer" ("stone of help"), saying, "Thus far the Lord has helped us" (1 Sam 7:12).

He ruled over Israel all his life

First Samuel 7:15–17 states, "Samuel judged Israel all the days of his life. He used to go annually on circuit to Bethel and Gilgal and Mizpah, and he judged Israel in all these places. Then his return was to Ramah, for his house was there, and there he judged Israel; and he built there an altar to the Lord."

In his old age Samuel made his sons, Joel and Abijah (1 Sam 8:1–2), judges over Israel. His sons, however, did not follow in the steps of their father's faith but took bribes and perverted justice (1 Sam 8:3). The sins of Samuel's sons were indelible blots in Samuel's life.

He anointed King Saul and King David

When Samuel's sons did not follow the ways of Samuel, all the elders of Israel came out and requested a king (1 Sam 8:4–5). Samuel opposed this idea, because the establishment of human kingship signified rejection of God's rule. In the end, however, God permitted Saul to be anointed king because the people were obstinate (1 Sam 8:7, 10–22; 10:1; 11:15).

When Saul disobeyed God's Word after becoming king, God proclaimed through Prophet Samuel, "Because you have rejected the word of the Lord, He has also rejected you from being king" (1 Sam 15:23; see also 1 Sam 15:22, 26). After this Samuel anointed David according to God's command and prepared him to be king in Saul's place (1 Sam 16:1, 13).

He was a conscientious leader who took strong measures against sin

Samuel was a conscientious leader. After Saul became king, Samuel testified that he had lived with integrity according to his conscience all his life (1 Sam 12:3, 5). The people also acknowledged his testimony, saying, "You have not defrauded us or oppressed us or taken anything from any man's hand" (1 Sam 12:4; see also 1 Sam 12:5). Samuel was a leader whose conscience was so pure that he could bear witness to his own integrity (see 2 Cor 4:2), and the people acknowledged it.

Samuel fiercely rebuked the people's sin of asking for a king and urged the people to live a life of total obedience to God's commands thereafter (1 Sam 12:13–15). In order to make the people understand how sinful it had been to ask for a king, Samuel prayed to God during a wheat harvest season when there would be no rain, asking for thunder and rain. When the Lord sent thunder and rain that day, all the people greatly feared the Lord and Samuel (1 Sam 12:16–18).

Furthermore, Samuel rebuked Saul when he sinned. Saul had disobeyed God's command, "Go and strike Amalek and utterly destroy all that he has, and do not spare him; but put to death both man and woman, child and infant, ox and sheep, camel and donkey" (1 Sam 15:3). Samuel pointed out Saul's sin and relayed a stern message of judgment that God had rejected Saul from being king (1 Sam 15:17–26).

Samuel's name is also listed in Hebrews 11, the "chapter of faith" (Heb 11:32). The basis of his faith lies in ceaseless prayer and the ministry of the Word. In 1 Samuel 12:23, he confessed, "As for me, far be it from me that I should sin against the Lord by ceasing to pray for you; but I will instruct you in the good and right way."

Samuel ministered according to the Word without selfish motives and upheld his calling faithfully with a pure conscience. He is indeed the model of a great leader for today's society, which is diffused with unrighteousness and corruption.

2. Solomon's Temple

Thirteen generations of high priests between 959 BC and 586 BC

David, who had earnestly desired to build the temple, could not do so because he had shed too much blood in battlefields; but he prepared everything needed for the construction of the temple (1 Chr 28:2–3, 11–19). Then Solomon began the construction of the temple in the month of Ziv (second month) in the fourth year of his reign, and he completed it after six years and six months, in the month of Bul (eighth month) in the eleventh year of his reign (1 Kgs 6:1, 37–38). Solomon's temple was the first stationary temple in the history of Israel (2 Sam 7:5–7). It was built on a mountain in Moriah, where Abraham had offered up Isaac (Gen 22:2). It had also been the threshing floor of Ornan, where David had repented and made an offering to the Lord (2 Chr 3:1).

With the construction of Solomon's temple, the priests and the Levites no longer needed to carry the tabernacle and all the utensils for its service (1 Chr 23:25–26). The temple was the place of God's presence and the center of the divine reign (1 Kgs 9:3; 2 Chr 7:15–16) for about 373 years (959–586 BC) until it was destroyed by Nebuchadnezzar of Babylon in 586 BC (2 Kgs 25:13–17; Jer 52:13).

11th Generation

1. **Zadok**	צָדוֹק	"righteousness"

Zadok was Ahitub's son (בֵּן, *ben*; 2 Sam 8:17; 1 Chr 6:8, 52–53; 18:16) and Ahimaaz's father (1 Chr 6:8). The name "Zadok" is צָדוֹק (*tsadoq*) in Hebrew and means "righteousness." Zadok served from the time of David's reign until the early years of Solomon's reign.

***First*, Zadok worked at David's side while David was fleeing from Absalom.**

When David was fleeing because of Absalom's rebellion, Zadok wanted to carry the ark of God together with Abiathar and all the Levites and follow David (2 Sam 15:24). However, David had fully acknowledged that Absalom's rebellion was God's punishment toward him for taking Bathsheba, Uriah's wife (2 Sam 12:9–12), and thus sent Zadok back to Jerusalem along with the ark of God (2 Sam 15:25).

This was an act based on faith. David did not want the ark of God—which symbolizes God's presence—to wander about with him as he began his life of a fugitive because of his sin. He believed that he would be able to see the ark and its place again if he found favor with God, but even if God were to give him up at the crucial moment, he confessed that he would still trust completely in God's will and obey Him, saying, "Behold, here I am, let Him do to me as seems good to Him" (2 Sam 15:26). Even in the worst of situations, David did not despair and did the best he could, asking Zadok to inform him about the circumstances in Jerusalem (2 Sam 15:27–29). Thus Zadok and Abiathar returned the ark of God to Jerusalem as David had commanded and remained there. With the help of David's friend Hushai, they played a crucial role in defeating the counsel of Ahithopel, who had sided with Absalom (2 Sam 17:15–23).

***Second*, Zadok actively helped David in his return to the palace.**

After Absalom's death, all the tribes of Israel wanted to bring David back to the palace in Jerusalem (2 Sam 19:9–10). When David heard this news, he sent Zadok and Abiathar to request that the tribe of Judah take the lead in his return to the palace (2 Sam 19:11–12). As a result, the hearts of the people of Judah were moved, and David was able to return safely to the palace (2 Sam 19:14–15). Zadok played a significant role in moving the hearts of the people of the tribe of Judah.

***Third*, Zadok established Solomon as king.**

When David's son Adonijah attempted to take the throne in Solomon's place, the priest Abiathar sided with Adonijah, while Zadok sided with David and Solomon until the end (1 Kgs 1:7–8). Together with Prophet Nathan, Zadok anointed Solomon and made him king as David had commanded (1 Kgs 1:32–39). First Kings 1:39 states, "Zadok the priest then took the horn of oil from the tent and anointed Solomon. Then they blew the trumpet, and all the people said, 'Long live King Solomon!'"

***Fourth*, Zadok established the lineage of the high priests for generations.**

Until this point in time, two lines of high priests—the line of Eleazar and the line of Ithamar (1 Chr 24:1–5)—had held the office of high priesthood together. Until Solomon finished building the temple, the tabernacle was at Gibeon (1 Kgs 3:2–4; 1 Chr 21:29; 2 Chr 1:3, 13), and the ark of the covenant was at the city of David (2 Sam 6:17; 1 Chr 15:1; 16:1; 2 Chr 8:11). Since sacrifices were offered to God at both places, priests served at both places (1 Chr 16:37–39; 2 Chr 1:3–6).

At the time of Solomon's enthronement, Zadok was the priest from the line of Eleazar and Abiathar from the line of Ithamar. However, Abiathar was divested of the high priesthood because he sided with Adonijah the traitor. First Kings 2:26–27 states, "To Abiathar the priest the king said, 'Go to Anathoth to your own field, for you deserve to die; but I will not put you to death at this time, because you carried the ark of the Lord God before my father David, and because you were afflicted in everything with which my father was afflicted.' So Solomon dismissed Abiathar from being priest to the Lord, in order to fulfill the word of the Lord, which He had spoken concerning the house of Eli in Shiloh."

Now what does "in order to fulfill the word of the Lord, which He had spoken concerning the house of Eli" mean? God had prophesied that the house of the priest Eli would forever lose the priesthood because of his and his sons' sins. First Samuel 2:30 states, "Therefore the Lord God of Israel declares, 'I did indeed say that your house and the house of your father should walk before Me forever'; but now the Lord declares, 'Far be it from Me.'" In accordance to this prophecy, Hophni and Phinehas—the two sons of Eli from the line of Ithamar—were killed on the same day (1 Sam 2:34; 4:17), but the succession of the high priesthood was actually cut off after Abiathar, who became the last priest in the lineage. From this time on, the sons of Zadok, from the line of Eleazar, monopolized the high priesthood.

Later on, during the period of the Babylonian captivity, Prophet Ezekiel prophesied that the priests from the line of Zadok would minister in the new temple that he saw in a vision (Ezek 40:46; 43:19). Ezekiel 44:15 states, "'The Levitical priests, the sons of Zadok, who kept charge of My sanctuary when the sons of Israel went astray from Me, shall come near to Me to minister to Me; and they shall stand before Me to offer Me the fat and the blood,' declares the Lord God."

Zadok faithfully served David and Solomon and fulfilled his duties well. God said that he would cut off the family of Eli from the priesthood but would "raise up for [Himself] a faithful priest" (1 Sam 2:35). This faithful priest refers to Samuel at the time, but also historically, to Zadok. The word "faithful" is אָמַן (*aman*) in Hebrew and means "to believe," "to confirm," or "to put trust in." Zadok was a person on whom God could rely, and he firmly fulfilled the calling that was entrusted to him. Ezekiel 48:11 identifies the portion that the sons of Zadok would receive: "It [the holy allotment] shall be for the priests who are sanctified of the sons of Zadok, who have kept My charge, who did not go astray when the sons of Israel went astray as the Levites went astray."

How was Zadok able to carry out his duties so faithfully? It was because Zadok was a seer. Second Samuel 15:27 states, "The king said also to Zadok the priest, 'Are you not a seer?'" A seer is רוֹאֶה (*roeh*) in Hebrew and means "one who sees," referring to a person who learns of God's will beforehand and proclaims it. Thus Zadok was faithful in carrying out his calling by trying to make judgments righteously according to God's will and doing his best to fulfill them.

12th Generation

2. Ahimaaz אֲחִימַעַץ "my brother is wrath"

Ahimaaz was Zadok's son (2 Sam 15:27, 36; 18:19–30; 1 Chr 6:8, 53) and Azariah's father (1 Chr 6:9). The name "Ahimaaz" is אֲחִימַעַץ (*ahimaats*) in Hebrew, a combination of the words אָח (*ah*, "brother") and מַעַץ (*maats*, "wrath"), and means "my brother is wrath."

***First*, Ahimaaz informed David about Absalom's schemes.**
Zadok's son Ahimaaz and Abiathar's son Jonathan were given the task of delivering to David news from the king's house in Jerusalem during Absalom's rebellion (2 Sam 15:36). When David was fleeing from Absalom, Ahithophel counseled Absalom that he should strike David immediately (2 Sam 17:1–3), and Hushai, David's friend, counseled Absalom that he should strike David slowly, after gathering many people first (2 Sam 17:11–14). Absalom accepted Hushai's counsel. When his counsel was rejected by Absalom, Ahithophel foresaw that he would die a wretched death for conspiring to get rid of David, and he went to his home, set his house in order, and strangled himself to death (2 Sam 17:23).

At the most urgent moment, Hushai informed the two priests, Zadok and Abiathar, that David should cross over the Jordan immediately and escape (2 Sam 17:15–16). Zadok's son Ahimaaz and Abiathar's son Jonathan, fearful that they might be seen entering Jerusalem, were staying at En-rogel (עֵין רֹגֵל, *en rogel*, "fountain of the spies"). While they were in En-rogel, a maidservant who acted as their informant brought them the news from Zadok and Abiathar (2 Sam 17:17). At this time Ahimaaz and Jonathan were discovered by Absalom's spy, so they ran quickly and went into the house of a man in Bahurim. There they escaped danger by hiding inside a well in the man's courtyard. After great difficulty they succeeded in sending their message to David (2 Sam 17:18–20). Ahimaaz the priest had risked his life to help David.

***Second*, Ahimaaz informed David of the news of victory.**
When Absalom died, Ahimaaz wanted to quickly bring the news to David, so he asked Joab the army commander to send him to David (2 Sam 18:19). Joab, however, sent a Cushite to bring the news. Ahimaaz thus made another request to Joab and then departed to bring the news. Although Ahimaaz departed much later than the Cushite, his fervent loyalty for David led him to run by the way of the plain, pass the Cushite, and bring the news of victory to David first. Nevertheless, he could not bring himself to tell David that Absalom had died (2 Sam 18:23, 28–29).

In accordance with his name, Ahimaaz was a man full of holy wrath. That is why he risked his life to inform David of Hushai's counsel and was the first person to bring David the news of victory. We too need attitudes like Ahimaaz's so we may also be filled with holy wrath and take the lead when it comes to doing God's work (2 Cor 7:11).

13th Generation

3. **Azariah**	עֲזַרְיָה	"the Lord has helped"

Azariah was Ahimaaz's son and Johanan's father (1 Chr 6:9). The name "Azariah" is עֲזַרְיָה (*azaryah*) in Hebrew, a combination of עָזַר (*azar*, "to help") and יָה (*yah*, shortened form of *Yahweh*), and means "the Lord has helped."

The Bible contains no particular records regarding Azariah's works.

14th Generation

4. **Johanan**	יוֹחָנָן	"the Lord has been gracious"

Johanan was Azariah's son, and his son's name was also Azariah (1 Chr 6:9–10). The name "Johanan" is יוֹחָנָן (*yohanan*) in Hebrew, a combination of the Hebrew words יְהוָה (*YHWH*) and חָנַן (*hanan*, "to be gracious"), and means "the Lord is gracious."

The Bible contains no particular records regarding Johanan's works.

The six generations of high priests 9th Amariah, 10th Ahitub, 11th Zadok, 12th Ahimaaz, 13th Azariah, and 14th Johanan were omitted from Ezra's genealogy (Ezra 7:1–5).[29]

15th Generation

5. Azariah | עֲזַרְיָה | "the Lord has helped"

Azariah was Johanan's son and Amariah's father (1 Kgs 4:1–2; 1 Chr 6:10–11; Ezra 7:3). The name "Azariah" is עֲזַרְיָה (*azaryah*) in Hebrew, a combination of the words עָזַר (*azar*, "to help") and יָהּ (*yah*, shortened form of *Yahweh*), and means "the Lord has helped."

Regarding Azariah, 1 Chronicles 6:10 states, "Johanan became the father of Azariah (it was he who served as the priest in the house which Solomon built in Jerusalem)." It is understood that a priest was to serve in the temple in Jerusalem; however, the above verse emphasizes this obvious point in order to highlight Azariah's faithfulness in carrying out his priestly duties. The word "served" in the phrase "served as the priest" is in the piel (intensive) stem of כָּהַן (*khahan*, "ministered as priest") in Hebrew and shows that Azariah ministered faithfully as a priest.

16th Generation

6. Amariah | אֲמַרְיָה | "the Lord speaks"

29 While four of the six names omitted are listed in Ezra 7:1–5 (Amariah, Ahitub, Zadok, and Azariah), these are other priests with the same names. These six priests are omitted between Meraiaoth (8th generation) and Azariah (15th generation) in Ezra 7:3.

Amariah was Azariah's son and Ahitub's father (1 Chr 6:11). The name "Amariah" is אֲמַרְיָה (*amaryah*) in Hebrew and is a combination of the words אָמַר (*amar*, "say") and יָהּ (*yah*, shortened form of *Yahweh*) and means "the Lord speaks."

King Jehoshaphat, the fourth king of the southern kingdom of Judah (871–847 BC), established a central judicial court in Jerusalem and allowed the knowledgeable high priest Amariah to handle the trials over religious issues. Thus 2 Chronicles 19:11 states, "Amariah the chief priest will be over you in all that pertains to the Lord." Jehoshaphat instituted a judicial system based on faith, and Amariah the high priest was respected enough to take charge of this duty.

17th Generation

7. **Ahitub** אֲחִיטוּב "my brother is goodness"

Ahitub was Amariah's son (1 Chr 6:11–12; Ezra 7:2–3). The name "Ahitub" is אֲחִיטוּב (*ahituv*) in Hebrew, a combination of the words אָח (*ah*, "brother") and טוּב (*tuv*, "goodness"), and means "my brother is goodness."

The Bible contains no particular records regarding Ahitub. When we compare the life and times and chronologies of Judah's kings and high priests, however, we can infer that Ahitub is, in fact, the high priest Jehoiada, who was active during the reign of King Joash (Jehoash), the eighth king of Judah. The following reasons lead to this conclusion.

Ahitub's father, Amariah, served as high priest during the reign of Jehoshaphat (871–847 BC), the fourth king of Judah (2 Chr 19:11). Azariah was high priest during the reign of Uzziah (Azariah), the tenth king (791–739 BC; 2 Chr 26:16–20). Fifty-six years passed between Jehoshaphat's death and Uzziah's accession, which is about the length of time two high priests could have served.

Two priests served during this period, according to the records of the high priests who took the office between the high priest Amariah during the time of Jehoshaphat's reign and the high priest Azariah during the time of Uzziah's reign. They were high priests Jehoiada and Zechariah, his son, during the reign of Joash (835–796 BC), the eighth king of Judah (2 Kgs 12:2–15; 2 Chr 24:2–14, 20). Jehoiada was the husband of Jehoshabeath, who hid Joash the prince when Athaliah attempted to destroy all the royal offspring of the house of David (2 Chr 22:10–11). Ultimately he made a great contribution in continuing the royal lineage of David by executing Athaliah and establishing the then seven-year-old Joash as king (2 Kgs 11:4–21; 2 Chr 23:1–21).

Moreover, 1 Chronicles 9:11 and Nehemiah 11:11, which record the genealogy of the priests who returned from the Babylonian captivity and settled in Jerusalem, lists Meraioth as Ahitub's son:

> *Azariah the son of Hilkiah, the son of Meshullam, the son of Zadok, the son of Meraioth, the son of Ahitub, the chief officer of the house of God . . . (1 Chronicles 9:11)*

> *Seraiah the son of Hilkiah, the son of Meshullam, the son of Zadok, the son of Meraioth, the son of Ahitub, the leader of the house of God . . . (Nehemiah 11:11)*

The Hebrew text for this verse reveals that the phrase "the chief officer of the house of God" refers to Ahitub, not Azariah (Seraiah). The New International Version translates 1 Chronicles 9:11 as, "Azariah son of Hilkiah, the son of Meshullam, the son of Zadok, the son of Meraioth, the son of Ahitub, the official in charge of the house of God . . ." From the phrase "the chief officer of the house of God" (1 Chr 9:11), the word "chief" is נְגִיד (*negid*) in Hebrew and means "leader" (1 Sam 9:16, NLT). This is the construct form of the word נָגִיד (*nagid*), meaning "ruler" (2 Sam 5:2), and it most likely refers to the high priest who was in charge of the house of God. Azariah in the above verse shares the same name with the grandfather of Jehozadak, who was among those taken to Babylon when Jerusalem fell (1 Chr 6:14–15). It is possible that he could be another descendant of the house of

Azariah and was named after his ancestor.

"The chief of the house of God" refers to the high priest. Considering that this expression was used to describe Ahitub, it seems to emphasize that Ahitub carried out his duties more faithfully than any other high priest. This also supports the conjecture that Jehoiada (יְהוֹיָדָע, "the Lord knows"), who was one of the most faithful of all the high priests in this time period, is the same person as Ahitub.

The Bible records that Jehoiada reached a ripe old age and died at the age of 130 (2 Chr 24:15). This implies a long period of priesthood for Jehoiada, who succeeded his father Amariah, the high priest during Jehoshaphat's time. Regarding this, John Lightfoot asserts that Ahitub was Jehoiada and that Meraioth was Jehoiada's son Zechariah.[30]

Amariah (1 Chr 6:11; 2 Chr 19:11)	**Amariah**
Ahitub (1 Chr 6:11–12)	**Jehoiada** (or Berechiah; Matt 23:35)
Meraioth (1 Chr 9:11; Neh 11:11)	**Zechariah**
Azariah (2 Chr 26:16–20)	**Azariah**

The name "Meraioth" is מְרָיוֹת (*meraywoth*) in Hebrew, derived from the word מְרָיָה (*merayah*, "rebellion"), and means "rebellion." Customarily no one from the lineage of the holy high priests gave his children names with negative meanings. Presumably, this name meaning "rebellion" came about as the succeeding generations began to call Zechariah by the name "Meraioth," denouncing the wickedness of his generation, namely, the latter part of King Joash's reign. It was a period when people were wicked enough to stone to death a priest who proclaimed the Word of God. Jesus also mentioned this

30 John Lightfoot, *The Whole Works of the Rev. John Lightfoot, D.D., Master of Catherine Hall, Cambridge*, ed. John Rogers Pitman (London: J. F. Dove, 1823), 28.

incident while He was rebuking the rebelliousness of the scribes and Pharisees (Matt 23:35).

If Jehoiada was Ahitub and Zechariah was Meraioth, then it becomes evident that they both died one year before Joash's death. After the death of Jehoiada the high priest, Joash began to worship idols. When Jehoiada's son Zechariah rebuked his idol worship, Joash killed him. Then Joash died one year later, in 796 BC. Thus Zechariah was martyred in 797 BC (2 Chr 24:20–25).

18th Generation

8. **Zadok**	צָדוֹק	"righteousness"

Zadok was the high priest listed after Ahitub (1 Chr 6:12; Ezra 7:2). The name "Zadok" is צָדוֹק (*tsadoq*) in Hebrew and means "righteousness." The Bible contains no particular records regarding Zadok's works.

19th Generation

9. **Shallum**	שַׁלּוּם	"retribution, peace"

Shallum was the high priest listed after Zadok (1 Chr 6:12–13; Ezra 7:2). The name "Shallum" (שַׁלּוּם, *shallum*) is derived from שָׁלַם (*shalam*), which means "to recompense" or "to be safe." The Bible contains no particular records regarding Shallum's works.

20th Generation

10. **Hilkiah**	חִלְקִיָּה	"my portion is the Lord"

Hilkiah was the high priest listed after Shallum (1 Chr 6:13; Ezra 7:1–2). The name "Hilkiah" is חִלְקִיָּה (*hilqiyyah*) in Hebrew, a combination of the words חֵלֶק (*heleq*, "portion") and יָהּ (*yah*, shortened form of *Yahweh*), and means "my portion is the Lord."

Hilkiah was high priest during the reign of Josiah, the sixteenth king of Judah (640–609[b] BC). While he was taking the money brought to the temple for the temple repairs according to the king's command, he discovered the book of the law and delivered it to the king through Shaphan the scribe (2 Kgs 22:3–10; 2 Chr 34:8–18). As soon as King Josiah heard the message written in the book of the law, he ripped his clothes and repented. He then carried out an extensive religious reformation not only in all Judah but also in the regions belonging to the northern kingdom of Israel (2 Kgs 22:11–23:20; 2 Chr 34:19–33). The book of the law that the high priest Hilkiah discovered became the impetus for the religious reformation, and Hilkiah faithfully led the reforms (2 Kgs 23:4–7).

21st Generation

11. **Azariah** עֲזַרְיָה "the Lord has helped"

Azariah was the high priest listed after Hilkiah (1 Chr 6:13–14; Ezra 7:1). The name "Azariah" is עֲזַרְיָה (*azarya*) in Hebrew, a combination of the words עָזַר (*azar*, "to help") and יָהּ (*yah*, short form of *Yahweh*), and means "the Lord has helped." The Bible contains no particular records regarding Azariah's works.

22nd Generation

12. **Seraiah** שְׂרָיָה "the Lord is ruler"

Seraiah is the high priest listed after Azariah (1 Chr 6:14; Ezra 7:1). The name "Seraiah" is שְׂרָיָה (*serayah*) in Hebrew, a combination of the words שָׂרָה (*sarah*, "have power") and יָהּ (*yah*, shortened form of *Yahweh*), and means "the Lord is ruler."

Seraiah was the high priest during the reign of King Zedekiah, the last king of Judah (597–586 BC). When Judah fell at the hands of King Nebuchadnezzar of Babylon, Nebuzaradan, the captain of the guard, captured Seraiah and took him before the king. The king then put him to death at Riblah in the land of Hamath (2 Kgs 25:18–21; Jer 52:24–27).

23rd Generation		
13. **Jehozadak** (Jozadak)	יְהוֹצָדָק	"the Lord is righteous"

Jehozadak is the high priest listed after Seraiah (1 Chr 6:14–15). The name "Jehozadak" is יְהוֹצָדָק (*yehotsadaq*) in Hebrew, a combination of the words יָהּ (*yah*, shortened form of *Yahweh*) and צֶדֶק (*tsedeq*, "be righteous"), and it means "the Lord is righteous." In some places in the Bible "Jehozadak" is recorded as "Jozadak" (יוֹצָדָק, "the Lord is righteous"; Ezra 3:2, 8; 5:2; Neh 12:26).

First Chronicles 6:15 states, "Jehozadak went along when the Lord carried Judah and Jerusalem away into exile by Nebuchadnezzar." Here the word "carried" is in the hiphil stem of the word גָּלָה (*galah*, "to uncover, send into exile"). This means that God uncovered the people of Judah and sent them into exile, indicating that Judah's captivity to Babylon was God's punishment. No other biblical records of Jehozadak's works exist besides his being taken into Babylonian captivity. The historian Josephus records Jehozadak as a high priest (*Ant.* 10.153; 20.231).

Jehozadak's (Jozadak's) son Joshua (Jeshua) was the high priest who returned to Jerusalem along with Zerubbabel and participated in the construction of the temple (Ezra 3:2, 8–9).

The high priests omitted between **Ahitub** (17th generation) and **Zadok** (18th generation)

The high priests who historically ministered between Ahitub and Zadok have been omitted in the genealogy in 1 Chronicles 6.

The first high priest omitted is Jehoiada's son, Zechariah, who is presumed to have been the same person as Meraioth (1 Chr 9:11; Neh

11:11), who was discussed in the section for the seventeenth generation. The second high priest omitted is Azariah (2 Chr 26:16–20); the third, Urijah (2 Kgs 16:10–16); and the fourth, Azariah (2 Chr 31:10, 13).

Azariah	עֲזַרְיָה	"the Lord has helped"

Azariah was the high priest who served after Meraioth. The name "Azariah" is עֲזַרְיָה (*azaryah*) in Hebrew, a combination of the words עָזַר (*azar*, "to help") and יָהּ (*yah*, shortened form of *Yahweh*), and means "the Lord has helped."

Azariah was the high priest during the reign of King Uzziah, the tenth king of Judah (2 Chr 26:17, 20). King Uzziah became leprous around 750 BC and lived in a separate house, and his son Jotham was his coregent (2 Kgs 15:5; 2 Chr 26:21). This came upon Uzziah because his heart became proud when he became strong. He acted corruptly and sinned against God by entering into the temple of the Lord and burning incense on the altar of incense himself. In order to stop the king, the high priest Azariah brought eighty courageous priests and told him to leave the sanctuary, for only the priests from the descendants of Aaron could offer incense. Nevertheless, King Uzziah was unwilling to listen and became enraged with the priests. Immediately, leprosy broke out on his forehead (2 Chr 26:16–20).

As evident from this incident, Azariah was the high priest in 750 BC. If he had begun to serve in 797 BC, when Zechariah was martyred, he would have held the office for forty-seven years by this time. If not, there must have been another high priest between Zechariah and Azariah.

Urijah	אוּרִיָּה	"flame of the Lord"

Urijah was the high priest who served after Azariah. The name "Urijah" (אוּרִיָּה) is a combination of the words אוּר (*ur*, "flame") and יָהּ (*yah*, shortened form of *Yahweh*), meaning "flame of the Lord." Urijah was the high priest during the reign of King Ahaz (731–715 BC), the twelfth king of Judah. Ahaz copied the pattern of the altar of the idols he had seen in Damascus of Assyria and built the altar in front of the house of the Lord. He made the priest make offerings on this altar and changed the pattern of the temple as he wished. Urijah followed these commands submissively (2 Kgs 16:10–18). Considering the fact that Urijah was in a position to take direct orders from the king, it can be presumed that he was a high priest.

Azariah עֲזַרְיָה "the Lord has helped"

Azariah was the high priest who served after Urijah. The name "Azariah" is עֲזַרְיָה (*azaryah*) in Hebrew, a combination of the words עָזַר (*azar*, "to help") and יָהּ (*yah*, shortened form of *Yahweh*), and means "the Lord has helped."

Azariah served as high priest during the reign of King Hezekiah, the thirteenth king (729[b]–686 BC; official reign twenty-nine years, from 715 BC to 686 BC; 2 Chr 31:10, 13). In the process of the religious reformation that Hezekiah led, he commanded the people who lived in Jerusalem to give the portion of the burnt offerings that was due the priests and the Levites that they might devote themselves to the law of the Lord. The sons of Israel brought in the tithe so abundantly that what they brought was placed in heaps (2 Chr 31:4–8). Azariah, the high priest from the house of Zadok, reported to Hezekiah, "Since the contributions began to be brought into the house of the Lord, we have had enough to eat with plenty left over, for the Lord has blessed His people, and this great quantity is left over" (2 Chr 31:10). The description of Azariah in 2 Chronicles 31:13, "the chief officer of the house of God," also reflects that he was the high priest.

3. Zerubbabel's Temple

Six generations of high priests between 515 BC and 320 BC

When the southern kingdom of Judah fell at the hands of Babylon in 586 BC, Solomon's temple, which had been the center of the Israelites' lives for about 370 years, was also destroyed (2 Kgs 25:8–17; 2 Chr 36:17–19; Jer 52:12–23). In 537 BC, the Israelites began to come back in their first return from captivity. In 536 BC, they began to rebuild the temple, but the work came to a halt due to interference from their enemies. The construction was finally completed in 516 BC (Ezra 3:8; 4:1–5; 6:15; Hag 1:14–15).

This temple was called Zerubbabel's temple because Zerubbabel, the leader of the first group to return from exile, led its construction (Zech 4:9). This new temple paled in comparison to Solomon's temple, but it was still adequate as the center of the Israelites' life of faith after their return.

24th Generation

1. **Joshua** or Jeshua	יְהוֹשֻׁעַ	"the Lord is salvation"

Joshua was the son of Jehozadak who was taken captive to Babylon (Hag 1:1). The name "Joshua" is יְהוֹשֻׁעַ (*yehoshua*) in Hebrew, a combination of the words יְהוָה (*YHWH*, "Yahweh") and יָשַׁע (*yasha*, "to save"), and means "the Lord is salvation." Joshua is also called "Jeshua," יֵשׁוּעַ (*yeshua*; Ezra 3:2, 8; 5:2; 10:18; Neh 12:1).

The Bible clearly records many times that Joshua was a high priest (Hag 1:1, 12, 14; 2:2, 4; Zech 3:1, 8; 6:11). He was most likely born when his father, Jehozadak, was taken captive to Babylon. Frank M. Cross asserts that Joshua was born around 570 BC. If so, Joshua was about thirty-three years old during the first return of the Jews to their home in 537 BC and fifty years old when the halted reconstruction of the temple resumed. He must have been about fifty-four years old when the temple was completed in 516 BC and officially began to serve as high priest from this time until 490 AD. He presumably lived until age eighty.[31]

***First*, Joshua was the first high priest in the postexilic era following the first return.**

The Jews were taken captive to Babylon with the fall of Jerusalem in 586 BC. The first group returned from the Babylonian exile in 537 BC under the leadership of Zerubbabel the governor and Joshua the high priest. The decree of restoration was proclaimed in the first year (538 BC) of Cyrus the king of Persia, and in 537 BC, a total of 49,897 people returned to the land of Judah (Ezra 2:1–65; see Neh 7:66–67; 49,942 people).

***Second*, Joshua was a leader who took the lead in the reconstruction of the temple.**

Joshua returned from the Babylonian exile with Zerubbabel (Ezra 2:2; Neh 7:7; 12:1). They first built an altar to the Lord to offer burnt offerings on it (Ezra 3:2–6) and began to rebuild the temple. Ezra 3:8 states, "In the second year of their coming to the house of God at Jerusalem in the second month, Zerubbabel the son of Shealtiel and Jeshua the son of Jozadak and the rest of their brothers the priests and the Levites, and all who came from the captivity to Jerusalem, began the work and appointed the Levites from twenty years and older to oversee the work of the house of the Lord."

The Israelites who returned from Babylon in 537 BC laid the foundations for the temple in the second month of 536 BC and began the construction work (Ezra 3:8–13). Nonetheless, disruptions by enemies halted the work for about sixteen years until it resumed in 520 BC. The following was the process through which the construction resumed.

31 James C. VanderKam, *From Joshua to Caiaphas: High Priests after the Exile* (Minneapolis: Augsburg Fortress, 2004), 19–20.

First, in the second year of King Darius, on the first day of the sixth month, the word of the Lord came to Zerubbabel and Joshua through Prophet Haggai (Hag 1:1). Zerubbabel, Joshua, and the people realized that they had sinned by letting the construction work come to a halt and leaving the house of God in desolation (Hag 1:2–11).

Second, in the second year of King Darius, on the twenty-fourth day of the sixth month, the Lord stirred up the spirit of Zerubbabel, Joshua, and all the people to begin working on the house of the Lord again (Hag 1:14–15). Here the word "stirred" is the hiphil (causative) stem of עוּר (*ur*, "to rouse oneself, awake"), signifying that God had awakened their spirits (רוּחַ, "heart"). We cannot do God's work if He does not awaken us.

Third, in the second year of King Darius, on the twenty-first day of the seventh month, the word of the Lord came by Haggai (Hag 2:1) to take courage even though the new temple might seem like nothing in comparison to the former (Hag 2:3–5). The Lord declared, "They [nations] will come with the wealth [Jesus Christ] of all nations," and "the latter glory of this house will be greater than the former" (Hag 2:7, 9).

This reconstruction progressed with King Darius's active support (Ezra 6:1–12) until it was completed on the third day of the month of Adar (twelfth month) in 516 BC, that is, in the sixth year of King Darius (Ezra 6:14–15). This great event had finally taken place after the long seventy-year period since the temple of Jerusalem had been destroyed in 586 BC. All this was possible through the mighty power of God's Word given to Zerubbabel and Joshua (Zech 4:6–10).

25th Generation

2. Joiakim יוֹיָקִים "the Lord raises up"

Joiakim was the son of Joshua the high priest and the second high priest of the postexilic period. Nehemiah 12:10 states, "Jeshua became the father of Joiakim," and Nehemiah 12:26 states, "These served in the days of Joiakim the son of Jeshua, the son of Jozadak, and in the days of Nehemiah the governor and of Ezra the priest and scribe."

The name "Joiakim" (יוֹיָקִים) is the shortened form of "Jehoiakim" (יְהוֹיָקִים) and is a combination of the words יְהוָה (*YHWH*, "Yahweh") and קוּם (*qum*, "to rise, arise"), meaning "the Lord raises up."

***First*, Joiakim the high priest presumably came back in the first return.**

Nehemiah 12:26 states, "These served in the days of Joiakim the son of Jeshua, the son of Jozadak, and in the days of Nehemiah the governor and of Ezra the priest and scribe." Ezra was the leader of the second return, and Nehemiah was the leader of the third return. The fact that Joiakim's name is listed along with these names shows that Joiakim ministered as high priest after the return from the exile. Joiakim must have come back in the first return (537 BC) along with the leader Joshua and become high priest before the second return (458 BC). Nehemiah 12:12 and 12:26 reveal the genealogical list and clearly differentiate the periods.

***Second*, it is likely that Joiakim assisted in the reconstruction of Zerubbabel's temple.**

Ezra 3:9 states, "Jeshua with his sons and brothers stood united with Kadmiel and his sons, the sons of Judah and the sons of Henadad with their sons and brothers the Levites, to oversee the workmen in the temple of God." Joiakim was probably included in the reference to "Jeshua with his sons." Joiakim returned with his father, Joshua, and worked hard on rebuilding the temple; he was most likely then appointed as the high priest to succeed Joshua before the second return took place (458 BC).

26th Generation

3. Eliashib אֶלְיָשִׁיב "God restores"

Eliashib was Joiakim's son and the third high priest of the postexilic period. Nehemiah 12:10 states, "Joiakim became the father of Eliashib." The name "Eliashib" is אֶלְיָשִׁיב (*elyashiv*) in Hebrew, a combination of the words אֵל (*el*, "God") and שׁוּב (*shuv*, "to return"), meaning "God restores."

***First*, Eliashib was a leader in repairing the northern walls of Jerusalem.**

After the third group of Jews returned from Babylon, Jerusalem's city walls were rebuilt under the direction of Nehemiah. The Tower of the Hundred and the Tower of Hananel belonged to the northern wall, the most dangerous area, where the threat of attack was the highest. Eliashib, however, was the first to lead the work to rebuild the northern wall. Nehemiah 3:1 states, "Eliashib the high priest arose with his brothers the priests and built the Sheep Gate; they consecrated it and hung its doors. They consecrated the wall to the Tower of the Hundred and the Tower of Hananel." As the high priest, Eliashib encouraged the people by taking the lead in rebuilding the wall and setting an example for them.

Nehemiah 3:14–19 contains the list of the main contributors to the construction of the city wall on the southeastern part of Jerusalem, leading to the front of the ascent of the armory at the Angle, while verses 20–32 contain the list of main contributors to the construction of the city wall on the eastern part of Jerusalem from the Angle to the Sheep Gate. The biggest number of people listed represents the contributors to the eastern wall, because that wall stretched the longest at about 650 meters. The work on this section of the wall was led by Baruch the son of Zabbai (Neh 3:20). Zabbai had married a Gentile and repented (Ezra 10:28), and Baruch was a priest (Neh 10:6–8). Baruch, along with Eliashib the high priest, participated in the building of the Sheep Gate, which is part of the northern city wall (Neh 3:1). He not only built the Sheep Gate but also rebuilt the wall from the Angle to the doorway of the house of Eliashib the high priest.

According to Nehemiah 3:21, Meremoth rebuilt the section from the doorway of the house of Eliashib, who was high priest at the time, to the end of his house. This shows not only that the house of the high priest was large but also that there was extensive damage to the house and that a great amount of work was needed.

***Second*, Eliashib prepared a large room in the temple for Tobiah.** Nehemiah served as the governor of Judah for about twelve years (444–433 BC). He returned to Persia but came back to Judah about one year later, in 432 BC. While Nehemiah was away, the high priest Eliashib built a relationship with Tobiah the Ammonite, who tenaciously disrupted the rebuilding of the city walls (Neh 2:10, 19, 4:3, 7–8, 6:1, 12–14, 17–19), and gave Tobiah a large room in the house of God (Neh 13:4–7). When Nehemiah became aware of this, he threw all Tobiah's household goods out of the room and cleansed the room. He then returned the utensils of the house of God with the grain offerings and the frankincense to the room (Neh 13:8–9). Nehemiah's holy wrath is reminiscent of Jesus Christ driving out the merchants from the temple (Matt 21:12–13; Mark 11:15–17; Luke 19:45–46; John 2:13–17).

***Third*, Eliashib allowed his grandson to become Sanballat's son-in-law.** Nehemiah 13:28 states, "Even one of the sons of Joiada, the son of Eliashib the high priest, was a son-in-law of Sanballat the Horonite, so I [Nehemiah] drove him away from me." When the Israelites had returned from the exile in Babylon, they had vowed that they would not intermarry with the Gentiles (Neh 10:29–30; see Ezra 9:1–10:44; Neh 13:23–27). Nonetheless, the vow had been broken by the high priest's household. Moreover, they had intermarried with the family of Sanballat (Neh 2:10, 19; 4:1–2, 7–8; 6:1–9, 12–14), who had interfered with the rebuilding of Jerusalem's walls. This was truly a grave sin (Lev 21:14–15).

At first Eliashib set an example for the people by taking the lead in the work to rebuild the city walls; but later he sinned greatly before God by intermarrying with a Gentile family that was an enemy of Israel.

27th Generation

4. **Joiada**	יְהוֹיָדָע	"the Lord knows"

Joiada was Eliashib's son and the fourth high priest of the postexilic period. Nehemiah 12:10 states, "Eliashib became the father of Joiada." Nehemiah 12:22 also mentions "the days of Eliashib, Joiada, and Johanan and Jaddua" and records the genealogy of the high priests in order. After Eliashib's death, Joiada succeeded his father as high priest (*Ant.* 11.297).

The name "Joiada" is the same as יְהוֹיָדָע (*yehoyada*) in Hebrew, a combination of the words יְהוָה (*YHWH*, "Yahweh") and יָדַע (*yada*, "to know"), and means "the Lord knows."

Joiada allowed one of his sons to become Sanballat's son-in-law (Neh 13:28). This was an act of defiling the priesthood and breaking the covenant (Neh 13:29). Nehemiah drove out the son of Joiada who had married Sanballat's daughter. From the phrase "drove him away," the words "drove away" are in the hiphil (causative) stem with the waw-consecutive form of the word בָּרַח (*barah*), indicating that Nehemiah immediately drove him away. The person driven out was not Joiada the high priest but his son. Sin had to be driven out immediately in order to preserve the holiness of the community.

The last prayer of Nehemiah, who had acted decisively with regard to sin, was "Remember me, O my God, for good" (Neh 13:31). This is a courageous prayer that only someone who preserved the purity of the community of the chosen people could offer up.

28th Generation			
5.	**Johanan** or	יוֹחָנָן	"the Lord has been gracious"
	Jonathan	יוֹנָתָן	"God has given"

Johanan was Joiada's son and the fifth high priest of the postexilic period (Neh 12:22). In Nehemiah 12:22, "Eliashib, Joiada, and Johanan and Jaddua" are listed according to their lineage. Also, Nehemiah 12:23 states, "The sons of Levi, the heads of fathers' households, were registered in the Book of the Chronicles up to the days of Johanan the son of Eliashib." The name "Johanan" is יְהוֹחָנָן (*yehohanan*) in Hebrew and means "the Lord has been gracious." It is recorded as יוֹנָתָן ("*Jonathan*," "given of God") in Nehemiah 12:11; Josephus recorded him as "Joannes" (*Ant.* 11.297–302).

Johanan served during the rule of Artaxerxes II (404–359 BC). The Elephantine Papyri—literary remains discovered in the Elephantine Island of Egypt—contains records of the lifestyle of the Jews in Egypt around the fifth century as well as their petition to build a temple there. It also documents the letter the Jews in Elephantine had sent to Johanan.[32] Part of the text recounts the following:

> *In the month of Tammuz [fourth month], year fourteen [410 BC] of King Darius [Darius II, 423–404 BC], when Arsames . . . conspired . . . to wipe out the temple of the god Yaho from the fortress of Elephantine . . . We have also sent a letter before now, when this evil was done to us, [to] our lord and to the high priest Johanan and his colleagues the priests in Jerusalem . . . To this day, we have been wearing sackcloth and fasting . . . Also, from then to now, in the year seventeen of King Darius [407 BC], no meal-offering, incense, nor burnt offering have been offered in this temple.*

32 James B. Pritchard, ed., *Ancient Near Eastern Texts Relating to the Old Testament* (Princeton: Princeton University Press, 1958), 491–92.

This period coincides with the period in which Johanan served as high priest (410–371 BC).

Johanan was an ungodly man who became high priest after killing his younger brother named Jesus during an argument inside the temple. According to Josephus's writings, Artaxerxes's general Bagoses, who had been close to Jesus, promised Jesus that he would take the high priesthood from Johanan and give it to him. Enraged by this, Johanan killed Jesus and became high priest (*Ant.* 11.298–99). Arguments among priests and murder inside the temple are quite shocking. Bagoses, never having seen such a primitive act of sin (a priest killing his younger brother inside the temple), was traumatized and asked, "Have you had the impudence to perpetrate murder in the temple?" Thus using this incident as an excuse, Bagoses defiled the temple and imposed a tax on the Jews, afflicting them for seven years (*Ant.* 11.300–301).

29th Generation

6. Jaddua יַדּוּעַ "knowing"

Jaddua was Johanan's son and the sixth high priest of the postexilic period. Nehemiah 12:22 lists the lineage as "Eliashib, Joiada, and Johanan and Jaddua," and Nehemiah 12:11 states, "Jonathan became the father of Jaddua." The name "Jaddua" originated from the Hebrew word יָדַע (*yada*) and means "knowing." Josephus also writes that when Jonathan died, his son Jaddua succeeded him as high priest (*Ant.* 11.302).

Jaddua was the last high priest recorded in the Old Testament. He served during the reigns of Darius III, the last king of Persia (336/335–331 BC), and Alexander the Great of Greece (336–323 BC).

No biblical records of Jaddua's works exist, but a few historical events are recorded in Josephus's writings.

Josephus writes that Jaddua had a younger brother named Manasseh, who married Nicaso, the daughter of Sanballat, the Samaritan governor (*Ant.* 11.302–3; see Neh 13:28). The elders of Jerusalem, fearing another wave of intermarriages with the Gentiles, opposed Manasseh serving as priest in the temple alongside Jaddua, for Manasseh was married to a Gentile. They warned that Manasseh should either get a divorce or refrain from approaching the altar. Jaddua was also enraged with Manasseh and drove him away from the altar. When Manasseh told his father-in-law of his intent to divorce Nicaso, Sanballat promised him that he would allow Manasseh to keep his priesthood. He also promised that he would appoint him governor of Samaria and build him a temple on top of Mount Gerizim, the highest mountain in Samaria, under the condition that he continued to live with his daughter. Thus Manasseh drew closer to Sanballat, and consequently chaos ensued as many priests and people intermarried with Gentiles (*Ant.* 11.310–11).[33]

The high priest during the latter years of the Persian Empire was the head not only of religion but also of political and military affairs. The high priest played the role of the highest ruler who communicated with the empire's central government. When Alexander was on his way to attack Tyre after defeating Darius at the Battle of Issus (333 BC, battle between Darius III of Persia and Alexander of the Great), he asked for support from Jaddua the high priest. Alexander's request to the high priest for resources as well as military support indicates not only that Judah must have possessed great military strength at the time but also that the high priest even held supreme command over the military.

Jaddua refused this request, but Sanballat seized the opportunity and betrayed King Darius. He took eight thousand soldiers with him to assist Alexander and asked Alexander to build a temple in Samaria in return. Alexander agreed to build a temple because he be-

---

33 Sanballat from Jaddua's era is a different person from "Sanballat the Horonite" mentioned in Nehemiah 13:28. According to Josephus, Sanballat who built the temple in Samaria during Jaddua's time lived during the rule of Darius III (336/335–331 BC; *Ant.* 11.302). Thus there were at least two governors of Samaria named "Sanballat" under Persian Rule.

lieved Sanballat's words that another temple in Samaria would divide the Jews and make it easier to control them. In the end, an additional temple was built on Mount Gerizim in Samaria, and Manasseh became its first high priest. After this the dissension between the Jews and the Samaritans grew until they stopped having any dealings with one another (John 4:9). About two hundred years later, in 128 BC, John Hyrcanus I attacked Samaria and destroyed this temple on Mount Gerizim (*Ant.* 13.254–56).

On the other hand, Jaddua, who was overcome with fear after refusing Alexander's request, had an unexpected dream in which God told him to stand on Alexander's side. Consequently, all the Jews welcomed Alexander when he came into Jerusalem, and Alexander happily accepted their welcome. This was because Alexander believed that Daniel's prophecy of the Greek who would destroy the Persian Empire was referring to him (Dan 8:21; 11:3), and thus he had come to believe that God would help him. Hence Alexander readily accepted Jaddua's request to allow the Jews to continue living in accordance with their laws and customs (*Ant.* 11.326–39).

4. Herod's Temple

Among all the high priests who served in Zerubbabel's temple, Jaddua was the last person mentioned in the Old Testament. However, more high priests served until 63 BC, when the Romans devastated Zerubbabel's temple. Most of the high priests who served in Zerubbabel's temple came from the Hasmonean dynasty.

Herod's temple was built during the period of Roman rule, and it was built with a political motive from the start. Herod the Great, a Gentile from Idumaea (Edom), built the temple in order to ease the animosity of the Jews and win their favor so that the Roman emperor would acknowledge him as a competent ruler. Therefore, only the high priests appointed by Herod's royal family—that is, those who supported Herod's reign—were put in charge of the temple. Offerings became a mere ritual and formality, and the religious leaders became extremely corrupt. Consequently, many of the temple's original functions were lost. Thus the high priests after the Old Testament period are not classified by the temple in which they served. The high priests from Jaddua to the priest prior to King Herod's reign are classified by era, while the high priests from the time of King Herod onward are classified by their appointers.

The following is a broad summary of Herod's temple.

Around 20 BC (see John 2:20), King Herod started reconstruction work on the Zerubbabel's temple that had been captured by the Roman general Pompey in 63 BC. It was finally completed about eighty-four years later, in AD 64. Herod's temple was the third and last temple built in the history of Israel. Although the temple was also known as the Second Temple, the name that reflects the hope of the Jews, it was actually the third temple.[34] When Pompey captured Jerusalem, he entered the temple to assert his authority but took no plunder, thus showing his respect for it. The history of Zerubbabel's temple closed when Herod, having carefully preserved it from any major damage when he gained control over Jerusalem in 37 BC, began to dismantle it in about 21 BC in preparation for the construction of his own grand temple.[35] Herod's temple was built in the contemporary Greco-Roman architectural style. Hence it must be regarded as distinct from Zerubbabel's temple.[36]

Herod's temple was not only the center of Israel's religious life but also the main stage of Jesus' public ministry. When Jesus had just

---

34 "The reason the Christians here follow the Jews is because of the prophecy of Haggai (2:6, 9), which they expound of the Messiah's coming to the second or Zorobabel's temple, of which they suppose this of Herod to be only a continuation, which is meant, I think, of his coming to the fourth and last temple, or to that future, largest, and most glorious one . . . ; whence I take the former notion ["Second Temple"), how general soever, to be a great mistake" (*Ant.* 15.380, footnote).

35 Walter A. Elwell and Barry J. Beitzel, *Baker Encyclopedia of the Bible*, vol. 2 (Grand Rapids: Baker, 1998), 2025.

36 Ibid., 2026.

begun His public ministry, He went up to Jerusalem and stood before Herod's temple, which was still unfinished even though a great multitude of people had been working on it for forty-six years. He then told the people to destroy the temple (John 2:19), for He would raise it up in three days. None of the Jews understood the meaning of Jesus' statement and mocked and condemned Him, saying, "It took forty-six years to build this temple, and will You raise it up in three days?" (John 2:20).

Herod's temple was such a beautiful and spectacular work of architecture that it is considered the greatest of Herod's achievements during his reign. The temple was built with marble, of which some pieces were as tall as twelve meters and as heavy as one hundred tons. The roof was covered with pure gold plates that reflected the sun from morning until evening so that anyone who looked at the temple could not help but admire it (Matt 24:1–2; Mark 13:1–2; Luke 21:5–6).

Later the Judean governor Florus (AD 64–66) took some treasures from the storehouse in Herod's temple and triggered the Judean war, which ultimately led to the destruction of Judea. Although its grandeur seemed as if it would last forever, Herod's temple was completely destroyed in AD 70 by the Roman General Titus, only about seven years after its completion. It happened exactly as Jesus had prophesied. This was clearly the price of the high priests' and religious leaders' sin of killing Jesus (Matt 27:24–26). While destroying Herod's temple, the Roman soldiers tore down each stone as unconfirmed rumors spread that huge amounts of silver and gold could be found between the stones. This was in fulfillment of Jesus' prophecy, "As for these things which you are looking at, the days will come in which there will not be left one stone upon another which will not be torn down" (Luke 21:6).

When the temple itself was totally destroyed (AD 70), the role of the high priest became nominal, and his power collapsed to the ground. From this time on, the center of Jewish society shifted from the priesthood to Pharisaic beliefs, which concentrated on the study of the law.

CHAPTER

13

The History of High Priests Classified by Time Period

The Old Testament ends with the book of Malachi. After Jaddua, the last high priest to be recorded in the Old Testament (Neh 12:11, 22), we find very few records of appointed high priests from 320 BC to AD 70. The New Testament records only a few of them: Annas, Caiaphas, and Ananias. The history of the high priests after Jaddua can be found in *Antiquities of the Jews* and *The Jewish War*, written by the Jewish historian Flavius Josephus. The books of the Maccabees also contain accounts of the high priests; although they are part of the Apocrypha, their historicity is well recognized.

The oldest and most important record of Jewish history after the era of Persian rule is *Antiquities of the Jews* (*Ant.*) by Flavius Josephus (AD 37–100).[37] For four years, from AD 66 to AD 70—the latter years of Emperor Nero's reign—the Jews engaged in armed resistance against

37 Flavius Josephus was a Jewish historian. He was born in AD 37 (the year Gaius Caligula became emperor of Rome) and lived until the early second century. In his autobiography he introduced his family as the chief family of the first of the twenty-four courses (divisions) of priests. He also reveals that he was of royal blood by his mother (*The Life of Flavius Josephus,* 1).

the Romans to drive them out of Judea (Israel) and gain independence. At the heart of this Jewish resistance was Josephus, from the lineage of the high priests. However, Josephus surrendered to Roman forces in a siege led by Vespasian, who was a Roman general at the time. After his release from imprisonment, he wrote *The Jewish War* (seven volumes), *Antiquities of the Jews* (twenty volumes), and *Against Apion* (two volumes) while living in Rome. Among existing Jewish history books, these contain the most comprehensive account of Jewish history beginning with the fall of Persia and are considered must-reads to learn the history of Rome and Judea during that period.[38]

In particular, Josephus records in his books a list of the high priests. He explained that his ancestors were zealous in preserving their records and passing them down to their descendants. Since he was a priest from a prominent family of priests, his records are considered reliable.[39] As evidence, Josephus wrote in *Against Apion*,

> *As to our forefathers, that they took no less care about writing such records (for I will not say they took greater care than the others I spoke of), and that they committed that matter to their high priests and to their prophets, and that these records have been written all along down to our own times with the utmost accuracy; nay, if it be not too bold for me to say it, our history will be so written hereafter;—I shall endeavor briefly to inform you.* (Apion 1.29)

Furthermore, Josephus pointed out the importance of preserving the "stock of the priests" unmixed and pure, hence the need to archive such information (*Apion* 1.30–35). He also made the following conclusion regarding the genealogy of the high priests:

---

38 Raymond F. Surburg, *Introduction to the Intertestamental Period* (St. Louis: Concordia, 1975), 161–62.

39 VanderKam, *From Revelation to Canon: Studies in the Hebrew Bible and Second Temple Literature* (Leiden: Brill, 2000), 239.

> *What is the strongest argument of our exact management in this matter is what I am now going to say, that we have the names of our high priests, from father to son, set down in our records, for the interval of two thousand years.* (Apion 1.36)

Josephus provided lists of the high priests in two places within his writings in addition to many individual references (*Ant.* 10.152–53; 20.224–51). It is clear that Josephus recorded the names of the high priests without omission in order to prove the veracity of their history.[40]

The books of 1 and 2 Maccabees recount the history from the Jews' return from the Babylonian exile until the fall of Jerusalem. As the last history books after the Old Testament era, their historicity is acknowledged.[41] Raymond F. Surburg asserts that 1 and 2 Maccabees are accepted as important books for the study of intertestamental history. He states that 1 Maccabees, in terms of its value as a history book, has been highly regarded for the reliability of its content. Its redactional method of recording history is characterized by direct expressions and truthfulness.[42]

The following are noteworthy evaluations of the books of the Maccabees:

> ***First Maccabees** is the most important historical writing in the Apocrypha. It is the primary resource for writing the history of the period that it covers, 180 to 134 BC.*[43]

> *The books of 1 and 2 Maccabees are two of the most important works relating to Jewish history during the Greek period* (see Jew-

40 Ibid.

41 Merrill C. Tenney, *New Testament Survey* (Grand Rapids: Eerdmans, 1985), 102.

42 Surburg, *Introduction to the Intertestamental Period*, 119.

43 Clayton Harrop, "Apocrypha, Old Testament," ed. Chad Brand et al., *Holman Illustrated Bible Dictionary* (Nashville, TN: Holman Bible Publishers, 2003), 81

ish History: Greek Period). Virtually all that we know about Seleucid rule, the Maccabean revolt and the rise of the Hasmonean kingdom come from them. Their value is further enhanced in that they seem to have been written relatively soon after the events they purport to describe.[44]

That the author of 1 Maccabees aims at giving a correct narrative, and that on the whole his account is correct, is the opinion of practically all scholars. The simple, straight-forward way in which he writes inspires confidence, and there can be no doubt that we have here a first-class authority for the period covered (175–135 BC). It is the earliest Jewish history which dates events in reference to a definite era, this era being that of the Seleucids, 312 BC, the year of the founding of that dynasty.[45]

The books of the Maccabees cover the times of the high priest Onias III's ruling (185–175 BC), the independence movement of Mattathias and his sons, and the defeat of Seleucus until the foundation of the Hasmonean dynasty. Regarding the high priests, it records the extremely wicked high priests under the control of Seleucus (Jason, Menelaus, and Alcimus) as well as the high priests of the Hasmonean dynasty.

Thus the books of the Maccabees and the works of Josephus are essential for understanding the intertestamental period. They are the most important and only source of information concerning the

44 Lester L. Grabbe, "1 and 2 Maccabees," *Dictionary of New Testament Background: A Compendium of Contemporary Biblical Scholarship* (Downers Grove, IL: InterVarsity Press, 2000), 657.

45 T. Witton Davies, "Maccabees, Books Of," ed. James Orr et al., *The International Standard Bible Encyclopaedia* (Chicago: The Howard-Severance Company, 1915), 1948.

46 Emil Schürer, *A History of the Jewish People in the Time of Jesus Christ*, second division, vol. 1 (Edinburgh: T&T Clark, 1890), 35.

political history of that period.[46]

In discussing the history of the high priests after the Old Testament era, this book cites references in the following short form: Josephus's *Antiquities of the Jews* as "*Ant.*," *The Jewish War* as "*War*," *Against Apion* as "*Apion*" and the books of the Maccabees as "1 Macc." and "2 Macc."

1. The Period of the Ptolemaic and Seleucid Reigns

The seven generations of high priests between 320 BC and 175 BC

In the fourth century BC, Alexander the Great from Macedonia (336-323 BC) emerged and conquered the entirety of Persia, Egypt, and the main dominant powers of that time, building the new Greek Empire. Nonetheless, Alexander the Great died shortly afterward, and Greece was divided among his four generals: Ptolemy, Seleucus, Lysimachus, and Cassander. Among them the Ptolemaic dynasty (323–30 BC) and the Seleucid dynasty (312–64 BC), respectively, ruled over Judea. The Ptolemaic dynasty ruled over Judea from about 320 BC until the Seleucid dynasty took it over after Antiochus III, the Seleucid king of the north, defeated Ptolemy V of the south in the Battle of Paneas in 198 BC (Dan 11:15–16).

The Ptolemaic dynasty adopted a policy by which it enjoyed financial benefits from the subjugated nations but did not concern itself with their domestic affairs. Thus the Jews enjoyed religious and cultural freedom under the Ptolemaic reign. It was during this time that they completed the Septuagint (LXX), the translation of the Old Testament into the Greek language, in the city of Alexandria, the center of Greece.

During this time the office of the high priest—the chief leader of the people of Judea—had to be approved by the Greeks or Romans who ruled over Judea. The high priests of the Zadokite lineage, who had served since the time of King Solomon, kept their office until just before the reign of Antiochus IV of the Seleucid dynasty. Among the high priests appointed after the reign of Antiochus IV, however, Jason, Menelaus, and Alcimus were extremely wicked even though they were genealogical descendants of Aaron.

30th Generation

1. **Onias I** Son of Jaddua	320–280 BC	forty years

Onias I was the son of Jaddua, the last high priest to be recorded in the Old Testament and the first high priest during the period of Greek rule. After the high priest Jaddua died following the death of King Alexander, his son Onias succeeded him (*Ant.* 11.346–47). The name "Onias" means "the Lord is gracious," and Onias served as high priest for about forty years, from 320 BC to 280 BC.

The first book of Maccabees gives an account of a letter from King Arius of Sparta to Onias the high priest that conveys his desire to live as brothers, because the Spartans and the Jews are both descendants of Abraham (1 Macc. 12:20–23). Since Arius I ruled from 309 BC to 265 BC, we can confirm the period during which Onias I served as high priest.[47]

31st Generation

2. **Simon I** Son of Onias I	280–260 BC	twenty years

As the son of Onias I, Simon I served for twenty years, from 280 BC to 260 BC (*Ant.* 12.42). The name "Simon" means "God has heard."

Simon exerted great effort in repairing the temple that had been destroyed during the reign of Ptolemy I and was greatly revered by the people for his many achievements. "Simon the high

47 VanderKam, *From Joshua to Caiaphas*, 127–28.

priest, the son of Onias, . . . in his life repaired the house again, and in his days fortified the temple" (Ecclesiasticus 50:1). He was called "righteous" (*Ant.* 12.42), because he was righteous before God and merciful to the people (Ecclesiasticus 50:1–29).[48] The Mishnah[49] (m.*Parah* 3:5) records "Simon the Righteous" in the list of the seven high priests who slaughtered the red heifer and prepared the water of ashes that removes impurity (Num 19:1–10).[50]

32nd Generation

3. **Eleazar**	Brother of Simon I	260–245 BC	fifteen years

When Simon I died, leaving behind only a young son named Onias II, Simon's younger brother Eleazar served as high priest (*Ant.* 12.43–44). This was probably done in accordance with what was written in Numbers 27:8–9: "If a man dies and has no son, then you shall transfer his inheritance to his daughter. If he has no daughter, then you shall give his inheritance to his brothers."

Eleazar served as priest for fifteen years during Ptolemy II Philadelphus's reign (285–246 BC). By God's special providence, it was during this time that Jewish scholars received support from Ptolemy II to translate the Old Testament, originally in the Hebrew language, into Greek—the *lingua franca* (i.e., a language adopted as a common language between speakers whose native languages are different) at the time. This translation became known as the Septuagint (LXX, actually translated by seventy-two people). According to the *Letter of Aristas*, the letter from Ptolemy II to the high priest Eleazar, Ptolemy II asks Eleazar to send six people from each of the twelve tribes, a total of seventy-two persons, in order to translate the Old Testament into the Greek lan-

48 Ibid., 147.

49 *Mishnah*, meaning "repetition," originates from the Hebrew word *shanah*, meaning "to study and review." The Mishnah is a commentary written according to the themes of the Old Testament; it not a new law but a compilation of laws passed down through oral tradition.

50 VanderKam, *From Joshua to Caiaphas*, 147.

guage (*Ant.* 12.44–50).

The fact that the king of a nation personally sent a letter to the Jewish high priest indicates that even the Gentiles acknowledged the high priest's role as the chief ruler of Judea. Furthermore, the fact that the high priest Eleazar was able to answer the king's questions on the law implies that he was proficient in the law. Since no records of other rulers besides Eleazar exist, it is highly possible that the high priest also played the role of a political leader.[51]

33rd Generation

4. **Manasseh** Brother of Onias I 245–240 BC five years

When Eleazar died, Manasseh, Onias I's brother, succeeded Eleazar as high priest and served for about five years, from 245 BC until 240 BC (*Ant.* 12.157). Presumably, Simon the Righteous's son Onias II could not serve as high priest, either because he was too young or some political influence hindered him.[52] Among ancient Jewish historians, Josephus is the only one who mentioned Manasseh in his writings, and he gave no detailed records regarding Manasseh's achievements or deeds.

34th Generation

5. **Onias II** Son of Simon I 240–218 BC twenty-two years

Onias II was Simon I's son, and he served as high priest for twenty-two years, from 240 BC until 218 BC (*Ant.* 12.157). He was a minor when his father Simon I died. Hence his uncle Eleazar and then his great-uncle Manasseh officiated for him until he was able to assume

51 Ibid., 160.

52 Ibid., 168.

the high priesthood (*Ant.* 12.42–44, 157). He was probably named according to the practice of papponymy, the custom at the time to name a grandson after his grandfather in the family of the high priests.

According to Josephus, Onias II had an excessive attachment to money and was very greedy (*Ant.* 12.158–59). Under Ptolemaic rule, the most important duty of the high priest was to collect annual taxes and pay tribute. When Onias II refused the duty of paying taxes, King Ptolemy gave the duty to the family of Tobiah (*Ant.* 12.160–61, 175–78).[53] Tobiah was an Ammonite who opposed the rebuilding of Jerusalem's walls along with Sanballat the Horonite during Nehemiah's time (Neh 2:10; 4:1–3; 6:1–19). The descendants of Tobiah profited greatly both politically and economically in those days under Ptolemaic rule.

35th Generation

6. **Simon II**	Son of Onias II	218–185 BC	thirty-three years

Simon II was Onias II's son as well as Onias III and Jason's father (*Ant.* 12.224). Simon II served as high priest during a period of upheaval (198 BC, after the Battle of Paneas), when Ptolemaic rule over Judea ended and Seleucid rule began.

In the midst of the intense conflict between the Ptolemaic and Seleucid dynasties, Ptolemy IV (221–203 BC) defeated Antiochus III of the Seleucid dynasty in the Battle of Raphia (217 BC), which took place near the end of the fourth Syrian War (Dan 11:11–12). It is recorded in the Maccabees that the high priest Simon II went out as the representative of the Jews to receive Ptolemy IV, since Judea had no other rulers. At his arrival in Jerusalem, however, Ptolemy IV went to

53 The high priests' responsibility in paying Judea's tribute reflects their "authority" in political as well as religious leadership, which was described as *prostasia* (προστασία: "the chief political office") in the early Hellenistic era (*Ant.* 12.4.1–2, §§158, 161).

the temple to give an offering and attempted to enter into the holy of holies. Simon II tried to dissuade him and stop him from entering. As he persisted, Simon II and the people lifted up supplication to God Most High. God answered their prayers by shaking Ptolemy IV to and fro so that he was left lying on the ground powerless (3 Macc. 1:1–2:24).

36th Generation

7. **Onias III**	Son of Simon II	185–175 BC	ten years

Onias III was Simon II's son (*Ant.* 12.225) and the last legitimate high priest from the line of Zadok. Accounts of Onias III are found in the book of Daniel as well as in 2 Maccabees and 1 Enoch. He served sometime between 187 BC and 175 BC.[54]

Onias III solemnly kept the laws, as he was a pious high priest. Jerusalem enjoyed peace under Onias III, and Seleucus IV made payments for temple offerings from his own income (2 Macc. 3:1–3). However, a temple governor by the name of Simon clashed with Onias III over the regulations governing the city market in Jerusalem. Simon reported to Apollonius, the governor of Coele-Syria and Phoenicia, that the treasury in the temple of Jerusalem was full of money that was not being used for the sacrifices, so the king was free to take it (2 Macc. 3:4–6). Thus the king immediately sent his financial official, Heliodorus, to seize the temple treasury. Heliodorus threatened Onias III under the pretense of a treasury inspection in order to enter the temple (Dan 11:20). Greatly troubled, Onias III and all the people prayed together. Suddenly Heliodorus, who was drawing near the treasury, fainted, and the treasury was preserved (2 Macc. 3:7–40).

Some time later Seleucus IV died, and Antiochus IV (Epiphanes) succeeded the throne. Then Jason, Onias III's younger brother, bribed the king and seized his brother's high priesthood (2 Macc. 4:7–

54 VanderKam, *From Joshua to Caiaphas*, 189.

10). Three years later Onias III was murdered at the instigation of his other brother, Menelaus, who had usurped the high priesthood from Jason (2 Macc. 4:23–34). The Jews regard Onias III's death as the greatest turning point in the history of the postexilic period. They view his death as the fulfillment of the prophecy in Daniel 9:26: "Then after the sixty-two weeks the Messiah will be cut off and have nothing." They also believe Onias III to be the "prince of the covenant" mentioned in Daniel 11:22.

2. The Extremely Wicked High Priests During the Seleucid Reign

Three generations of high priests between 175 BC and 159 BC

Antiochus IV (175–163 BC) of the Seleucid dynasty severely oppressed Judaism by forbidding all worship and religious activities, including circumcision, keeping of the Sabbath, and abiding by the law. He went as far as to place the image of Zeus in the temple of God and call the temple the temple of Zeus (*Ant.* 12.248–56, *War* 1.34–35). He built temples for idol worship in various places in Judea and burned many books of the law. Anyone who opposed this was ruthlessly executed. Furthermore, anyone who did not discard everything related to Judaism and adopt Hellenism was considered an outlaw. Such an outlaw underwent great miseries and inhumane bitter torments until eventual death. As a result, all Jews trembled in dreadful terror. Even in the midst of all this, those who were faithful to God's covenant to the end despite the threat of death kept their faith and chose the path of martyrdom (1 Macc. 1:62–64). The book of Hebrews offers a vivid account of such faith (Heb 11:35–38).

The image of Zeus—the "abomination of desolation" (Dan 11:31; Matt 24:15; Mark 13:14)—remained in the temple for three years, from the twenty-fifth day of the twelfth month in 167 BC until the twenty-fifth day of the twelfth month in 164 BC, when Judah Maccabee, the son of Mattathias, rose up and cleansed the temple (1 Macc. 4:36–39). Jerusalem was finally recovered on the twenty-fifth day of the month of Kislev (the twelfth month in solar calendar) in 164 BC (1 Macc. 4:52), and an eight-day dedication feast was held after the purification of the temple. This feast became the origin of the Hebrew "festival of lights" known as *Hanukkah* ("dedication"), or the Feast of the Dedication (John 10:22; *Ant.* 12.285, 316–325).

During this period the rulers of the Seleucid dynasty appointed wicked people such as Jason, Menelaus, and Alcimus (Jakim) who were sympathetic to their policies and gave them great financial assistance.

High priests were supposed to preserve the holiness of the temple, bear the entire nation upon their shoulders, and offer up whole sacrifices to God for the people. Yet these wicked priests betrayed and abused God's name, the temple, and the nation for their own wealth, honor, and power. They were so thoroughly corrupt that they became shameless thieves who devoured people's precious tax money.

37th Generation

1. **Jason** Younger brother of Onias III 175–172 BC three years

Jason was Simon II's son and Onias III's younger brother. He served as the high priest for three years (175–172 BC; 2 Macc. 4:7). Onias IV, the son of Onias III, was still an unweaned baby at this time and could not serve as high priest (*Ant.* 12.237). By changing his original name, "Jesus," to the Hellenistic name "Jason" (*Ant.* 12.239), he became the first high priest to use a Hellenistic name rather than the Semitic name. At this time Seleucus IV was assassinated by his subordinate Heliodorus, and Antiochus IV (Epiphanes) became king (175 BC; see Dan 11:21) in accordance with the prophecy, "Within a few days he will be shattered, though not in anger nor in battle" (Dan 11:20). Jason paid Antiochus IV an extensive bribe in exchange for his appointment as high priest to replace his brother Onias III. He secured the high priesthood by vowing that he would wholeheartedly support Antiochus's policy to Hellenize Judea (2 Macc. 4:7–9).

Jason actively introduced ways of life that conflicted with Jewish law, causing a heavy influx of foreign customs (2 Macc. 4:10–17). Many Jews who had been proud of the law and the offerings that had been passed down from their ancestors began to hanker after the Hellenistic culture. Some even removed their marks of circumcision in order to mingle with the Greeks (*Ant.* 12.241; 1 Macc. 1:15). Ultimately, Jason completely overthrew his duties as God's high priest and acted as a puppet controlled by the Seleucid dynasty. From this time on, the high priest's role became greatly perverted to that of exercising political power. Daniel describes such traitors who led the movement toward Hellenism as "transgressors" (Dan 8:23).

Jason lost the high priesthood to Menelaus and went to the land of Ammon (2 Macc. 4:26). During this time he heard the false rumor that Antiochus IV had died during a second military expedition to Egypt (170–168 BC). He then took over one thousand soldiers and attacked Jerusalem by surprise and recklessly slaughtered his own people (2 Macc 5:5–6).

Later Jason was forced to flee from his brother Menelaus and hide in Ammon. Despised as an oppressor of his own nation and people, he wandered from city to city until he was ultimately driven out to Egypt. He had banished many people, and now he was banished to foreign countries, going from Ammon to Egypt and then on a ship to Sparta, and he ultimately died in a foreign country. Jason died with no one mourning for him, no funeral, and no burial among his ancestors (2 Macc. 5:7–10).

38th Generation

2. **Menelaus** Younger brother of Onias III or Brother of Simon (governor of the temple)

172–162 BC | ten years

Menelaus was Onias III's and Jason's younger brother (*Ant.* 12.238) and Onias IV's uncle (*Ant.* 12.387). He is also recorded as the brother of Simon, the governor of the temple, from the house of Bilgah (2 Macc. 3:4; 4:23). Bilgah belonged to the fifteenth division among the twenty-four divisions of the high priests that had been established by David (1 Chr 24:14; Neh 12:5, 18). Menelaus served as high priest for ten years, from 172 BC until 162 BC (*Ant.* 12.385).

Menelaus enticed Antiochus IV with the lie that he would outbid his brother Jason by three hundred talents of silver, and thus he secured the high priesthood (2 Macc. 4:24–27). Although the high priesthood could not be established or abolished by man's will (Heb 5:4), Antiochus IV was set against the holy covenant and replaced high priests as he wished (Dan 11:28). Menelaus did not possess the character befitting a high priest; he had the temperament of a cruel tyrant and the rage of a wild beast (2 Macc. 4:25).

While Antiochus IV was away in Cilicia, Menelaus had Andronicus kill Onias III, who was hiding in the temple of a foreign god. Menelaus also incited Antiochus IV to profane the temple and urged him to slaughter Menelaus's own people. Antiochus IV entered the holy of holies to plunder it, and it was the high priest Menelaus who guided him (2 Macc. 5:15–16, *Ant.* 12.246). Antiochus IV stole from the temple money and goods equivalent to 1,800 talents (2 Macc. 5:11–21).

In 162 BC, Lysias—Antiochus V's guardian and regent—told the king that Menelaus was the person who had incited the king's father (Antiochus IV, 175–163 BC) to force the Jews to give up the religion of their ancestors and had caused conflict. Lysias said that Menelaus had to be killed in order to prevent an uprising of the Jews (*Ant.* 12.384). Although Antiochus IV had persecuted the people and defiled the temple, his wicked deeds fell on Menelaus, because he had encouraged Antiochus IV's evil acts during his ten-year office as high priest. This stunning truth was clearly testified through the mouth of Lysias, commander-in-chief of the Seleucid Gentile nation.

While Menelaus was in office, not once did he show the disposition of a high priest; he had no sense of calling, self-sacrifice, or intercession on behalf of the people. He was a traitor who betrayed his country and people in order to secure power for himself. He was a wicked and filthy man who defiled God's laws and temple. Antiochus V sent Menelaus to Berea in Syria and executed him there (*Ant.* 12.385). This was God's severe punishment against Menelaus for bringing chaos to the nation and committing all sorts of unpatriotic treachery for ten years.

39th Generation		
3. **Alcimus** (Jakim) Descendant of Aaron	162–159 BC	three years

Alcimus was appointed after the death of Menelaus. He was known as a descendant of Aaron (1 Macc. 7:5, 9, 14; *Ant.* 12.385–387; 20.235). His Hebrew name is "Jakim," which means "God will rise." "Alcimus" is his Greek name, meaning "valiant," "brave," and "heroic."

Prior to Alcimus's appointment, Antiochus IV died in the spring or summer of 163 BC (1 Macc. 6:16; 2 Macc. 9:3–28; *Ant.* 12.356–357; *War* 1.40). Following his death, his commander-in-chief, Lysias, proclaimed Antiochus V, Antiochus IV's son, king (*Ant.* 12.360–61; 1 Macc. 6:17). When the king advanced with his army to attack Judea, he heard that Philip (a confidant of Antiochus IV, whom Antiochus IV had approved as king) was gaining power in his own country (Antioch). The king suddenly offered peace to the Jews and promised to allow them to live according to their law so he could use them to keep Philip's power in check (1 Macc. 6:55–59; *Ant.* 12.379–381). Nonetheless, he broke his promise with the Jews when he saw that the temple of Jerusalem could be used as a secure fortress. He tore down the walls of Jerusalem and took the high priest Menelaus captive (1 Macc. 6:62; *Ant.* 12.383). After putting Menelaus to death, Antiochus V appointed Alcimus high priest (*Ant.* 12.385).

Onias IV, the son of the last Zadokite high priest Onias III, fled to King Ptolemy when he saw that Alcimus, who was not from a legitimate high-priest lineage, had become high priest. There Onias IV built a temple similar to the temple in Jerusalem and offered sacrifices (*Ant.* 12.387–88).

Alcimus enticed many people in order to strengthen his power and gained many followers, but those who followed him were mostly ungodly people and apostates who had turned away from the law of God (*Ant.* 12.398–99). They used Alcimus's power to commit all sorts of evil acts against the Jews, and the damage they caused was incomparably extreme next to that caused by the Gentiles (1 Macc. 7:21–25). Furthermore, Alcimus led the initiative to kill sixty pious Hasideans through deception in order to maintain the high priesthood (*Ant.* 12.394–96; 1 Macc. 7:10, 13–16).

Since the family of Judas Maccabeus had cleansed and restored the temple in 164 BC, the people who followed him—"the soldiers and the people" (*laos*, a multitude set apart from the organizations that exercised political pressure on the government for their own benefit)—presumably had already bestowed the high priesthood upon Judas Maccabeus (*Ant.* 12.414). With Demetrius I's order to kill Judas, Nicanor, the king's general, went seeking Judas among the priests who were serving in the temple (2 Macc. 14:31–33). This also supports the belief that Judas had been serving as high priest. It is conjectured that although he had not been officially appointed as high priest, he was serving as an unofficial priest among the people.[55]

Alcimus put to death anyone who was discovered to be a supporter of Judas Maccabeus and slaughtered virtuous and pious Jews (*Ant.* 12.399–400). Because of his evil ways, he could not maintain his position as high priest, and he went to the king for support. He lied to Demetrius I, saying, "As long as Judas lives, it is impossible for the state to be at peace," in order to incite the king's anger against the Maccabees (2 Macc. 14:10). Thus Demetrius I believed that he too would be in danger if Judas Maccabeus gained greater power, and he

55 Ibid., 243.

appointed Nicanor the general as governor of Judea. Then he gave the order to invade Judea a second time, kill Judas Maccabeus, disperse his followers, and annihilate all the Jews; he also reappointed Alcimus as high priest (1 Macc. 7:26; *Ant.* 12.402). Nicanor, however, died during the battle against Judas Maccabeus on the thirteenth day of the month of Adar in 160 BC (1 Macc. 7:43; *Ant.* 12.409). The temple was miraculously protected from assault by the Gentile king of Seleucid, which threat had been instigated due to the accusation of the high priest Alcimus, the national traitor (*Ant.* 12.401, 412; 1 Macc. 7:43–49).

Not long after this, in the spring of 160 BC, Demetrius I dispatched Bacchides to battle against Judas Maccabeus; this was the dynasty's third attempt to destroy the Maccabees. This time Judas was defeated and killed in battle (1 Macc. 9:3, 17–18; *Ant.* 12.430). After this the family of Maccabees endured extreme persecution.

The heinously evil Alcimus met a wretched end. He received God's punishment and died while destroying the wall of the sanctuary (the inner court of the temple) to remove the works of the prophets. In the fifth month of 159 BC, Alcimus began to tear down the wall to remove the railing that divided the court of the Gentiles from that of the Israelites, but he suddenly fainted, and the work stopped. His mouth became paralyzed and his tongue hardened, and he died after many days of great torment (1 Macc. 9:54–56; *Ant.* 12.413). The land of Judea enjoyed peace for two years after Alcimus's wretched death (1 Macc. 9:57; *Ant.* 13.22).

3. The Seven-Year Interlude in the High Priesthood

Between 159 BC and 152 BC

An approximately seven-year interlude took place in the high priesthood after Alcimus was punished by God and died in 159 BC, three years after he had been appointed high priest in 162 BC, until 152 BC (*Ant.* 20.237). This was the first interlude in the high priesthood since the time of Zerubbabel's temple. Jonathan, Mattathias's fifth son, was appointed high priest after the interlude on the Feast of Booths in the seventh month of the year 160 BC according to the Seleucid calendar (1 Macc. 10:21; *Ant.* 13.46), which is equivalent to 152 BC.

The offerings made on the Day of Atonement each year cannot be carried out without a high priest (Exod 30:10; Lev 16:29–34; Heb 9:7). It is possible that the high priesthood was left empty because no suitable candidates could be found, and thus the priest of the second-order made the offerings as deputy high priest.[56]

4. The Period of Judean Independence (The Hasmonean Dynasty)

Nine generations of high priests between 152 BC and 37 BC

After the wicked high priests—Jason, Menelaus, and Alcimus, whose legitimacy as high priests was questionable—tyrannized Israel during the period of Seleucid rule, an interlude occurred in the high priesthood for about seven years, from 159 BC until 152 BC. Then the Hasmonean dynasty, established by the sons of the Maccabees family who had led Judea's revolution for independence, rose to become the ruling dynasty of Judea and succeeded the high priesthood.

When Jonathan Apphus, Judas Maccabeus's youngest brother, succeeded him as general after his death, internal conflict over the throne took place within the Seleucid dynasty between Alexander Balas, Antiochus IV's son, and Demetrius I, Seleucus IV's son. Jonathan seized this opportunity to become high priest and king of Judea.

56 Second priests (the priests of the second-order) were appointed in case the high priest could not carry out his duties. In the absence of the high priest, the second priest oversaw all the work in the temple as well as the duties of the priests. Second Kings 25:18 and Jeremiah 52:24 record, "Seraiah the chief priest and Zephaniah the second priest." Here the word "second" is מִשְׁנֶה (*mishneh*) in Hebrew and means "second," "copy," or "replica."

This was the first step leading to the rise of the Maccabean dynasty (1 Macc. 10:1–21; *Ant.* 13.35–46).

Judea gained independence when Jonathan's older brother Simon succeeded him and became the political and religious leader of the Jews. After Simon's murder in 135 BC, his son John Hyrcanus I seized both the high priesthood and the kingship, finalizing Judea's independence.

During this time Judean society was divided into two factions: the Sadducees of the priestly class, who supported Hellenization, and the Pharisees, who opposed it. Later an extreme conflict boiled up between the two factions over the throne. In 67 BC, the two sons of the Hasmonean dynasty, Hyrcanus II and Aristobulus II, engaged in an intense struggle over the throne. They involved Rome in their conflict, which resulted in the conquest of Jerusalem in 63 BC by the Roman general Pompey.

Israel, which had been called Judah during the Old Testament period, began to be called Judea after the Babylonian exile (see Ezra 5:8, KJV). The name "Judea" had referred only to a small region during the Persian era; this region of Judea later maintained its status as an independent nation for a short period during the Hasmonean dynasty. After its conquest by Rome in 63 BC, Judea became the name for all Israel, and Herod was the first to use the official title "king of Judea" (Luke 1:5). Judea, Samaria, and Galilee were together called Palestine during this period.

40th Generation

1. **Jonathan Apphus** Youngest son of Mattathias	152–142 BC	ten years

Jonathan was Mattathias's youngest son, and he lived in a town called Modein to the northwest of Jerusalem. Mattathias led the Maccabean revolt during the reign of Antiochus IV (Epiphanes) of the Seleucid dynasty (1 Macc. 2:1–5). He was the descendant of Asamonaios ("Hasmonai" according to rabbinic literature) from the house of Jehoiarib (1 Chr 9:10; 24:7; 1 Macc. 2:1), the first division among the twenty-four divisions of priests, and a native of Jerusalem (*Ant.* 12.265). Josephus refers to the Judean independence era as the Hasmonean independence era, because Asamonaios, or Hasmon, was Mattathias's great-grandfather (*Ant.* 12.265; 16.187; 17.162; *War* 1.19).

During David's time, when the lot was cast to divide the priests into twenty-four divisions, sixteen were chosen from the line of Eleazar and eight from the line of Ithamar (1 Chr 24:1–5). The division of Jehoiarib, which was the first to be chosen, is presumed to have been from the line of Eleazar. Furthermore, Mattathias's reference to Phinehas as "our ancestor" reveals that the high priests from the Hasmonean family belonged to the line of Zadok, among Aaron's descendants (1 Macc. 2:26, 54).

After Judas Maccabeus died in 160 BC, those who had turned away from the law began to resurface (1 Macc. 9:23). The Seleucid general Bacchides tortured, abused, and killed anyone who had followed or supported Judas Maccabeus. This was the greatest tribulation for the Jews since the return from Babylon (1 Macc. 9:27; *Ant.* 13.5). It was at this time that Jonathan rose as a leader at the request of the people.

Although he had already been appointed by the Seleucid king, because the ungodly people of that time who did not fear God and Jewish traitors who rejected the law rose from all sides to harm the Jews and exert evil influence on them, it was actually the Jews who had requested that Judas Maccabeus's brother Jonathan become their king. Thus Jonathan accepted the people's request with the resolution that he would also die for his nation (*Ant.* 13.5–6).

Jonathan reigned as king in relative peace for about seven years (160–153 BC) after the death of Judas Maccabeus (*Ant.* 13.34). He held the high priesthood for ten years, from 152 BC to 142 BC (*Ant.* 13.212; 20.238). The name "Jonathan" means "God has given"; his nickname, "Apphus," means "pretense" or "the diplomat" and is an allusion to his adept diplomatic character by which he hid his true intentions in order to benefit in dealing with others.

Around 152 BC, a struggle ensued between Demetrius I, the king at the time, and Alexander Balas, the son of Antiochus IV, for the throne. In 150 BC, Demetrius I was defeated and killed in battle against Alexander Balas, and the eleven-year Seleucid reign came to an end (*Ant.* 13.61). Alexander Balas wrote to Jonathan, calling him one of his closest friends, and made him high priest and governor of the province (1 Macc. 10:17–20, 65). Thus Jonathan was able to hold the high priesthood and political leadership concurrently. From this time forth, the characteristic of the leader of Judea officially changed from that of high priesthood concentrating on religion to that of a king and military commander concentrating on politics.[57]

Around 145 BC, when Demetrius II became king, the Jews conspired against Jonathan. Nevertheless, Jonathan used his superior diplomatic skills to win Demetrius II's heart and even received an exemption from paying tribute and further strengthened his high priesthood (1 Macc. 11:19–29; *Ant.* 13.120–126).

In 142 BC (see 1 Macc. 13:41), however, Trypho (*Ant.* 13.131), the general of Alexander Balas's army, attempted to destroy Jonathan's army and attack the land of Judea. When his plans failed, he killed Jonathan in Baskama, a town northeast of the Lake of Gennesaret (1 Macc. 13:12–24). Simon III took the body of his younger brother Jonathan and buried it in Jonathan's birthplace of Modein (*Ant.* 13.210; 1 Macc. 13:25).

41st Generation

2. **Simon (III) Thassi** Older brother of Jonathan	142–134 BC	eight years

57 Deborah W. Rooke, *Zadok's Heirs: The Role and Development of the High Priesthood in Ancient Israel, Oxford Theology and Religion Monographs* (New York: Oxford University Press, 2000), 289.

Simon III, the high priest Jonathan's older brother, was the last survivor from the family of Mattathias (1 Macc. 13:4). The high priesthood was supposed to be passed down from the father to the son (Num 3:2–4) or a brother if there was no son (see Num 27:8–9). Yet Jonathan's older brother, Simon III, succeeded the priesthood, even though Jonathan had sons.

It is unclear whether or not Jonathan's sons were dead. When Trypho had taken Jonathan captive, he had deceitfully promised to free him in return for hostages, and Simon III had sent Jonathan's two sons as hostages (1 Macc. 13:16–19; *Ant.* 13.204, 206). In the end, Trypho had still killed Jonathan as he had planned (142 BC). Nothing more is known of his two sons.

During the time Jonathan was being held hostage, the situation became critical as Trypho mobilized a great army to attack Jerusalem. Simon assembled the people, who had been trembling in terror, in the temple and encouraged them with faith (1 Macc. 13:2–3). The people regained their strength and asked Simon to become their leader and fight for them (1 Macc. 13:7–9). They thus established Simon as their leader (*Ant.* 13.201).

Simon III served as high priest for eight years, from 142 BC to 134 BC (*Ant.* 13.228). First Maccabees 14:27 indicates that "the eighteenth day of Elul, in the one hundred and seventy-second year" was "the third year of Simon the great high priest." The "one hundred and seventy-second year" in this passage is according to the Seleucid calendar, which is calculated to be 140 BC. Since it was the third year of Simon the high priest, Simon became high priest in 142 BC. Simon died in the one hundred seventy-seventh year, in the month of Shebat, or the eleventh month (i.e., the second or third month in 134 BC; 1 Macc. 16:14).

In the year that Simon became high priest, he led Judea to independence from the Seleucid rule, and a new era began (1 Macc. 13:36–41). The Israelites no longer used the Seleucid calendar, and all official documents and contracts began with the header "In the first year of Simon the great high priest and commander and leader of the

Jews" (1 Macc. 13:42; *Ant.* 13.213–214). Simon urged the people to tear down the citadel in Jerusalem that had been built and used by the surrounding enemies as their garrison. The people spent three years working night and day to demolish the citadel of their enemies and leveled the ground so that the temple would be the highest building in Jerusalem, as it had been in the past (*Ant.* 13.217). The destruction of the citadel, which was symbolic of the Seleucid reign, was like a declaration of independence for Jerusalem. On the twenty-third day of the second month in the year 171 on the Seleucid calendar (i.e., the beginning of the seventh month in 141 BC), the Jews waved palm branches, lifted their voices in joyful cheer, and sang praises to the sound of harps, cymbals, and lyres. This day was celebrated each year (1 Macc. 13:51). Judea enjoyed the greatest prosperity and peace during Simon's rule; Simon kept the law and took care of the temple, and the people respected him (1 Macc. 14:4–15; *Ant.* 13.214).

On the eighteenth day of the month of Elul (the sixth month), three years after Simon III became high priest, Simon was officially proclaimed high priest before the people, the priests, the leaders of the people, and the elders. The priests and the people engraved a statement on a brass tablet, a part of which read, "The Jews and the priests were well pleased that Simon should be their leader and high-priest for ever, until a faithful prophet should arise. . . . And all the people consented to ordain for Simon that it should be done according to these words" (1 Macc. 14:25–49). Demetrius II, the Seleucid king, also approved Simon as high priest (1 Macc. 14:38). Through this the high priesthood moved from the house of Onias to the Hasmonean dynasty.[58]

Per Simon's father Mattathias's dying charge, "Behold, I know that your brother Simon is a man of counsel, give ear unto him always: he shall be a father unto you" (1 Macc. 2:65), Simon acted wisely and was like a father to his brothers. He was also the leader who

58 VanderKam, *From Joshua to Caiaphas*, 281.

brought independence and peace to the nation.

42nd Generation

3. **John Hyrcanus I** Son of Simon III	134–104 BC	thirty years

Hyrcanus I was the third high priest from the Hasmonean dynasty and Simon III's son. Simon III, who had opened the era of the Hasmonean dynasty, was killed as a result of his son-in-law's betrayal, and his son Hyrcanus I became king (1 Macc. 16:12–24). Hyrcanus I reigned thirty-one years, the longest of any king in the Hasmonean dynasty (*Ant.* 13.299).

Hyrcanus I promoted circumcision and held fast to the observance of the law. He aspired to restore the Davidic kingdom and acquired the largest territory since King Solomon's time. He destroyed the two-hundred-year-old temple of Samaria, which had been built around 330 BC on Mount Gerizim (*Ant.* 13.254–56). After Antiochus VII, the Seleucid king, died in battle against the Parthians (Arsacid king) in 129 BC, Hyrcanus I saw that Judea had no king and seized the opportunity to conquer the Idumean cities of Adora and Marisa. Hyrcanus I promised the Idumeans that they could stay in their land as long as they would be circumcised and keep Jewish law and tradition. The Idumeans abided and were thence Judaized (*Ant.* 13.257–58).

However, Hyrcanus became increasingly corrupt as his territory enlarged and his power strengthened. He Hellenized his children's names as well as the culture of the royal family. Also, the policy he had carried out for the Idumeans brought about a fatal result for Judea later. The family of Herod, who was an Idumean, executed all the Hasmonean royal family and ruled over Judea for more than one hundred years. The Jews were greatly afflicted during this period until they ultimately met their tragic end in AD 70 when the Romans destroyed them.

43rd Generation

4.	**Aristobulus I** First son of Hyrcanus I	104–103 BC	one year

Aristobulus I had the shortest reign, about one year, in the Hasmonean dynasty. His Hebrew name was "Judah," and he was the first among the five sons of Hyrcanus I (*Ant.* 20.240).

Hyrcanus I entrusted the nation to his wife and the high priesthood to his firstborn, Aristobulus I. Nevertheless, Aristobulus I was greedy for the throne and changed the ruling structure from government to kingdom; thus he was the first to wear a diadem on his head since the Babylonian exile. He was the first person to concurrently hold the titles of king and high priest (*Ant.* 13.301; 20.241). Still unsatisfied, he imprisoned his mother and starved her to death; he imprisoned his brothers; and he believed (wrongly) that his most beloved brother, Antigonus, was vying for his throne and cruelly killed him (*Ant.* 13.302–9). He did not hesitate to slaughter even his own family, acting as if he were going to enjoy his powers forever. After a mere one-year reign, Aristobulus I suffered an extreme mental illness as he regretted his past deeds, and he died tragically from a vicious disease (*Ant.* 13.316–17).

44th Generation

5.	**Alexander Jannaeus** Brother of Aristobulus I	103–76 BC	twenty-seven years

Alexander Jannaeus was the fifth high priest of the Hasmonean dynasty and Aristobulus I's younger brother. He married Salome Alexandra, the wife of Aristobulus I. When Aristobulus had died, Alexandra had released all the brothers Aristobulus I had imprisoned and made one of them, Alexander Jannaeus, king (*Ant.* 13.320). As soon as Alexander Jannaeus became king, he killed one brother who had aspirations for the throne and kept alive the one who was not ambitious for the throne (*Ant.* 13.323).

Through many military campaigns Alexander Jannaeus expanded the Judean territory to the size it had been during the period of Israel's united monarchy. However, the people had to supply him with material resources and manpower, and their discontentment increased to the extent that they reviled him as a son of a captive, unworthy of the priesthood. At this Alexander Jannaeus slew sixty thousand people in rage (*Ant.* 13.372–73). Furthermore, in five or six battles of civil war, he slew more than fifty thousand Jews in a period of six years (*War* 1.91).

The Jews who turned their backs against Alexander Jannaeus sought the help of Demetrius III of the Seleucid dynasty (*Ant.* 13.376), but six thousand Jews took pity on Jannaeus, who had fled to the mountains, and they suddenly turned to his side. Shocked by this, Demetrius III withdrew (*War* 1.95; *Ant.* 13:379). Later Alexander Jannaeus conquered the city of Bethome and besieged those Jews who rebelled against him. He then brought them to Jerusalem, and as he feasted with his concubines, he ordered the crucifixion of eight hundred of them. While they were still alive, he ordered the throats of their children and wives to be cut before their eyes (*Ant.* 13.380). His justification for this slaughter was that the Jews had called in a foreign army (Demetrius III) to put him in a predicament (*Ant.* 13.375–81).

Just before Alexander Jannaeus died, he was mindful of the eight hundred Pharisees he had crucified. Thus he asked his wife Alexandra to express his apology by giving the Pharisees key positions so that she would receive their support.

Alexander Jannaeus ruled twenty-seven years (103–76 BC). He entrusted the throne to his wife and died at the age of forty-nine (*Ant.* 13.398–404).

45th Generation		
6. **Hyrcanus II** First son of Alexander Jannaeus	76–67 BC	nine years

Hyrcanus II was the sixth high priest of the Hasmonean dynasty and Alexander Jannaeus and Salome Alexandra's first son.

Although Alexander Jannaeus had two sons, Hyrcanus II and Aristobulus II, he committed the throne to his wife, Salome Alexandra, for the reason that Hyrcanus II was incompetent (*Ant.* 13.407). Since Alexandra was a woman, she appointed her older son Hyrcanus II as high priest, and she ruled for nine years, until she died at the age of seventy-three (*Ant.* 13.408, 430). Alexandra reconciled with the Pharisees in accordance with her husband's dying words, and from this time forth the Pharisees became members of the Sanhedrin. On the other hand, the Sadducees, who were the Pharisees' opposing party, began contacting the younger son Aristobulus II.

Later Hyrcanus II died by the hands of Herod the Great (*Ant.* 15.173).

46th Generation		
7. **Aristobulus II** Second son of Alexander Jannaeus	67–63 BC	three years, three months, or three years, six months

Aristobulus II was Alexander Jannaeus and Salome Alexandra's younger son and the seventh high priest of the Hasmonean dynasty. He served as high priest from 67 BC until 63 BC, for about three years and three months (or three years and six months; *Ant.* 14.97; 20.244).

After Alexander Jannaeus died, his wife ruled in place of her husband, and she appointed her older son, Hyrcanus II, as high priest. Aristobulus II, however, wanted the rulership and high priesthood for himself. When Queen Alexandra died, Aristobulus II rebelled against his older brother and defeated him; he made an agreement with his older brother, Hyrcanus II, and acquired both the throne and the high priesthood (*Ant.* 14.4–6). The Jews sent a letter to Rome's Pompey to denounce the conflict between the two leaders from the line of priests (*Ant.* 14.41). Ultimately Pompey conquered Jerusalem in 63 BC, three years and three months (or three years and six months) after Aristobulus II began his rule. Pompey took the priesthood from Aristobulus II and returned it along with the ruling authority to Hyrcanus II, but he did not allow Hyrcanus II to wear the diadem (*Ant.* 20.244). This was because Pompey had already established the Idumean Antipater (Herod's father) as governor of Judea.

The Seleucid dynasty disappeared from history once Pompey made Syria a Roman province in 63 BC.

47th Generation

8. **Hyrcanus II** First son of Alexander Jannaeus	63–40 BC	twenty-three years

Hyrcanus was reappointed by Rome's Pompey as the eighth high priest of the Hasmonean dynasty. He served for about twenty-three years, from 63 BC to 40 BC.

Rome began to govern Judea after Pompey conquered Jerusalem in 63 BC. Pompey had established Herod's father, Antipater, as governor of Judea and Hyrcanus II as high priest, outwardly acknowledging Judea's independence. However, Hyrcanus II could exert barely any influence, since the Jews were obligated to pay taxes to Rome and under strict restrictions.

During the power struggle between Pompey and Julius Caesar, Hyrcanus II supported Julius Caesar. In 47 BC, Julius Caesar officially announced Hyrcanus II ruler of Judea. In reality, however, Antipater the Idumean, who was procurator of Judea, secured all the actual power (*Ant.* 14.143; *War* 1.199–203).

In the winter of 48–47 BC, Caesar was besieged by Ptolemy's army, but he was able to escape safely with Antipater's help. Caesar remembered Antipater's faithful deed and bestowed special authority to the people of Judea.

48th Generation

5.	**Antigonus** Son of Aristobulus II	40–37 BC	three years

Antigonus was Aristobulus II's son (*Ant.* 20.245) and the ninth high priest of the Hasmonean dynasty. Upon his return to Judea with help from the Parthians, he cut off the ear of his uncle Hyrcanus II so that he could no longer serve as high priest (*Ant.* 14.365–66; Lev. 21:17–24).

In 40 BC, when Antigonus seized Judea, Herod went to Rome for assistance, and the Roman senate appointed him king (seventh month, 40 BC; *Ant.* 14.381–89). In the third month of the third year of Antigonus's reign, the Roman general Socius, along with Herod, seized Antigonus and took him captive to Rome. According to Josephus, this was "on the third month, on the solemnity of the fast" of 37 BC (*Ant.* 14.389, 487–88). Antigonus was taken in chains to Antioch and decapitated by Anthony as requested by Herod. Thus the 126-year Hasmonean dynasty came to an end (*Ant.* 14.490; 20.246). The value of the Hasmonean dynasty lay in the fact that its priests were actual descendants of Aaron, and they thus preserved the priesthood. Nevertheless, they lost their royal authority to Antipater's son Herod, who was of a common family, because of their own internal conflicts (*Ant.* 14.491).

CHAPTER

14

The History of High Priests Classified by Appointers

AFTER HEROD THE GREAT

Judea had twenty-eight high priests from the time of Herod until AD 70, when the Roman general Titus seized Jerusalem (*Ant.* 20.250). Josephus's record of the twenty-eight priests includes Joseph the son of Ellemus, who took Mattathias's place as high priest once on the Day of Atonement, and Ananel and Joasar, who were reappointed to second terms but counted only once. Hence, Judea actually had thirty generations of high priests during this period.

1. Herod the Great

Appointed seven high priests between 37 BC and 4 BC

Herod the Great was born around 73 BC as the second son of Antipater, a descendant of Esau (Edom); he became king in 37 BC. His name means "son of a hero." Around 40 BC, when Rome was intervening in Judean internal affairs, the Parthians conquered Syria, and Antigonus, the son of Aristobulus II, bribed the Parthians and became high priest and king. When this happened, Herod fled to Rome, where the senate appointed him king. In 37 BC, Herod usurped Antigonus with military support from Antony and reigned over Judea as king.

When Herod divorced his wife Doris and married Hyrcanus II's granddaughter Mariamne I, Hyrcanus II became in-laws with his friend Antipater (procurator of Judea in 47 BC, father of Herod the Great). Herod, being a commoner, was seeking to secure the legitimacy of his throne by joining the priestly family (*War* 1.241; *Ant.* 20.248).

Herod the Great ruled over all Palestine and an extensive part of the Trans-Jordan. He showed great leadership and had many large-scale architectural projects in Caesarea Philippi as well as other places. However, out of constant fear that he might lose his throne, he purged anyone who was a threat—whether it was his wife, son, mother-in-law, mother-in-law's father who had served as high priest, or brother-in-law (*War* 1.431–44). His pathological anxiety and brutality were clearly demonstrated in his massacre of all male children in Bethlehem under the age of two in an attempt to kill Jesus Christ, who had been born the king of the Jews (Matt 2:1–16). For this reason the Bible sums up the time in which Jesus was born as "in the days of Herod the king" (Matt 2:1). During Herod's reign strife arising from conspiracy and accusations among his ten wives and family members did not cease. In his latter years, he became even more violent as his chronic disease worsened. His sin-stained life ended at the age of seventy (*War* 1.665; *Ant.* 17.191).

For more than one hundred years, from the death of Herod the Great until AD 70, the people of Judea were under the rule of the Herodian dynasty, which appointed most of the high priests during that period. Herod the Great appointed seven high priests during his thirty-four-year reign (37–4 BC). The high priests appointed by the Herodian dynasty were extremely corrupt and under the protection of political power. They were not permitted to perform priestly duties independently, even though they were high priests. Moreover, no sign of purity and godliness as religious leaders was found in them.

Year	Roman Emperor	Governors of Judea	High Priests of Judea	High Priests Appointed By
General Pompey captures Jerusalem, 63 BC				
48	Pompey's death, Caesar's tyranny		**Hyrcanus II** 63–40 BC	**Julius Caesar** 63–59 BC, Consul 59–58 BC, Procurator 58–49 BC, Governor of Gallia, 48–44 BC, Dictator
44	Caesar's death			
40				
(43) –31	Rule of the second triumvirate (Antony, Octavian, Lepidus)		**Antigonus** 40–37 BC	Antigonus's rebellion 40–37 BC
37			1 **Ananel** 37–35 BC	**Herod the Great** 37–4 BC
35			2 **Aristobulus III** 35–34 BC	
31	Battle of Actium, Octavian's victory		3 **Ananel** 34–30 BC *reappointed	
27			4 **Jesus** 30–24 BC son of Phabi	
24			5 **Simon** 24–5 BC son of Boethus	
5	**Octavian is given regnal title "Augustus" (the Roman Empire begins) 27 BC–AD 14**		6 **Matthias** 5–4 BC son of Theophilus	
4			**Joseph** son of Ellemus *one-day substitute	**Herod Archelaus** Tetrarch of Judea 4 BC–AD 6
			7 **Joasar** 4 BC son of Boethus	
			8 **Eleazar** 4 BC son of Boethus	

6	**Augustus** 27 BC–AD 14	**Coponius** AD 6–9	9 **Jesus** 4 BC–AD 6 son of Sie 10 **Joasar** AD 6 son of Boethus *reappointed	
9		**Marcus Ambivulus** AD 9–12	11 **Annas** AD 6–15 son of Seth	**Quirinius** Governor of Syria AD 6–9
12				
14		**Annius Rufus** AD 12–15		
15	**Tiberius** AD 14–37			
26		**Valerius Gratus** AD 15–26	12 **Ishmael** AD 15–16 son of Phabi 13 **Eleazar** AD 16–17 son of Annas 14 **Simon** AD 17–18 son of Camith	**Gratus** Governor of Judea AD 15–26
34		**Pontius Pilate** AD 26–36	15 **Joseph Caiaphas** AD 18–36 son-in-law of Annas	
36				**Vitellius** Governor of Syria AD 35–39
37		**Marcellus** AD 36–37	16 **Jonathan** AD 36–37 son of Annas	
39	**Caligula** AD 37–41	**Marullus** AD 37–41	17 **Theophilus** AD 37–41 son of Annas	
41			18 **Simon Cantheras** AD 41–42 son of Boethus	
42	**Claudius** AD 41–54	**Interregnum** AD 41–44	19 **Matthias** AD 42–43 son of Annas	**Herod Agrippa I** AD 37–44
44			20 **Elioneus** AD 43–45 son of Cantheras	
46		**Cuspius Fadus** AD 44–46	21 **Josephus** AD 45–48 son of Camei	**Herod of Chalcis** AD 41–49
48		**Tiberius Julius Alexander** AD 46–48		
52		**Ventidius Cumanus** AD 48–52	22 **Ananias** AD 48–59 son of Nedebaius	

54	**Nero** AD 54–68	**Antonius Felix** AD 52–60	23 **Ishmael** AD 59–61 son of Phabi	**Herod Agrippa II** AD 50–100
60				
62		**Porcius Festus** AD 60–62	24 **Joseph Cabi** AD 61–62 son of former high priest Simon	
			25 **Annas II** AD 62 son of Annas	
64		**Lucceius Albinus** AD 62–64	26 **Jesus** AD 62–63 son of Damneus	
			27 **Jesus** AD 63–64 son of Gamaliel	
66		**Gessius Florus** AD 64–66	28 **Matthias** AD 64–66 son of Theophilus	
67			29 **Phannias** AD 67–70 son of Samuel	**Chosen by casting lots** After the Jewish Revolution (AD 66)
69	**Galba / Otho / Vitellius** AD 69			
70	**Vespasian** AD 69–79			

Jerusalem falls at the hands of General Titus, son of Emperor Vespasian
April–August AD 70

49th Generation

1. **Ananel** From Babylon		37–35 BC	two years

Ananel was the first high priest appointed during Herod's time. A descendant from the Hasmonean family (Aristobulus III, son of Alexander II; *Ant.* 15.23–24) was available to serve as high priest after the death of Antigonus; nevertheless, Herod the Great decreased the influence of the Hasmonean family, since they had thus far held great power in ruling concurrently as king and high priest. He wanted to place the high priest under his command and sought out an unknown person for the position. At last he called his close friend Ananel from Babylon and appointed him (*Ant.* 15.22, 39; 20.247).

50th Generation

2. **Aristobulus III** Grandson of Aristobulus II	35–34 BC	one year

Aristobulus III was the last descendant of the Hasmonean royal family and the second person King Herod appointed to the high priesthood (*Ant.* 15.41). Aristobulus III was born to Alexandra, the daughter of Hyrcanus II, and Alexander II, the son of Aristobulus II; he was also the younger brother of Mariamne I, the wife of Herod the Great. In 35 BC, he became high priest at the young age of seventeen through Herod, but he died about one year later, in 34 BC, at the age of eighteen (*Ant.* 15.50–51, 56).

Before Aristobulus III's appointment in 35 BC, Alexandra, Herod's mother-in-law and Hyrcanus II's daughter, had protested to Herod the Great that appointing Ananel as high priest had been a disgrace to the Hasmonean family. She used her close relationship with Cleopatra VII from the Ptolemaic dynasty to compel Herod to depose Ananel from the high priesthood and appoint her son Aristobulus III in his place (*Ant.* 15.23–24).

Another reason Herod appointed Aristobulus III as high priest was that Aristobulus III was winning the favor of Mark Antony, who held great power in Rome at the time. Hence in order to prevent Aristobulus III from going abroad, Herod wanted to tie him down with temple duties (*Ant.* 15.28–31).

In the tenth month of 35 BC, Aristobulus III was robed in the garments of the high priest according to the law and made sacrifices on the altar during the Feast of Tabernacles. He was exceedingly handsome, and it was apparent from his countenance that he was of noble birth. His appearance reminded the people of his grandfather, Aristobulus II, and the people's affections toward him increased incessantly (*Ant.* 15.50–52). Herod decided to kill Aristobulus III when the people who came up to Jerusalem began praising him. He sent his servant to drown Aristobulus III while he was swimming in a pond near the palace of the Hasmonean dynasty located in Jericho. Aristobulus III was only eighteen at the time (*Ant.* 15.50–56). After this Herod never again appointed anyone from the Hasmonean royal family as high priest (*Ant.* 20.249).

51st Generation

3. **Ananel** From Babylon	34–30 BC	four years

Ananel had been the first to be appointed high priest during Herod's time, and he was reappointed after the death of Aristobulus III (*Ant.* 15.22, 56).

52nd Generation

4. **Jesus** Son of Phabi (from Egypt)	30–24 BC	six years

Herod the Great dismissed Ananel and appointed Jesus the son of Phabi as high priest (*Ant.* 15.322). The name Phabi was found on a tombstone in Leontopolis, Egypt, which leads to the inference that Phabi was a name of a family that originated from Egypt.[59] Just as Herod had appointed Ananel to gain the support of the Jews in Babylon, he probably chose a Jewish high priest from Egypt in order to gain the Jews' political support. With this the high priesthood was no longer regarded as a lifetime position in which succession was based on blood lineage; the high priesthood had lost its original power and status.

Three high priests served from the Phabi family out of the twenty-eight high priests (thirty generations) from the period after Herod the Great until AD 70, when Jerusalem fell at the hands of the Romans:

- Jesus 30–24 BC / six years
- Ishmael 15–16 AD / one year
- Ishmael 59–61 AD / two years

53rd Generation

5. **Simon** Son of Boethus	24–5 BC	nineteen years

Herod the Great was mesmerized by the beauty of Mariamne II,[60] the daughter of Simon the priest from Jerusalem, and he appointed Simon as high priest in order to marry her. With the wedding drawing near, he sought to raise the status of the future bride's family by quickly deposing Jesus and appointing his future father-in-law as high priest (*Ant.* 15.320–22). As such, Herod the Great appointed and deposed the high priest as he pleased for his own self-interest.

Simon was appointed in 24 BC and served as high priest for about nineteen years, which was the longest period of any high priest

59 VanderKam, *From Joshua to Caiaphas*, 406.

60 She was called Mariamne II in order to avoid confusion with Herod's ex-wife of the same name (Hyrcanus II's granddaughter from his daughter).

during the Herodian rule. It was during Simon's office that Herod began to build the temple. Around 5 BC, Mariamne II connived against Herod with his first wife, Doris, her son Antipater, and Herod's brother Pheroras to kill the king. As a result, Herod divorced her and deposed her father, Simon the high priest (around 5 BC; *Ant.* 17.68–78).

Boethus, the father of Simon the high priest, was from Alexandria of Egypt, where many Jews dwelt (*Ant.* 15.320). In 24 BC, in the thirteenth year of Herod's reign, an unprecedented drought continued for an extended period of time (*Ant.* 15.299–300). Gaius Petronius, the Egyptian prefect (24–21 BC), provided grain to help. This was the year that Herod and Mariamne II got married and Simon became high priest. Other high priests served from the house of Boethus besides Simon: four high priests (five generations) from the house of Boethus served from the time of Herod the Great until AD 70, when Jerusalem was destroyed by the Romans:

- Simon (24–5 BC; nineteen years)
- Joazar (4 BC, reappointed in AD 6; total two years)
- Eleazar (4 BC; one year)
- Simon Cantheras (AD 41–42; one year)

  Note: The wife of Jesus, son of Gamaliel (AD 63–64; one year), was from the house of Boethus.

54th Generation

6. **Matthias** Son of Theophilus	5–4 BC	one year

Matthias is recorded as the son of Theophilus from Jerusalem (*Ant.* 17.78). In 5 BC, he became the fifth high priest appointed by Herod the Great and was deposed on the third month of 4 BC (*Ant.* 17.164).

On the day before the Day of Atonement, Matthias dreamt of having relations with a woman and thus became unclean. Hence, he had his cousin Joseph the son of Ellemus serve as high priest in his place just for the Day of Atonement (*Ant.* 17.165–67; see Lev 22:2–3).

Matthias is presumed to have been the high priest during the time of Jesus' birth. Herod the Great and all Jerusalem were thrown into tumult after they heard the news of Jesus' birth from the wise men from the East in 4 BC.[61] Herod gathered all the chief priests and scribes of the people and inquired of them where the Christ would be born. They answered, "In Bethlehem of Judea," in accordance with the prophecy in Micah 5:2 (Matt 2:5; see Matt 2:3–6).

After this incident, Herod became extremely sick, and two prominent scholars of the law in Judea incited the people to tear down a golden statue of an eagle that Herod had placed inside the temple. Herod held Matthias responsible for this incident and deposed him (*Ant.* 17.149–64, 167).

According to Josephus, a lunar eclipse occurred on the night of the day Herod deposed Matthias (from the night of the twelfth of March in 4 BC to the early morning of the thirteenth day; *Ant.* 17.167).[62] Some time after the lunar eclipse, Herod killed his son Antipater, and Herod himself died five days later (*Ant.* 17.187, 191).

55th Generation		
7. **Joasar** Son of Boethus (from Alexandria, Egypt)	4 BC	one year

Joasar was the brother of Herod's wife, that is, the son of Simon, Herod's father-in-law. He was the second high priest from the house of Boethus and the last high priest appointed by Herod (*Ant.* 17.164).

---

61 Alfred Edersheim, *The Life and Times of Jesus the Messiah, Vo. 1* (London: Longmans, Green, and Co., 1896), 218.

62 A lunar eclipse was seen from Palestine on March 23 and September 15 in AD 5; on March 12 in AD 4; and on January 10 in AD 1 (Jack Finegan, *Handbook of Biblical Chronology* [Peabody, MA: Hendrickson, 1998], 294–95).

In early 4 BC, Herod the Great deposed Matthias and appointed Joasar, and Herod died just before the Passover that year. Herod Archelaus (4 BC–AD 6), who succeeded Herod, mourned for his father for seven days. The Feast of Passover was celebrated not too long afterward (*Ant.* 17.200, 213); a riot took place among the people who gathered, and Archelaus's army killed three thousand civilians (*Ant.* 17.213–18). Herod Archelaus deposed Joasar not long after his appointment, but Joasar was reappointed in AD 6.

While Herod's sons—Archelaus and Antipater (Herod Antipus, called Herod the tetrarch)—were involved in a power struggle, the Roman emperor Caesar divided the Palestinian region into three parts and allowed Archelaus, Antipater, and Philip II to rule over each part separately (Matt 2:22; 14:1; Luke 3:1). As soon as Archelaus returned to Judea from Rome, having been appointed ruler over Judea, Samaria, and Edom, he deposed the high priest Joasar, suspecting that he supported the direct rule of Rome, and appointed Joasar's brother Eleazar in his place (*Ant.* 17.339).

2. Herod Archelaus

Appointed three high priests between 4 BC and AD 6

Herod Archelaus was born to Herod the Great and Malthace the Samaritan, and Herod appointed him as his principal heir before his death. For about ten years, from 4 BC to AD 6, Herod Archelaus ruled over Judea, Samaria, and Edom—about half the regions Herod had ruled over—and appointed three high priests.

Nevertheless, the Jews' resentment toward Herod Archelaus built up because of his deeds, such as indiscriminately slaughtering about three thousand Jews from the crowds that showed signs of rebellion during the Passover in the first year of his reign (4 BC), deposing the high priest under the pretense that the high priest supported the rioters, and divorcing his wife and unrighteously remarrying.

Eventually, the Jews reported charges against him to the Roman Emperor, and Herod Archelaus was banished to Vienne, one of the cities in Gaul (*War* 2.111). From this time forth, governors were commissioned from Rome to rule over the Judean regions.

The Bible records that Jesus' parents, Joseph and Mary, heard that Herod Archelaus had succeeded his father, Herod the Great, as ruler of Judea and were afraid to go there. Thus they moved to the regions of Galilee and lived in the city of Nazareth (Matt 2:22–23).

56th Generation		
1. **Eleazar** Son of Boethus (from Alexandria, Egypt)	4 BC	one year

Eleazar was the third high priest from the house of Boethus and the first high priest appointed by Archelaus in 4 BC (*Ant.* 17.339).

The Jews had sent an envoy to the Roman emperor, Caesar Augustus, petitioning for liberty to live according to their own law. They had complained against the unlawfulness of Herod Archelaus and requested that Judea be annexed to Syria so it would be ruled by a governor commissioned by Rome, not by a king or a similar form of government (*Ant.* 17.300–314). Archelaus deposed Joasar the high priest with accusations that he had assisted these people, and he appointed Joasar's brother Eleazar (*Ant.* 17.339).

Archelaus violated the laws of the ancestors and married Glaphyra, the wife of his older brother Alexander and the daughter of King Archelaus of Cappadocia, and had three children with her (*Ant.* 17.340–41; *War* 2.114; see Lev 18:16; 20:21). The Jews despised him even more because of this matter.

Eleazar was deposed from the high priesthood within one year, and Jesus the son of Sie was appointed high priest (*Ant.* 17.341).

57th Generation

2. Jesus Son of Sie | 4 BC–AD 6 | ten years

Jesus is recorded as "the son of Sie" (*Ant.* 17.341). Four high priests with the name Jesus were appointed after the time of Herod the Great:

- Jesus, the son of Phabi (30–24 BC; six years)
- Jesus, the son of Sie (4 BC–AD 6; ten years)
- Jesus, the son of Damneus (AD 62–63; one year)
- Jesus, the son of Gamaliel (AD 63–64; one year)

58th Generation <reappointed>

3. Joasar Son of Boethus | AD 6 | one year

Joasar was the fourth high priest from the house of Boethus. He served as high priest for about one year in 4 BC, and it appears that he was reappointed by Archelaus in AD 6 (*Ant.* 18.3). After Archelaus was exiled, however, Quirinius—the governor of Syria—accused Joasar of abusing his powers and deposed him (*Ant.* 18.26).

The Roman emperor Caesar Augustus often issued decrees to take a census to impose tax on the assets of the Jews. Quirinius, the governor of Syria at the time, was assigned to conduct a tax census (*Ant.* 18.2; see Acts 5:37). As this happened shortly before Joasar's deposition, Joasar persuaded the Jews who strongly opposed the taxation to calm down (*Ant.* 18.3). Josephus wrote that the census was completed in "the thirty-seventh year of Caesar's victory over Antony at Actium [31 BC]," which was AD 6 (*Ant.* 18.26).

3. Quirinius, the Governor of Syria

Appointed one high priest between AD 6 and AD 9

Quirinius's full name was Publius Sulpicius Quirinius. He gained fame after he successfully suppressed the small population of a nation in Asia near Galatia after he became consul of Rome in 12 BC (*Ant.* 18.1). After Herod Archelaus was banished in AD 6, Judea, Samaria, and Idumea were annexed to Syria. Quirinius was then commissioned as governor of Syria, and he ruled until AD 9. He imposed a tax on the Jews, disposed of Herod Archelaus's assets, and appointed Annas as the high priest of Judea. Coponius, one of the knights who came with him, was appointed the first governor of Judea.

59th Generation

1. **Annas** Son of Seth | AD 6–15 | nine years

Annas was the son of Seth and was appointed high priest by Quirinius in AD 6 (*Ant.* 18.26; Luke 3:2; John 18:13–24; Acts 4:6).

Annas was the first high priest appointed by the governor of Syria. He is mentioned numerous times in the New Testament as well as in rabbinic literature. In the fifteenth year of the reign of Emperor Tiberius, both Annas and Caiaphas were high priests (Luke 3:1–2), and Caiaphas was Annas's son-in-law (John 18:13). Originally only one high priest served at a time, but the New Testament refers to both Annas and Caiaphas as high priests simultaneously (John 18:19, 24; Acts 4:6). This indicates that they were the most influential people in the Judean region at the time.

Annas's office ended in AD 15, but he continued thereafter to exercise great influence as he established his sons as high priests. Around AD 29, after Jesus was arrested, He received His first interrogation from Annas (John 18:12–13, 19–24); even at this time Annas was still called the high priest.

Acts 4:1–6 also record that Annas was "of high-priestly descent."[63] Annas served for nine years in the office. Valerius Gratus, governor of Judea, deposed Annas from the high priesthood in AD 15, but he did not exclude Annas's family members from becoming successors. Annas's five sons and even his son-in-law successively served as high priests. Annas's five sons, Eleazar (sixty-first generation; one year), Jonathan (sixty-fourth generation; one year), Theophilus (sixty-fifth generation; four years), Matthias (sixty-seventh generation; one year), and Annas II (seventy-third generation; three months) were appointed to the office. His son-in-law, Joseph Caiaphas, enjoyed the longest term in office as high priest (sixty-third generation; eighteen years).

4. Valerius Gratus, the Governor of Judea

Appointed four high priests between AD 15 and AD 26

After Caesar Augustus banished Herod Archelaus, Rome began to directly govern Judea and Samaria, the regions Archelaus had ruled. The Roman governors generally controlled the law, public security, and taxation; other matters were entrusted to the Sanhedrin, Judea's self-governing body. The governors employed many tax collectors to gather taxes and carried out large-scale taxation censuses, which provoked great opposition from the Jews (Acts 5:37). In addition, the governors exercised the authority to appoint high priests so they could rule over Judea more effectively.

Valerius Gratus was appointed governor of Judea by Emperor Tiberius and succeeded Annius Rufus. He appointed four high priests during his eleven-year term. His last appointment was Joseph Caiaphas, Annas's son-in-law, who gave Jesus up to crucifixion (John

63 Those of priestly lineage were probably members of the Sanhedrin (VanderKam, *From Joshua to Caiaphas*, 421–22, cf. 179-180).

18:13–14).

Gratus was succeeded by Pontius Pilate (AD 26–36), who knew that Jesus was blameless but still handed Him over to be crucified under the authority of the Roman governor (John 19:1–16).

60th Generation

1. **Ishmael** Son of Phabi | AD 15–16 | one year

Ishmael was the second high priest from the house of Phabi. He was the first high priest appointed by the Judean governor Gratus and was deposed not long after his appointment (*Ant.* 18.34).

The *Mishnah* (m.*Parah* 3.5) lists the names of seven high priests who prepared the ashes of the red heifer to make the "water to remove impurity" (see 19:1–10). The list includes Moses, Ezra, Simon the Righteous, Johanan the high priest, Elioenai, Ananel, and Ishmael the son of Phabi. Ishmael is believed to be the high priest on this list.[64]

61st Generation

2. **Eleazar** Son of Annas | AD 16–17 | one year

Eleazar was the first of Annas's five sons to become high priest. He was appointed by Gratus the governor of Judea in AD 16 and served for about one year, until AD 17 (*Ant.* 18.34).

62nd Generation

3. **Simon** Son of Camith | AD 17–18 | one year

64 Ibid., 179–180, 397–398.

Simon, the son of Camith, was appointed by Gratus the governor of Judea in AD 17 and served for about one year, until AD 18 (*Ant.* 18.34).

The Talmud records that Simon the high priest went before a Gentile king of Arabia to speak to him on the night before the Day of Atonement and became unclean when the Gentile king's saliva fell upon his priestly garment. Thus his brother Judah went into the holy place on the Day of Atonement and ministered in his place (t.*Yoma* 3:20, m.*Yoma* 7:4). He was deposed without ever having ministered on the Day of Atonement, the most important duty performed as high priest once a year. This indicates that the Jews regarded the garments of the high priest as very sacred.

63rd Generation

4. **Joseph Caiaphas** | AD 18–36 | eighteen years
Son-in-law of Annas

Joseph Caiaphas was Annas's son-in-law and the third high priest from the house of Annas (Matt 26:3, 57; Luke 3:2; John 11:49; 18:13–14, 24, 28; Acts 4:6). In AD 18, he was appointed by Governor Valerius Gratus, Pontius Pilate's predecessor, and was later deposed by Vitellius, the governor of Syria. He was not deposed when Gratus left and Pontius Pilate (AD 26–36) came as the new governor; he continued to serve as high priest for about eighteen years, from AD 18 to AD 36 (*Ant.* 18.35). He was the chief religious leader of Judea and exhibited great political and diplomatic skills.

Luke 3:1–2 states that Caiaphas was high priest during the time Pilate was governor. In John 11:47–53, Caiaphas appeared when the chief priests and the Pharisees convened a council to discuss how they would do away with Jesus. Regarding Caiaphas, the Bible also states, "The chief priests and the elders of the people were gathered together in the court of the high priest, named Caiaphas" (Matt 26:3). Matthew 26:59 states, "Now the chief priests and the whole Council kept trying to obtain false testimony against Jesus, so that they might put Him to death." The "whole Council" mentioned in this verse refers to the Sanhedrin, and Caiaphas, being the high priest at the time, was the official leader of the Sanhedrin. The death sentence of Jesus Christ came from the decision of the Sanhedrin led by the high priest.

5. Vitellius, the Governor of Syria

Appointed two high priests between AD 35 and AD 39

Lucius Vitellius was appointed by Emperor Tiberius as Roman consul in AD 34 and as governor of Syria in AD 35, and he ruled as governor until AD 39. During his four years as governor, he appointed and deposed two high priests.

In AD 35, Vitellius commanded Pontius Pilate to return to Rome and then went up to Jerusalem during Passover. Vitellius won the people's favor by pardoning their taxes and returning the priestly garments, which had been under Roman custody, to the care of the high priests. Afterward he deposed Caiaphas and appointed Jonathan, the son of Annas, as high priest (*Ant.* 18.95; see *Ant.* 18.90).

Herod Antipas repudiated his first wife, the daughter of King Aretas IV of Nabatea, and married Herodias, the wife of his half brother, Herod Philip I. This triggered a battle between Herod Antipas and King Aretas IV, in which King Aretas IV was victorious (*Ant.* 18.109–14). Upon hearing this news, Emperor Tiberius dispatched Vitellius to attack King Aretas IV (*Ant.* 18.115), and Vitellius sought to march through the land of Judea. The high-ranking officials of Judea did not approve this, however, because Vitellius's ensigns contained images banned under Jewish law. Vitellius's army acquiesced (*Ant.* 18.121–22).

At this time Vitellius went up to Jerusalem with Herod and his friends in order to celebrate a traditional feast of the Jews and offer sacrifices to God. He received a special welcome from the multitudes in Judea (*Ant.* 18.122). During his first three days there, he deposed Jonathan the high priest and appointed his brother Theophilus (*Ant.* 18.123). On the fourth day he received a letter informing him of Emperor Tiberius's death (March 16 in AD 37), and he dismissed his army to return to their respective homes (*Ant.* 18.124).

64th Generation

5. **Jonathan** Son of Annas | AD 36–37 | one year

Jonathan was the son of Annas and the fourth high priest from the house of Annas. Vitellius, the governor of Syria, appointed him and also deposed him.

Around this time Vitellius visited Jerusalem. The Judean governor Pontius Pilate returned to Rome, and Marcellus succeeded him (AD 36).

In AD 36, the first instance of Christian persecution occurred with the martyrdom of Stephen (Acts 7:1–8:1).[65] Stephen was a true martyr who testified of the gospel of Jesus Christ until his life's end (Acts 6:8–7:60). Many opponents were unable to stand up against this one man, Stephen, who spoke with wisdom and the Spirit (Acts 6:10). Thus the multitude established false witnesses and plotted against Stephen and brought him before the council of the Sanhedrin (Acts 6:11–15). Upon hearing the false witnesses, the high priest, who was the head of the Sanhedrin, asked him, "Are these things so?" (Acts 7:1). This high priest was Jonathan, the son of Annas, who had taken the initiative in having Jesus killed.

Stephen testified that Jesus Christ was the Messiah before the high priest and those who brought charges against him (Acts 7:2–53).

---

65 "Stephen, Saint," *Britannica Concise Encyclopedia* (Chicago: Encyclopaedia Britannica, 2006).

At the conclusion of his sermon, Stephen said to the people who had brought charges against him, "You men who are stiff-necked and uncircumcised in heart and ears are always resisting the Holy Spirit; you are doing just as your fathers did. Which one of the prophets did your fathers not persecute? They killed those who had previously announced the coming of the Righteous One, whose betrayers and murderers you have now become; you who received the law as ordained by angels, and yet did not keep it" (Acts 7:51–53). In the scope of God's work of redemption, the evil acts of the Jews reached its peak when they betrayed and murdered Jesus (Acts 7:52).

The murder of Stephen was incited by Jonathan the high priest and carried out illegally, for he was tried by the Sanhedrin, not in the court of the governor (Acts 6:8–8:1). Although he was not guilty of any charges, he was stoned to death outside the city (Acts 7:58; see Lev 24:14).

Later, while Vitellius was in Jerusalem in order to battle against King Aretas IV, he deposed Jonathan the high priest and appointed his brother Theophilus instead (*Ant.* 18.123). Even after his deposition, Jonathan continued to be very influential. During Herod Agrippa I's time, Cantheras the high priest (AD 41–42) was deposed, and Jonathan was reappointed, but Jonathan refused the appointment (*Ant.* 19.313–16).

Some time later the tyrant Felix (AD 52–60) became governor of Judea through Jonathan's support. However, he brutally oppressed the Jews as their insurrections became more frequent and systematic after Nero (AD 54–68) became emperor of Rome. Felix, believing that Jonathan was behind these uprisings, used Jonathan's most trusted friend, Doras, to have him killed by brigands (*Ant.* 20.162–64).

65th Generation

5. **Theophilus** Son of Annas | AD 37–41 | four years

Theophilus was Annas's son and the fifth high priest from the house of Annas. This relatively unknown name "Theophilus" was mentioned in the inscription on an ossuary of his granddaughter, Yehohanah. Its epitaph read, "Yehohanah granddaughter of Theophilus, the High Priest." Since the name "Yehohanah" does not appear in the list of high priests in the first century AD, the "high priest" on the epitaph is certainly referring to Theophilus.[66]

Theophilus was appointed by the Syrian governor Vitellius and served as high priest from AD 37, when Emperor Tiberius died, until AD 41, when Herod Agrippa I became tetrarch. Herod Agrippa I deposed Theophilus and appointed Simon Cantheras as high priest (*Ant.* 18.123–24; 19.297).

6. Herod Agrippa I

Appointed three high priests between AD 41 and AD 44

Herod Agrippa I was the son of Aristobulus—the son of Herod the Great and Miriamne I from the Hasmonean dynasty—and hence the grandson of Herod the Great. His siblings were Aristobulus, Herodia ("Herodias"; Matt 14:3–11; Mark 6:17–28; Luke 3:19), and Herod of Chalcis. He received Herod Philip's territory in AD 37 because of his close friendship with Emperor Caligula. When Claudius became emperor in AD 41 (Acts 11:28; 18:2), he also gave Judea and Samaria to Herod Agrippa I, such that his territory expanded to become as large as that of Herod the Great.

During the following three years (AD 41–44), Agrippa I appointed and deposed three high priests. He also executed Apostle James, the son of Zebedee, and imprisoned Apostle Peter, persecuting Christians in order to earn the trust of the Jews (Acts 12:1–5).

---

66 VanderKam, *From Joshua to Caiphas*, 442-443.

He acted proudly when the people deified him, however, and suddenly, in AD 44, he was eaten by worms and died (Acts 12:21–23). Acts 12:23 states, "Immediately an angel of the Lord struck him because he did not give God the glory, and he was eaten by worms and died." His first sin was in deifying himself, and his second sin was in persecuting the church and killing the apostles (Acts 12:1–2; see Mal 2:2; 1 Cor 10:31).

Agrippa I's daughters, Bernice and Drusilla, are both mentioned in Acts 25:13 and 24:24, respectively.

66th Generation

1. **Simon Cantheras** Son of Boethus	AD 41–42	one year

Simon Cantheras was the fourth from the house of Boethus, following Simon (24–5 BC), Joasar (4 BC), and Eleazar (4 BC). When Claudius became emperor of Rome in AD 41, he gave Agrippa I dominion over Judea and Samaria. At this time Herod Agrippa I deposed Theophilus and appointed Simon Cantheras the son of Boethus as high priest (*Ant.* 19.297). However, he deposed him about one year later (*Ant.* 19.313).

67th Generation

2. **Matthias** Son of Annas	AD 42–43	one year

Matthias was the son of Annas and the sixth high priest from the house of Annas. Agrippa I appointed Matthias after he deposed Simon Cantheras (*Ant.* 19.313, 316), and Matthias served as high priest for about one year, from AD 42 to AD 41. Considering that Matthias was chosen at the recommendation of his brother Jonathan (the sixty-fourth high priest), it appears that Jonathan was quite influential in those days.

68th Generation

3. **Elioneus** Son of Cantheras | AD 43–45 | two years

In AD 43, Herod Agrippa I deposed Matthias and appointed Elioneus, the son of Cantheras, as high priest. Elioneus served about one year after the death of Herod Agrippa I in AD 44 and was deposed by Herod of Chalcis (now Lebanon) in AD 45 (*Ant.* 19.342).

The governor Cuspius Fadus (AD 44–46) was commissioned to Judea after the death of Herod Agrippa I. He entrusted custody of the sacred vestments of the high priest to the Roman officials in the city of Antonia. The Jewish religious leaders made an entreaty to the Roman emperor Claudius in AD 45, and Herod Agrippa II, the son of Herod Agrippa I, persuaded the emperor to allow the Jews to regain custody of the sacred vestments of the high priests (*Ant.* 20.6–10).

7. Herod, King of Chalcis

Appointed two high priests between AD 44 and AD 49

Herod of Chalcis (now Lebanon) was the grandson of Herod the Great and the younger brother of Herod Agrippa I. He married his niece Bernice, the daughter of Herod Agrippa I (Acts 25:13, 23; 26:30). He was called the king of Chalcis, a small territory located on the inclined plane west of the Lebanon mountain range. After the death of Agrippa I, he made requests to Emperor Claudius and received authority to govern the temple, manage the offerings, and appoint the high priest. He appointed and deposed two high priests between AD 44 and AD 49 (*Ant.* 20.15).

After the death of Herod of Chalcis (AD 49), Agrippa II (AD 50–100) began to govern Chalcis at the Emperor Claudius's command (*Ant.* 20.104). Although Agrippa II did not directly govern Judea, he exercised the authority to appoint and depose high priests as well as manage the temple storage houses and the sacred vestments of the high priests until the Jewish revolt in AD 66. Moreover, he remained influential within Jewish society from AD 70, when Judea fell to the Romans, until AD 100.

Thus for about one hundred years, from AD 37, the era of Herod the Great, until AD 66, when the Jewish revolt occurred, the Herodian dynasty greatly influenced the appointments and depositions of the Jewish high priests.

69th Generation

1. **Josephus** Son of Camei | AD 45–48 | three years

Herod of Chalcis appointed Josephus, the son of Camei, as high priest and also deposed him (*Ant.* 20.16, 102). Since Herod of Chalcis deposed him just before Herod died in AD 49, which was the eighth year of Claudius's reign (*Ant.* 20.103), Josephus probably served as high priest until AD 48.

70th Generation

2. **Ananias** Son of Nedebaius | AD 48–59 | eleven years

In AD 48, just before his death (AD 49), Herod of Chalcis deposed Josephus the son of Camei from the high priesthood and appointed Ananias, the son of Nedebaius. Ananias served for eleven years, until AD 59, when Agrippa II deposed him (*Ant.* 20.103, 203).

Acts 24:2–21 recounts the charges brought against Paul by Tertullus the orator.[67] Acts 24:27 states, "After two years had passed, Felix was succeeded by Porcius Festus, and wishing to do the Jews a favor, Felix left Paul imprisoned." Felix finished his term as governor in AD 60, so two years prior to this, when the Sanhedrin brought

67 "Orator": a public speaker, especially one of great eloquence

charges against Paul (Acts 24:1), must have been AD 58. Toward the end of Felix's term as governor, Herod Agrippa II appointed Ishmael the son of Phabi as high priest (*Ant.* 20.179), so Ananias must have served as high priest until AD 59. Ananias served the longest term as high priest (eleven years) after Simon the son of Boethus (nineteen years) and Joseph Caiaphas (eighteen years).

According to Josephus, Ananias was a brutal and violent man who collected tithes from the other priests and appropriated these funds as his personal assets; he also offered generous bribes to Rome's high officials (*Ant.* 20.206–7). Even his wicked servants used violence to take the tithes from the threshing floor, which belonged to the priests. They harshly beat anyone who refused to cooperate. No one could stop their lawless deeds (*Ant.* 20.206). Other priests followed the evil deeds of the servants, and as a result, some of the elderly priests who had been living by these tithes starved to death (*Ant.* 20.207).

Ananias served as high priest during the ministry years of Apostle Paul (see Acts 23:1–5; 24:1). Using his power as high priest, Ananias used violence to stop the gospel preached by Apostle Paul.

While listening to Paul, the high priest Ananias commanded those standing beside Paul to strike him on the mouth (Acts 23:2). Paul rebuked him, saying, "God is going to strike you, you whitewashed wall! Do you sit to try me according to the Law, and in violation of the Law order me to be struck?" (Acts 23:3). He called Ananias a "whitewashed wall" because Ananias accepted the glory of the high priesthood while he himself was extremely evil and unrighteous. It was truly hypocritical that he, who was supposed to guide righteously according to the law, commanded people to strike the innocent Paul. The high priest in Jewish society at that time possessed the great authority to serve God on behalf of the people, but Apostle Paul daringly denounced him as a whitewashed wall. The bystanders rebuked Paul, saying, "Do you revile God's high priest?" and Paul explained, "I was not aware, brethren, that he was high priest" (Acts 23:4–5).

In Acts 24:2–3, Tertullus the lawyer, whom the high priest Ananias had brought with him, praised Felix the governor: "Since we have through you attained much peace, and since by your providence reforms are being carried out for this nation, we acknowledge this in every way and everywhere, most excellent Felix, with all thankfulness." This was cunning flattery, which he used to lift Felix's spirit so that Felix might listen seriously to his accusations against Apostle Paul. The lawyer incited the Roman government, which valued peace, with the following charge against Apostle Paul: "We have found this man a real pest and a fellow who stirs up dissension among all the Jews throughout the world, and a ringleader of the sect of the Nazarenes" (Acts 24:5). They also accused Apostle Paul of having desecrated the temple (Acts 24:6) and thus sought the Romans' approval for Paul's death sentence. However, Apostle Paul defended himself, saying, "They found me occupied in the temple, having been purified, without any crowd or uproar" (Acts 24:18), and he stated that he had only said, "There shall certainly be a resurrection" (Acts 24:15; see Acts 24:10–21). Despite knowing that Apostle Paul was without blame, Felix kept Paul imprisoned for two years until he left office because he wanted to win the favor of the Jews (Acts 24:27).

In Ananias were found no traces of godliness or compassion as a high priest; he was cruel, a skillful conjurer, and a leech on the Romans. When war with Rome began in AD 66, the Jewish zealots set fire to the house of the high priest Ananias and the palaces of Agrippa and Bernice. Ananias and the leaders fled. Ananias hid in an aqueduct in the palace of Herod the Great, but he was found and killed along with his older brother (*War* 2.441).

8. Herod Agrippa II

Appointed six high priests between AD 50 and AD 66

Herod Agrippa II was the son of Herod Agrippa I and was raised in the court of the Roman emperor Claudius. He was the young age of seventeen when his father Agrippa I died (AD 44), so Claudius kept him in Rome and sent a Roman governor to rule Judea once again. Without a tetrarch in Judea from this time on, the Roman governor began to exercise supreme power over the entire Judean region. From AD 44 until AD 66, before the Jewish revolt, seven governors were commissioned, in the following order: Fadus (AD 44–46), Alexander (AD 46–48), Cumanus (AD 48–52), Felix (AD 52–60), Festus (AD 60–62), Albinus (AD 62–64), and Florus (AD 64–66).

Around AD 50, Agrippa II became king of Chalcis, which had been ruled by his uncle Herod. From this time on until the Jewish revolt in AD 66, Agrippa II exercised his authority to appoint the high priests, and he appointed and deposed six high priests.

Agrippa II received the territory of Herod Philip from Emperor Claudius, and Nero, who became emperor in AD 54, also gave him the regions near Galilee. In AD 60, Agrippa II, accompanied by his younger sister Bernice, went to pay respects to Festus after Festus became governor of Judea (Acts 25:13). Agrippa II continued to be faithful to the Roman emperor and preserved the emperor's territory. Even when Jerusalem was destroyed in AD 70, Agrippa II stood by the Romans as their praetor. He died childless around AD 100, and the Herodian dynasty ended with his death.

71th Generation

2. **Ishmael** Son of Phabi | AD 59–61 | two years

Ishmael was the third high priest from the house of Phabi. He was the first high priest appointed by Agrippa II in AD 59 (*Ant.* 20.179) and served as high priest while Festus (AD 60–62) was governor of Judea. Another person of the same name and household had served as high priest in AD 15–16.

In Jerusalem at this time, sedition between the high priest and the principal men of the multitude of Jerusalem arose and led to a violent incident. As a result, the nation was thrown into extreme chaos, a state like that of anarchy that completely prevailed over justice and righteousness (*Ant.* 20.180). The high priests, who had become extremely corrupt, sent their servants onto the threshing floors to ruthlessly seize the tithes due to the priests (*Ant.* 20.180–81).

Ishmael is the high priest who brought charges against Apostle Paul when Festus became governor in AD 60 (Acts 25:1–2).

The sentence for Apostle Paul, who had been imprisoned by Felix the governor of Judea for two years (AD 58–60), was put off when Emperor Nero (AD 54–68) appointed Festus to succeed Felix as governor of Judea (Acts 24:27; 25:1). When Festus went up to Jerusalem after his appointment, the high priests and leading men of the Jews brought charges against Apostle Paul (Acts 25:1–2). These high priests refer to the members of the Sanhedrin, such as Ishmael and his predecessor, Ananias (Acts 24:1).

Although Festus confirmed that Apostle Paul had committed no crime worthy of the charge against him (Acts 25:24–25), to buy the favor of the Jews, he asked Paul if he would be willing to go up to Jerusalem and stand trial before the Sanhedrin (Acts 25:9). Paul answered, however, that he wanted to be questioned before Caesar since he was a Roman citizen, and Festus consented (Acts 25:10–12). Several days later Herod Agrippa II, who ruled the northern regions of Galilee, came with his sister Bernice to pay respects to Festus, and Festus entrusted the issue of Paul's trial to Herod (Acts 25:13–27). Festus, who heard Paul's defense, cried out in a loud voice, "Paul, you are out of your mind! Your great learning is driving you mad" (Acts 26:24). Agrippa II only said, "In a short time you will persuade me to become a Christian" (Acts 26:28), and did not find any fault in Paul. Ultimately, the king, the governor, Bernice, and all those sitting with them acknowledged Paul's innocence (Acts 26:30–32).

Apostle Paul stood before the Jews (Acts 22:1–21), the Sanhedrin council (Acts 23:1–6), Felix (Acts 24:10–21), Festus (Acts 25:8, 10–11), and Agrippa II and boldly testified not only of his own innocence but also of the gospel of Jesus Christ (Acts 26:1–23). He also appealed to the Roman emperor in order to seize an opportunity to preach the gospel (Acts 25:11; see Acts 23:11). The innocent Apostle Paul was falsely accused of all sorts of things and tried before the king, the governor, and other high government officials. However, without losing his composure, he seized the opportunity to boldly testify of the Word of God. Likewise, as people indebted to the gospel, we must boldly testify of the Word both in season and out of season (Rom 1:14–15; 1 Cor 9:16; 2 Tim 4:2).

Agrippa II built a building at a location higher than the temple, and from there he monitored all the activities of the temple. Offended by this, the leaders who lived in Jerusalem built a high wall, but Festus commanded them to tear down this wall. Ten Jews went to inquire of Emperor Nero regarding this issue, and Ishmael the son of Phabi was one of those persons. Nero allowed the Jews to preserve the wall in accordance with the ten Jews' request. However, Ishmael was taken hostage at this time, and Agrippa II appointed Joseph Cabi as high priest in his place (*Ant.* 20.195–96).

72nd Generation

2. **Joseph Cabi** Son of Simon | AD 61–62 | one year

Although Simon the father of Joseph Cabi is also known as Simon Canteras, the name "Cabi" suggests that Joseph Cabi is more likely the son of Simon Camit.[68] He was appointed by Agrippa II in AD 61 and deposed in AD 62 when Albinus became governor of Judea after Festus's death (*Ant.* 20.196–97).

73rd Generation

3. **Annas II** Son of Annas | AD 62 | three months

Annas II was the son of Annas (served AD 6–15) and the seventh and

68 VanderKam, *From Joshua to Caiaphas,* 476.

last high priest from the house of Annas. He was appointed by Agrippa II in AD 62 (*Ant.* 20.197) but was deposed only after three months (*Ant.* 20.203). Caesar appointed Albinus (AD 62–64) as governor of Judea after hearing that Festus (AD 60–62) had died (*Ant.* 20.197).

During his short tenure Annas II was arrogant and extremely merciless. He was a member of the Sadducees, who were rigid in judging offenders (*Ant.* 20.199). While the governor was being changed, Annas II seized the opportunity to assemble the council of the Sanhedrin and put to trial James the brother of Jesus and some others. When he had formed an accusation against them as breakers of the law, he delivered them to be stoned (*Ant.* 20.200). Before Jesus had been crucified on the cross, He had been bound by the Roman cohort, the commander, and the officers of the Jews and then taken to Annas II's father, Annas (Caiaphas's father-in-law), to be questioned and insulted by Annas's officers (John 18:12–14, 19–24). Now James the brother of Jesus was put to death by Annas's son, Annas II, in the short three months he served.

At that time several Jews went to Albinus the governor of Judea (AD 62–64) as well as Agrippa II and appealed to them concerning this matter. Consequently, Annas II, who had committed all kinds of evil deeds for three months, was deposed by Agrippa II (*Ant.* 20.203).

Annas II was killed by the Idumeans when they joined with the Zealots, who had started the Jewish riots in AD 66 (*War* 4.314–25).

74th Generation

4. **Jesus** Son of Damneus | AD 62–63 | one year

Agrippa II next appointed Jesus the son of Damneus as high priest (*Ant.* 20.203). Jesus served as high priest while Albinus (AD 62–63) was governor of Judea. During this time Ananias, the former high priest (son of Nedebaius; served AD 48–59), was still influential (*Ant.* 20.204–7).

Some time later Agrippa II deposed Jesus the son of Damneus and appointed Jesus the son of Gamaliel, but great strife erupted between the predecessor and the successor over the high priesthood. These two high priests fought with each other regardless of Agrippa II's command; this suggests that the Jews disliked Agrippa II for the probable reason that he had seized the people's assets to beautify a foreign city (*Ant.* 20.211–14).

75th Generation

5. **Jesus** Son of Gamaliel	AD 63–64	one year

Jesus was the son of Gamaliel (*Ant.* 20.213). Acts 5:34 refers to a man named Gamaliel: "A Pharisee named Gamaliel, a teacher of the Law, respected by all the people." It is uncertain, however, if they are the same person. Jesus was appointed by Agrippa II in AD 63 and deposed after about one year, not too long after the temple of Herod was completed in AD 64 (*Ant.* 20.213, 223).

After Jesus was deposed, he was tragically killed by the Idumeans along with Annas II (the son of Annas) during the revolt of the Zealots in AD 66 (*War* 4.314–25).

76th Generation

6. **Matthias** Son of Theophilus	AD 64–66	two years

It is possible that Matthias's father, Theophilus, was the high priest who had served from AD 37 to AD 41. If so, Theophilus was probably part of the house of Annas, which was influential in the Judean regions during the first century.[69]

Theophilus means "beloved by God" or "friend of God." Matthias the son of Theophilus was the last high priest to be appointed in ordinary custom before the Romans completely destroyed the

69 Ibid., 487.

temple. Agrippa II deposed Jesus the son of Gamaliel and appointed Matthias the son of Theophilus. During the high priesthood of Matthias, war broke out between Judea and Rome (*Ant.* 20.223).

9. Chosen by the Rebels (Zealots) by Casting Lots

The last high priest, AD 67

Revolts often occurred in Judean society while it was under the rule of the governors commissioned by Rome. These revolts were usually led by the Zealots, and many assassins arose to kill leading officials from the Roman government (Acts 21:38). When the last governor, Florus (AD 64–66), stole several pieces of treasure from the temple treasury (*War* 2.293), the Jews regarded this as a desecration of the temple and led a large-scale revolt in order to liberate themselves from Roman rule.

General Vespasian suppressed the Jewish revolt to a certain extent, but when he became emperor of Rome in AD 69, his son Titus began a campaign to conquer Jerusalem. Titus besieged Jerusalem from the third month of AD 70, when the Passover was being observed, until the city finally fell five months later. According to Josephus's writings, more than one million Jews were killed, and seventy thousand were taken captive. The temple was completely destroyed by fire set by a Roman soldier. All this happened merely seven years after the temple of Herod had been completed in AD 63.

As the Jewish revolt swept across Judea, the Zealots began to take power. During this turbulent period the Zealots chose the last high priest, Phannias, by lot.

77th Generation		
1. **Phannias** Son of Samuel	AD 67–70	three years

Phannias the son of Samuel was the last high priest of Judea. He was not from a high-priestly family but rather chosen by lot by a representative of the Zealots (*Ant.* 20.227). The Zealots had sought the authority to appoint the high priest by craftily imitating the way David had chosen the twenty-four divisions, which he had done by lot (1 Chr 24). This was a display of the extreme corruption of the Jews during those times. Wanting the high priest to become an accomplice to their deeds, the Zealots broke the tradition of the law and appointed the priest as they pleased (*War* 4.147–50). They cast lots, seeking to appoint a high priest from the priestly family of Eniachim, but the lot fell upon Phannias, the son of Samuel, of the village of Aphthia (*War* 4.155).

This ludicrous ending was a clear manifestation of the long period of corruption in the high priesthood. The people stubbornly cast lots to choose a high priest for themselves. However, their new high priest, Phannias, was not only logically unworthy of the high priesthood, but he did not even know what the high priesthood was. Just as a clown gets dressed up before going onstage, the Jews clothed Phannias with the high-priestly garment and instructed him as to what he was to do in each process of the sacrifice. They enjoyed the sacrifice worship as if acting a play upon a stage. The sacred dignity of the high priest was completely dissolved, and sacrifices became a spectacle and a joke. Some priests standing at a distance could not contain their flowing tears as they watched Phannias performing the sacrifices; they sorely lamented as they watched the ritual and proceedings of the holy sacrifices turn into a spectacle (*War* 4.156–57).

The Jewish historian Josephus wrote that no one, not even a king, could become a high priest, if he was not of the Aaronic line, and he did not write further of Phannias (*Ant.* 20.226). The Jewish War broke out while Phannias was high priest (*Ant.* 20.227), and Phannias served until AD 70, when Jerusalem was destroyed by General Titus, the son of Emperor Vespasian. The people who led the revolt used the holy of holies in the temple as their headquarters, displaying how people had utterly neglected and trampled upon God's temple and its holiness.

Concluding Remarks: The Priest Is the Lamp of Redemptive History

Representing the people of Israel before God, the high priests had the duty to properly guide the people with the Word of God. However, our survey of the seventy-seven generations of high priests reveals that the high priesthood was passed down through the Aaronic line in accordance to God's covenant only in the beginning; that covenant was not kept in the latter generations. The covenant of the priesthood was broken, because the majority of priests did not listen to God's Word, abused their position, and became extremely corrupt (Neh 9:34–35; Mal 2:8).

With the passage of time, many of the Aaronic high priests became extremely wicked as they grew greedy for money and power and oppressed the people. Starting from Ananel (forty-ninth generation), the high priests were appointed through political power regardless of the Aaronic lineage; all the priests lost the essence of the high priesthood and became corrupt. Not only were they unable to fulfill their calling, but they also rebelled by delivering the true eternal high priest, Jesus Christ, to be crucified. Particularly in the case of the house of Annas, seven people—Annas, his five sons, and his son-in-law Caiaphas—successively held the high priesthood for a long period of about thirty-five years. Among them, Caiaphas, Annas, and a multitude of wicked high priests became closely knit in order to play a leading role in capturing and killing Jesus.

Jesus had warned His disciples that He would suffer at the hands of the high priests before He suffered on the cross. Matthew 16:21 states, "Jesus began to show His disciples that He must go to Jerusalem, and suffer many things from the elders and chief priests and scribes, and be killed, and be raised up on the third day."

Although Jesus was without sin, He was accused because of the jealousy of the extremely corrupt priests and high priests of that time (Matt 26:57–68; 27:12, 18; Mark 14:53–65; 15:3, 10–11; Luke 22:66–71; John 18:19–24). Knowing this, Pilate sought to free Jesus according to the custom of releasing a prisoner during the feast, but again the high priests incited the multitude so that the people shouted in a loud voice to crucify Jesus. Ultimately Barabas, who had incited a revolt, was released, and Jesus was handed over to the cross (Mark 15:6–15; Luke 23:13–25; John 18:35, 38–40; 19:6). Pilate tried hard to release Jesus, who was guiltless, but the high priests shouted, "We have no king but Caesar" (John 19:15), so Pilate handed Jesus over to them so that they could do as they wished (Matt 27:26; Luke 23:25; John 19:12–16) and their demand would be granted (Luke 23:24) because he wished to satisfy the crowd.

While Jesus was being questioned by Annas, one of the officers struck Jesus with his hands (John 18:22). After Jesus' sentencing was confirmed, the officers spat in His face, covered His face with a towel, and struck His face and mocked Him saying, "Prophesy to us, You Christ; who is the one who hit You?" Even the officers slapped His face (Matt 26:68; see Matt 26:66–68; Mark 14:64–65). After He endured indescribable humiliation and affliction as a prisoner, He was taken to the governor's palace, the Praetorium (Mark 15:16), and mocked before the whole army (Matt 27:26–30; Mark 15:15–20; John 19:1).

Even as Jesus hung on the cross, His whole body torn, battered, and bloodied from the whippings, the high priests mocked Him, saying, "Let Him now come down from the cross, and we will believe in Him" (Matt 27:42; see Matt 27:41–43; Mark 15:31). The chief priests and the Pharisees, who were afraid that Jesus would resurrect, as He had often prophesied, received Pilate's permission to seal Jesus' tomb with a great stone and set soldiers to secure the place until the third day (Matt 27:62–66). The corruption of the high priests was the result of their forgetting the covenant and not upholding their calling as the lamp of the times. They did not recognize Jesus, the true high priest, and gave Him over to be crucified.

Psalm 132:17 states, "There [in Zion] I will cause the horn of David to spring forth; I have prepared a lamp for Mine anointed." In this verse "for Mine anointed" refers to a descendant who would succeed the throne in David's place (1 Kgs 11:36; 15:4), ultimately the

Messiah (Christ, "anointed One"). The word "prepared" is written in the perfect tense of the word עָרַךְ (*arakh*) in Hebrew, which means "to arrange" or "set in order." This means that another prepared lamp would replace the lamp before it went out so that the light would burn continually without going out. This is the promise that God would continue to fill the throne with the descendants of David until the coming of the Messiah.

It was the priests who prepared the lamps so that they burned continually; the priests always kept the temple lamps in order so that they did not dim all night. This was the perpetual statute. Leviticus 24:3–4 states, "Outside the veil of testimony in the tent of meeting, Aaron shall keep it in order from evening to morning before the Lord continually; it shall be a perpetual statute throughout your generations. He shall keep the lamps in order on the pure gold lampstand before the Lord continually." Exodus 27:21 states, "In the tent of meeting, outside the veil which is before the testimony, Aaron and his sons shall keep it in order from evening to morning before the Lord; it shall be a perpetual statute throughout their generations for the sons of Israel."

In this light the high priests and priests were the lamps of the nation. When the priests allowed the temple lamps to dim, then the nation's lamp also dimmed. Israel's history shows that a priest who obeyed God's Word was a lamp that gave life to the period in which he lived, but a priest who disobeyed God's Word was a lamp gone out, and he led his period through sin and death.

First Samuel 3:3 states, "The lamp of God had not yet gone out, and Samuel was lying down in the temple of the Lord where the ark of God was." In actuality, the temple lamps were supposed to be lit twenty-four hours (Exod 27:20–21; 30:7–8; Lev 24:3–4). This means that Samuel was called during the deep night before sunrise. Symbolically, since Eli the priest's eyesight had grown dim so that he could not see well and his sons had committed sins and had become spiritually dark (1 Sam 2:12–17; 3:2), this was a prophecy that the lamp of the nation would be brightly lit through Samuel.

Historically, after the intertestamental period, while Judea was being ruled by foreigners, the high priests were appointed by the rulers. Especially after Ananel, whom King Herod appointed in AD 37, Zadokite priests were no more, and people who had nothing to do with the covenant of God succeeded the high priesthood. When God established the house of Levi as priests, He said through Moses in Leviticus 8:35, "Keep the charge of the Lord, so that you will not die, for so I [Moses] have been commanded." Just as death comes when this eternal statute is broken, so Israel experienced total spiritual darkness when Herod the Great began to appoint false high priests.

All saints, as members of the chosen nation and a royal priesthood (1 Pet 2:9), must become spiritual lamps that light this darkened world. Proverbs 6:23 states, "The commandment is a lamp and the teaching is light; and reproofs for discipline are the way of life." Thus royal priests who light the lamp of the Word brightly are those people who have been called as the light that gives life to the world.

Matthew 5:14–15 states, "You are the light of the world. A city set on a hill cannot be hidden; nor does anyone light a lamp and put it under a basket, but on the lampstand, and it gives light to all who are in the house." Lamps have to be kept at a high place in order to brighten their surroundings. Today we must also raise high the lamp of the covenant and advance each day toward that high place. A church that turns to worldliness cannot fulfill its calling as priests who bring light to the world. I hope we become a church that always rises high toward God, that rises high each day through spiritual thoughts and through the bread of life from heaven so we can all become true priests who brighten the whole universe with the lamp of the Word.

The Family Tree of the Hasmonean Dynasty (High Priest) and the Herodian Clan (Rulers of Judea)

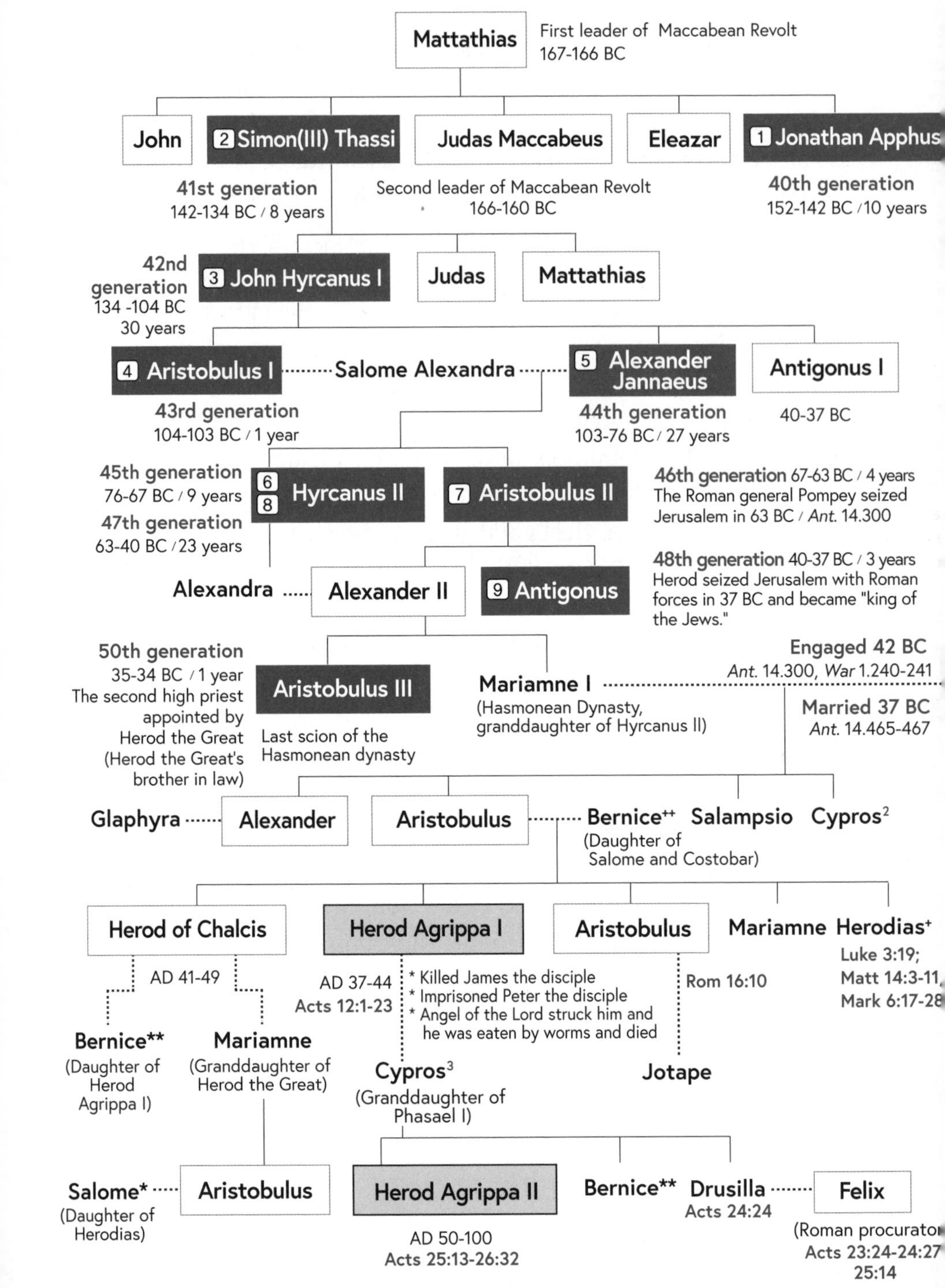

After Rome conquered Jerusalem in 63 BC, Hyrcanus ll was made high priest and Antipater the Idumaean was de procurator of Judea (*Ant.* 14. 137-139). Antipas skillfully used the largely incompetent Hyrcanus ll in order ecome governor of Judea in 55 BC and then procurator of Judea in 47 BC. He made his sons Phasael I and od governors of Jerusalem and Galilee respectively. From this time, the royal family of Herod began to rcise authority in the region of Judea.

In 40 BC, Antigonus (son of Aristobulus ll) ruled as high priest and king for about three years with the help of Parthians. However, Herod seized Jerusalem with Roman forces and in 37 BC, became "King of the Jews." h the death of Anigonus at this time, the reign of the Hasmonean Dynasty, which had lasted about 126 years, e to an end. On the other hand, in 42 BC, Herod, who was not of noble birth, became engaged to Mariamne I, last Hasmonean princess, in an attempt to unite himself with the family (*Ant.* 14.300, *War* 1.240-241). He rried her in 37 BC (*Ant.* 14.465-467), but he wiped out the royal family of the Hasmonean Dynasty by killing brother-in-law, Aristobulus lll the last Hasmonean prince, and his wife Mariamne I, because they were a threat his throne (*War* 1.435-437, 443).

The unity of the Hasmonean Dynasty and the Herodian Dynasty, which began with Alexander Jannaeus and wife Alexandra establishing Antipas the Idumaean as governor of Idumaea (*Ant.* 14.10), continued with the rriage of Herod the Great and Mariamne l. Thus, the Idumaeans (Idumea: "Edom"), who had once been forced ollow Judean policies under the rule of John Hyrcanus I (135-104 BC) were now ruling over Judea. The people udea suffered under the rule of the Idumaeans until it was destroyed at the hands of the Romans in AD 70.

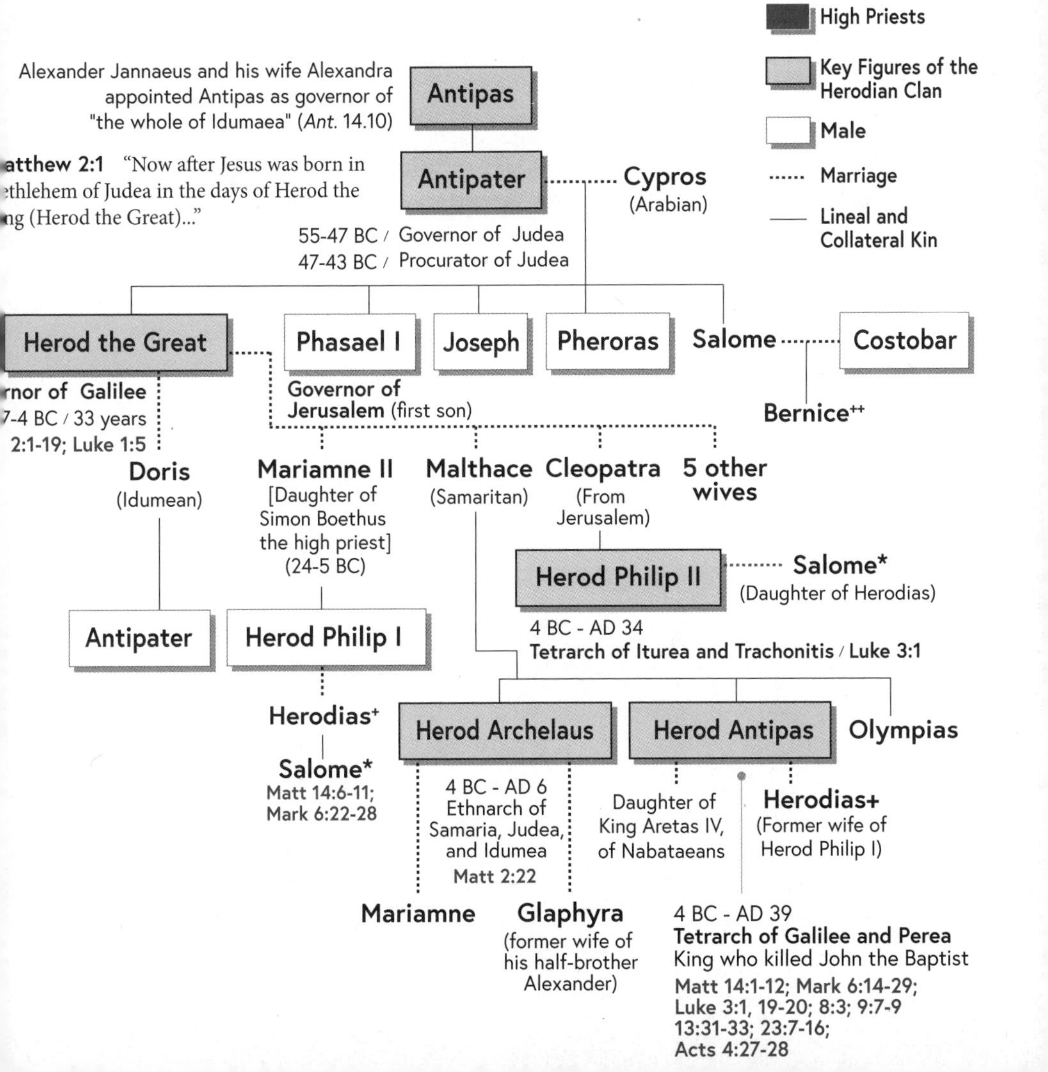

ים המלח
עמלק
מדבר צין הוא קדש
הר ההר
קדש ברנע
מדבר סיני
מדבר פארן
מדבר שור
ארץ פלשתים
עתר
מקדה
עיר כרמל
שבט
הצור
מולדה
אלתולד
שרון
באר שבע
שמעון
גת
פתם
אלכסנדרי
לוח המסעות במדבר
אשר על פי ה׳ יסעו ועל פי ה׳ יחנו
א׳ רעמסס טו׳ רתמה כט׳ חר הגדגד
ב׳ סכת טז׳ רמן פרץ ל׳ יטבתה
ג׳ אתם יז׳ לבנה לא׳ עברנה
ד׳ פי החירת יח׳ רסה לב׳ עציון גבר
ה׳ מרה יט׳ קהלתה לג׳ מדבר צין
ו׳ אילם כ׳ הר ספר לד׳ הר ההר
ז׳ ים סוף כא׳ חרדה לה׳ צלמנה
ח׳ מדבר סין כב׳ מקהלת לו׳ פונן
ט׳ דפקה כג׳ תחת לז׳ אבת
יוד׳ אלוש כד׳ תרח לח׳ דיבן גד
יא׳ רפידם כה׳ מתקה לט׳ עלמן דבלתים
יב׳ מדבר סיני כו׳ חשמנה מ׳ הרי עברים
יג׳ קברות התאוה כז׳ מסרות מא׳ ערבת מואב
יד׳ חצרות כח׳ בני יעקן

PART

V

The Garments and Duties of the High Priest

PART V

Even within the tribe of Levi, Aaron's direct descendants received the special position of high priest (Exod 28:1). The high priest was "appointed to offer both gifts and sacrifices" (Heb 8:3). The garments of the high priest outwardly manifested the special position of the high priesthood. These garments were precious and beautiful with multi-colored threads, golden threads, and rare jewels wonderfully harmonized together. Clothes reflect the character, status, and duties of the one wearing them. Thus God clothed His specially chosen high priests with garments holy, glorious, and beautiful in order to distinguish them from the multitude. Exodus 28:2 states, "You shall make holy garments for Aaron your brother, for glory and for beauty."

Although the high priest is an imperfect being, God clothed him with beautiful garments so his every movement would reveal only God's glory. Indeed, the high priest had the greatest calling on earth—the duty to reveal God's glory. Hence he was the most precious being on earth. Special sanctification and special duties were required of the high priest, all of which embodied the image of Jesus Christ, who would come as the eternal high priest.

CHAPTER

15

The Garments of the High Priest

God commanded the high priests to wear special garments in order to reveal the glory, holiness, beauty, and redemptive ministry of the high priesthood. The garments of the high priest included a breastpiece, an ephod, a robe, a tunic of checkered work, a turban, and a sash. In Exodus 28:4, God said, "These are the garments which they shall make: a breastpiece and an ephod and a robe and a tunic of checkered work, a turban and a sash, and they shall make holy garments for Aaron your brother and his sons, that he may minister as priest to Me." The list also included linen breeches (Exod 28:42). Both the high priests and the priests wore the tunic of checkered work, the sash, the turban, and the linen breeches. However, only the high priest could wear the specially made ephod, the band of the ephod, the robe, and the breastpiece.

Each time we hear and read about the beautiful and splendid garments of the priests and the high priests, we must fathom the depths of God's heart, as He longs for us to live holy and beautiful lives of faith. We must also truly understand the redemptive administration of our high priest Jesus Christ.

1. The Garments Worn by Both Priests and High Priests

The priestly garments are mentioned in three different places in the Old Testament. First, in Exodus 28 God instructed Moses on how to make the garments. All the instructions were in the command form: "you shall" and "you shall make." Second, Exodus 39 recounts how Moses did "just as the Lord had commanded" regarding the priestly garments. The phrase "just as the Lord had commanded Moses" appears seven times (Exod 39:1, 5, 7, 21, 26, 29, 31). Exodus 39:41–43 says that the people brought to Moses "the woven garments for ministering in the holy place and the holy garments for Aaron the priest and the garments of his sons, to minister as priests. So the sons of Israel did all the work according to all that the Lord had commanded Moses. And Moses examined all the work and behold, they had done it; just as the Lord had commanded, this they had done. So Moses blessed them." Third, Leviticus 8:6–9 is an account of the investing of Aaron and his sons with the priestly garments in preparation for the ordination.

The garments that the priests must wear

Tunic	כְּתֹנֶת	*kethoneth*
Exodus 28:39–40; 29:5, 8; 39:27; Leviticus 6:10; 8:7, 13		

Characteristics

The "tunic of checkered work" (Exod 28:39) is also described as "tunics of finely woven linen" (Exod 39:27; see also Lev 8:7) and the "linen robe" (Lev 6:10). The tunic was a one-piece garment worn inside the robe next to the flesh; its sleeves came down to the wrist and its length down to the heels.

The priestly tunics and all other ordinary tunics were one-piece garments. After Jesus was crucified on the cross, the Roman soldiers divided up His garment into four parts, and each soldier took one; but the tunic was seamless, woven in one piece, so they did not divide it but cast lots for it, and one person took it (Matt 27:35; John 19:23–24; see Ps 22:18).

Materials

Fine linen was used to make the tunic. Exodus 28:39 states, "You shall weave the tunic of checkered work of fine linen, and shall make a turban of fine linen, and you shall make a sash, the work of a weaver." The noteworthy expression here is "fine linen," which demonstrates that the tunic of the priest was finely woven with the finest of linen threads. The Hebrew word "checkered" is written in the piel (intensive) stem, the perfect tense of the word שָׁבַץ (*shavats*), which means "to weave in checkered work." Thus the expression "checkered" emphasizes the weaving rather than the pattern of the linen.

Redemptive-historical significance

In Hebrew the word "tunic" is כְּתֹנֶת (*kethoneth*), which means "to cover," but it originates from an unused root. The tunic was not used only during Moses' time; Adam and Eve were also clothed with this garment. They lived in the garden of Eden, not knowing shame, because they were clothed in the glory of God. After they sinned, however, they felt shame because of their nakedness and sewed fig leaves together to make loin coverings (Gen 2:25; 3:7). So God made garments of skin for them and clothed them with the garments instead of the sewn fig leaves (Gen 3:21). The word for the loin coverings (Gen 3:7) made of sewn fig leaves is חֲגוֹר (*hagor*) in Hebrew, and it refers to a garment that barely covers the loins. The "garments of skin" mentioned in Genesis 3:21, however, is כְּתֹנֶת (*kethoneth*) in Hebrew; it was just like the tunic of the priests, a long garment that covered from the shoulders down to the feet. Manmade garments are useless in covering the shame of sin. God shed the blood of an animal in order to make the *kethoneth* for fallen man. This foreshadows Jesus Christ, who would come as the high priest. He would shed His precious blood and offer the atoning sacrifice, thereby completely covering the sin and transgression of fallen mankind and clothing them with garments of righteousness (Isa 53:4–6; Matt 20:28; Mark 10:45; Rom 13:14; Gal 3:27).

Jesus was stripped three times before He was crucified. First, the Roman soldiers stripped Him and put a scarlet robe on Him. They put a crown of thorns on His head and a reed in His hand, and mocked Him, saying, "Hail, King of the Jews" (Matt 27:28–29). After they mocked Him, they took the scarlet robe off and put His own garments back on Him and led Him out to be crucified (Matt 27:31). When Jesus was about to be nailed to the cross, they removed His clothes again (Matt 27:35). They divided His garment into four parts, and each person took a piece, but only one person took the tunic (John 19:23–24). This was in fulfillment of the prophecy in Psalm 22:18, "They divide my garments among them, and for my clothing they cast lots."

Jesus was stripped and subjected to all sorts of shame and punishment in order to clothe us sinners with the garments of righteousness (Isa 53:11; Jer 23:6; Rom 3:21–26; 5:6–9). Jesus' whole body was covered with deep gashes resembling furrows (Ps 129:3), and His thick blood covered His entire body like a garment. He endured such suffering and death to redeem us from our transgression and sin (Isa 53).

Sash (for tunic)	אַבְנֵט	*avnet*
Exodus 28:39; 39:29; Leviticus 8:7, 13		

Characteristics

Because the tunic of the high priest was a loose-fitting, seamless, one-piece garment, he wore a sash to make it easier for him to perform his priestly duties while wearing the tunic (*Ant.* 3.154). The sash was tied around the chest once and hung loosely down to the ankles (*Ant.* 3.155). Leviticus 8:7 states, "He put the tunic on him and girded him with the sash." The word "girded" is חָגַר (*hagar*) in Hebrew and means "to gird oneself."

Materials

The sash for the tunic was made of fine twisted linen woven with blue, purple, and scarlet material (Exod 39:29; see also Exod 28:39). Among the four-colored threads, the fine twisted linen is the most noteworthy. Fine linen was also used to make the tunic (Exod 28:39), and the screen for the doorway of the tent was also made of blue, purple, and scarlet material and fine twisted linen woven together (Exod 26:36; 27:16; 36:37; 38:18).

The "fine twisted linen" (Exod 39:29) that was used to make the sash is שֵׁשׁ מָשְׁזָר (*shesh mashzar*) in Hebrew and was a thread that took a great amount of labor to make. Flax stalks, harvested at the proper time, were boiled, steamed, and dried. They were then soaked in water, and their fibers were separated, strand by strand. Each strand was connected to a long thread, and the strands were twisted together so the thread would not break. In order to change the colors of the coarse linen into a pure white color, the linen was soaked in lye for two nights, rinsed, and dried in the sun. The process by which the flax stalks growing in the fields became finely twisted linen threads is reminiscent of God's meticulous hands that change sinners into precious people. The pure white color represents righteousness. The faith of chosen saints becomes mature through righteous acts they do through God's perfect intervention within us. These acts are prepared to become fine linen, bright and clean, through God's boundless grace (Rev 19:8).

Redemptive-historical significance

The sash that is tied around the waist shows the attitude of the one with a calling (2 Kgs 4:29; 1 Pet 5:5). First Peter 1:13 (RSV) states, "Gird up your minds." Those who had special callings were commanded, "Gird up your loins" (2 Kgs 9:1). Like soldiers headed for war, they were to gird their loins, which refers to being fully ready to take swift action (Exod 12:11). Jesus too said, "Let your loins be girded" (Luke 12:35; RSV). He also said to be on the alert "like men who are waiting for their master . . . so that they may immediately open the door to him" (Luke 12:36). A person with a calling has to gird the loins all the time. Jeremiah (Jer 1:17) as well as John the Baptist girded their loins and lived according to their callings (Matt 3:4). A priest cannot fulfill his calling without girding the loins with the sash of his calling (Eph 4:4; 6:14).

Cap	מִגְבָּעָה	*migbaah*
Exodus 28:40; 29:9; 39:28; Leviticus 8:13		

Characteristics

Exodus 39:28 refers to the caps of the priests as "decorated caps." Here the word "decorated" is מִגְבָּעָה (*migbaah*) and originates from גִּבְעָה (*givah*), which means "mountain" or "hill." Thus the "decorated caps" had pointed tops like a mountain and were different from the caps of the high priests. The "turban" of the high priests, which is mentioned in the beginning of Exodus 39:28, was wound around and sewn so it could be worn on the head (Exod 28:39). It was different from the caps of the priests, making it easy to differentiate between the two positions.

Materials

The caps of the priests were made of fine linen. Exodus 39:27–28 states, "They made . . . the decorated caps of fine linen." Thus the caps of the priests were different from the golden crowns of the worldly kings.

Redemptive-historical significance

The caps of the priests revealed glory and beauty. Exodus 28:40 states, "For Aaron's sons you shall make tunics; you shall also make sashes for them, and you shall make caps for them, for glory and for beauty." The cap made of fine linen was white in color and looked plain to the human eye. Nonetheless, the Bible says that the caps were "for glory and for beauty." This reflects that God's righteousness, signified by the fine linen, is most glorious and beautiful before God.

Linen breeches	מִכְנָס	*mikhnas*
Exodus 28:42; 39:28; Leviticus 6:10; 16:4		

Characteristics

The linen breeches were worn closest to the flesh and were like linen trousers worn in order to cover the lower part of the body or the flesh of the high priest. We refer to such garments today as underwear or loose drawers. They started at the waist and came down to the thighs. Exodus 28:42 states, "You shall make for them linen breeches to cover their bare flesh; they shall reach from the loins even to the thighs." Leviticus 6:10 states, "The priest is to put on his linen robe, and he shall put on undergarments next to his flesh."

Materials

The breeches were made of fine twisted linen. Exodus 39:27–28 states, "They made . . . the linen breeches of fine twisted linen." The Bible likens linen to the righteous acts of the saints who have put on the righteousness of Christ (1 Cor 1:30; 2 Pet 1:1) and live righteously by faith (Rev 19:8). Prophet Isaiah said, "All our righteous deeds are like a filthy garment" (Isa 64:6). However, we have put on Jesus Christ's garment of righteousness without price through the redemption of the cross (Rom 3:24; Eph 1:7; 2:8).

Redemptive-historical significance

In the Old Testament, the phrase "to uncover one's nakedness" at times referred to committing adultery. Ezekiel 23:18 speaks of the betrayal of Oholibah, who represents Israel. She betrayed God by allying with a Gentile nation, and Ezekiel describes it, saying, "She uncovered her harlotries and uncovered her nakedness."

Thus covering the priest's nakedness with linen breeches is symbolic of how the priest must not commit adultery but must live a physically pure life. A priest's pure life is possible only when he puts on the righteousness of Jesus Christ, which the linen symbolizes (Rev 19:8; Rom 13:14; Gal 3:27).

The spiritual garments that a priest must wear

In a broad sense, the whole nation of Israel was a priestly nation during Old Testament times. In Exodus 19:6, the Lord said to Israel, "'You shall be to Me a kingdom of priests and a holy nation.' These are the words that you shall speak to the sons of Israel."

The actual priests were the sons of Aaron, from the tribe of Levi, from among the twelve tribes. The Lord instructed Moses, "Bring near to yourself Aaron your brother, and his sons with him, from among the sons of Israel, to minister as priest to Me—Aaron, Nadab and Abihu, Eleazar and Ithamar, Aaron's sons" (Exod 28:1). Aaron's four sons were "the anointed priests, whom he [Moses] ordained to serve as priests" (Num 3:3).

Today, however, those who are acknowledged as priests are the saints who have been redeemed by Jesus Christ's blood on the cross. Here on earth they are the ones who come before God and worship Him by the merit of Jesus Christ's precious blood; in the future they will reign with Christ in the kingdom of God (Rev 20:6). First Peter 2:9 states, "You are a chosen race, a royal priesthood, a holy nation, a people for God's own possession." Revelation 5:10 declares, "You have made them to be a kingdom and priests to our God; and they will reign upon the earth." Revelation 1:6 further clarifies: "He has made us to be a kingdom, priests to His God and Father—to Him be the glory and the dominion forever and ever. Amen."

Prophet Isaiah prophesied that new priests and new Levites would be established in the new age (Isa 66:21). Isaiah 61:6 states, "You will be called the priests of the Lord; you will be spoken of as ministers of our God. You will eat the wealth of nations, and in their riches you will boast."

What kinds of garments must we wear since we have been called as the priests of the gospel of Jesus Christ?

The priests of Old Testament times wore a tunic of checkered work, a sash, a cap, and linen breeches. The saints of Jesus Christ today do not need to wear the same garments that the priests wore. However, we must understand how the priestly garments foreshadow Christ's work of redemption as well as what spiritual garments the saints with a calling in Christ must wear. Thus although the saints today do not wear the same physical priestly garments the Old Testament priests did, they must wear the corresponding spiritual garments. What, then, are the spiritual garments that must be worn by saints who have become royal priests in Jesus Christ?

***First*, a priest must wear the garment of righteousness.**
Psalm 132:9 states, "Let Your priests be clothed with righteousness, and let Your godly ones sing for joy." Psalm 132 contains Solomon's thanksgiving for the construction of the temple (Ps 132:8–10), and it corresponds with Solomon's prayer during the temple dedication in 2 Chronicles 6:41–42. It contains Solomon's confession of his emotion when the ark of the covenant was set in the holy of holies after the completion of the temple.

Before a priest performed the priestly duties, he first changed into garments fit for his duties. The priests had to wear the designated garments and officiate over the sacrifice offerings. As people who have been called to worship God and become mediators for the people, the saints today who have the priestly calling must wear garments befitting their calling. Job, who was a priest for his family, also confessed the following while enduring extreme tribulation: "I put on righteousness, and it clothed me; my justice was like a robe and a turban" (Job 29:14). Prophet Isaiah also said, "Righteousness will be the belt about His loins" (Isa 11:5) and he said in his prayer, "He has wrapped me with a robe of righteousness" (Isa 61:10).

"Righteousness" is the best garment the saints can put on. A saint must put on righteousness in order to become a true priest. The saints must be accustomed to righteousness such that it becomes their habits, thoughts, and character. When a person has no righteousness, his or her relationship with God is also cut off. That person is no longer the Lord's priest (2 Chr 6:41; Ps 132:9) but a dead priest whose spiritual life is lost, whose light has gone out. Such a person cannot even protect his or her own soul (Mal 2:7–9).

The garment of righteousness that the saints must wear is the grace of redemption, which is the cleansing that comes through Jesus Christ's blood on the cross (Rom 3:24; 4:6–8; 13:14; Gal 3:27).

Our garments become clean when we wash them in the blood of Jesus Christ the Lamb (Rev 7:14). The bride of the Lamb must wear the "fine linen, bright and clean," and this linen is the righteous acts of the saints (Rev 19:8), which is δικαίωμα (*dikaiōma*) in Greek. In Revelation 19, He who sits on the white horse as well as the armies of heaven following Him appear. The armies of heaven are also clothed in fine linen, white and clean (Rev 19:11–14). Indeed, the fine linen, white and clean—or the garment of righteousness—is the garment of calling that the saints who have become God's priests must wear in the end times (Rev 16:15).

***Second*, a priest must wear the garment of salvation.**

A priest must wear the garment of salvation. Psalm 132:16 states, "Her priests also I will clothe with salvation," and 2 Chronicles 6:41 states, "Let Your priests, O Lord God, be clothed with salvation." Psalm 132:9 proclaims, "Let Your priests be clothed with righteousness," and Psalm 132:16 promises that God will clothe the priests with "salvation." "Garment of salvation" is closely associated with the garment of righteousness.

Those who put on clothes of righteousness will put on the clothes of salvation. Isaiah 61:10 states, "He has clothed me with garments of salvation, He has wrapped me with a robe of righteousness." In Psalm 98:2, the words "salvation" and "righteousness" are used interchangeably. Even in the New Testament, the one who wears Jesus Christ's garment of righteousness will wear the garment of salvation. Romans 5:9 also states, "Much more then, having now been justified by His blood, we shall be saved from the wrath of God through Him," and the passage goes on to speak of righteousness (justification) in connection with salvation (Rom 10:10).

The priests who are clothed with the garment of salvation must now become messengers and the channel of salvation for the world. Psalm 71:15 states, "My mouth shall tell of Your righteousness and of Your salvation all day long; for I do not know the sum of them." The psalmist confesses that he has received immeasurable grace and put on the robe of righteousness and salvation; now he pledges to speak of that salvation all day long. Here "all day long" is כָּל־הַיּוֹם (*kal-hayyom*) and means "all the days." It refers to one's "whole life" and "throughout one's life" rather than all day long. In addition, the word "tell" is the piel (intensive) stem of סָפַר (*safar*, "to recount, to declare") written in the imperfect tense. This word demonstrates the psalmist's firm resolve; he was so moved by God's immeasurable righteousness and salvation that he wanted to proclaim it without ceasing for the rest of his life. We, the saints, who have become the royal priesthood, must proclaim the "excellencies of Him who has called [us] out of darkness into His marvelous light" (1 Pet 2:9). Through our proclamation we can pass the "garment of salvation" to others as well, and God's redemptive administration will continue to be fulfilled every day.

***Third*, a priest must wear garments of joy and gladness.**

If the priests have already put on the garments of righteousness and salvation, now they must put on the garments of joy and gladness. Psalm 132:9 states, "Let Your priests be clothed with righteousness, and let Your godly ones sing for joy," and Psalm 132:16 states, "Her priests also I will clothe with salvation, and her godly ones will sing aloud for joy." Here the word "godly" is חָסִיד (*hasid*) and refers to the "godly man" (Deut 33:8) and "godly ones" (1 Sam 2:9).

The phrase "sing for joy" in Psalm 132:9 is the piel (intensive) stem of the Hebrew word רָנַן (*ranan*) written in the imperfect tense. This expression emphasizes the continuity of utmost joy, overflowing joy, and shouts of joy bursting forth (2 Sam 6:15; 2 Chr 6:41). The laughter of joy abounds for those who wear garments of righteousness and salvation, and their overflowing joy and gladness do not cease. Like the psalmist, when joy that comes from above overflows, we will clap our hands in joy and sing praises of thanksgiving even on our beds at night (Ps 149:5; see also Job 35:10–11).

Apostle Paul overflowed with this kind of joy and gladness. He was in prison, his clothes torn, and his whole body bloodied and bruised from the beatings, but he still prayed and praised the Lord (Acts 16:22–25). Indeed, no pain could block the joy and delight of salvation that burst out from the depths of Paul's heart. Furthermore, Paul energetically preached this salvation to the other prisoners: "Believe in the Lord Jesus, and you will be saved, you and your household" (Acts 16:31).

What was the basis of this proclamation? Second Chronicles 6:41 states, "Let Your priests, O Lord God, be clothed with salvation and let Your godly ones rejoice in what is good." Grace is the source of joy for the holy and godly saints. The word "grace" is בַּטּוֹב (*vattov*) in Hebrew and means "in good." This "good" refers to God, who is absolute goodness itself. Thus the saints must be able to proclaim joy and gladness in any situation. Prophet Habakkuk confessed, "Though the fig tree should not blossom and there be no fruit on the vines, though the yield of the olive should fail and the fields produce no food, though the flock should be cut off from the fold and there be no cattle in the stalls, yet I will exult in the Lord, I will rejoice in the God of my salvation" (Hab 3:17–18).

The type of priest God wants is not one who is dressed up in magnificent and special garments. God delights in upright priests wearing garments of righteousness, true priests wearing garments of salvation, and holy priests wearing garments of joy and gladness in the Lord. We have one true high priest: Jesus Christ the eternal high priest. Thus only those who have Christ in their hearts and love Him deeply can become true priests on the earth.

2. Holy Garments Worn Solely by the High Priest

Overview of the garments of the high priest

God made holy garments for Aaron the high priest (Exod 28:2). Holy garments played the role of covering Aaron's human nature and sin. In order to enter into God's presence, a priest, who was a sinner, needed holy garments that covered his sins. Moreover, the high priest must adorn himself with a character that was holier and nobler than that of the priests. Without holy garments, they could not enter the holy of holies, the place of God's presence (see Lev 16:4).

The garments of the high priest were incomparably superior to the garments of the priests. Unlike the priests, the high priest wore the golden plate, the robe of the ephod, the ephod, and the breastpiece of judgment. The high priest's magnificent garments brought out the glory of the high priest. The garments of the high priest were made of the highest quality, using the best techniques, with the utmost care and finest wisdom.

Thus the garments of the high priest typified the perfect and holy character of Jesus Christ, who is "holy, innocent, undefiled, separated from sinners and exalted above the heavens" (Heb 7:26). They also signified "wisdom from God, and righteousness and sanctification, and redemption" in Jesus Christ (1 Cor 1:30). Aaron the high priest outwardly displayed dignity through garments that were suitable for his position. Jesus Christ, however, possessed wisdom, righteousness, holiness, and boundless love even from before eternity. Through these innate characteristics, He possessed in abundance the glory and dignity of the nations, such as is befitting an eternal high priest (Rev 15:3–4). Indeed, only Jesus Christ is our perfect and eternal high priest.

First, the names of the garments of the high priest

The garments of the high priest were differentiated from the garments of the priests and were often called "holy garments" (Exod 28:2, 4), "Aaron's garments" (Exod 28:3), "holy garments which were for Aaron" (Exod 39:1), and "holy garments for Aaron" (Exod 39:41). These garments were finely woven (Exod 39:1) and displayed beauty (Exod 28:2), glory (Exod 28:2), and holiness (Exod 28:2; 39:1).

During normal times the high priest wore garments that displayed the dignity and glory of his position, garments that were magnificent and beautiful. However, on the Day of Atonement, when he entered the holy of holies, he did not wear the ephod of gold, blue, purple, and scarlet material and fine twisted linen or the breastpiece of judgment or the golden plate (Lev 16:3–4, 23–24). Because he took the blood of the sacrifice into the holy of holies to receive atonement for the sins of the people on this day, he had to take off the magnificent priestly garments. Instead he put on a white linen robe, symbolizing purity, and entered with a humble heart.

***Second*, holy garments appointed as a perpetual statute**

The high priest must wear these garments when performing priestly duties (Exod 28:1–4, 41; 39:41). God said that he must wear these garments so that he would not die when he entered the tent of meeting or approached the altar to minister in the holy place. God said that this should "be a statute forever" to the high priest and his descendants after him (Exod 28:43).

God commanded that the high priest must not under any circumstance tear these "holy garments" that God had ordained as a perpetual statute:

> *The priest who is the highest among his brothers, on whose head the anointing oil has been poured and who has been consecrated to wear the garments, shall not uncover his head nor tear his clothes. (Leviticus 21:10)*

The high priest Caiaphas, however, who was questioning Jesus tore his robes before Jesus in excitement, saying, "He has blasphemed!" (Matt 26:65; see also Mark 14:63–64). Since Caiaphas broke the law that prohibited the tearing of the priestly garments, Caiaphas was actually the one who blasphemed the law.

***Third*, those who made the holy garments**

God commanded that those who made the garments of the high priest be persons fully endowed with the spirit of wisdom. In Exodus 28:3, God said to Moses, "You shall speak to all the skillful persons whom I have endowed with the spirit of wisdom, that they make Aaron's garments to consecrate him, that he may minister as priest to Me." God led these persons with the spirit of wisdom in order to make Aaron holy so that he could perfectly perform the duties of the priest as God had commanded.

Oholiab was one of the persons especially called for this work. God inspired Oholiab's (אָהֳלִיאָב, "father's tent") heart (Exod 35:34–35) and filled him with the skill (Exod 31:6) and understanding (Exod 36:1). Thus Moses called "every skillful person in whom the Lord had put skill, everyone whose heart stirred him" to come to the work and perform it in accordance with God's command (Exod 36:2).

All work done according to God's command and all things fulfilled according to His will are the outcome of the skill, ability, and understanding that God has given to the persons with the calling. God even fully stirs their hearts so that they desire to perform the work (Phil 2:13). Thus God's work cannot be performed through human will or emotion but only through the wisdom given by God.

The Bible emphasizes numerous times that those who make the "holy garments" must be filled with the spirit of wisdom from God. The Holy Spirit of God is the Spirit who fills a person with wisdom; and when a person is filled with wisdom, he can discern God's will and follow His Word perfectly without leaving anything out.

The garments worn only by the high priest

A high priest is a person especially called by God. The garments of the high priest outwardly signified the special status of the high priesthood and reflected God's redemptive providence.

Turban	מִצְנֶפֶת	*mitsnefeth*
Exodus 28:39; 29:6; 39:28; Leviticus 8:9; Zechariah 3:5		

Characteristics

The high priest's turban had a few special characteristics.

First, its shape was different from the priests' caps. Exodus 28:39 states, "You shall weave the tunic of checkered work of fine linen, and shall make a turban of fine linen, and you shall make a sash, the work of a weaver." Here the Hebrew word מִצְנֶפֶת (*mitsnefeth*) for the word "turban" originates from the word צָנַף (*tsanaf*), meaning "to wrap, to wind up together, and to wind around." The turban of the high priest was presumably headwear made by winding cloth and sewing the pieces together. According to the Talmud, a turban consisted of eight yards (about 7.3 m) of linen.[70]

Second, a golden plate was placed on the front of the turban (Exod 28:36–38; 29:6; 39:30–31). The words "Holy to the Lord" were engraved on the plate (Exod 28:36; 39:30). This golden plate was then fastened to the front of the turban using a blue cord (Exod 28:37; 39:31). Exodus 28:36–37 states, "You shall also make a plate of pure gold and shall engrave on it, like the engravings of a seal, 'Holy to the Lord.' You shall fasten it on a blue cord, and it shall be on the turban; it shall be at the front of the turban." The word "plate" is צִיץ (*tsits*) in Hebrew and means "blossom," "flower," and "shining object" (Ps 132:18). Exodus 39:30 describes it as a "plate of the holy crown," and Numbers 6:7 refers to it as a symbol of "separation to God."

Materials

The turban of the high priest was made of fine linen. Exodus 28:39 states, "Make a turban [*mitsnefeth*] of fine linen." Also, the plate with the engraved words "Holy to the Lord" was made with pure gold (Exod 28:36).

---

70 M. G. Easton, *"High Priest," Easton's Bible Dictionary* (New York: Harper & Brothers, 1893).

Redemptive-historical significance

First, the turban of the high priest symbolizes holiness. Leviticus 8:9 refers to the turban as a "holy crown," and Zechariah 3:5 states, "Let them put a clean turban on his head." This is the scene in which Prophet Zechariah asks God to place a turban on the head of Joshua the high priest. Here the word "clean" is טָהוֹר (*tahor*) in Hebrew, meaning "clean" and "purity," and refers to holiness that is flawless, clean, and pure.

Jesus the high priest was holy and wore a crown of glory and honor. Hebrews 2:9 states, "We do see Him who was made for a little while lower than the angels, namely, Jesus, because of the suffering of death crowned with glory and honor, so that by the grace of God He might taste death for everyone." When Jesus died on the cross, He wore the crown of thorns of scorn, humiliation, and suffering, but the resurrected and ascended Jesus will wear a crown of glory and honor before God (see Isa 62:1–3).

Prophet Isaiah prophesied that Jesus Christ will adorn Himself with a garland (פְּאֵר, *peer*, "headdress, turban") as the bridegroom of the saints (see Isa 62:4–5; 2 Cor 11:2; Eph 5:22–25):

> *I will rejoice greatly in the Lord, my soul will exult in my God; for He has clothed me with garments of salvation, He has wrapped me with a robe of righteousness, as a bridegroom decks himself with a garland, and as a bride adorns herself with her jewels.* (Isaiah 61:10)

We who have been grafted into Jesus the high priest will also in the future put on the holy crown along with Him. At the second coming, those who have been faithful to God for His glory and for the name of the Lord will receive the crown before God's throne (Rev 3:11). This crown is the "crown of righteousness" (2 Tim 4:8), the "crown of glory" (1 Pet 5:4), the "imperishable" crown (1 Cor 9:25), and the "crown of life" (Jas 1:12; Rev 2:10). The twenty-four elders took off their crowns and threw them before the throne of God and gave glory before God (Rev 4:10–11).

On the other hand, the high priest wore a turban and covered his head before God as a gesture of total abandonment of his own thoughts and will and of complete obedience to God. Jesus, our high priest, was God Himself, but He emptied Himself and took on the form of a bondservant and became a man. He fully obeyed God the Father, even until He died on the cross (Matt 26:39; Phil 2:6–8). A true life of faith is faithfulness unto death, total obedience to God, and all glory ascribed only to God.

Second, the plate of the high priest represents purity. The plate of gold has the words "Holy to the Lord" engraved on it (Exod 28:36; 39:30). The word "holy" is קֹדֶשׁ (*qodesh*) in Hebrew, meaning "consecrated," and God gave the high priest the plate of holiness and proclaimed him holy. God said that He would receive Aaron's offerings only if the plate was always on his forehead. Exodus 28:38b states, "It shall always be on his forehead, that they may be accepted before the Lord." This means that without this plate, God would not accept anything.

Since the forehead represents a person's character, a high priest must always live a holy life through God's Word and prayer (1 Tim 4:5). This is a stern lesson that without a holy life, no sacrifice (worship) will be accepted by God.

Prophet Zechariah prophesied that the words engraved on the plate of the high priest, "Holy to the Lord," will be inscribed even on the bells of the horses (Zech 14:20). The bells of the horses were small bells attached to the horses' necks and very common during ancient times. The fact that the words "Holy to the Lord" were to be engraved even on common objects means that there will come a time when holiness to the Lord will cover the whole world. This means that there will come a day when people will worship in spirit and in truth within the new covenant of Jesus Christ, and the knowledge of the Lord will fill this world, just as the waters cover the sea, so that all the world will become holy under God's reign (Isa 11:9; Jer 31:34; Hab 2:14).

God's will for us is holiness (consecration; Lev 11:44; 19:2; 1 Pet 1:16). The high priest must be set apart from all defilements and offer up himself to God first and then be fully devoted to serving for God's glory. In addition, "Holiness to the Lord" must be imprinted on the bodies, hearts, and minds of all those serving in God's temple. God's power leaves the high priest the moment he loses his holiness; all honor disappears instantly, and he becomes no different from a dead man who has lost his life. When Achan was not holy, Israel was defeated in the battle of Ai (Josh 7:1, 13), and the invincible Samson became powerless when he lost his holiness as a Nazirite (Judg 16:17, 19–20). David was greatly cursed when he took Bathsheba, and he lost his holiness: the sword did not leave his house forever; other men lay with his wives in broad daylight; and the son Bathsheba bore died (2 Sam 12:1–14).

God receives worship only from those who have thoroughly consecrated themselves. Thus, as the end draws near, we must become consecrated people (separated as holy). Hebrews 12:14 states, "Pursue peace with all men, and the sanctification without which no one will see the Lord."

Ephod אֵפוֹד *efod*

Exodus 28:6–14; 29:5; 39:2–7; Leviticus 8:7

Characteristics

The אֵפוֹד (*efod*) was one of the holy garments worn while the high priest was performing his duties (Exod 28:2; 39:1; Lev 8:7–9; see 1 Sam 2:28). It was a sleeveless apron-like garment that came down to the knees and was worn on top of the outer robe (the robe of the ephod). The following are the characteristics of the ephod.

First, the front and back panels were firmly fastened together by two shoulder pieces. Regarding the ephod of the high priest, it was written, "They shall also make the ephod . . . It shall have two shoulder pieces joined to its two ends, that it may be joined" (Exod 28:6–7; 39:4). Here the word "joined" is the pual (intensive passive) stem of the Hebrew word חָבַר (*havar*), meaning "to unite" and "to be joined," with a conjunction, so it is written as "and so it shall be joined together" (KJV). Considering these kinds of descriptions of the ephod, the ephod was comprised of two parts—front and back panels that were joined at the top of the shoulders. The sash for the ephod was also tied around the body over the ephod and below the breastpiece such that the front and back panels of the ephod stayed close to the body and did not become loose. Hence the ephod was not a one-piece garment but a simple garment whose back and front panels were joined by two shoulder pieces.

Second, two onyx stones were set on the shoulder pieces. On the shoulder pieces of the high priest were two onyx stones carved and set in filigree settings of gold. On each stone were engraved six names of the sons of Israel in order of age (Exod 28:9–11; 39:6). The two stones were placed on the shoulder pieces of the ephod as memorial stones for the sons of Israel (Exod 28:12; 39:7; see "Excursus 5: The Garments of the High Priest").

Materials

The ephod of the high priest was skillfully made of gold, blue, purple, and scarlet material and fine twisted linen (Exod 28:6; 39:2–3). Unlike the white linen ephod of the other priests, this ephod was beautiful and magnificent.

Exodus 39:3 explains in detail how the gold threads were made: "They hammered out gold sheets and cut them into threads." Garments made with the gold threads as part of its material were the ephod (Exod 28:6; 39:2), the sash worn on top of the ephod (Exod 28:8; 39:5), and the breastplate (Exod 28:15; 39:8). The sash and the breastplate worn on top of the ephod were skillfully made "like the work of the ephod" with gold, blue, purple, and scarlet material and fine twisted linen (Exod 28:15; see also Exod 28:8; 39:5, 8). The gold thread was not used, however, in making the sash for the tunic (Exod 39:29).

The ephod of the priests, called "the linen ephod," was differentiated from the ephod of the high priest (1 Sam 22:18). The young Samuel wore the linen ephod (1 Sam 2:18). David also wore the linen ephod as he brought the ark of the covenant into the city of David (2 Sam 6:14; 1 Chr 15:27). Samuel was able to wear the ephod despite his young age because he had been dedicated to serving the Lord all his life (1 Sam 1:28). It is presumed that David, as the king of Israel, the priestly nation of God, wore the priestly garment, the ephod, during a national feast in order to raise the dignity of the priests.

Redemptive-historical significance

The phrase "to wear the ephod" was used to mean "to become a priest" or "to perform priestly duties." In 1 Samuel 22:18, Doeg the Edomite attacked and killed the priests, and the verse narrates that he killed "men who wore the linen ephod." Moreover, the phrase "without ephod" indicated living without a priest or living a godless life (Hos 3:4). Based on such usages, it can be assumed that the word "ephod" was mainly used in reference to priests.

During David's life of refuge from Saul, he used the ephod to inquire whether the people of Keilah would surrender him to Saul (1 Sam 23:9–12). He also used it to ask if he would be victorious if he attacked Amalek (1 Sam 30:7–8).

During the period of the judges, the ephod was used to satisfy the personal greed of fallen human beings (Judg 17:5; 18:14). All Israel played the harlot with the golden ephod that the judge Gideon had made with gold seized from the Midianite soldiers, and it became a snare to Gideon and his household (Judg 8:26–27). The ephod Gideon made was extremely expensive. Judges 8:27 states that "it" (אוֹתוֹ, *otho*) was used to make the ephod. "It" refers to the gold earrings weighing 1,700 shekels of gold that had been seized (Judg 8:24–26), which amounted to about forty-four pounds (704 ounces, or twenty kilograms). According to today's price of gold (about $1220 USD per ounce), it would be worth more than a quarter of a million dollars.

Furthermore, Micah the Ephraimite had a shrine and placed there a graven image and a molten image, which his mother had made with two hundred pieces of silver. He also made an ephod and household idols for the shrine and consecrated one of his sons so he might become his priest (Judg 17:1–5).

Also, when Saul inquired of God to find out who had disobeyed the command to fast, he commanded Ahijah the priest to bring the "ark of God" (1 Sam 14:18). However, since the ark of God was located in Kiriath-jearim at the time (1 Sam 7:1–2), it is presumable that Ahijah brought the ephod and not the ark. First Samuel 14:3 states that Ahijah was "wearing an ephod" while Saul was camped along with the people of Israel, facing the Philistine army. Here the word "wearing" is נָשָׂא (*nasa*), meaning "to lift" or "to carry." This demonstrates that Ahijah carried the ephod around in order to inquire regarding the will of the Lord concerning the battle against the Philistines. It is evident, however, that the northern kingdom of Israel also made the ephod for the purpose of worship (Hos 3:4). The Lexham Bible Dictionary states that the ephod was synonymous with the ark, and the ephod itself was a miniature temple and regarded as such. It states that it was clear that the ephod was used as a means to receive oracles or a portable object used by priests to receive God's command (1 Sam 14:3, 18–19; 23:9).[71]

Two onyx stones sat, one on each side of the high priest's shoulder, with the names of the twelve tribes engraved on them. The high priest was to bear all Israel's sins on his shoulders and stand before God as a mediator. The shoulders represent the ample strength and

---

71 Ronald D. Roberts, "Ephod," ed. John D. Barry and others, *Lexham Bible Dictionary* (Bellingham, WA: Lexham, 2016).

power required to take on this responsibility (see Deut 33:12). This image of the high priest is reminiscent of Jesus Christ, who bore the cross on His shoulders in order to atone for all the sins of mankind. Prophet Isaiah prophesied that the government would rest on the shoulders of the child who was to come as the Messiah (Isa 9:6). Through the parable of the shepherd searching persistently for the one lost sheep among the one hundred until he finally finds it and brings it back on his shoulders, Jesus explained how He receives sinners and takes responsibility for them until the end (Luke 15:3–5). Jesus Christ, our high priest, has engraved our names on His shoulders, and all those whose names have been engraved will surely be saved.

Skillfully woven band of the ephod

חֵשֶׁב אֲפֻדָּת *heshev afuddath*

Exodus 28:8; 29:5; 39:5; Leviticus 8:7

Characteristics

The band of the ephod is described as "the skillfully woven band, which is on it [the ephod]" (Exod 28:8; see also 39:5), and it was to be worn around the waist and tied in the front. Besides the band of the ephod, there was also a sash for the tunic (Exod 28:39; 39:29; Lev 16:4).

Leviticus 8:7 states, "He put the tunic on him and girded him with the sash, and clothed him with the robe and put the ephod on him; and he girded him with the artistic band of the ephod, with which he tied it to him." The band of the ephod was a beautifully woven band. For this reason it is described as an "artistic band" (Lev 8:7) and "skillfully woven band of the ephod" (Exod 28:27–28; see also 39:20–21).

Materials

The band of the ephod was woven with gold, blue, purple, and scarlet material and fine twisted linen "like its [the ephod's] workmanship" (Exod 28:8; 39:5). The sash for the tunic was made of the same material, excluding the gold (Exod 39:29).

Redemptive-historical significance

The sash that was tied around the tunic and worn by both the high priest and the priests was not made with gold. However, the high priest's band of the ephod was made with gold material. Daniel 10:5 describes a certain man by the river Chebar as "dressed in linen, whose waist was girded with a belt of pure gold of Uphaz" (see Rev 1:13). The word "girded" is חָגַר (*hagar*) in Hebrew and means "to gird," "to arm," or "dressed." Thus this manifests Jesus, our high priest, who is working continuously for the completion of the work of redemption (John 5:17).

Robe of the ephod

מְעִיל הָאֵפוֹד *meil haefod*

Exodus 28:31–35; 29:5; 39:22–26; Leviticus 8:7

Characteristics

The following are the characteristics of the robe of the ephod.

First, the whole robe was blue. The blue robe worn over the white tunic symbolized the dignity and authority of the position of the high priest. The blue color was used for the veil, the curtains, the gate of the tabernacle, and the gate of the court. The cord that tied the plate of pure gold onto the priest's head, as well as the cord that connected the breastplate and the band of the ephod, were also blue. Just as we remember God's immense love and grace whenever we look up to the expansive blue sky, the blue robe of the high priest also represented the abundant grace of Jesus Christ, our high priest (John 1:14, 16).

Second, an opening for the head was made between the two shoulders of the robe, but it was made with special care so that it did not become torn or tattered as it was put on and taken off. Exodus 28:32 states, "Around its opening there shall be a binding of woven work, like the opening of a coat of mail," which means to make a woven work around the collar just like the collar of armor. God made a special request to make a woven collar around the opening of the neck so that the robe would not tear as one put it on.

Third, pomegranates of blue, purple, and scarlet material were made all around on the robe's hem, and bells of gold were attached between the pomegranates at an equal distance (Exod 28:33–34; 39:24–26).

The Bible does not record the exact number of bells of gold and pomegranates, and there have been various views.[72] However, considering that the sound of the bells must be heard from the outside, it can be conjectured that eighteen bells of gold were attached between eighteen pomegranates. Pomegranates were one of the seven fruits of the land of Canaan; it is also one of the fruits that the twelve spies brought back with them (Num 13:23). Inside its skin, which is round and inflated like a balloon, a pomegranate is packed with seeds covered in deep red flesh. The fruit is full of white seeds, it is about the size of an orange, and the juice tastes sweet and tangy. For this reason, even from ancient times, pomegranates have symbolized abundance and prosperity. Our lives can also bear abundant fruit only in Jesus Christ (John 15:7–8).

72 Peter Schegg, *Biblische Archäologie*, ed. Wirthmüller (Freiburg: Herder, 1887), 545. Also see, *Zevachim* 88[b].

Materials

This "robe of the ephod" is an outer robe worn under the ephod, and it was all blue and plain without pattern (Exod 28:31; 39:22). It was longer than the ephod and was a one-piece seamless robe that fell from top to bottom (Exod 28:32; 39:23). It was woven with blue material. Exodus 39:22 states, "He made the robe of the ephod of woven work, all of blue." The Good News Translation (GNT) states, "The robe that goes under the ephod was made entirely of blue wool."

Redemptive-historical significance

While the sacrifices were offered in the holy place, the golden bells attached to the hem of the robe of the ephod rang every time the high priest moved. This probably prompted the people listening outside to put on a solemn and reverent heart as they waited attentively. Moreover, while the high priest was inside the holy place, the ringing of the bells was an indication that the high priest was alive (Exod 28:35). The melodious sounds of the golden bells attached between the woven pomegranates resonated inside the holy place. It was the sound of good news, wonderful news, and blessed news (Ps 40:9; Isa 40:9; 41:27; 52:7; Luke 1:19; Rom. 10:15). The sound of the Word of Jesus the high priest is the blessed news of salvation, and the fruit of life springs forth wherever this news is preached. We must all become golden bells that continuously make the beautiful sounds of the gospel as we perform God's work.

Breastpiece of judgment

חֹשֶׁן מִשְׁפָּט *hoshen mishpat*

Exodus 28:15–30; 29:5; 39:8–21; Leviticus 8:8

Characteristics

The breastpiece, as is evident from its name, was worn on the chest on top of the ephod. It was so splendid, magnificent, and mysterious that its appearance was quite conspicuous. The following are characteristics of the breastpiece.

First, twelve precious stones representing the twelve tribes lay on the outer layer of the breastpiece (Exod 28:17–21; 39:10–14), and the Urim and Thummin were in the space between the outer and the inner layer (Exod 28:29–30; Lev 8:7–8). The Urim and Thummin were used to inquire regarding the will of God before a decision was made on a national issue (see 1 Sam 23:9–12). It was a tool used to entrust all decision-making powers to God. The breastpiece was also called the "breastpiece of judgment," because the Urim and Thummin were kept inside a pouch of the breastpiece (Exod 28:15).

The breastpiece with the twelve stones was attached at the top, with gold chains, to the two gold filigree settings of the onyx stones on the shoulder pieces of the ephod. The lower part was tied with a blue cord to the high priest's band of the ephod so that it did not come loose from the ephod (Exod 28:22–28).

Second, four rows of three stones were mounted on the perfectly square breastplate (Exod 28:16–20; 39:9–13). Each stone was set in gold filigree (Exod 39:13), and the names of the twelve tribes of Israel were engraved on the twelve stones (Exod 28:21; 39:14). No records exist of the order in which the names of the twelve tribes were engraved on the twelve stones, but they were probably written in the order in which God commanded the Israelites to march in the wilderness (Num 10:11–28). Numbers 10 records the order in which the twelve tribes set out from their camps when they marched in the wilderness.

Each name of the twelve tribes was engraved on each of the twelve stones like the engravings of a seal (Exod 28:21; 39:14). The high priest was to enter the holy place with these twelve engraved stones attached to his chest. The ministry of the priest was never for himself;

it was the intercessory work of bearing the sins of the people before God.

Human beings, who possess nothing good but are only full of sin (Ps 14:1; Isa 1:4; Rom 7:18; 1 Tim 6:4–5; 2 Tim 3:8), are weak beings who can never go before God without the atoning work of Jesus Christ. Thus they can be acknowledged as righteous only when they go forth with the holiness of Jesus Christ.

Third, the breastpiece with the twelve stones were tied to gold rings and attached to the gold filigree on the shoulder pieces with the onyx stones. It was also tied to the high priest's waistband. A total of six gold rings were connected to the high priest's garment. Four rings were at each of the four edges of the breastpiece (Exod 28:23, 26; 39:16, 19), and two were on either side of the band of the ephod (Exod 28:27; 39:20). Of the gold rings on the four edges of the breastpiece, the two rings at the top were connected to the shoulder pieces, and the two lower rings were connected to the band of the ephod. No gold rings were on the shoulder pieces, however, so the gold chains were attached to the gold filigree around the onyx stones (Exod 28:9–14; 39:15–18).

The upper part of the breastpiece and the shoulder pieces were connected with gold chains (Exod 28:22–24; 39:15–17), and the lower part of the breastpiece was connected to the band of the ephod with a blue cord (Exod 28:28; 39:21). The blue cord was also used to attach the gold plate to the front of the turban (Exod 28:37; 39:31).

The two gold rings at the bottom of the breastpiece were specifically placed on the inside edges of the breastpiece (Exod 28:26; 39:19) to secure the breastpiece to the ephod (Exod 28:28).

Materials

The breastpiece was an exquisite and beautiful piece of work made with the same materials as the ephod (Exod 28:15; 39:8). It was square—a span (a half cubit, or about 8.86 inches [22.5 centimeters]) in length and a span in width. It was made with gold, blue, purple, and scarlet material and fine twisted linen and was folded double (Exod 28:15–16; 39:8–9). The squareness of the breastpiece signifies the fact that the intercessory ministry of the priests must be fair, without partiality.

Redemptive-historical significance

Just as the breastpiece with the twelve stones with the names of the twelve tribes was attached to the top of the ephod, the names of the chosen saints will certainly be recorded in the book of life (Rev 21:27). Only when Jesus, our high priest, embraces us, just as a hen embraces its chicks in its bosom, will we be remembered by God and abide in His love (Matt 23:37). We are inscribed not only on God's "palm" (Isa 49:16) but also in the heart of Jesus Christ, our mediator (Song 8:6). The fact that the twelve stones with the names of the twelve tribes were on the chest of the high priest means that God was protecting the Israelites with great love (see John 13:23). All the names of the saints are inscribed in the heart of Jesus Christ our high priest, and He protects us completely with the fervent love of His heart.

In the same way that the twelve stones on the breastplate were set in their appointed places, so the saints must never leave their place of calling. Moreover, as the stones possessed various shapes and hues, the saints must also glorify God and be faithful to Him according to the talent He has entrusted to each person. As we do so, then, just as the stones radiantly shone from the high priest's breast, God will also receive great glory through His children (Phil 1:20; 1 Cor 10:31).

Because the high priest loved and cherished the breastpiece the most, he always looked over it carefully. This means that not only the church but all its members also are made to live before Jesus Christ our high priest as members of His body (1 Cor 12:12–31). The saints must never leave the church, and the church must never leave Christ.

As we have just observed, the ephod, breastpiece, and shoulder pieces were attached together with gold rings, the blue cord, and gold chains so that they became one harmonious garment. The work of the high priest, the mediator between God and mankind under the first covenant, foreshadows the work of Jesus Christ, the mediator of the new covenant (Heb 8:6).

Jesus Christ, the only begotten Son who is in the boundless loving bosom of God, took all the sins and infirmities of mankind upon His two shoulders and bore them (Matt 8:16–17; John 1:18). Jesus is truly eternally unchanging and is the golden chain of God's love that no one can break. He is heaven's blue cord of life and knows no death forever (Rom 8:35–39).

When God gave orders concerning the garments of the high priest, He gave thorough and detailed instructions regarding the connecting rings, the shape of the collar of the tunic, the length and even the colors of each garment, all according to their uses. None of God's Words were recorded without meaning—not even one.

God, who is the same yesterday, today, and forever, intervenes in the lives of His children, the saints; He understands and protects them (Heb 13:8). Thus those who are inside Jesus' bosom are forever safe and will enjoy peace (John 14:27). When the saints remain in God's bosom, like the precious stones sparkling with their own brilliant hue, they will live monumental lives that shine forever and ever.

CHAPTER

16

The Duties of the High Priest

The word *duty* refers to the task that a person in charge must faithfully perform. The duties of the high priest reveal the image of Jesus Christ, the true high priest.

1. As the Representative of the People, the High Priest Was in Charge of All Things Related to the Sacrifice

The high priest was the head of the Levitical priests and performed work related to sacrifices in the tabernacle. He represented the people of Israel before God and oversaw all things related to the sacrifice. Hebrews 8:3 states that the high priest was appointed "to offer both gifts and sacrifices." He also managed all the money that came in and went out of the house of God (2 Kgs 12:10; 22:4; 2 Chr 24:12).

Jesus Christ is the representative of all saints who are a royal priesthood. This is why Jesus Christ is called the head of the church (Eph 1:22; 5:23; Col 1:18). We must be ruled by Jesus Christ in all aspects of life such as in matters of wealth, marriage, child-rearing, and so forth.

2. He Entered the Holy of Holies on One Day of the Year

The high priest offered sacrifices in the holy of holies on one day of the year, the Day of Atonement, which was the tenth day of the seventh month (religious calendar). This was the climax of all sacrifices, as it was the sacrifice that procured the forgiveness of sins for all the people of Israel. The Day of Atonement was called the "sabbath of solemn rest" (Lev 16:31) and a "permanent statute" (Lev 16:29, 31, 34). Leviticus 16:34 states, "You shall have this as a permanent statute, to make atonement for the sons of Israel for all their sins once every year." Of Aaron's four sons, Nadab and Abihu offered strange fire before the Lord, which He had not commanded them; and fire from the Lord came out and consumed them, and they died (Lev 10:1–7). Then, through Moses, God especially visited the house of Aaron, which had been consumed with fear and a sense of guilt (Lev 16:1), and spoke to Aaron regarding the statute of the Day of Atonement. When God revealed the statute of the Day of Atonement, Aaron and his household became the mediators between God and the people of Israel.

On the Day of Atonement, the high priest offered a sin offering for himself and for his household (Lev 16:11–14) as well as for the people (Lev 16:15–19). Then he offered a burnt offering for himself and another for the people and made atonement (Lev 16:23–24). Hebrews 9:7 states, "Into the second [tabernacle], only the high priest enters once a year, not without taking blood, which he offers for himself and for the sins of the people committed in ignorance."

Aaron prepared a bull for a sin offering and a ram for a burnt offering for himself. Then for the people of Israel he took two male goats for a sin offering and one ram for a burnt offering and prepared them (Lev 16:3, 5).

On the Day of Atonement, the high priest bathed his body with water and clothed himself with the holy linen tunic and the linen breeches, girded himself with the linen sash, and put the linen turban on his head (Lev 16:4). He entered the holy of holies alone and sprinkled the blood of the sin offering for himself and for the people of Israel. During ordinary times the dignity of the high priest was on display through the magnificent garments he wore (Lev 8:7–9). When he entered the holy of holies, however, he did not put on the ephod, the breastpiece of judgment, or the robe of the ephod but only the linen robe that symbolized purity. The humble image of the high priest wearing the linen robe foreshadows the image of Jesus Christ, who purifies all sins by serving as the mediator between God and man.

Entry into the holy of holies on this day was forbidden for all laymen and even for the priests. Leviticus 16:2 states, "The Lord said to Moses: 'Tell your brother Aaron that he shall not enter at any time into the holy place inside the veil, before the mercy seat which is on the ark, or he will die; for I will appear in the cloud over the mercy seat.'" Here the place "inside the veil" refers to the holy of holies, the area inside the veil that separated the holy place and the holy of holies. Entry into this area was forbidden to all except the high priest without exception (Lev 16:2), and the high priest was allowed to enter this area only one day a year.

Leviticus 16 contains several references to the high priest's entry inside the veil: "inside the veil" (Lev 16:12, 15) and "when he goes in to make atonement in the holy place" (Lev 16:17).

In actuality, the high priest entered the holy of holies four times during the Day of Atonement. Hebrews 9:7 states, "Into the second [tabernacle], only the high priest enters once a year," but this did not mean that the high priest entered the holy of holies only one time on the Day of Atonement but rather only one day a year, the Day of Atonement.

The following was the procedure for the high priest's entry into the holy of holies on the Day of Atonement.

***First*, he took the firepan full of coals of fire from upon the altar before the Lord and two handfuls of finely ground sweet incense and entered the holy of holies (Lev 16:12).**

He escaped death by putting the incense on the fire before the Lord so that the cloud of incense covered the mercy seat that was on the ark of the testimony (Lev 16:13). The act of covering the mercy seat with the cloud of incense reveals that mankind is frail and cannot see God face to face (Exod 33:20; Deut 5:24–27).

***Second*, the high priest, after he burned incense, came out of the holy of holies; then he took some of the blood of the bull inside the holy of holies and sprinkled it with his finger on the mercy seat on the east side.**

Then he sprinkled some of the blood in front of the mercy seat with his finger seven times (Lev 16:14). Here "mercy seat on the east side" is עַל־פְּנֵי הַכַּפֹּרֶת קֵדְמָה (*al-pene hakkapporeth qedemah*) and means "the top of the front of the east side of the mercy seat." This is where the blood was sprinkled. The high priest sprinkled the blood one time on the top side of the mercy seat toward the front and seven times on the front side of the mercy seat. This was an entreaty to God to look upon the blood and forgive the people's sins. The sprinkling of the blood seven times symbolized Jesus Christ's complete forgiveness of sins (Heb 7:27; 9:12; 10:10). The east of the temple is the direction through which God's presence came (Ezek 10:18–19; 11:22–23; 43:1–5). The sprinkling of the blood was for the forgiveness of the sins of the high priest and his household (Lev 16:6, 11, 14).

An important point to focus on regarding the offerings on the Day of Atonement is that the atonement for the high priest himself had to precede that of the entire people. This is written seven times in Leviticus 16 alone. Verse 6 states, "The sin offering . . . is for himself, that he may make atonement for himself and for his household" (two times). Verse 11 states, "Then Aaron shall offer the bull of the sin offering which is for himself and make atonement for himself and for his household, and he shall slaughter the bull of the sin offering which is for himself" (three times). Verse 17 states "that he may make atonement for himself and for his household and for all the assembly of Israel" (one time). Then verse 24 states that he would "offer his burnt offering and the burnt offering of the people and make atonement for himself and for the people" (one time).

***Third,* he took the blood of the goat of the sin offering and brought it to the holy of holies.**

He then sprinkled the blood on the mercy seat and in front of the mercy seat in the same way as in the second step (Lev 16:15). This sprinkling of the blood was for the atonement of the sins of the people. This goat was one of the two goats prepared for the sin offering but not the goat that would be sent out into the wilderness (Lev 16:21–22; "Azazel"; Lev 16:10, 18, 26, ESV).

After sprinkling the blood of the goat, the high priest came out of the holy of holies, went to the altar before the Lord, and made atonement for the altar. He did so by taking some of the blood of the bull and the blood of the goat and putting them on the horns of the altar on all sides; and with his finger he sprinkled some of the blood on the altar seven times (Lev 16:18–19; see Exod 30:10). It was important to consecrate the altar thus from the impurities of the people of Israel (Lev 16:19) and to make atonement for the holy of holies, the tent of meeting, and the altar (Lev 16:20, 33). If the altar was defiled, then God would accept none of the offerings made on it throughout the coming year. Hence God emphasized the consecration of the altar above all else (Exod 29:37). The emphasis on the purification of the altar of burnt offering is particularly evident in the new temple of Prophet Ezekiel. God said that a newly built altar must be consecrated for seven days before making offerings on it. Ezekiel 43:26–27 states, "'For seven days they shall make atonement for the altar and purify it; so shall they consecrate it. When they have completed the days, it shall be that on the eighth day and onward, the priests shall offer your burnt offerings on the altar, and your peace offerings; and I will accept you,' declares the Lord God."

After consecrating the altar, the high priest laid both his hands on the head of the live goat and sent it away into the wilderness (Lev 16:21). Then he went into the tent of meeting, took off the linen garment he had worn when he went into the holy of holies, and left it there. He then washed himself in water in the holy place, put his clothes on, and came out (Lev 16:23–24). His clothes here refer to the garments in Leviticus 8:7–9—the magnificent garments that he normally wore when he performed the duties of the high priest.

The high priest, after changing his clothes, atoned for himself and for the people by offering his burnt offering and the burnt offering of the people. He then offered up in smoke the fat of the sin offering on the altar (Lev 16:24–25). The atonement made in the holy of holies was for the atonement of the fundamental sins of mankind, while the atonement made by the burnt offerings cleansed the filth that appeared after the fundamental sins were atoned for.

***Fourth and finally,* it is conjectured that the high priest reentered the holy of holies in order to remove the incense and the fire.**

Details on the high priest's fourth entry into the holy of holies are well recorded in Jewish literature. According to the Mishnah (*Yoma* 5:1; 8:4) and *The Book of Our Heritage*, which was written by Eliyahu Kitov, the high priest changed into new white linen garments after the process of entering the holy of holies three times and after the burnt offering for the atonement was completed. These new white linen garments were not the garments he had previously worn and taken off; they were new linen garments. Before he changed into the new garments, the high priest consecrated himself by washing his hands and feet, took off his clothes, and washed his body. Then, after changing into the new linen garments, he washed his hands and feet again and entered the holy of holies in order to remove the incense and the fire.[73]

73 Eliyahu Kitov, *The Book of Our Heritage: The Jewish Year and Its Days of Significance*, vol. 1, *Tishrey-Shevat* (New York: Feldheim, 1997), 96–97.

It is no longer necessary to offer painstakingly complicated offerings on the Day of Atonement. When Jesus died on the cross, the veil between the holy of holies and the holy place was torn from top to bottom (Matt 27:51). This veil refers to Jesus' flesh (Heb 10:20). As the high priest, Jesus accomplished eternal atonement on the cross with His own blood and entered the holy of holies once and for all (Heb 10:10–14). Hebrews 9:12 states that "not through the blood of goats and calves, but through His own blood, He entered the holy place once for all, having obtained eternal redemption." Because Jesus' body was torn on the cross, all our sins were completely removed, and the wall between God and mankind came crumbling down. Now, through the mediation of Jesus Christ, the true high priest, anyone can go before God at any time (Rom 5:1–11; Eph 2:14–18; 1 Tim 2:5–6; Heb 10:19–20).

Jesus is the high priest who was promised with an oath (Heb 7:20–21; see also Ps 110:4), the eternal high priest according to the order of Melchizedek (Heb 5:6; 6:20; 7:17). Therefore, being empowered by Jesus Christ, the eternal high priest of the covenantal oath, may we all be more than able to enter into the kingdom of heaven.

3. He Adjudicated Using the Urim and the Thummim

Deuteronomy 33:8 states, "Let Your Thummim and Your Urim belong to Your godly man." The Urim and the Thummim were placed inside the breastpiece of judgment that was attached to the ephod the high priest wore (Exod 28:29–30; Lev 8:7–8). This was the means through which the high priest, who had been entrusted with God's spiritual authority, received answers regarding God's judgment when resolving various issues.

The Urim and the Thummim were often used as the instrument for casting lots when the high priest inquired of God regarding important national issues (see Num 27:21; Deut 33:8; 1 Sam 23:6, 9–11; 28:6).

Although the exact shape of the Urim and the Thummim is unclear, it is presumed that one lot represented a positive answer and the other represented a negative answer. The word "Urim" (אוּרִים) means "lights," as it is the plural form of the word אוֹר (*ur*), meaning "light." "Thummim" (תֻּמִּים) means "perfection," as it is the plural form of the word תֹּם (*tom*), meaning "completeness." The judgment of God—who is light and perfection itself—is His eternally unchanging will, so it must be totally obeyed.

The Septuagint (LXX) of 1 Samuel 14:41 also mentions the Urim and the Thummim. It asks the Lord to "give a perfect lot"; this phrase is הָבָה תָמִים (*havah thamim*) in Hebrew and means "show us perfection."

The word "Urim" begins with the first character of the Hebrew alphabet, א (*alef*), and "Thummim" begins with the last letter, ת (*tav*). This reveals Jesus Christ, who is the first and the last (Rev 1:8, 17; 2:8; 21:6; 22:13) and the cause and the effect of all history.

The Urim and the Thummim were holy instruments, a channel through which the ultimate judgment was entrusted to the absolute sovereignty of God while precluding any human judgment (Ezra 2:63; Neh 7:65). During Nehemiah's time an inspection was made of the genealogies of the returnees of the first return from exile. It revealed that some priests could not prove their ancestral registration (the sons of Habaiah, Hakkoz, and Barzillai). Regarding them the governor commanded that "they should not eat from the most holy things until a priest stood up with Urim and Thummim" (Ezra 2:63; see also Neh 7:65). The New King James Version comes closest to the original meaning of the Hebrew text and translates it as, "They should not eat of the most holy things till a priest could consult with the Urim and Thummim." However, it is presumed that the Urim and the Thummim vanished when the high priest's ephod, which held them, was lost when the Babylonians burned down the Jerusalem temple in 586 BC or when the high priest Seraiah was captured and taken to the king of Babylon and killed (2 Kgs 25:8–9, 18–21). For this reason the governor in Nehemiah's time said that if a high priest rose who could judge with the Urim and the Thummim, then he could ask God if the sons of the three men were indeed sons of priests. However, considering that this is the last mention of the Urim and the Thummim, it appears as though the sons of Habaiah, Hakkoz, and Barzillai—who could not find their names in the genealogy—were stripped of their priesthood forever (Ezra 2:61–63; Neh 7:63–65).

We seek to live according to God's will, but many times we do not properly know God's will. The way to resolve this issue is through prayer and waiting for His answer so we can work it out. The surest way is to find the solution through the Old and New Testaments, which are like the Urim and the Thummim. Psalm 119:105 states, "Your word is a lamp to my feet and a light to my path." The whole Bible, which was written through the inspiration of God, is "profitable for teaching, for reproof, for correction, for training in righteousness" (2 Tim 3:16). Thus when we continue in the things we have learned and become convinced of, we become adequate as people of God and equipped for every good work (2 Tim 3:14–17).

Only the judgment of the Old and New Testaments are just and perfect to reveal light. The perfect judgment will be proclaimed to all mankind during the judgment of the great white throne, which will take place after the second coming of Jesus Christ, the eternal high priest (Rev 20:11–15).

4. He Saved Those Who Had Fled to the City of Refuge

City of refuge is עִיר מִקְלָט (*ir miqlat*) and means "a city of asylum" or "a city of intaking." A city of refuge was a city that took in a person who had committed murder to guarantee his safety. A person who had unintentionally murdered another could escape death at the hands of his victim's relatives by fleeing to the city of refuge. However, a person who had murdered intentionally must be taken even from the altar and killed (Exod 21:12–14).

Three cities of refuge could be found to the east of the Jordan River and three to the west of the Jordan River. To the east of the Jordan were Bezer (Josh 20:8; 21:36), Ramoth in Gilead (Josh 20:8; 21:38), and Golan in Bashan (Josh 20:8; 21:27). To the west of Jordan were Kedesh (Josh 20:7; 21:32), Shechem (Josh 20:7; 21:21; 1 Chr 6:67), and Hebron (Josh 20:7; 21:13). The cities of refuge were located about thirty miles (approximately forty-eight kilometers) from any given city within a region so they could be reached within one day. According to Jewish tradition, signs written with the words "city of refuge" were posted at various points on the path to the cities of refuge. The roads that led to the cities of refuge were usually paved and about 15.3 yards (approximately fourteen meters) wide (see Deut 19:3).

According to the law of Moses, a person who unintentionally killed should remain in the city of refuge to escape the avenger of blood. When the high priest died, the person was forgiven of his sin and could live freely outside the city of refuge (Num 35:25–28; Josh 20:6). This was because the death of the high priest, who was in charge of the atonement of the people, was regarded as payment for the blood of the manslayer. Likewise, through the death of Jesus Christ, our eternal high priest, all of us who believe have been granted remittance from our debt of sin, given liberation from the bondage of sin and death, and gifted with eternal salvation (Heb 5:8–10).

ים המלח
מדבר צין הוא קדש
עמלק
מדבר סיני
קדש ברנע
מדבר פארן
מדבר שור
ארץ פלשתים
שבט
שבט שמעון
באר שבע
עיר כרמל
אשקלון
גת
פתם
ארץ גשן
אלכסנדרי
לוח המסעות במדבר
אשר על פי ה׳ יסעו ועל פי ה׳ יחנו
א״ רעמסס טו״ רתמה לט״ הרהגדגד
ב״ סכת טז״ רמן פרץ ל״ יטבתה
ג״ אתם יז״ לבנה לא״ עברנה
ד״ פיהחירת יח״ רסה לב״ עציון גבר
ה״ מרה יט״ קהלתה לג״ מדבר צין
ו״ אילם כ״ הר ספר לד״ הר ההר
ז״ ים סוף כא״ חרדה לה״ צלמנה
ח״ מדבר סין כב״ מקהלת לו״ פונן
ט״ דפקה כג״ תחת לז״ אבת
יו״ אלוש כד״ תרח לח״ דיבן גד
יא״ רפידם כה״ מתקה לט״ עלמן דבלתים
יב״ מדבר סיני כו״ חשמנה מ״ הרי עברים
יג״ קברות התאוה כז״ מסרות מא״ ערבת מואב
יד״ חצרת כח״ בני יעקן

CONLUSION

JESUS CHRIST,

THE ETERNAL HIGH PRIEST WHO CAME ACCORDING TO THE ORDER OF MELCHIZEDEK

Ever since the history of sin began with the fall of Adam, the only way for man to go before God was through a sacrifice in which blood was shed, for the life of the flesh is in the blood (Lev 17:11; Heb 9:22). In order to offer a sacrifice, several things were needed: an offering, a sanctuary, and a priest. The offering had to be an animal that was blameless, flawless, and clean. Moreover, the sons of Aaron from the tribe of Levi were consecrated and set apart specifically to perform the priestly duties. Unfortunately, the offering, the tabernacle, and the priests of the Old Testament were limited by the fact that they could not garner complete and fundamental atonement for sin.

Jesus Christ, however, became the perfect offering, the greater and more perfect temple, and the great high priest who achieved the complete forgiveness of sins for the people (John 2:19–21; Heb 4:14; 9:11; 10:14). Jesus gave up His perfect and blameless body for all time in place of all other offerings, thereby becoming the perfect sin offering and peace offering (Rom 3:25; 1 John 2:2). As the true high priest, He did away with all the sins of mankind once and for all (Heb 7:27; 9:12, 26, 28; 10:10). As a result, not only were all our sins forgiven, but we also secured our eternal redemption, and the path to God was opened (Heb 4:16; 6:19–20; 7:25; 10:19–22).

To the Jewish converts who sought to return to Judaism because they could not endure persecution from their fellow countrymen, the author of Hebrews offered the testimony that Jesus was the Messiah. He made reference to Melchizedek in Genesis 14 and the various religious processes of the Day of Atonement in Leviticus 16 in order to testify to the superiority of Jesus Christ as the high priest. He proclaimed, "Consider Jesus, the Apostle and High Priest of our confession" (Heb 3:1). The book of Hebrews refers to Jesus as the "priest" (ἱερεύς, *hiereus*) eight times and as the "high priest" (ἀρχιερεύς, *archiereus*) ten times.[74]

---

74 Priest (Heb 5:6; 7:11, 15, 17, 20 (in context), 21; 8:4; 10:21); high priest (Heb 2:17; 3:1; 4:14,15; 5:5, 10; 6:20; 7:26; 8:1; 9:11).

Two unique expressions that the book of Hebrews employs to refer to Jesus' priesthood are "great high priest" (ἀρχιερέα μέγαν, *archierea megan*; Heb 4:14) and "great priest" (ἱερέα μέγαν, *hierea megan*; Heb 10:21). Here the word "great" is μέγας (*megas*), which means "head," "great," or "preeminent" when describing a personal being. Jesus Christ is the head among the priests and the greatest among all high priests, who are already the chiefs among the priests. Thus no matter how great a high priest from the house of Aaron may be, he is fundamentally different from Jesus Christ.

In what ways is Jesus Christ the great high priest? Let us examine this according to the order of the book of Hebrews.

1. Jesus Christ Is the High Priest Who Sympathizes With Our Weaknesses

Hebrews 4:14–10:18 testifies of the superiority of Jesus' high priesthood from various perspectives, and Hebrews 4:14–16 proclaims in its introduction that Jesus Christ is the high priest.

Hebrews 4:15 states, "We do not have a high priest who cannot sympathize with our weaknesses, but One who has been tempted in all things as we are, yet without sin." Here the word "weaknesses" is ἀσθένεια (*astheneia*), and it refers to all types of human imperfections such as poverty, hunger, sickness, and mental and physical suffering. The word "sympathize" describes "a person in a higher position knowing and caring about the difficulties of someone in a lower position and saving him." The word also signifies "sharing in the pain and suffering of another with compassion and pity on the person." It means "understanding another person's situation and circumstances personally and holistically." In Greek "sympathize" is συμπαθέω (*sympatheō*) and means "to share the same emotion," "to identify with," or "to have compassion."

How often does the phrase "He felt compassion for them" appear in the four Gospels (Matt 9:36; see also 14:14; 15:32; 20:34; Mark 1:41; 6:34; Luke 7:12–13)? While Jesus was with us in the flesh, He experienced our weaknesses before we did, and He Himself was tempted in all the ways we are tempted. From the time He came upon the earth until He died on the cross, He experienced the sorrow of poverty (Luke 2:22–24; see Lev 12:6–8), the sorrow of hunger (Matt 21:18; Mark 11:12), the cold shoulder and rejection from the people of His hometown (Matt 13:54–58), and the sorrow of homelessness (Matt 8:20). He cried when He received news that a beloved person was sick or had died (John 11:3–35, 38). He lamented over the future of the nation (Luke 19:41–44). Though Jesus was without sin, He was falsely accused and sentenced to death (Matt 26:65–66). He was even betrayed by His own beloved disciples (Matt 26:56). His short thirty-three-year life was a continuous series of unfathomable suffering.

Jesus was tempted in all things as we are (Luke 4:13; 22:28; Heb 4:15). The word "tempted" in the phrase "One who has been tempted" in Hebrews 4:15 is in the passive perfect tense of the Greek verb πειράζω (*peirazō*). It means "he has been tempted." Jesus, throughout His life, was tempted by Satan or those who opposed Him, but He overcame the temptations through the Word. Thus Jesus can sufficiently help us when we are tempted and help us obtain victory. Hebrews 2:18 states, "Since He Himself was tempted in that which He has suffered, He is able to come to the aid of those who are tempted." Hebrews 4:16 describes this as the "grace to help." Here the word "help" is βοήθεια (*boētheia*), and in the Bible it is used often to describe a person who runs to assist someone who is in trouble after hearing his cry for help (Matt 15:25; Acts 16:9). When we are confronted with a great temptation or a dangerous situation and cry out for His helping grace, Jesus Christ the great high priest will come in our "time of need" (at the right time, before it is too late), and out of His compassion for us, He will certainly help us (Heb 4:16). Such help cannot come from another human being, nor can we expect it to. How can a human being who continuously struggles with his own weaknesses and mistakes come in the time of need to lend a helping hand? For this reason Psalm 146:3 states, "Do not trust in princes, in mortal man, in whom there is no salvation" (see Isa 2:22).

Indeed, no high priest in the Old Testament times could sympathize with the weaknesses of mankind. The high priests, who were supposed to give comfort and hope to the people, became corrupt and even cut off people's hopes. They were like billowing waves and sought to satisfy their own greed (Ezek 34:8; Rom 16:18; Phil 3:19; Jude 1:12–13). Jesus Christ, however, is the great high priest who knows well our weaknesses (John 2:24–25) and can sympathize with everything we face.

We may be overwhelmed by physical and mental weaknesses. We may face various temptations. We may be afflicted by illnesses in our minds and bodies. We may find ourselves struggling financially. Yet Jesus the high priest, who sympathizes with us in all these things, will partake in our suffering; He will give us strength, and He will solve our problems (Isa 63:9). Since we have such a great high priest among us, we must continue to "draw near with confidence to the throne of grace, so that we may receive mercy and find grace to help in time of need" (Heb 4:16).

2. Jesus Christ Is the Only High Priest Who Possesses the True Qualifications of the High Priesthood

Hebrews 5:1–10 discusses the qualifications of a high priest. As a representative of the people of God, a high priest must make atonement for sins by entering the holy of holies alone to offer sacrifices according to God's command. His duty is to guide the people so that they can build a proper relationship with God. Two main qualifications exist for the high priest.

The high priest must be taken from among men

Hebrews 5:1 speaks of "every high priest taken from among men." Jesus was without sin (Heb 4:15), yet He became a man in order to redeem the sins of all mankind (John 1:14). If there is a difference between Jesus and the other high priests, it is that the others were originally human beings, but Jesus was originally God who came to the earth as a man (Phil 2:6–7).

Jesus, the Word who became flesh (John 1:14), while in the flesh offered up "both prayers and supplications with loud crying and tears to the One able to save Him from death, and He was heard because of His piety" (Heb 5:7). This refers to Jesus' prayer in the garden of Gethsemane the night before He bore the cross for the redemption of mankind. Jesus was so heavily laden with grief and anguish in his heart (Matt 26:37–38; Mark 14:33–34) that he prayed fervently with loud crying until His sweat became like drops of blood (Luke 22:43–44).

The high priest must be appointed by God

Hebrews 5:4 states, "No one takes the honor to himself, but receives it when he is called by God, even as Aaron was." Aaron and his descendants became honorable high priests because they received God's calling (Exod 28:1; Lev 8:1–13; Num 20:25–29; 25:10–13). Christ also did not take upon Himself the glory of becoming a high priest (Heb 5:5; see John 8:50). God said, "You are My Son, today I have begotten You" (Heb 5:5), and, "You are a priest forever according to the order of Melchizedek" (Heb 5:6; Ps 110:4). However, God never said to the other high priests, "You are My son," or, "You are a priest forever."

As the high priest, Jesus learned obedience and was made perfect. Hebrews 5:8–9 states, "Although He was a Son, He learned obedience from the things which He suffered. And having been made perfect, He became to all those who obey Him the source of eternal salvation." This does not mean that Jesus learned something He did not know but that He practiced obedience in what He had known. This also does not mean that Jesus was imperfect and then made perfect but that He perfected His redemptive work as the high priest through the suffering and obedience of the cross. Jesus always obeyed the command of God the Father, believing that it was eternal life (John 12:50). He humbled Himself, even to the point of death on a cross, and was obedient to the end (Phil 2:8). Through this kind of obedience, Jesus became the source of eternal salvation for all those who obey Him (Heb 5:9).

Through prayer Jesus overcame the extreme suffering that led to death. He also learned obedience and fully obtained all the qualifications of the high priest. Ultimately He was "designated by God as a high priest according to the order of Melchizedek" (Heb 5:10). The word "designated" uses the past participial form of the word προσαγορεύω (*prosagoreuō*) in the passive voice and means "to address" or "to call by name." Although Jesus existed in the form of God and was God Himself (Phil 2:6), He did not seek glory for Himself; He was designated by God as the high priest.

Jesus Christ was crucified high on a cross in Golgotha and offered the perfect sacrifice for sinners once and for all. Even now He is still at the right hand of God, continuously interceding for His people until their salvation is perfected (Rom 8:34; Heb 7:25; 8:1; 1 John 2:1). Thus He can "save forever those who draw near to God through Him" (Heb 7:25). No one can receive salvation without Jesus the high priest (John 14:6).

Because we have been called as priests of the gospel to fulfill the administration of redemption, we also need to offer up earnest prayers in reverence to God. It is absolutely necessary for us to adopt the attitude of obedience unto death—by being ready to give ourselves up at any time and follow God's will.

3. Jesus Christ Is the High Priest Who Is the Anchor of Our Souls

Hebrews 5:11–6:20 is placed between Hebrews 5:1–10, which discusses the qualifications of the high priest, and Hebrews 7:1–10:18, which discusses the work of Jesus Christ as the perfect high priest according to the order of Melchizedek. The passage urges the spiritual growth of the saints in relation to the high priest.

The Bible testifies that those who do not understand Melchizedek have yet to attain full spiritual maturity. The people of Israel during Jesus' time did not realize that Jesus was the eternal high priest who had come according to the order of Melchizedek. Those who do not possess the understanding of Melchizedek are like infants who need milk; they are not accustomed to the Word of righteousness and cannot discern good and evil (Heb 5:11–14; 1 Cor 3:1–2). Thus in order to leave spiritual immaturity, they must leave the elementary teaching about the Christ and press on to maturity (Heb 6:1–3). They must also realize the fearful consequence of apostasy (Heb 6:4–6) and absorb the rain of grace that God often bestows so that they may produce vegetation useful to those for whose sake it was cultivated (Heb 6:7).

There is no injustice with God; He does not forget the good works and love that His saints show toward His name as they serve (Heb 6:10). Thus His saints must not be sluggish but "show the same diligence so as to realize the full assurance of hope until the end." They must become imitators of those who have inherited the promise through faith and patience (Heb 6:11–12).

Abraham is an example of one who received blessings through faith and patience. God promised to Abraham, "I will surely bless you and I will surely multiply you," and having patiently waited, Abraham finally received the promise (Heb 6:14; see Heb 6:13–15).

Hebrews 6:19–20, which is the conclusion of Hebrews 5:11–6:20, states, "This hope we have as an anchor of the soul, a hope both sure and steadfast and one which enters within the veil, where Jesus has entered as a forerunner for us, having become a high priest forever according to the order of Melchizedek."

An anchor is a hook-shaped metal object tied to the end of a rope or chain on a vessel and sunk into the ocean floor to prevent the vessel from drifting away from its port. The author of Hebrews metaphorically explained that our souls have to be secured tightly by such an anchor.

The two anchors of our faith are the unchanging truths—God's promise and oath (Heb 6:17–18)—and these are our firm hope. God revealed His promise and oath to Abraham as well. Hebrews 6:13 states that when God "made the promise to Abraham, . . . He swore by Himself." For Abraham the reality of this covenantal oath was Isaac. God promised and made an oath that through Isaac Abraham's descendants would multiply like the stars in the sky and the sand in the sea, and these people to be born would become a great nation (Gen 22:16–17; Heb 6:13–14).

God even guaranteed the promise that He made to Abraham. Hebrews 6:17 states that God "interposed with an oath" (see Ps 119:122). Here the word "interposed" means "surety" (Ps 119:122), and it describes the act of assuming full responsibility for the fulfillment of another's debt and becoming liable if the other defaults. An oath is a promise that guarantees the truthfulness of the words spoken through the mouth. Hebrews 6:16 proclaimed that "an oath given as confirmation is an end of every dispute." This means that there will be no more modifications to the promise. This promise of God to Abraham, which He guaranteed with an oath, was fulfilled through Jesus Christ, who came as a descendant of Abraham, as well as through many of His believers in faith.

Just as God's anchor of the covenant oath held Abraham, it holds the souls of all the saints today. There is not a moment of peace in the sea, which represents the world. The harsh waves of sin come crashing to capsize the ships of the saints, and the ships reel to and fro, unable to gain stability (Ps 107:26–27). The ships of the saints, however, are securely docked at their desired haven by the anchor of God's sworn covenant, so they will never drift from that haven (Ps

107:28–30). It is the anchor of agape love, which does not let go until the end (John 13:1), and the anchor of life and strength, which sufficiently overcomes the power of death (Rom 8:31–39).

This haven is the holy of holies inside the veil, the kingdom of God, and the place in which Jesus has "entered as a forerunner for us, having become a high priest forever according to the order of Melchizedek" (Heb 6:19–20). When Jesus bore all our sins as the high priest and died on the cross, the veil was torn in half from top to bottom (Matt 27:51; Mark 15:38; Luke 23:45). A new and living way was inaugurated for us through the veil, and that veil is the flesh of Jesus Christ (Heb 10:20).

Thus through Jesus Christ we can let down the anchors of our souls into the kingdom of God, which cannot be shaken, and at last we shall enter into that kingdom (Heb 12:28).

4. Jesus Christ Is Another High Priest Who Came According to the Order of Melchizedek

Jesus Christ is the eternal high priest according to the order of Melchizedek. Hebrews 7:1–28 testifies of the superiority of Jesus Christ the high priest according to the order of Melchizedek by reintroducing the contents of Hebrews 5:10, which states that He was "designated by God as a high priest according to the order of Melchizedek." Hebrews 7:1–3 especially reveals who Melchizedek is, and Hebrews 7:4–10 reveals Melchizedek's superiority in comparison to the Levitical priests.

The word "order" in Hebrews 5:10 is τάξις (*taxis*) in Greek. It is a military term that implies "orderly arrangement" and means "affiliation," "order," "align," or "rank." Also, the phrase "according to" is κατά (*kata*) in Greek and is a preposition with the meaning "according to" or "after." Thus "according to the order" means "standing in the same line." We must understand Jesus who came according to the order of Melchizedek and stand in the line of faith that wholly follows Him.

Who is Melchizedek?

***First*, Melchizedek was the king of peace and the king of righteousness.**

Melchizedek is the one who greeted Abraham and blessed him when Abraham returned after defeating Chedorlaomer and the kings who were with him (Gen 14:17–20).

Melchizedek is the king of Salem (Gen 14:18; Heb 7:1). "Salem" is שָׁלֵם (*shalem*) in Hebrew and means "peace"; therefore, Melchizedek is "king of peace." "Melchizedek" is מַלְכִּי־צֶדֶק (*malki-tsedeq*) in Hebrew and means "king of righteousness" (Heb 7:2). Melchizedek is the king of peace and the king of righteousness, and this name reflects a vivid image of Jesus, who is the prince of peace (Isa 9:6) and the prince of righteousness (Isa 9:7). Peace and righteousness are Jesus' attributes. He gives true peace to mankind (Mic 5:4–5; John 14:27) and rules with justice (Deut 32:4; Ps 89:14; 119:137).

***Second*, Melchizedek blessed Abraham with bread and wine.**

Melchizedek blessed Abraham with bread and wine (Gen 14:17–20). Likewise, Jesus blessed His disciples with bread and wine during the last supper (Matt 26:26–28; Mark 14:22–24). Luke 22:19–20 states, "When He had taken some bread and given thanks, He broke it and gave it to them, saying, 'This is My body which is given for you; do this in remembrance of Me.' And in the same way He took the cup after they had eaten, saying, 'This cup which is poured out for you is the new covenant in My blood.'" The bread from the last supper represents the holy body of Jesus, which would be torn on the cross, and the wine represents the new covenant established with His blood.

The order of Aaron is the order that follows the old covenant (Heb 8:7; 9:18), and the order of Melchizedek is the order that follows the new covenant (Heb 9:15). The order of Aaron is weak and follows the unprofitable old commandment (Heb 7:18). It is the first covenant with fault (Heb 8:7) and the first one that is becoming obsolete, growing old, and ready to disappear (Heb 8:13). However, the order of Melchizedek is connected to the "better covenant" (Heb 7:22; 8:6), "a new covenant with the house of Israel" (Heb 8:8), and the "eternal covenant" (Heb 13:20). Today we must believe in the new covenant and receive blessings through Jesus Christ who came according to the order of Melchizedek.

***Third*, Melchizedek received a tithe from Abraham and blessed him.** Melchizedek received a tithe from Abraham and blessed him (Gen 14:20; Heb 7:4). The Levitical priests received tithes from the people of Israel (Num 18:21, 24, 28; Heb 7:5). Nevertheless, when Abraham offered the tithe to Melchizedek, it is as if the Levitical priests also took part in giving that offering, because they came from the loins of Abraham (Heb 7:9–10). The Aaronic priests and the Melchizedekian priest both received tithes; but those who received the tithe in the order of Aaron were mortal men, while the One who received the tithe in the order of Melchizedek was He "of whom it is witnessed that he lives on" (Heb 7:8). Thus the order of Melchizedek is superior to the order of Aaron.

It is said that the lesser is blessed by the greater (Heb 7:7). The fact that Abraham was blessed by Melchizedek means that Melchizedek is greater than Abraham. The tribe of Levi was a distant descendant of Abraham. Thus the order of Melchizedek is incomparably greater than the order of Aaron, which belongs to the tribe of Levi (Heb 7:4–10).

Since Jesus is the high priest according to the order of Melchizedek, He receives the tithe and blesses all mankind (Prov 10:22; Mal 3:10). Thus when we offer the "whole tithe" (Mal 3:10) to Jesus and receive blessings, we can also become people who are according to the order of Melchizedek.

Another high priest

Hebrews 7:11–19 emphasizes the need for another priest, this one according to the order of Melchizedek, not from the imperfect Levitical priesthood, whose office is based on the law (Heb 7:11, 15). Hebrews 7:11 states, "If perfection was through the Levitical priesthood (for on the basis of it the people received the Law), what further need was there for another priest to arise according to the order of Melchizedek, and not be designated according to the order of Aaron?" According to this passage, another priesthood was established because perfection could not be achieved through the Levitical priesthood. "Perfection" is τελείωσις (*teleiōsis*) and refers to fulfilling or completing certain work with perfection. Such perfection, however, cannot be achieved through the Levitical priesthood, because that priesthood is continuously changing. Regarding the imperfection of the Levitical priesthood, Hebrews 7:12 states, "The priesthood being changed, of necessity there is also a change of the law" (NKJV). What is perfect does not change, but what is imperfect changes continuously.

The word "another" is ἕτερος (*heteros*) in Greek, and it refers to something that is intrinsically different. As the high priest who achieves perfection, in what ways is Jesus Christ "another" priest?

***First*, Jesus Christ is not a high priest of the line of Aaron but another high priest from the tribe of Judah.**

The high priesthood in the Old Testament was succeeded by the sons of Aaron, from the tribe of Levi. A high priest could never come from another tribe. People naturally assumed that the high priest would come from the tribe of Levi. Contrary to such assumptions, God raised up the true priest from the tribe of Judah.

Jesus was of the tribe of Judah, a tribe "from which no one has officiated at the altar" (Heb 7:13). Hebrews 7:14 states, "It is evident that our Lord was descended from Judah" (see Gen 49:10; 2 Sam 7:12; Isa 11:1; Mic 5:2). Hebrews 7:14 also states that Judah was "a tribe with reference to which Moses spoke nothing concerning priests." Moses never spoke about the priesthood from the tribe of Judah. It is evident, however, that another priest in the likeness of Melchizedek "descended from Judah" (Heb 7:14; see also Heb 7:15).

Here the word "descended" is ἀνατέλλω (*anatellō*) in Greek, and this word is used to describe the rising of the sun or stars (Mark 16:2; Jas 1:11; 2 Pet 1:19). Just as a righteous branch came forth from the stem of Jesse (Isa 11:1), Christ our Sun (Luke 1:78) rose from an earthly tribe called Judah (Mic 5:2; Matt 1:3; Luke 3:33; Rev 5:5). In the fullness of time, God raised the most holy and eternal high priest from the tribe of Judah, which He had all along treated as if it had nothing to do with the priesthood.

Hebrews 7:15 states, "It is yet far more evident if, in the likeness of Melchizedek, there arises another priest" (NKJV). Here the word "arises" is ἀνίσταται (*anistatai*), which is the middle voice of the word ἀνίστημι (*anistēmi*), meaning "to raise up," "to come to life again from death," or "to establish someone into a position." This is an expression that emphasizes Christ's sudden emergence at a certain point in history to perform the final duties of the high priest (see Judg 5:7; Deut 18:18; Luke 1:69; Acts 3:22). The arising of a priest from the tribe of Judah and not the tribe of Levi is also the fulfillment of the prophecy in Psalm 110:4 that the Messiah would come as the eternal priest according to the order of Melchizedek. Jesus Christ's priesthood has no relation to any human lineage, because it is the fulfillment of the covenant within God's sovereignty.

Never in its wildest dream did the tribe of Judah think that the new priest according to the order of Melchizedek would arise from it. This is God's redemptive providence that is truly difficult for mankind to fathom. God did not reveal this redemptive providence beforehand; it was His mysterious and profound providence to prevent Satan from hindering the path of the coming of Jesus Christ, the covenant offspring (Deut 29:29; Rom 16:25–26; 1 Cor 2:7; Eph 1:9).

***Second*, Jesus Christ is another high priest according to the power of an indestructible life** (Heb 7:16).

The law stipulates that priests can come only from Aaron's descendants from the tribe of Levi (Exod 28:1; 40:12–15; Num 3:2–4; 17:8; 25:11–13). This statute was so strict that no tribe other than the tribe of Levi dared to minister at the altar or enter the tabernacle to minister. However, this physical lineage stipulated by the law was irrelevant when Jesus became a priest. Hebrews 7:16 states that Jesus became another high priest "not on the basis of a law of physical requirement." Here the "law of physical requirement" refers to the physical requirement and lineage under the law for those who would become priests (Exod 40:12–15; Lev 21:17–23). Jesus did not become another high priest according to this law but according to "the power of an indestructible life" (Heb 7:16).

The expression "power of an indestructible life" emphasizes Jesus' divinity. Just as Melchizedek was without father and mother, so Jesus Christ was not conceived through natural relations between a man and his wife. He was conceived by the Holy Spirit and became the Word incarnate (Matt 1:18, 20; John 1:14).

The genealogy of Jesus Christ is recorded in two places—Matthew 1 and Luke 3— but in truth, Jesus does not have a genealogy because He was not born through natural means. When Jesus asked, "Who is the Christ?" the Pharisees answered, "The son of David." Jesus then asked them, using the words of Psalm 110:1, "How does David in the Spirit call Him 'Lord,' saying, 'The Lord said to my Lord, "Sit at My right hand, until I put Your enemies beneath Your feet"'?" (Matt 22:42–44). That is right. Physically Jesus was born through the genealogy of Abraham and David (Matt 1:1). Fundamentally, however, He existed even before Abraham was born (John 8:58), and He is David's Lord and the root of David (Rev 5:5; 22:16). Jesus Christ cannot be confined within a genealogy. He exists from eternity to eternity, without a beginning or an end to life (Heb 1:12; 13:8). He is the eternal Alpha and the Omega, who is and was and will come again (Isa 41:4; 44:6; 48:12; Rev 1:8, 17; 2:8; 21:6; 22:13).

Ultimately, Jesus' high priesthood according to the power of an indestructible life transcended the law that stipulated that priests must come from the tribe of Levi. This was the fulfillment of God's profound providence within the amazing administration of redemption that had been unknown to mankind.

5. Jesus Christ Is the Eternal High Priest of the Covenantal Oath

After Hebrews 7:11–19 proves the superiority of the high priest Jesus Christ over the Levitical priests who received the office based on the law, Hebrews 7:20–28 demonstrates that Jesus Christ's high priesthood is based on the covenantal oath and that it is eternal.

The high priest of the covenantal oath

Hebrews 7:20–21 states that "it was not without an oath (for they indeed became priests without an oath, but He with an oath through the One who said to Him, 'The Lord has sworn and will not change His mind, "You are a priest forever"')." God never had second thoughts after He made His oath. He always fulfills what He has spoken once, without changing His mind, and He does not know how to lie (Heb 6:17–18).

The word "change" in Psalm 110:4 is the imperfect tense of the word נָחַם (*naham*, "to be sorry"). Thus "will not change His mind" means that after God has made an oath, He will remain unchanged. The lives of deceitful human beings are full of regrets, but God, who is upright, has no regrets (Num 23:19; Rom 11:29).

God established Aaron and his sons as high priests with His command and the ordination. In Exodus 29:9 God commanded, "You shall gird them with sashes, Aaron and his sons, and bind caps on them, and they shall have the priesthood by a perpetual statute. So you shall ordain Aaron and his sons."

Aaron and his sons did not possess special qualifications to become high priests. Aaron was a man with a tainted past; he had made a golden calf and made the people commit the sin of idolatry. In His endless love and grace, however, God called Aaron and entrusted him with the glorious high priesthood. Hebrews 5:4 speaks of being "called by God, even as Aaron was." Yet even though Aaron was called by God, he was not established with an oath (Heb 7:21). Jesus Christ is the only person on Earth established as high priest with an oath (Heb 7:20–21).

An oath is a final confirmation that puts an end to every human dispute (Heb 6:16; see Exod 22:11). Thus an oath that God swears once is forever unchangeable and steadfast.

Hebrews 7:20–21 is based on Psalm 110:4: "The Lord has sworn and will not change His mind, 'You are a priest forever according to the order of Melchizedek.'" The word "sworn" is שָׁבַע (*shava*) and means "to repeat a promise seven times." The number "seven" symbolizes perfection. Human beings are limited by time and space and weak regarding temptations. Hence their promises are imperfect from the beginning and can easily be broken. God's oath, however, will never change.

Hebrews 6:17 states, "God, desiring even more to show to the heirs of the promise the unchangeableness of His purpose, interposed with an oath." Here the word "oath" is ὅρκος (*horkos*) in Greek and means "something promised with an oath." This is a word used when entreating God to curse or punish a person who has made a false statement (see Num 5:21; Deut 29:21). A covenanted oath, therefore, is certain.

Hebrews 7:28 compares the Aaronic high priesthood, which was established without an oath, with Jesus' high priesthood that was established with an oath, saying, "The Law appoints men as high priests who are weak, but the word of the oath . . . appoints a Son, made perfect forever." Since the Aaronic high priests appointed by the law are men with weaknesses, they cannot truly save us. Jesus Christ, however, appointed by the word of the oath can save us completely. He is the source of eternal salvation (Heb 5:9; 7:25).

The eternal high priest

Jesus is the eternal high priest who came according to the order of Melchizedek (Ps 110:4; Heb 5:6; 6:20; 7:17, 21). What are the reasons for His eternal nature?

***First*, Jesus Christ is the same yesterday, today, and tomorrow and is alive forever (Heb 13:8).**

Hebrews 7:25 states, "He always lives to make intercession for them." Jesus Christ was crucified on the cross and then resurrected. He ascended into heaven after forty days, and even now He is at the right hand of God's throne making intercession for us as the high priest (Rom 8:34; Heb 8:1).

***Second*, Jesus Christ's priesthood does not change but is forever.** Hebrews 7:24 states, "Jesus, on the other hand, because He continues forever, holds His priesthood permanently." The word "permanently" is ἀπαράβατος (*aparabatos*) and means "unchangeable," "inviolable," "without a successor," and "not transferable."

There were many Levitical priests, because all men die, and one man could not continuously serve as priest (Heb 7:23). Jesus Christ, however, is immortal and lives forever. Because He overcame death, He is eternal life itself; hence He holds his priesthood permanently and cannot be succeeded by anyone else (Heb 5:6; 6:20; 7:17, 21, 23–24).

6. Jesus Christ Is the High Priest Who Mediates for Us

According to Hebrews 8:1–13, Jesus Christ is the mediator of the new covenant (Heb 8:13; 9:15; 12:24). The mediator of the new covenant is the mediator of a better covenant enacted on better promises (Heb

8:6). This is different from the first covenant, which contains fault (Heb 8:7). The new covenant is not inscribed on tablets of stone, as the old covenant was, but it is inscribed on the tablets of human hearts, according to the Word of God (Heb 8:8–12; 2 Cor 3:3).

Hebrews 8:1 states, "We have such a high priest, who has taken His seat at the right hand of the throne of the Majesty in the heavens." Romans 8:34 states, "Who is the one who condemns? Christ Jesus is He who died, yes, rather who was raised, who is at the right hand of God, who also intercedes for us." After Jesus broke the power of death and darkness, He resurrected and ascended into heaven. He is at the right hand of God, continuously mediating for the church and its saints, whom He purchased with His precious blood (Acts 20:28; Heb 7:25; 1 John 2:1).

The word "mediation" refers to the act of peacefully reconciling antagonistic or hostile parties (Job 9:32–34; Prov 18:19; Isa 38:14). The Bible uses the word "mediation" in reference to the act of reconciling the relationship between God and men, thus bringing peace (1 Tim 2:5; Heb 8:6; 9:15; 12:24).

In this world the one and only true mediator between God and men is Jesus Christ. First Timothy 2:5 states, "There is one God, and one mediator also between God and men, the man Christ Jesus." Jesus Christ is a qualified mediator because He is truly God and at the same time a true man.

Jesus Christ's offering of Himself on the cross once and for all was the completion of His selfless redemptive work, and His intercessory prayer in heaven is His continuing high priestly ministry.[75] Intercessory prayer is ἔντευξις (*enteuxis*) in Greek and means "to turn to" or "to meet with"; it refers to the act of clinging to someone with an entreaty. Even today Jesus speaks and prays in heaven on our behalf (Rom 8:34), and He will continue His intercessory prayer until He

75 Douglas F. Kelly, *Systematic Theology: The Beauty of Christ –A Trinitarian Vision,* vol. 2 (Fearn: Mentor, 2014), 510.

returns in glory and power to judge the living and the dead.

The following are characteristics of Jesus Christ's intercessory prayer.[76]

***First*, Jesus' intercessory prayer is powerful.**

James 5:16 states, "The effective prayer of a righteous man can accomplish much." However, there is no one righteous, not even one (Rom 3:10); only Jesus is truly righteous (Rom 3:26; 1 Pet 3:18; 1 John 2:1). Thus the perfect, faultless prayer of Jesus Christ is the most powerful prayer, and its efficacy is everlasting.

***Second*, Jesus' intercessory prayer is continuous.**

Hebrews 7:25 states, "He always lives to make intercession for them." Jesus Christ's prayer will continue without ceasing until His second coming. Likewise, we must follow Jesus' example and live lives of continuous prayer (1 Sam 12:23; 1 Thess 5:17).

***Third*, Jesus' intercessory prayer is active.**

Jesus' intercessory prayer is not a mere formality, but it is an active and determined prayer based on love. Before He died on the cross, Jesus went to the garden of Gethsemane, and "being in agony He was praying very fervently; and His sweat became like drops of blood, falling down upon the ground" (Luke 22:44).

***Fourth*, Jesus' intercessory prayer is with authority.**

Jesus received all authority in heaven and on earth from God the Father (Matt 28:18; Eph 1:22; Col 2:9–10). Thus Jesus' prayer possesses an absolute authority that cannot be violated even by the angels in heaven, let alone the people of this world.

---

76 Youngyup Cho, *Christology* (Seoul: Word of Life Press, 2007), 422–27.

***Fifth*, Jesus' intercessory prayer is special.**

Jesus' intercessory prayer is not like the ordinary intercessory prayers of the saints for one another. Jesus' prayer is a universal prayer that saves all God's people and fulfills God's redemptive-historical administration. In John 17, even before going up to the Garden of Gethsemane, Jesus prayed for the safety and unity of all the saints (John 17:11, 21–22), for the fullness of His joy in them (John 17:13), and for their protection from the evil one (John 17:15). He also prayed for their holiness (John 17:17, 19), the evangelism of the gospel to the world (John 17:20–21), their perfection (John 17:23), and their future in heaven (John 17:24).

***Sixth*, Jesus' intercessory prayer is preventive.**

Jesus makes intercession in advance so that the saints do not sin. While we are clothed with the flesh, at times we sin because of our corruptible nature (1 John 2:15–16). Jesus Christ, however, works together with the Holy Spirit to prevent us from sinning (Rom 8:26, 34). Jesus' prayers include great indignation against the sins we have committed, exhortation, and rebuke, and they also provide us the strength to sin no more and live victorious lives. First John 2:1 states, "My little children, I am writing these things to you so that you may not sin. And if anyone sins, we have an Advocate with the Father, Jesus Christ the righteous." I earnestly hope that from now on, we all remember Jesus, who earnestly prays on our behalf, and that we make greater effort to strive against sin and overcome it (Heb 12:3–4).

7. Jesus Christ Is the High Priest of the New Covenant

Jesus' work as high priest is superior to the work of the Old Testament priests. Hebrews 8:6 describes it as "a more excellent ministry." The words "more excellent" are διαφορωτέρας (*diaphorōteras*) in Greek and mean "preeminent" or "surpassing." The following is a close study of Hebrews 8, which discusses the reasons Jesus' high priesthood is superior to the Levitical high priesthood.

***First,* Jesus Christ is in the heavenly tabernacle.**

A high priest is appointed to offer gifts and sacrifices (Heb 5:1; 8:3). This priest offers gifts on this earth according to the law (Heb 8:4). Jesus, conversely, is the high priest who offered Himself as the sacrifice (Heb 7:27; 9:26, 28; 10:10, 12, 14); He is the high priest who ministers in the heavenly tabernacle and not on the earth. Hebrews 8:1–2 states, "We have such a high priest, who has taken His seat at the right hand of the throne of the Majesty in the heavens, a minister in the sanctuary and in the true tabernacle, which the Lord pitched, not man."

The tabernacle built through Moses is a copy and shadow of the true sanctuary in heaven (Heb 8:5). Thus the Levitical high priesthood, whose members served in the imperfect tabernacle on Earth, is also imperfect, while the high priesthood of Jesus Christ, who serves in the heavenly tabernacle, is perfect.

***Second,* Jesus Christ is the mediator of a better covenant.**

Hebrews 8:6 states, "He has obtained a more excellent ministry, by as much as He is also the mediator of a better covenant, which has been enacted on better promises." The Greek word "mediator" is μεσίτης (*mesitēs*) and refers to "someone who brings about reconciliation between parties" or "someone who uses his own assets as collateral in order to guarantee someone else's repayment of debt." A high priest who is according to the law cannot be a true mediator. However, Jesus Christ the high priest is according to the new covenant that is better than the law, and He offered Himself as a propitiation, thereby reconciling God and mankind (Rom 3:25; 1 John 2:2). Because He reclaimed us from the hands of Satan with the price of His own blood (Acts 20:28; 1 Cor 6:20), He is indeed the true mediator. The new covenant was enacted on promises rather than the law (Heb 8:6), and these promises were made in Jeremiah 31:32–34.

***Third*, Jesus Christ is the high priest of a faultless new covenant.** Hebrews 8:7 states, "If that first covenant had been faultless, there would have been no occasion sought for a second." The law was an imperfect promise, but the new covenant is faultless. The word "faultless" in Greek is ἄμεμπτος (*amemptos*) and means "blameless" or "without fault."

The new covenant is also written on the heart. Hebrews 8:10 states, "I will put My laws into their minds, and I will write them on their hearts" (see Jer 31:31–33). If the old covenant inscribed the law on stone tablets (2 Cor 3:7), then the new covenant inscribes the Word of God on the heart (2 Cor 3:3) in order to establish a proper relationship between God and His people (Heb 8:10; Jer 31:33).

In addition, in the new covenant everyone will know God, from the least to the greatest. Hebrews 8:11 states, "They shall not teach everyone his fellow citizen, and everyone his brother, saying, 'Know the Lord,' for all will know Me, from the least to the greatest of them." The issue of sin will be completely resolved on the day when the new covenant is consummated (Heb 8:12), and the people of the new covenant will have a perfect fellowship with God (see Isa 11:9; Hab 2:14). Thus the old covenant becomes obsolete, grows old, and disappears, but the new covenant is eternal (Heb 8:13).

8. Jesus Christ Is the High Priest Who Offered a Perfect Sacrifice

The ministry of Jesus Christ is superior to the ministry of the Old Testament priests. First, it is because His ministry is based on the new covenant (Heb 8:1–13), but next, it is because a perfect sacrifice is offered in place of an imperfect sacrifice (Heb 9:1–28). Why is the sacrifice of Jesus Christ a perfect sacrifice?

***First*, His sacrifice achieved eternal redemption.**

Hebrews 9:1–10 explains the tabernacle and the sacrifices of the Old Testament and their limitations. Afterward Hebrews 9:12 states, "Not through the blood of goats and calves, but through His own blood, He entered the holy place once for all, having obtained eternal redemption" (see Heb 9:26, 28; 10:12). By offering Himself once and for all, Jesus Christ cleansed our consciences from dead works with His blood so that we may serve the living God (Heb 9:14).

Thus Jesus Christ "became to all those who obey Him the source of eternal salvation" (Heb 5:9). That is why He is able "to save forever those who draw near to God through Him" (Heb 7:25). The sacrificial system and weak mortal high priests of the Old Testament could not achieve eternal redemption. Only the eternal high priest, Jesus Christ, can achieve perfect redemption.

***Second*, His sacrifice gives the eternal inheritance as a promise.**

Hebrews 9:15 states, "He is the mediator of a new covenant, so that, since a death has taken place for the redemption of the transgressions that were committed under the first covenant, those who have been called may receive the promise of the eternal inheritance." Now anyone who believes in Jesus Christ the eternal high priest is guaranteed the eternal inheritance. This faith to believe is completely a gift of grace from God (Eph 2:8). This faith does not come from mankind but from God, who calls all His children who were chosen from before the foundation of the world (Eph 1:4–5). "Those who have been called" will become possessors of the eternal inheritance (Heb 9:15).

The outcome and assurance of this promise from God is certain, because it is a promise guaranteed with an oath (Heb 6:17). Thus if we hold fast the beginning of our assurance until the end, we will become partakers in the eternal inheritance along with Jesus Christ (Heb 3:14).

***Third*, His sacrifice was offered once and for all.**

The Levitical priests could not completely resolve the issue of sin, so they had to repeatedly offer the same sacrifices over and over again (Heb 10:11). The sacrifice offered by Jesus, however, was made "once for all," so it does not need to be repeated (Heb 9:12; 10:10; see also Heb 9:26, 28; 10:2), and He does not need to enter the holy place often, as the high priest did year by year with blood that was not his own (Heb 9:25; 10:1). By His sacrifice made once and for all, Jesus perfected for all time those who are sanctified (Heb 10:14, 18). Hebrews 10:12 states, "He, having offered one sacrifice for sins for all time, sat down at the right hand of God." The sacrifice "for all time" is the sacrifice made once and for all, and its efficacy is eternal (Heb 7:27; 9:12, 26, 28; 10:10, 12).

Jesus' eternal sacrifice offered once and for all is incomparable to the sacrifices offered beforehand. Truly Jesus Christ is the "better hope" (Heb 7:19), the "guarantee of a better covenant" (Heb 7:22), the "mediator of a better covenant" (Heb 8:6), and the "better sacrifice" (Heb 9:23).

9. Jesus Christ Is the High Priest of Suffering Who Gave His Own Body As a Sacrifice

As the conclusion of Hebrews 4:14–10:18, which proves the superiority of Jesus Christ the high priest, Hebrews 10:1–18 reiterates what has been proven thus far.[77] Hebrews 10:18 concludes, "Where there is forgiveness of these things, there is no longer any offering for sin."

77 The content of Hebrews 10:1 summarizes Hebrews 8:5 and 9:8–10. Hebrews 10:2–4 and 10:11 summarize Hebrews 9:1–22. Hebrews 10:5–10 summarizes Hebrews 7:27 and 9:23–28. Hebrews 10:12 summarizes Hebrews 8:1. Hebrews 10:13–14 summarizes Hebrews 9:28. Hebrews 10:15–17 summarizes Hebrews 8:8–12.

Hebrews 10 especially emphasizes that Jesus became an "offering." Hebrews 10:14 states, "By one offering He has perfected for all time those who are sanctified." The high priest was appointed to offer gifts and sacrifices (Heb 8:3), but the Aaronic priests were not able to become sacrifices themselves. Not only were they unable to become sacrifices themselves, but they needed to make an offering for their own sins before they made the sacrifices (Lev 16:6, 11, 17, 24; Heb 5:3; 7:27; 8:3; 9:7). Hebrews 5:3 states that the Aaronic priest was "obligated to offer sacrifices for sins, as for the people, so also for himself."

Jesus, however, was without sin (Heb 4:15) and did not need to offer a sacrifice for Himself; instead He became a perfect sin offering on our behalf. He is the Word incarnate, who came as the perfect high priest and offered His body—which is without sin—as a ransom. First John 2:2 states, "He Himself is the propitiation for our sins; and not for ours only, but also for those of the whole world" (see Rom 3:25).

According to the Old Testament law, an offering must be without blemish or spot (Exod 12:5; 29:1; Lev 1:3; 22:19–25; Num 6:14; 19:2). Jesus possessed the perfect qualifications of an offering, because He never committed sin (1 Pet 2:22), He did not know sin (2 Cor 5:21), and was without sin (Heb 4:15; 1 John 3:5). No one could convict Jesus of sin (John 8:46) or find any guilt in Him (John 18:38). He obeyed to the point of death on the cross by shedding His precious blood (Phil 2:8; Heb 5:7–9). He was truly an unblemished offering fully sufficient to redeem sinners (1 Pet 1:18–19).

Hebrews 7:26 lists five reasons why it is fitting for us to have Jesus as our high priest. First, He is "holy" (ὅσιος, *hosios*, "pious"). Second, He is "innocent" (ἄκακος, *akakos*, "pure"). Third, He is "undefiled" (ἀμίαντος, *amiantos*, "guiless, genuine"). Fourth, He is "separated from sinners" (κεχωρισμένος ἀπὸ τῶν ἁμαρτωλῶν, *kechōrismenos apo tōn hamartōlōn*, "set apart from the sinners"). Fifth, He is "exalted above the heavens" (ὑψηλότερος τῶν οὐρανῶν γενόμενος, *hypsēloteros tōn ouranōn genomenos*, "having reached the highest above the heavens"). Hence we must not follow the Levitical high priests, who are with fault and full of weaknesses, but

Jesus Christ our true high priest, who is faultless (John 1:14; Heb 4:14).

On the Day of Atonement, the high priest sprinkled the blood of the sin offering on the altar and burned the flesh of the sacrificed animal outside the camp (Lev 16:14–15, 19, 27; Heb 13:11). The phrase "outside the camp" refers to the area outside the place where the Israelites pitched their tents. Just like the offerings that were burnt outside the camp, so Jesus also suffered on the hill of Golgotha outside the city gate. Hebrews 13:12 states, "Jesus also, that He might sanctify the people through His own blood, suffered outside the gate." Jesus became an offering on the hill of Golgotha and not within the city of Jerusalem. He climbed up the hill of Golgotha with His holy body whipped and His flesh torn. As the ruthless Roman soldiers kicked Him, He could no longer bear the weight of the cross, and He fell by the roadway. As Jesus took each heavy step carrying the cross for the redemption of mankind, His whole body became drenched with blood and sweat (Matt 27:31–32; John 19:17).

The author of Hebrews described Jesus' suffering as a "reproach" (Heb 13:13). The word "reproach" is ὀνειδισμός (*oneidismos*) in Greek, and it means "condemnation," "rebuke," "contempt," or "ridicule." Jesus who bore the cross and walked toward Golgotha became the object of condemnation and ridicule before a countless number of people and endured unbearable contempt.

In truth, Jesus' thirty-three-year life was the life of a high priest marked with all kinds of suffering. Jesus' entire life—from the time He came until He left—was the walk of a high priest covenanted with an oath. The life of our high priest, Jesus Christ, entailed a walk of tears, of suffering through bearing the sins of mankind, and of the forgiveness of sins. In the end, however, Jesus saved all humanity and was full of the joy of God. Seeing that salvation would be completed through Him, He walked the path in thanksgiving. How our eternal high priest came to this earth and poured out His blood, tears, sweat, and heart in His walk! He was the high priest according to the eternal order of Melchizedek. He was the one and only eternal high priest in heaven and on earth established by God with an oath.

By being the high priest and the sacrifice at the same time, Jesus Christ achieved eternal redemption on the cross once and for all and sanctified the saints (Heb 10:10). Ephesians 5:2 states that Christ "gave Himself up for us, an offering and a sacrifice to God as a fragrant aroma" (see Rom 4:25; Heb 7:27; 9:14; 10:12). Here the word "offering" is προσφορά (*prosphora*) in Greek; it refers to all sorts of offerings sacrificed and connotes Jesus' whole life. Jesus' entire life was a life of obedience offered up to God as a sacrifice (see Phil 2:8). The word "sacrifice" is θυσία (*thysia*) in Greek and means "a sacrifice." It indicates how Jesus was ultimately sacrificed on the cross.

In addition, the phrase "fragrant aroma" modifies both "offering" and "sacrifice." The word "fragrant" is εὐωδία (*euōdia*), and "aroma" is ὀσμή (*osmē*); both words mean "fragrance." The successive use of the two words signifies the "fragrance of fragrance" or "the greatest fragrance." The fact that Jesus' whole life was fragrant means that God received His entire life as the greatest fragrance with the greatest joy (see Gen 8:21; Exod 29:18; Lev 1:9; 3:5; Phil 4:18). Jesus' whole life was full of the fragrance of absolute obedience and of eternal life (John 12:50; Phil 2:8; see 2 Cor 2:14–16).

Having offered one sacrifice of eternal redemption once and for all for our sins (Heb 7:27; 9:12, 26, 28; 10:10), Jesus Christ sat down at the right hand of God. Since then He has been praying on our behalf and waiting until His enemies are made a footstool for His feet (Rom 8:34; Heb 8:1; 10:12–13).

Jesus is the Savior of all sinners, the eternal life of this world, the hope of all peoples, and "the wealth of all nations" (Hag 2:7; 2 Cor 4:7). Since we have been saved once and for all by such a high priest (Heb 7:27; 10:10), how could we truly be more blessed? Because He has saved us, He has called us—who are like earthen vessels—His treasured possessions (Deut 26:18). If there is a way for us to repay this grace, it is only by following Jesus' footsteps and obeying completely the Word God has commanded (Heb 5:9; 1 Pet 2:21). Wherever our steps take us, in all our words, deeds, and thoughts, we must exude the holy fragrance of Christ and leave behind only beautiful and precious impressions (2 Cor 2:14–16). We must deeply engrave in our hearts Jesus Christ, the high priest who has saved us, always desiring that our whole lives will become perfect sacrifices to be offered up before God.

Concluding Remarks: Eschatological Outlook of the High Priest

After Israel's first return from exile, God showed eight visions to Prophet Zechariah. In the fourth vision, Zechariah saw the high priest Joshua standing before an angel, and Satan stood at his right hand to accuse him (Zech 3:1). The Lord rebuked Satan, saying that the high priest Joshua was like a brand plucked from the fire (Zech 3:2); the passage states that Joshua's holy garments were filthy (Zech 3:3). This was a reflection of the dismal reality of the Israelites, who had just returned from exile. Nevertheless, God said, "See, I have taken your iniquity away from you and will clothe you with festal robes," and He placed a clean turban on Joshua's head and clothed him with festal garments (Zech 3:4). Then the angel of the Lord testified, "Thus says the Lord of hosts, 'If you will walk in My ways and if you will perform My service, then you will also govern My house and also have charge of My courts, and I will grant you free access among these who are standing here'" (Zech 3:7). This signifies that God had clothed the high priest Joshua, the representative of the chosen people of Israel, with the grace of forgiveness and promised that Joshua would continue to minister in the temple and freely come and go before the Lord.

In addition, Zechariah 3:8 refers to Joshua the high priest and his friends as "men who are a symbol." What kind of symbol were these men? Joshua the high priest was a symbol of the eternal high priest Jesus, and his priest friends were symbols of the saints who have become priests through Jesus' work of redemption (1 Pet 2:9; Rev 1:6; 5:10).

Furthermore, the book of Zechariah contains two expressions regarding Jesus who is to come as the eternal high priest. In Zechariah 3:8, it states, "I am going to bring in My servant the Branch," and in Zechariah 3:9, God says, "Behold, the stone that I have set before Joshua."

Jesus the high priest will come as a branch

Zechariah 3:8 states, "I am going to bring in My servant the Branch." Here the word "branch" is צֶמַח (*tsemah*) and refers to a shoot that has just budded from a branch or a sprout coming out of the ground. Various verses in the Old Testament use the word *tsemah* to refer to the Messiah. The expressions "a man whose name is Branch" (Zech 6:12), "the Branch of the Lord" (Isa 4:2), and "a righteous Branch" (Jer 23:5; 33:15) all refer to Jesus Christ. These expressions reveal that Jesus Christ would come with a weak, insignificant, and humble appearance. Isaiah 53:2 prophesies regarding Jesus, "He grew up before Him like a tender shoot, and like a root out of parched ground; He has no stately form or majesty that we should look upon Him, nor appearance that we should be attracted to Him."

When Jesus was conceived by the Holy Spirit and born through Mary, He was laid in a manger that reeked of animal feces, because there was no room in the inn (Luke 2:7). As soon as He was born, an angel of the Lord instructed Joseph and Mary to flee since King Herod sought to kill the child, so He journeyed far and took refuge in Egypt (Matt 2:13–15). Jesus was born in His own land (John 1:11), but the land of Judea, which was ruled by King Herod, was a parched ground that He could not set foot on even for a day (Isa 53:2). Even after He returned from Egypt, He lived as the son of a carpenter in Nazareth in Galilee and not in the land of Judea (Matt 2:22–23; 13:55; Mark 6:3).

This "Branch," however, would later build the temple. Zechariah 6:12 states, "Behold, a man whose name is Branch, for He will branch out from where He is; and He will build the temple of the Lord."

This signifies that Jesus would come and establish the New Testament church through His redemption on the cross and the victory of His resurrection (John 2:19–22). In the end He will come again and establish the eternal kingdom of God (Zech 6:13).

Jesus the high priest will come as "one stone"

Zechariah 3:9 states, "'Behold, the stone that I have set before Joshua; on one stone are seven eyes. Behold, I will engrave an inscription on it,' declares the Lord of hosts, 'and I will remove the iniquity of that land in one day.'" Here "one stone" refers to Jesus Christ (Isa 28:16; Dan 2:34–35, 45; Matt 21:42; 1 Cor 10:4; Eph 2:20–22; 1 Pet 2:6–8).

An inscription will be engraved on the one stone. The word "engrave" in Zechariah 3:9 is פָּתַח (*pathah*) and means "to open," "to tear," "to open the top," or "to swing open." The image of the one stone being torn reveals the suffering of Jesus Christ. Thick thorns tore into Jesus' head. His hands were torn by nails, His side pierced through by a spear (John 19:2, 34; 20:25, 27). From His holy body that was torn came forth the blood of the new covenant that would save all mankind (Matt 26:28; Mark 14:24; Luke 22:20; John 19:34). Each time Jesus' holy flesh was torn, extreme pain, indescribable with words, pulsated throughout His body. He was pierced because of our transgressions and crushed for our iniquities. He was chastened for our well-being and scourged so we could be healed (Isa 53:5).

As the consequence of the one stone being torn, the iniquity of the land was removed in one day. Zechariah 3:9 states, "I will remove the iniquity of that land in one day." The "one day" in this verse is the day of complete redemption as foreshadowed by the Day of Atonement. It was the day when Jesus Christ was crucified on the cross, and, ultimately, it is the day of the second coming. On that day all sins will be completely removed forever, not just from the land of Judea, but also from the whole world.

On that day "every one of you will invite his neighbor to sit under his vine and under his fig tree" (Zech 3:10). The expression "to sit under his vine and under his fig tree" refers to the greatest prosperity and peace enjoyed during King Solomon's time (1 Kgs 4:25). Jesus Christ achieved salvation by His crucifixion, and ultimately, on the day of the second coming, we will enjoy eternal peace and prosperity in the kingdom of God (Rev 21:25–26).

This "one stone" has "seven eyes" (Zech 3:9). The Lamb—the second-coming Christ—also has "seven eyes" (Rev 5:6). These seven eyes are "the eyes of the Lord which range to and fro throughout the earth" (Zech 4:10), and "the eyes of the Lord [that] move to and fro throughout the earth that He may strongly support those whose heart is completely His" (2 Chr 16:9). The seven eyes signify the omniscience and omnipotence of God. By His omniscience and omnipotence, the second coming of Christ will consummate the history of redemption, which has been ceaselessly advancing through all sorts of grief (Rev 21:6).

Moreover, the "seven eyes" are the "seven lamps" (Num 8:2-3) and the "seven spirits" (Zech 4:2; Rev 1:4; 3:1; 4:5; 5:6), which refer to God's perfect work of light and the perfect work of the Holy Spirit. Unlike the work He had revealed in portions during each era (Heb 1:1), now through the perfect work of the light and the Holy Spirit, God will remove the sins of this land in one day, expel the darkness of the entire universe, and shine the eternal light (see John 14:26; 15:26; 16:13). Although pitch darkness may cover the whole world and corrupt the spiritual world until the coming of Jesus Christ, the lamp of the Word of God will continue to burn brightly without ever being quenched (Ps 119:105). Ultimately, the work of the "seven eyes" and the "seven lamps" of the "one stone" will fulfill the prophecy in Zechariah 14:7: "It will be a unique day which is known to the Lord, neither day nor night, but it will come about that at evening time there will be light."

On that day, which is known to the Lord, the glorious day when Jesus returns, the Lord Himself will descend from heaven with a shout, with the voice of the archangel and with the trumpet of God (1 Thess 4:16) as prophesied in the Bible. On that day the prophecy "By one offering He has perfected for all time those who are sanctified" will be consummated (Heb 10:14). Through the resurrection and transfiguration, the saints will be changed into glorious and spiritual bodies that transcend the limitations of time and space (Rom 8:30; 1 Cor 15:51–54; 1 Thess 4:16–17). At that time all the world's darkness will disappear (Rev 21:25; 22:5), and the light of Jesus Christ will fill the entire universe. All the powers of evil will be completely destroyed (Rev 20:10, 14), and God's righteous rule will be perfected. Then God's redemptive administration, which has advanced throughout history, will finally be fulfilled completely.

What are the priestly duties of the saints who hope for this eternal day?

***First*, the saints must boldly go before the throne of grace.**

Hebrews 4:14–15 states, "We have a great high priest who has passed through the heavens, Jesus the Son of God. . . . We do not have a high priest who cannot sympathize with our weaknesses." Hebrews 4:16 continues, "Let us draw near with confidence to the throne of grace, so that we may receive mercy and find grace to help in time of need."

The moment Jesus Christ our high priest died on the cross, the veil between the holy place and the holy of holies tore from top to bottom (Matt 27:51; Mark 15:38; Luke 23:45). This signifies that the true holy of holies in heaven has been opened wide to the saints who have become priests in the New Testament era. Hebrews 10:19–20 states that "we have confidence to enter the holy place by the blood of Jesus, by a new and living way which He inaugurated for us through the veil, that is, His flesh."

Now we must draw near to the throne of grace with confidence in order to receive the grace to help us in time of need (Heb 4:16). This is a special privilege and calling for the saints who have become priests. The phrase "in time of need" is εὔκαιρος (*eukairos*) in Greek and means "timely" or "opportune time." Just as God sent the early and late rain in its season (Deut 11:14), so He bestows timely grace upon each person who comes before the throne of grace. Therefore, let us also draw near to God with sincere hearts in full assurance of faith (Heb 10:22).

***Second*, the saints must offer up a living sacrifice that God delights in.** Just as the priests of the Old Testament offered sacrifices to God, so the spiritual priests of the New Testament must also go directly before God and offer sacrifices. The sacrifices the saints must offer include the sacrifice of the body, the sacrifice of thanksgiving, and the sacrifice of praise.

As priests, the saints must present their bodies as sacrifices. Romans 12:1 states, "I urge you, brethren, by the mercies of God, to present your bodies a living and holy sacrifice, acceptable to God, which is your spiritual service of worship." Here the word "bodies" does not merely refer to the flesh but to the whole person, who has been reborn. Dead sacrifices were offered during the Old Testament times, but now living sacrifices or spiritual worship must be offered. Those who offer living sacrifices must not "be conformed to this world, but be transformed by the renewing of [the] mind, so that [they] may prove what the will of God is, that which is good and acceptable and perfect" (Rom 12:2). Thus those who can discern and live according to the will of God are offering living sacrifices and worshiping spiritually.

The saints must also offer sacrifices of thanksgiving. Psalm 50:14 states, "Offer to God a sacrifice of thanksgiving," and Psalm 50:23 states, "He who offers a sacrifice of thanksgiving honors Me." Thanksgiving is the saint's expression of gratitude for the grace God has bestowed upon him or her. Those who know God but do not honor Him as God or give thanks to Him will receive God's wrath (Rom 1:21). We have received indescribable, innumerable, and immeasurable grace from God. Each and every day we must express our gratitude with our hearts, bodies, lips, wealth, and deeds.

As priests, the saints must offer up sacrifices of praise. Hebrews 13:15 states, "Through Him then, let us continually offer up a sacrifice of praise to God, that is, the fruit of lips that give thanks to His name." The word "praise" is αἴνεσις (*ainesis*) in Greek, which originates from the word αἰνέω (*aineō*). The word *aineō* was used when the angels praised God (Luke 2:13) and when people praised God (Luke 2:20; 19:37; Acts 2:47; 3:8–9; Rev 19:5). Sacrifices of praise are the fruits of lips that testify of God's name. Thus if we do not testify of God's name, then we are not offering sacrifices of praises. We must testify of God's amazing name, always giving thanks for God's greatness and Jesus Christ's grace of redemption (Eph 5:19; Col 3:16).

***Third*, the saints must find the lost.**

The purpose of mankind's history lies in God's desire to find His lost people and save them (Matt 1:21). God is seeking the people whom He has appointed to salvation and eternal life from before the foundation of the world (Acts 13:48). Hence we must properly carry out our calling as priests, which is to find the lost. As the eternal high priest, Jesus Christ did not cease even for one moment in His work to find the lost. John 6:39 states, "This is the will of Him who sent Me, that of all that He has given Me I lose nothing, but raise it up on the last day." Matthew 18:14 states, "It is not the will of your Father who is in heaven that one of these little ones perish" (see Matt 9:13; Luke 15:7).

Jesus also said, "It is not those who are healthy who need a physician, but those who are sick; I did not come to call the righteous, but sinners" (Mark 2:17). He drew close to sinners and preached to them. Jesus' purpose in coming to this world was evangelism (Mark 1:38–39; Luke 4:43–44), and His purpose in calling the twelve disciples was so they too could preach (Mark 3:14). With His first words after He broke the power of death and resurrected, Jesus commanded His beloved disciples to preach the gospel (Matt 28:18–20). This work is to find the one lost sheep among the one hundred (Luke 15:4–7). It is to light the lamp and sweep the whole house to find one of the ten silver coins (Luke 15:8–10). It is to find the younger son who has left the house so he can live with his father again (Luke 15:11–32). This is precisely why Jesus traveled from place to place (Matt 4:23; 9:35) without taking time to eat (Mark 3:20; 6:31), seeking out the lost and preaching to them. He even went to the regions of the Samaritans, with whom the Jews did not have any dealings (John 4:3–4, 9). He also sought out Zaccheus, who was condemned as a national traitor, and said, "Zaccheus, hurry and come down, for today I must stay at your house" (Luke 19:5). Later that day He proclaimed, "Today salvation has come to this house, because he, too, is a son of Abraham. For the Son of Man has come to seek and to save that which was lost" (Luke 19:9–10).

In order to seek and to save that which was lost, Jesus completed His three-year public life and at last became a sacrifice for redemption on the cross. His death on the cross and resurrection were the climax of redemptive history. Even now, as the eternal high priest, the resurrected Jesus is at the right hand of God's throne, praying for us who are seeking the lost and preaching the gospel (Rom 8:34; Heb 7:25). Indeed, the high priestly work to seek and to save the lost is continuing without interruption until that one day when salvation will be completely fulfilled.

Apostle Paul followed in the footsteps of Jesus the eternal high priest his whole life. For this reason he confessed that he was the priest of the gospel. In Romans 15:16, he says that God gave him grace "to be a minister of Christ Jesus to the Gentiles, ministering as a priest the gospel of God, so that my offering of the Gentiles may become acceptable, sanctified by the Holy Spirit." In the Old Testament a priest had to go before God with a sacrifice. Apostle Paul confessed that he sought to preach to the Gentiles and offer them to God as an acceptable sacrifice.

He also confessed that proclamation of God's Word was a duty that had been entrusted to him according to the commandment of God our Savior (Titus 1:3). This was the work that had been entrusted to Apostle Paul; this was the only reason for his boasting (Rom 15:17). Apostle Paul traveled from Jerusalem as all the way around to Illyricum (modern day Albania) and fully preached the gospel of Christ (Rom 15:19). For the sake of the gospel, he was imprisoned, beaten numerous times, and faced dangers from rivers, from robbers, in the wilderness, and in the sea. He almost died many times and was hungry, thirsty, cold, and exposed (2 Cor 11:23–27). However, Apostle Paul confessed in Romans 1:14, "I am under obligation both to Greeks and to barbarians, both to the wise and to the foolish." Moreover, he confessed that he had nothing to boast of even if he preached the gospel, for He was under compulsion. In fact, woe would be upon him if he did not preach the gospel (1 Cor 9:16). His whole life was truly a life of evangelism (Eph 6:19–20).

God's sworn covenant—which appointed Jesus Christ as the eternal high priest according to the order of Melchizedek (Ps 110:4; Heb 7:21–22)—will one day be gloriously and perfectly fulfilled. Until that day we must have faith to the preserving of the soul (Heb 10:39) and hold fast the beginning of our assurance until the end (Heb 3:14). I pray that each one of us will show the same diligence until the end to fulfill our hope and inherit the promises through faith and patience (Heb 6:11–12).

If there is one thing we must do, it is to go before the throne of grace each day and offer our bodies as living sacrifices in spiritual worship. As we do this, we must persevere through all suffering (Heb 10:36; see 1 Thess 1:3; Jas 5:8, 11), give true thanks, and be faithful to our duties as priests to find the lost and preach the gospel.

I sincerely hope we all become eternal victors on the day when Jesus Christ, the eternal high priest of the covenantal oath, fulfills the entire administration of redemption.

Bibliography

Albright, William F. "Samuel and the Beginnings of the Prophetic Movement." *Interpreting the Prophetic Tradition*. Edited by Harry. M. Olinsky. New York: Ktav, 1969.

Barry, John D. et al., eds. *Lexham Bible Dictionary*. Bellingham, WA: Lexham, 2016.

Bergen, Robert D. *1, 2 Samuel: An Exegetical and Theological Exposition of Holy Scripture*. The New American Commentary. Vol. 7. Nashville: Broadman & Holman, 2001.

Brand, Chad et al., eds. *Holman Illustrated Bible Dictionary*. Nashville, TN: Holman Bible Publishers, 2003.

Cho, Youngyup. *Christology*. Seoul: Word of Life Press, 2007.

Craigie, Peter C. Jeremiah 1–25. *Word Biblical Commentary*. Vol. 26. Dallas, TX: Word, Incorporated, 1991.

Davies, T. Witton. *The International Standard Bible Encyclopaedia*. Chicago: The Howard-Severance Company, 1915.

DeVries, Simon J. 1 Kings. *Word Biblical Commentary*. Vol. 12. Dallas: Word, 2003.

Easton, M. G. *Easton's Bible Dictionary*. New York: Harper & Brothers, 1893.

Edersheim, Alfred. *The Life and Times of Jesus the Messiah*. London: Longmans, Green, and Co., 1896.

Finegan, Jack. *Handbook of Biblical Chronology*. Peabody, MA: Hendrickson, 1998.

Josephus, Flavius and William Whiston. *The Works of Josephus: Complete and Unabridged*. Peabody: Hendrickson, 1987.

Keil, Carl Friedrich and Franz Delitzsch, *Commentary on the Old Testament*. Vol. 3. Peabody, MA: Hendrickson, 1996.

Kelly, Douglas F. *Systematic Theology: The Beauty of Christ –A Trinitarian Vision*. Vol. 2. Fearn: Mentor, 2014.

Kim, Joong-Eun. "Priests' Index of Ethics (Lev 21–22)." *Christian Philosophy* 33. No. 12. Seoul: The Christian Literature Society of Korea, 1989.

Kitov, Eliyahu. *The Book of Our Heritage: The Jewish Year and Its Days of Significance*. Vol. 1, Tishrey-Shevat. New York: Feldheim, 1997.

Lee, Byung-Kyu. *Commentary on Jeremiah and Lamentations.* Seoul: Yum Kwang, 1995.

Grabbe, Lester L. "1 and 2 Maccabees." *Dictionary of New Testament Background: A Compendium of Contemporary Biblical Scholarship*. Edited by Craig A. Evans and Stanley E. Porter. Downers Grove, IL: InterVarsity Press, 2000.

Lightfoot, John. *The Whole Works of the Rev. John Lightfoot, D.D., Master of Catherine Hall, Cambridge.* Edited by John Rogers Pitman. London: J. F. Dove, 1823.

Neusner, Jacob. *The Babylonian Talmud: A Translation and Commentary.* Vol. 18b. Peabody, MA: Hendrickson Publishers, 2011.

Park, Abraham. *God's Profound and Mysterious Providence: As Revealed in the Genealogy of Jesus Christ from the Time of David to the Exile in Babylon.* Singapore: Periplus, 2011.

Park, Abraham. *The Covenant of the Torch: A Forgotten Encounter in the History of the Exodus and Wilderness Journey.* Singapore: Periplus, 2010.

Pratt, Richard L. *1 & 2 Chronicles: A Mentor Commentary*. Fearn: Mentor, 2006. Reprint, 1998.

Pritchard, James B., ed. *Ancient Near Eastern Texts Relating to the Old Testament.* Princeton: Princeton University Press, 1958.

Rooke, Deborah W. *Zadok's Heirs: The Role and Development of the High Priesthood in Ancient Israel, Oxford Theology and Religion Monographs.* New York: Oxford University Press, 2000.

Schegg, Peter. *Biblische Archäologie.* Edited by Wirthmüller. Freiburg: Herder, 1887.

Schürer, Emil. *A History of the Jewish People in the Time of Jesus Christ, Second Division.* Vol. 1. Edinburgh: T&T Clark, 1890.

Seder Olam: The Rabbinic View of Biblical Chronology. Translated by Heinrich W. Guggenheimer. Lanham, MD: Rowman & Littlefield, 1998.

Surburg, Raymond F. *Introduction to the Intertestamental Period.* St. Louis: Concordia, 1975.

Tenney, Merrill C. *New Testament Survey.* Grand Rapids: Eerdmans, 1985.

Thompson, J. A. *The Book of Jeremiah.* The New International Commentary on the Old Testament. Grand Rapids, MI: Wm. B. Eerdmans Publishing Co., 1980.

VanderKam, James C. *From Joshua to Caiaphas: High Priests after the Exile.* Minneapolis: Augsburg Fortress, 2004.

VanderKam, James C. *From Revelation to Canon: Studies in the Hebrew Bible and Second Temple Literature.* Leiden: Brill, 2000.

Elwell, Walter A. and Barry J. Beitzel, *Baker Encyclopedia of the Bible.* Vol. 2. Grand Rapids: Baker, 1998.

Won, Yong-kook. *Deuteronomy.* Seoul: Lifebook, 1993.

Index